THE GIANT BOOK OF
LOST
WORLDS

THE GIANT BOOK OF
LOST WORLDS

Edited by Damon Wilson

This edition published and distributed by Parragon, 1998

Parragon
Unit 13–17, Avonbridge Trading Estate
Atlantic Road, Avonmouth
Bristol BS11 9QD

Produced by Magpie Books,
an imprint of Robinson Publishing Ltd, London

Copyright © Robinson Publishing 1996

Cover illustration courtesy of Popperfoto

ISBN 0-75252-406-2

A copy of the British Library Cataloguing-in-Publication Data
is available from the British Library.

Printed and bound in the E.C.

CONTENTS

INTRODUCTION

The besieged inhabitants of Troy looked out from their walls one morning and saw that their attackers had gone. On the plains outside their city was a huge wooden effigy of a horse – an animal held sacred by the Trojans. This gift-offering by their Greek enemies was brought in triumph into the city. Unknown to the Trojans, the horse contained Greek warriors. Under cover of darkness the Greeks opened the city gates to their returning army and Troy was taken. According to ancient Greek legend, this famous trick brought to an end the 10-year siege of Troy and ended the conflict that began when Paris, a Trojan prince, abducted Helen, the beautiful wife of Menelaus, King of Sparta. Under the leadership of his brother King Agamemnon of Mycenae, Menelaus and many other Greek warriors set out to punish the Trojans.

The many strands of the legend have provided material for poets and dramatists from ancient times to our own day. In one epic poem, the *Iliad*, by the Greek poet Homer, who lived in the 8th century BC, a brief period in the war is described in vivid and moving detail. Another Homeric epic, the Odyssey, tells of the adventures of the Greek warrior *Odysseus* as he returns home from Troy. Dramatists of Greece's classical age, such as Sophocles and Euripedes, wrote tragedies based on the conflict. The story of two young Trojan lovers, Troilus and Cressida, was immortalised by Chaucer and Shakespeare. And a modern play by Jean Giradoux, *Tiger at the Gates*, uses the war as its theme.

The people of the ancient world accepted the story of Troy as historical fact. Alexander the Great, for instance, believed that one of the Greek heroes from the *Iliad*, Achilles, was his ancestor. After the Middle Ages, however, the story was consigned to the category of pure myth. Apart from the air of unreality created by the participation of the gods in the story, there were many inaccuracies in the text, scholars claimed. As for a city called Troy, if it had ever existed, it had long since vanished. Moreover, there was no real evidence that a Greek civilisation had existed before 1200 BC – the time around which the war was supposed to have taken place.

One can imagine the smiles among archaeologists in the 1860s when a rich German businessman with no training in archaeology set out for the Aegean with a copy of the *Iliad* to search for Troy. As a child, Heinrich Schliemann had been captivated by these heroic tales and was convinced that they were true. His dream of finding Troy and Mycenae had stayed with him throughout years of pursuing a successful career in business, and he was now, in his mid-40s, abandoning the world of commerce to discover the lost world of Troy. All he had was his copy of Homer, plenty of money to pay a small army of workmen, and boundless determination.

Arriving in Turkey, he first explored a site near the village of Burnarbashi, where, according to tradition, Troy was buried. But the site's location and some other of its features did not tally with descriptions in Homer, and Schliemann passed it by. Some distance away at Hissarlik he found a more promising site. There, about an hour's walk from the sea, a flat-topped mound dominated the surrounding plain. He started to dig.

His faith was well rewarded. Over the next few years he discovered not one city but nine, built one on top of another. The question was, which was Homer's Troy? Schliemann thought it was either the second or the third level from the bottom, where he found traces of fire and some massive walls that he identified as those surrounding King Priam's palace. Just before he concluded his excavation of Troy, Schliemann discovered, in this 'palace' area, a hoard of gold jewelry – Priam's treasure. More recent studies have shown that Troy was at a higher level, and that the treasure Schliemann discovered had belonged to a much earlier king. Nevertheless, he had achieved his goal; he had found Troy. The professional archaeologists who had smiled at this legend-obsessed amateur had to acknowledge that he had made a discovery of great significance.

Schliemann went on to make more discoveries. He excavated the ruins at Mycenae and found graves containing skeletons bedecked with gold. They were not, as he supposed, the bodies of Agamemnon and his family but royalty of an earlier age. But again he had proved that Homer was not merely a spinner of tales but also an historian. Furthermore, an impressive Greek civilisation based at Mycenae had existed as far back as 1450 BC – 250 years before Troy fell.

Other Greek legends concerned the island of Crete. Here, in a labyrinth in his palace, King Minos had kept a monster, half bull and half man, called the Minotaur, to which he sacrificed youths and maidens sent by Athens as tribute. In one of the best-known stories an Athenian prince, Theseus, kills the Minotaur and escapes with Minos' daughter Ariadne.

Were the stories of Crete entirely fictitious, or – as in the case of Troy and Mycenae – were they based on a real civilisation? Schliemann, of course, took the latter view, and he planned to excavate on the island. Circumstances prevented his doing so; but another man, Arthur Evans, a British archaeologist, had also become fascinated with the possibility of a Cretan civilisation and in 1899 he began to dig near the town of Knossos.

Almost immediately his efforts were rewarded. He discovered a magnificent royal palace – including a labyrinth that might have given rise to the legend – and abundant evidence that an advanced civilisation had existed on Crete several centuries before the Trojan War took place.

Ever since Schliemann and Evans made their startling discoveries, it has been less easy to dismiss legend as a source of historical fact. In England, for example, excavators continue to search for evidence of the legendary British hero, King Arthur. Perhaps the most persistent legend of all, that of Atlantis, continues to gain supporters and inspire controversy. The source of the

Lost Worlds

Atlantis legend is two of Plato's dialogues in which he describes life on an island utopia located somewhere in the Atlantic Ocean. According to the story, which Plato got from another source, Atlantis was destroyed by violent earthquakes that caused it to sink into the sea.

Many scholars dismiss the Atlantis story as impossible on various scientific grounds. This does not daunt the Atlantologists, however, who counter with their own evidence in support of its existence. Although most of them favour the view that Atlantis was located in the Atlantic Ocean, others have suggested that it might have been a Mediterranean island, or not an island at all but a mainland state.

Certainly, the past hundred years or so have demonstrated the existence of many previously unknown civilisations. Time and again, archaeologists and travellers have discovered the remains of some unknown culture lying in a remote part of the world. Their discoveries have answered many old questions and raised almost as many new ones.

Few of these archaeological finds have been more spectacular than the Maya ruins of Mexico and Central America. Here, in thick jungle, in the 1840s, John Lloyd Stephens, an American archaeologist, and the artist Frederick Catherwood, his English companion, found fantastically carved statues and temples and pyramids comparable to those of Egypt. Other explorers went on to reveal other pre-Columbian cultures, such as those of the Aztecs and Olmecs of Mexico and the Incas of Peru.

The Spanish invaders of the 16th century had discovered these civilisations, but their interest in them had been mainly predatory. They had confiscated the gold of the Aztecs and Incas and destroyed their cities. Only a few of them bothered to record what they saw, and their writings remained relatively unknown. It was not until the last century that archaeologists began to turn their attention to Central and South America and to rediscover pre-Columbian civilisations. Europeans and Americans (of both continents) who were accustomed to regard the Middle East as the original source of civilisation had to revise their view of the world. Separated from Western culture by thousands of miles of ocean, the Indians of the Americas had independently created their own civilisations.

Or had they? Some people, noting resemblances between the native American cultures and those of the Old World, have suggested that some contact had occurred between the two worlds centuries before the Spanish conquest. Also, there are Inca legends of a 'white god' called Viracocha who came from across the sea and brought civilisation to them. Artifacts have been found in South America that depict men with beards and narrow, beaked noses who look quite unlike Indians. Some of the people holding this 'diffusionist' theory of the development of pre-Columbian culture believe that the contact was made by Egyptians or other North Africans who sailed across the Atlantic in boats made of papyrus reeds. Others believe that the visitors from over the sea were Atlanteans.

Atlantis is not the only supposed lost continent. Lemuria, a continent that once, it is said, linked southern Asia with eastern Africa, is believed by some people to have been the original home of the human species. Yet another lost continent, called Mu, is supposed to have been located in the south Pacific in the area now dotted by the islands of Polynesia. The islands are said to be the mountaintops of the former continent. According to the theory, Mu's advanced civilisation produced the mysterious stone heads that stand on Easter Island.

Mysterious remains found anywhere in the world are usually interpreted by Atlantologists and other lost-continent adherents as evidence supporting their theory. There is certainly plenty of scope for speculation, for even known civilisations often present us with a mystery. About a hundred years ago, for example, the Hittites were identifiable only as an obscure tribe mentioned occasionally in the Bible. Today, thanks to archaeological detective work, we know that they were a powerful nation who once ruled a large part of the Middle East. Yet we still do not know where they came from originally, nor are we certain what happened to them after their empire collapsed.

We do know what happened to the Etruscans, those artistically gifted, pleasure-loving people who dominated ancient Italy: they were conquered and their civilisation extinguished by the Romans. Their language, however, has defied countless attempts to decipher anything more than a few names and seems to be unrelated to any other language, ancient or modern. Many scholars believe that the Etruscans were emigrants to Italy and point to numerous resemblances between Etruscan culture and religion and those of eastern peoples – though as yet there is no conclusive proof of this theory.

In southern Africa, the ruins of Zimbabwe still inspire wonder and controversy. Are these stone towers and enclosures the remains of the legendary Ophir, the land from which King Solomon obtained his gold? Or are they the products of a much more recent African civilisation – and, if so, what happened to the people who built them?

Now that we take myths a little more seriously than we did a few generations ago, the widespread stories of a world cataclysm are attracting some attention. The biblical account of a great flood that covered the earth and destroyed every living thing – except those on Noah's Ark – has parallels in the mythology of Babylonia, ancient Greece, India, Iceland, and many other countries. Their folklore contains harrowing stories of destruction by fire, or earthquake, or by a combination of natural forces. Of course, there are many possible explanations for these myths – the simplest being that to primitive people, a great natural disaster is viewed as an expression of divine wrath. The horror of the disaster is exaggerated with every retelling of the story. But it is just possible that these myths – like the Homeric legends – contain more truth than we suppose. Someday, perhaps, we will discover scientific evidence that some tremendous upheaval did occur in the remote past. Such evidence would make the story of Atlantis more believable than it is today.

One of the more fantastic variants of the Atlantis legend states that it was located on the site of the Sahara Desert – the rest of Africa, according to the theory, being covered with water. Geologists have shown, however, that the African continent has existed in its present shape for hundreds of thousands of years. If Plato's utopia was located there, it was not an island.

Yet the Sahara – one of the most inhospitable environments on earth – has yielded some surprising secrets. Tiny crocodiles live there in isolated desert pools, which they could not possibly have reached by migration. How did they get there? Ancient skeletons of elephants, giraffes, antelopes, and other animals have been found in this wasteland – thousands of miles from their present homes in the fertile parts of Africa. Human remains, too, have been discovered – not only skeletons thousands of years old but also flint tools and rock paintings and engravings. Some of the paintings show herds of cattle; others depict scenes of hunting, racing, and dancing. Obviously, at some time in its prehistory, the Sahara Desert was a fertile land.

Although exploration of the desert began during the last century, intensive study got underway only within the past few decades. In exploring dry canyons cut thousands of years ago by deep rivers, palaeontologists have found Old Stone Age tools dating back perhaps 500,000 years. The New Stone Age is estimated to have begun in the Sahara sometime between 8000 and 6000 BC, about the time that the climate became very rainy. At that time, too, more advanced peoples began migrating into this fertile area from all directions. Scientists believe that during this era the Sahara was the most densely populated region on earth. The communities appear to have had a fair degree of organisation; there is evidence, for example, of a distinct class of craftsmen who made the tools used by the hunters and stock raisers and who also made delicate ornaments in which these people evidently delighted.

Around 2000 BC, the Sahara began to dry up. The possible causes of this change in climate remain obscure. There may have been a disturbance in the zones of high and low pressure. But the increasing aridity of the region may also have been caused by the people who lived there, whose herds of cattle and goats must have consumed and destroyed enormous amounts of plant life. By the time the Sahara began to be mentioned by travellers it had become a dry region. In 450 BC, Herodotus, the Greek historian comments on the large areas of the Sahara lacking any vegetation and on the sand dunes dotted with oases. The fertile Sahara had died and the Sahara we know today – desolate and unfriendly – had taken its place.

Few parts of the world have been so radically transformed as the Sahara. Yet the flowering and dying of civilisations is a worldwide phenomenon. Stone temples that once echoed to the sound of bells and chanting now sit empty and silent in the midst of encroaching jungle. Splendid columns that lined avenues through which triumphant armies marched now lie crumbling in the sand. We may know little of the people who lived in these lost lands, but their fascination endures. Contemplating fragments of their culture, we are free to savour the mystery of a world that we can never know fully.

CHAPTER 1

THE EGYPTIAN MYSTERIES

The modern Egyptians pride themselves on being the oldest civilisation in the world. Foreign invasions, religious upheavals and Biblical plagues notwithstanding, the culture of Egypt has endured for thousands of years. Egypt may therefore seem a strange starting point for a study of lost civilisations, but down the millennia the Egyptians have forgotten more than other cultures ever knew. Two centuries ago, the temples, pyramids and hieroglyphic writings of the Nile valley were little more than the enigmatic survivals of a mythic age. It took a war to open Egypt to the new scientific discipline called archaeology, which would soon begin to sweep away the dust of the ages.

Ten thousand colourful horsemen turned out to defend the city of Cairo against Napoleon's expeditionary force on 12 July, 1798. This army of Mamelukes, the foreign mercenaries who ruled Egypt for the Turkish emperor, was a formidable sight. Exhorting his troops before the engagement that became known as the Battle of the Pyramids, Napoleon coined a memorable and rousing phrase. 'Soldiers,' he cried, 'remember that from the top of these monuments 40 centuries are looking down upon you.' In fact at that time the pyramids of Giza were about 4500 years old. But considering that Egyptology only began with Napoleon's conquest, 40 centuries wasn't a bad estimate.

The object of Napoleon's expedition to Egypt was to threaten British India. Militarily, however, it was a failure, but it had more success in its secondary purpose, which was to open up the ancient and mysterious land of Egypt to European scholarship. A contingent of nearly 200 scientists, scholars, and artists accompanied the army, and one of Napoleon's first acts when he entered Cairo was to requisition five large mansions to accommodate what he called the 'Institute of Egypt'. Over the next year the French troops pushed into Upper Egypt, but always they were accompanied by scientists and artists who collected, measured, investigated, and sketched the antiquities of the Nile valley.

Among these 'learned civilians' from France was a former courtier and diplomat named Vivant Denon. A dilettante in the arts, it was his work in Egypt that gained him lasting fame. He was enraptured by all that he saw. 'One has to rub his eyes to be sure that he is not in a dream,' he wrote on the day he first saw the ancient city of Thebes. Of the temple at Dendera he wrote: 'What uninterrupted power, what wealth, what abundance, what superfluity of resources must have belonged to a government that could raise an edifice like this.' But the awe of the tourist soon gave way to the passion of the artist, and Denon sketched all the relics he encountered in the minutest detail. Future Egyptologists were to be greatly indebted to him, for many of the things he drew were later pillaged or destroyed.

So painstaking was Denon's work that he copied exactly the mysterious inscriptions on the Egyptian monuments, though neither he nor any of the scholars of the Institute of Egypt had any idea what they meant. The ancient civilisation of the Egyptian pharaohs was as strange and remote to the inhabitants of Egypt as it was to their conquerors, but the Frenchmen sons of 18th-century European Enlightenment, were dedicated to the task of bringing all areas of human knowledge under their sway. They recognised that the script known as *hieroglyphics*, from Greek words *hieros* meaning sacred and *glyphein*, to carve, must be the key to the mysteries of this land of massive monuments.

It was in the summer of 1799 that one of Napoleon's officers of engineers made the most important find of the whole expedition. Pierre Bouchard was in charge of construction work at a French fortification near Rosetta, about 40 miles from Alexandria, when one of his soldiers drew his attention to a basalt stone that he had dug up. It was about the size of a tabletop and it was divided into three sections of engraved writing. The bottom section was in Greek, and therefore was readable. The top section was in the enigmatic hieroglyphic script in which figures of animals, birds, and human beings were mingled with abstract symbols. The middle section was in a kind of writing known as *demotic*, a simplified and popular form of hieroglyphic used for everyday purposes by the ancient Egyptians. It was a fair assumption that the three sections contained the same text. If this were so it might be possible to use the Greek to decode the hieroglyphics. The Rosetta stone was sent to Cairo and Napoleon gave orders for casts of it to be made. This made it possible for copies of the texts to be sent to France where excited scholars vied with each other to be the first to crack the code of the pharaohs. It was as well for French scholarship that the casts and copies were made. When the French had to capitulate to the British fleet at Alexandria in 1801 and negotiate for the safe conduct of their 'learned civilians' back to France, surrender of the Rosetta stone was part of the price. It is now in the British Museum in London.

One of the scholars on Napoleon's Egyptian expedition was the mathematician and physicist Jean-Baptiste Fourier. Soon after his return from Egypt, Fourier was inspecting a school in Grenoble when he came across an 11-year-old boy prodigy named Jean-Francois Champollion who had recently taken up the study of Hebrew after already mastering Latin and Greek. The boy spoke of his fascination with ancient languages, so Fourier invited him to his home and showed him his Egyptian collection. 'Can anyone read them?' Champollion asked when he saw the cryptic hieroglyphs. When Fourier told him that nobody could, the boy said solemnly, 'I am going to do it.'

With extraordinary single-mindedness, Champollion prepared himself to fulfill this ambition. He studied Denon's profusely illustrated account of his travels, and he added to his linguistic repertoire Arabic, Syrian, Chaldean, and then Coptic. This last was a language directly descended from ancient Egyptian. The initial optimism of scholars as to the possibility of deciphering the hieroglyphs with the help of the Greek text of the Rosetta stone had proved mistaken. Some small progress was made with the interpretation of parts of the demotic text – the middle and best preserved section of the Rosetta stone – by the French orientalist Sylvestre de Sacy and by a Swedish diplomat, Johann David Åkerblad. The top section of hieroglyphic script continued to baffle scholars.

The main reason why it baffled them was that they regarded the hieroglyphs as a form of picture-writing in which the recognisable figures stood for what they represented and the more abstract symbols had some religious significance. This view went back to a Greek writer of the 4th century AD named Horapollo, and because of its antiquity and plausibility nobody had thought to doubt it. After all, the very term 'hieroglyph' means 'holy writing'. Champollion's first important discovery was that there was a difference between the sacred sculptural emblems of the Egyptians and their hieroglyphic texts, although they both made use of animal and bird figures. Champollion formulated and worked on the assumption that the hieroglyphs were phonetic symbols, and it was his persistent following up of this idea that ultimately led to the breakthrough that made him the father of Egyptology.

In fact Champollion was not entirely original in his approach. Some writers have claimed that an Englishman named Thomas Young was the first man who saw the light. Young was a man of multiple talents who made significant contributions to theoretical physics as well as to the study of languages. He worked with the Rosetta stone and also with the text of an obelisk from Philae in Egypt which stood (and still stands) in the grounds of the country estate of a Mr Bankes at Kingston Lacey in Dorset, England. Young worked out that certain groups of symbols in the ancient texts, which were formed in oval 'cartouches', would be the names of rulers, and he proposed that names of foreign origin would have been rendered phonetically. Following this line of reasoning, Young correctly identified the names Ptolemy and Berenike. He also established other principles that were later proved correct. For instance, he suggested that hieroglyphic scripts could be read either from left to right or from right to left, and that the correct beginning of a line was indicated by the way the bird or animal figures faced. What he didn't see was that it was not only foreign names that were represented phonetically in the texts, but that the hieroglyphs were all phonetic symbols.

It was the text of the obelisk in Dorset that enabled Champollion to make his discovery of the key to the hieroglyphs. He identified on it, in another cartouche, the name Cleopatra. Then, when he compared the signs that rendered Ptolemy with those that rendered Cleopatra, he found that three of them were common to both names. Moreover these symbols occurred in roughly the positions corresponding with the positions of the letters P, O, and L in the names. Having found this lead, he was able to surmise or narrow down the possibilities of what other hieroglyphs stood for what letters in the names. In this way Champollion took his first steps toward translating the language of the ancient Egyptians. Turning his attention to another and older text, he was able to make out the signs that spelled the name Rameses which was given to eleven of the pharaohs. Therefore he established that phonetic symbols had not only been used for the names of foreign rulers but also for those of Egyptian rulers. Further long and patient research led him to the conclusion that hieroglyphics were not 'holy writing' but the written form of a real language that dealt with everyday things.

Champollion realized the ambition of his boyhood 20 years after he had announced it to Fourier. It was in 1822 that he read his historic paper on the hieroglyphs to a French learned society. Then in the years 1828–29 he led a scientific expedition to Egypt, where his ability to read the writing on the ancient stones astonished 19th-century Egyptians and enabled him repeatedly to confirm his ideas and to identify and date the great monuments and relics by reading their inscriptions. Champollion laid the foundations of Egyptology, although when he died at the age of 42 many European scholars mocked his ideas and dismissed him as mad. It was not until 1866, when another engraved text in the three languages of the Rosetta stone was found by a German, Richard Lepsius, that Champollion was proved right beyond dispute. Lepsius placed on one of the Giza pyramids a tablet bearing the name of the sponsor of his 1843–45 expedition, King Frederick William IV of Prussia, and written in hieroglyphic script – an act which paid tribute to the scholar Champollion quite as much as to the Prussian king.

While men like Champollion and Young were puzzling over the cipher that would open the mysteries of ancient Egypt, others were making a more direct approach to those mysteries, and at the same time making fortunes for themselves out of valuable Egyptian antiquities. One of the most important of these treasure seekers was an extraordinary Italian adventurer named Giovanni Belzoni who had started his career as a strong man in a London circus billed as 'The Patagonian Sampson'. But Belzoni's first experience among the monuments of the ancient Egyptians was typical of many later explorers. When, in 1818, he found his way into the burial chamber of Chephren, builder of the second pyramid of Giza, he found it empty. Robbers had taken its contents during the Middle Ages, so his only satisfactions were to scrawl his name boldly on the wall of the sacred place – the inscription is still there today – and to go down in history as the first man to discover an ancient Egyptian burial chamber in modern times. But Belzoni was a man who looked for more substantial rewards for his efforts. After all, he had gone to Egypt in the first place to seek his fortune, not to establish a scholarly reputation. He had the good fortune to meet and befriend the British consul general, Henry Salt, who was running a profitable sideline in buying Egyptian antiquities for patrons in England. Belzoni became Salt's chief collector, and in the course of travelling around Egypt looking for bargains he happened to make some important discoveries. He was not only the first modern European to explore the interior of a pyramid, but was also the first to enter the temple at Abu Simbel. He was also the discoverer of the tomb of Seti I in what became known as the Valley of the Kings near Thebes in Upper Egypt, where he acquired for Salt a *sarcophagus* or stone coffin which is today in the Soane Museum in London.

Many of the exhibits in the Egyptian gallery of the British

Museum are there thanks to Belzoni's energy. He was not daunted by size. One of his first commissions from Salt was to get a giant stone head of the pharaoh Rameses II that was lying in the sand at Thebes. Another was to bring an obelisk down the Nile by barge from Philae. On this second errand Belzoni came into conflict with the agents of the French consul general, Bernardino Drovetti, who was also in the looting and shipping business. Shots were fired, but Belzoni retained his trophy. In this way, the Italian adventurer contributed indirectly to the solution of the riddle of the hieroglyphs, for this particular obelisk was the one destined for Mr Bankes' estate in Dorset and which helped Champollion to make this breakthrough. On another occasion an obelisk Belzoni was transporting fell into the Nile, but while a less enterprising man would have left it there Belzoni managed to get it out again.

The massive size of many of his Egyptian acquisitions was a problem that never seemed to trouble Belzoni. Nor was the original purpose of the buildings and antiquities, whether religious or funerary. He never appears to have shown much curiosity about or admiration for the people who many thousands of years ago had built the magnificent temples, tombs, and statues of the Nile valley. He appears to have been completely without superstition or any other fear. The following extract from one of his accounts of a particularly tough tomb-looting expedition gives us a good idea of the man's nerve: 'I sought a resting place and found one; but when my weight bore on the body of an Egyptian, it crushed it like a band-box. I naturally had recourse to my hands to sustain my weight, but they found no better support; so that I sank altogether among the broken mummies, with the crash of bones, rags, and wooden cases, which raised such a dust as kept me motionless for a quarter of an hour.' If there ever was such a thing as 'the mummy's curse', which was said to threaten later robbers and explorers of the Valley of the Kings, the brash giant Belzoni must have been immune to it.

Between 1804 and 1844, the ruler of Egypt on behalf of the Turks was another adventurer, a former coffee dealer from Albania named Mehemet Ali. His chief concern was to get his country modernized and he had little interest in its antiquities. It was left to others to protest about the wholesale robbery of the land of the pharaohs, which at the rate it had reached in the 1820s and 1830s, would soon have scattered the relics so far and wide that scholars trying to solve the mysteries of ancient Egypt would have been frustrated. Remarkably preserved by the sand and the hot, dry climate was evidence of a great civilisation raised by men more than 4000 years ago that had flourished for thousands of years, a civilisation capable of engineering feats that would even discourage a modern contractor, and possessed of artistic and religious traditions that seemed strange to Europeans but were clearly consistent and long-established. The relics of this early peak of human civilisation had obviously been pillaged down the centuries, but in the first decades of the 19th century the rich and insatiable European and American collectors had encouraged the plundering. The traffic in treasures reached such proportions that before long there would be little left except the most massive and enigmatic relics of all, the great pyramids themselves. At this time two things were badly needed. First, some control of the traffic in Egyptian antiquities; secondly, some attempts to undertake systematic archaeological field work and to apply the new knowledge of hieroglyphic script to the task of understanding ancient Egyptian culture and history.

In the 1830s a British army officer, Colonel Richard Howard-Vyse, teamed up with a civil engineer, John Perring, to investigate the pyramids. This was one of the first expeditions motivated by the quest for knowledge rather than profit, but if Vyse's motives were more admirable than Belzoni's his methods were scarcely less crude. He identified the smallest of the Giza pyramids as that of the ancient king Mykerinos, but in an attempt to get into the burial chamber he damaged the pyramid with explosives.

It was the three-year expedition of Champollion's disciple Richard Lepsius in 1843–45 that was the first real archaeological exploration of the land of Egypt. Lepsius discovered the remains of 30 formerly unknown pyramids, which meant the total of known pyramids was 67. He travelled all over the land copying

down or taking casts of hieroglyphic inscriptions on buildings
and statues. By translating them and comparing and cross-
relating their sources, Lepsius gradually built up a view of the
panorama of Egyptian history. He explored no less than 130
mastabas, the strange rectangular buildings with sloping sides
that the ancient Egyptians had erected over the tombs of important people. On the vast empty plain where once had stood
Akhetaton, capital city of the heretic king and religious genius
Akhnaton, he found relics with inscriptions that provided insights
into the character and thought of that strange inspired ruler.
Lepsius took a wealth of information back to Germany with him
in 1845, as well as a wealth of antiquities which furnished the
Egyptian Museum in Berlin. In addition, he established the foun-
dations of the study of ancient Egyptian history with his books,
Egyptian Chronology (1849) and *The Book of Kings* (1850).

In 1850 a young Frenchman, Auguste Ferdinand Mariette,
arrived in Egypt on a mission to catalogue manuscripts in Coptic
monasteries and to buy for the Louvre Museum in Paris ancient
Egyptian documents known as *papyri*, from the material on
which they were written, made from thin strips of a grasslike
plant called papyrus, pressed together and dried. The monks were
suspicious of him, however, because some years before an
Englishman had gone around on a similar pretext and had
proceeded to get the monks drunk in order to steal their manuscripts. Having met resistance to his project everywhere, Mariette
went to Cairo, where one evening he climbed to the top of the
citadel and had an experience that changed his life. As he
described it later: 'Suffused in golden dust and in the fiery red
glow from the setting sun, the pyramids, massed together,
presented an imposing spectacle, which overwhelmed me and
absorbed me with a force almost painful in its violence.'

Giving up the hunt for manuscripts, Mariette boldly put the
funds the authorities of the Louvre had furnished him with to
another purpose. One day he was walking among the ruins of
Sekkara, a town about 15 miles from Cairo, when he noticed, near
the great step pyramid of Zoser, a sphinx partly buried in the
sand. On it he read a hieroglyphic inscription referring to Apis,

the sacred bull of a cult that had been centered at the nearby city of Memphis. Mariette then remembered a passage from the Greek geographer, Strabo, who was born in about 58 BC. Strabo described the burial ground of the sacred bulls of Memphis, where in his own day there had been an Alley of Sphinxes, most of them, even then, nearly buried in sand. Mariette had one of those intuitions that have often led to great archaeological finds. He felt sure that he was standing on the sacred site, and he backed his hunch by using his funds to hire Arab workers. He excavated an avenue 600 feet in length flanked by 140 sphinxes and with the remains of a temple at each end. In the temples and in several tombs he found a wealth of artifacts connected with the cult, as well as some fine statues such as the figure of a seated scribe which is today one of the treasures of the Louvre.

Not surprisingly, the French authorities approved Mariette's employment of their funds and provided him with more money to continue his excavations. In one of the temples he found a steep shaft leading down to the burial chambers where the succession of sacred bulls of Apis had been ceremonially buried over centuries. Eventually he excavated galleries stretching underground for about 1000 feet, opening onto burial chambers containing the immense stone sarcophagi in which the sacred bulls had lain. Each sarcophagus had been covered with a heavy stone slab, but most of these had been pushed aside by tomb robbers centuries ago. Only two of the sarcophagi were unopened, and in them Mariette found intact the original burial regalia of the sacred bulls.

The Serapaeum, as this site is called after the god Serapis, was in its day the most sensational excavated find in the history of Egyptian archaeology. With its discovery Mariette began a career of 30 fruitful years in Egyptology. He campaigned widely and successfully for conservation of the antiquities of Egypt, and when the Egyptian authorities formed an Institute of Egyptian Antiquities in 1857, Mariette was appointed its director and the chief supervisor of all excavations. He investigated many important sites, and made one other major find: the tomb of a great courtier and landowner named Ti. The tomb was situated near the

Serapaeum, but it was considerably older and was judged to date from about the same period as the great pyramids of Cheops, Chephren, and Mykerinos at Giza. Its chief interest was its wealth of well preserved decoration. The narrative friezes and reliefs on the walls of the burial chamber and the corridor leading to it gave a vivid and detailed picture of daily life in ancient Egypt. Here were depicted the activities of farmers, shipbuilders, foresters, stone masons, leather workers, and gold-smelters. Here too were illustrations of Ti's own domestic and official life which showed him to have been a very powerful lord in a feudal-type society. The tomb of Ti gave a fascinating insight into the life of the period when the pyramids had been built, but at the same time it increased the mystery of those colossal structures for it posed a central question: how could a people with only a rudimentary technology have succeeded in building them?

Mariette did not believe that much could be learned from the pyramids themselves, and it was not until a year before his death that he turned his attention to them. In 1880 he opened a minor pyramid at Sekkara, and he had a stroke of luck comparable to that of his first discovery. The small pyramid turned out to be a royal tomb.

It was Mariette's successor as director of the Institute, another Frenchman, Gaston Maspero, and his assistant Brugsch who made the next great discovery in Egyptian archaeology. The royal burial chambers in the great pyramids and in the Valley of the Kings all turned out to be empty when they were explored. It was naturally assumed that their contents, including the mummified royal remains, had all been pillaged centuries ago. Powdered mummy had been in great demand as a remedy for all kinds of diseases in the European Middle Ages. So when Maspero found intact the mummies of 36 kings, queens, princes, and high priests, including the illustrious Rameses II, Seti I, Tuthmose II, and Amenophis I, he won renown in the history of Egyptology.

The circumstances of Maspero's find were curious and dramatic. Noticing that some fine funerary objects and papyri were turning up regularly on the private market in Egyptian antiquities, Maspero decided that someone had found a rich tomb and was plundering it. His investigations led him to an Arab family, one of whose members was induced to talk and to lead the authorities to the secret hiding place of the loot. It was just outside the Valley of the Kings, and was a most cunningly concealed hiding place. Access was gained only by descending between the walls of a precipice to the hidden entrance to a well. Leading from the interior of the well there were underground passages which led eventually to a funerary chamber. Inside this chamber was an astonishing sight. Not only was the ground littered with valuable objects and works of art, but also from floor to ceiling were piled sarcophagi and boxes of mummies. All of these were carefully marked with their names and among them were some of the most famous rulers of Egyptian antiquity. When the contents of the royal mass tomb were transferred by barge down the Nile to Cairo, funeral salutes were fired by the Egyptian villagers, while women followed along the bank wailing and tearing their hair as if in mourning for their own rulers. Tomb plundering had been a problem at the very time when the royal tombs in the Valley of the Kings had been constructed. This fact is proved by surviving contemporary documents announcing dire punishments for tomb robbers. The royal tombs were probably situated together in the Valley so that the living successors of the royal dynasty would be able to protect them. After all it would be in their own interest to do so because they too in turn would need protection. There are indications that the system worked relatively well for a time, but with inevitable dynastic changes, wars, and the occasional accession of weak rulers, there was obviously no guarantee of the eternal repose for their mortal remains that the great kings had hoped for. It must have been at a time when a collapse of authority was foreseeable that a ruler, or possibly an assembly of priests, had removed the royal mummies that Maspero found to the obscure communal tomb outside the valley, for there they might have a chance of resting in peace even though not in the splendour they had originally provided for themselves. It is ironical that in this land where stood the most monumental tombs the world had ever seen, the rulers that enjoyed the longest uninterrupted repose after death

View of the treasury in Tutankhamen's tomb

had been bundled unceremoniously together in an obscure hole in the ground.

It seemed that nearly every new discovery in Egyptology raised some new question about the pyramids. Were they really just monumental tombs, the egomaniacal creations of ancient kings bent on feathering the nests of their eternal souls? Not every European scholar thought so. One man who thought that at least one of the pyramids at Giza was much more than this was the Astronomer Royal for Scotland, Charles Piazzi Smyth, who in 1874 published a curious and apparently scholarly book titled *Our Inheritance in the Great Pyramid*, which became an international best seller.

Wherever there are intriguing mysteries and reliable information is meagre, eccentric theories flourish. Nowhere has this been more true than in the case of the puzzle of the pyramids. Piazzi Smyth set out for Egypt in 1864. His object was to measure the exact dimensions of the Great Pyramid at Giza. Ten years later, when he published his book, he had decided that the Great Pyramid had great significance for Christians and that its structure could even reveal future events. Briefly, Piazzi Smyth found, in its dimensions and alignments and those of its internal chambers and passages, the encoded history of the human race from Old Testament Biblical times down to the future Second Coming of Christ. The Scot has had many followers down to modern times, and in recent years the so-called science of 'pyramidology' has enjoyed a boom. The ideas of the eccentric 19th-century astronomer have been combined with the theory of the modern German writer Erich von Daniken that the pyramids were built by space men. This makes a heady mix of speculation indeed. But perhaps Piazzi Smyth's major importance was that his theories brought to Egypt the man who was to become the greatest Egyptologist of all, the British archaeologist William Flinders Petrie. Petrie arrived in Egypt in 1880 at the age of 27. His father, a supporter of Piazzi Smyth's idea that the Great Pyramid was divine revelation in stone, encouraged him to make the trip. He believed that the young man, who had already made a reputation for himself with his precise and detailed survey of Stonehenge, would be able to confirm the measurements on which the Astronomer Royal's theories were based. But Petrie was, at the least, skeptical of Piazzi Smyth's and his own father's views, and so it was that he went to Egypt determined to settle once and for all the puzzle of the pyramids.

CHAPTER 2

THE PUZZLE OF
THE PYRAMIDS

The heart of the mystery of ancient Egypt lies on the Giza plateau, within sight of modern Cairo. Its three pyramids represent the pinnacle of Egyptian engineering achievement, but what do they represent beyond that? For over a hundred and fifty years the pyramidologists and their twentieth-century descendants have been at odds with Egyptologists over the matter. Egyptologists insist that the pyramids are simply tombs. Pyramidologists are certain they contain encoded messages from the past. Up to now, the Egyptologists, with their appeal to scientific evidence and common sense have had the best of it. But recent discoveries on the Giza plateau look as if they might change all that.

One still, moonlit night in 1880 a white figure emerged from one of the tombs near the base of the Great Pyramid of Cheops, scrambled over the great stones and climbed to the entrance to the chambers of the dead. Then it disappeared. An observer might well have thought that he had seen a ghost. What in fact he would have seen was a stark naked Englishman. William Flinders Petrie, just arrived at Giza, had encamped in one of the mastabas and was impatient to begin the survey of the Great Pyramid. He went naked because of the heat, and even so, when he emerged after midnight he was sweating profusely and had an aching head. He was satisfied with the night's work, though, when he went back to his mastaba. By the light of a smoking lamp he copied out and put in order the notes he had made inside the pyramid.

Night after night Petrie worked in the stifling corridors and chambers of the pyramids. His work led to the publication of his book, *Pyramids and Temples at Gizeh*, in 1883. His findings are generally considered to have demolished Piazzi Smyth's theory that mysteries and messages were encoded in the measurements of the Great Pyramid. But he had demonstrated that it was a building of sublime symmetry and proportions and a consummate feat of engineering genius. Petrie became the man most intimately acquainted with the pyramids of Egypt, and throughout his life he denounced the fantasies of pyramidologists. A tale he enjoyed telling was how he once caught a pyramidologist filing down a projecting stone in order to make its measurement conform to his theory.

One overwhelming fact that is difficult to reconcile with the claims of mystical pyramidology is that the Great Pyramid of Cheops is only one of more than 60 pyramids scattered throughout Egypt. This implies that it is a cultural artifact of a historical people and not a building raised on the precise instructions of God Almighty. Petrie, in his 60-year career in Egyptology, investigated all the pyramids, and put forward his own hypotheses as to when, how, and why they had been built.

The oldest structure, he believed, was the pyramid at Medum, which doesn't look much like a pyramid at all today, but more like an immense square tower. This tower structure, Petrie believed, was the central core of the building. Beneath and in the middle of it was the tomb chamber, the entrance to which was by way of a long sloping passage which leveled off below the chamber and then rose vertically into it through the floor. The building had been begun, he suggested, as a mastaba, which had been enlarged by heightening it and adding a coating. This process of heightening and extending had been repeated seven times, resulting in a high, stepped mass of masonry. The same process was exemplified more clearly in the better preserved step pyramid at Sekkara. The pyramid shape, Petrie thought, might have come about rather by chance as the original structure was added to. This idea was supported by the fact that the internal masonry lining the descending passage showed clear discontinuities at points corresponding to where the entrances would have been at the different stages of construction. This observation indicated that for a time the stepped structure had been regarded as the building's ultimate form. Eventually a true pyramid would have been achieved by adding a uniform slope of masonry from base to top. Whether this stage had actually been reached at Medum was dubious, though, for it was possible that the disaster of its collapse had occurred before the building was complete. The internal stresses set up in such an immense mass of masonry were such that the very precise calculations of angles, tolerances, and the load-bearing capacity of foundations needed to be made to ensure against collapse. Medum probably taught the pyramid builders valuable architectural lessons which they applied in the later construction of the pyramids at Giza.

Although they undermined the elaborate theories of Piazzi Smyth, Petrie's measurements confirmed an observation made by another founder of Biblical-Pyramidology: John Taylor. This London publisher had wondered why the angle of the Great Pyramid's flank sloped at almost 52 degrees (in fact, 51°51'). Then, after comparing the pyramid's height to its base length, he saw the answer: it had to slope at just that angle if the structure's height was to relate to its length by the same ratio as the radius of a circle to its circumference. In other words, the ancient Egyptians had understood the principle of pi (a mathematical discovery usually attributed to Pythagoras over two thousand years later).

This discovery led Taylor to believe that the ancient pyramid builders had constructed the monument to represent the proportions – if not the shape – of the northern hemisphere of the Earth. This theory appeared to be vindicated when Petrie's measurements confirmed that the base length of the Great Pyramid was one eighth of a minute of the Earth's circumference (i.e. if it is multiplied by eight, then sixty [the number of minutes in a degree] then 360 [the number of degrees in a circle] the figure of 25,000 miles is arrived at – the circumference of the Earth is 24,902 miles). So great a coincidence could not, Taylor thought, be a matter of accident. The designers of the pyramid must have left it as a hidden message for future generations. As to how the ancient Egyptians had known the exact size of the Earth – despite leaving no trace of an ocean-going navy or records of world circumnavigation – the explanation seemed obvious to a Christian fundamentalist like Taylor: they had been told by God. Flinders Petrie, and most subsequent Egyptologists, understandably rejected this explanation. Unfortunately, in doing so, they have all but ignored Taylor's mathematical findings. The answers to the mysteries of the pyramids lie, orthodox Egyptologists stress, in the history and beliefs of the men who built them. If something cannot be explained, it is simply because we don't yet know enough about the ancient Egyptians. The result is that, embarrassed by their early association with the pyramidologists, the Egyptologists have generally taken a conservative stance towards the pyramids, insisting that they are tombs *and nothing more*. Now it is true that this explanation fits the majority of pyramids in the Nile valley, which are basically burial chambers surrounded by a mountains of rubble, and whose other chambers seem designed to confuse grave-robbers. But the Great Pyramid of Cheops fails to fit the pattern. Its 'underground chamber' is simply a rubble-filled pit, and there is no sign that it was ever used as a tomb. Modern carbon-dating of its mortar placed it around 2400 to 2500 BC – about the time of the Pharaoh Cheops.

The Cheops' Pyramid was first thoroughly investigated in 820 AD by Caliph Al-Mamun, son of the fabled Haroun Al-Rashid. The Caliph had heard that the pyramid contained not only great treasure, but ancient star maps and terrestrial globes of the highest accuracy. As ruler of a trading empire, good maps were worth more to him than gold. At that time, the Great Pyramid's smooth outer casing of pure white limestone was still intact, showing no sign of an entrance. (It was not until an earthquake levelled Cairo in 1222 AD, that stone-hungry builders stripped the limestone slabs and revealed the rough blocks beneath, giving the Great Pyramid its present 'stepped' appearance.) Luckily, the Caliph had read about the travels of Strabo. When this Greek geographer had visited the Great Pyramid in 24 AD, he was shown a hinged door in the limestone that gave access to a 'vermin-infested pit' running down at an angle, deep beneath the pyramid.

Unfortunately, in the intervening centuries, the local Egyptians had forgotten the position of the hidden door, so all Al-Mamun could do was order his workers dig into the limestone facing at a likely spot.

After months of back-breaking work and one hundred feet into the pyramid, the Caliph came to suspect that the monument was solid, and prepared to abandon the attempt. It was at this point that a worker in the tunnel heard a thud coming from somewhere above him and to his left. Digging in the direction of the noise, the workmen found themselves in a sloping passage, sealed at its upper end by Strabo's hinged limestone slab. A prism shaped rock lay on the floor of the low tunnel. Unmoved for thousands of years, it had chosen just that moment to fall from the roof of the passage and alert the attentive workman. Lit by flickering torches, the explorers followed the new passage down into the depths beneath the pyramid.

One can imagine their disappointment when the tunnel ended in a half-finished chamber, empty of all but the droppings of the vermin Strabo had mentioned. Retracing their steps, they came upon the fallen, prism-shaped block again. Looking at the hole it had made in the ceiling, Caliph Al-Mamun saw that it was, in fact, the opening of a diagonally ascending passage, blocked with a granite plug. After weeks of hacking at it, the explorers squeezed past the plug, only to find the passage blocked by another. The process had to be repeated again and again, but the diggers worked with a will – the treasure must be great indeed to be hidden so thoroughly. At last they emerged into a horizontal passage running due south. At one end was a rectangular room with plastered walls and a gabled roof. Since Arabs buried their women in gabled tombs, the Caliph named it the Queen's Chamber.

But it contained no queen, or anything else, except a recess in one wall, and a half-inch deposit of sea salt on the plaster. The frustrated workmen began to bore into the recess but soon gave up.

When they returned to the diagonally ascending passage, they saw that it had originally continued upward, although a tall step now blocked the way. When they boosted one another up this step, they found themselves in a high roofed gallery, running up towards the centre of the pyramid.

Up to that point, they had been forced to squeeze through narrow passages, but when they clambered up to the Grand Gallery, Al-Mamun's men had room to stretch. It was seven feet wide at the floor, narrowing to about half that width at the ceiling, 28 feet above their heads. Scrambling 153 feet up the slippery limestone floor, which was angled at 26 degrees, they came to a stone block, eight feet high. Beyond that was an entrance and a short passage, leading to the centre of the pyramid.

Al-Mamun led the way into a large square chamber, three times taller than a man, constructed of polished red granite. Again he was to be disappointed. Apart from a red granite sarcophagus shaped like a lidless shoe box, the room, which he called the King's Chamber, was empty and had no other exits. They had explored the whole pyramid and found nothing but an empty stone bath tub. Had tomb robbers been there before them? No, it was impossible, the plugged, sloping passage was the only entry, and they had been the first to clear it. It seemed the pyramid had been sealed-up empty. Whatever else it was, it was not a tomb.

According to legend, Al-Mamun propitiated the exhausted workmen by having treasure carried into the pyramid by night, to be 'discovered' and distributed among them the next day. Al-Mamun was the only one who had gained nothing from the expedition; the star maps and globes were apparently mythical. Al-Mamun returned to Baghdad, where he continued to offend conservative Moslems with his rationalist attitudes, and after establishing a library called the House of Wisdom, died in 833 AD.

If he had explored a little more persistently, Al-Mamun might have discovered the answer to at least part of the riddle. There was indeed a second entrance: a narrow, well-like shaft leading directly from the Grand Gallery down to Strabo's verminous passage. This was not discovered until the adventurer Giovanni

Caviglia cleared the rubble that blocked it in the early nineteenth century. Was this the way the tomb robbers had entered to loot the King's and Queen's chamber? If so, why did they go to all the trouble of blocking their exit with rubble when they left?

In the 19th century, other strange features were discovered. For example, a series of five empty rooms, each only a few feet high, are stacked above the King's Chamber. These appear to be an anti-earthquake precaution, reducing the weight of stone on the ceiling of the King's Chamber to prevent possible collapse. It was also noted that the King's Chamber had nine inch sloping shafts in the north and south walls. Investigation of the outside of the pyramid revealed corresponding openings, and when the shafts in the King's Chamber were unblocked, air rushed in and kept the temperature at a constant 68 degrees. The Queen's Chamber had similar shafts, but these did not appear to reach the outside air. If, as it seemed, the shafts to the King's Chamber were for ventilation, why were the lower Queen's Chamber shafts – logically built first – uncompleted? Furthermore, why bother to air-condition a tomb?

One of the most interesting clues to the purpose of the Great Pyramid had been furnished by the 5th century Byzantine philosopher Proclus, who recorded that, during its construction, it had been used as an observatory. This notion was taken up in 1883 by an astronomer named Richard Anthony Proctor, who pointed out that the 'descending passage' would, in 2500 BC, have pointed directly at the Pole Star, which in those days was Alpha Draconis. (Due to the phenomenon known as precession of the equinoxes – caused by a wobble on the earth's axis – the stars slowly change their position.) If the rubble-filled pit had once contained a pool, the light of the Pole Star would be reflected in it as in the mirror of a modern telescope. Moreover, in the days before the Grand Gallery was finished and the King's Chamber constructed, its 'end' would have made an ideal slot through which to observe the transit of stars and make an accurate map of the heavens. Once the heavens had been mapped, the Pyramid could be completed, and its builders could make their exit through the top, leaving the upward-sloping passage to the King's Chamber sealed with granite plugs.

All this is not to suggest, of course, that most of the pyramids of Egypt were not designed a tombs. The ancient Egyptians have been described by one writer as a people with a national death fixation. Perhaps it might be more accurate to say a life-after-death fixation. Their religion revolved around the notion of the pharaoh as a god-king, who would intercede with his fellow gods to ensure immortality for every one of his people. The transition of the soul from this world to the Egyptian afterworld lay at the core of their faith, and the correct method of burial, with suitable grave goods and decorations, was of central importance to rich and poor alike – a point that is demonstrated by one of the most widely-publicised Egyptological discoveries of all time.

No archaeological discovery has cast more light on the ancient Egyptian cult of the dead than that of the tomb of Tutankhamen. Excavated in the years 1922-26 by a former assistant of Petrie's, Howard Carter, this site yielded the richest-ever find in the history of Egyptology and made the obscure adolescent pharaoh the best-known figure from Egyptian history. For a century Egyptologists had dreamed of finding the pharaoh's tomb unmolested by robbers, and the possibility that such a thing existed was beginning to look very remote indeed when Carter made his incredibly fortunate strike. The astonishing wealth of this tomb of a ruler who could never have been more than a puppet of the powerful priesthood made people wonder what fabulous treasures must have furnished the sepulchral chambers of more illustrious pharaohs. It also helped them to understand the lure that had driven the tomb robbers to overcome all the difficulties that had been put in their paths.

In 1914 a British amateur in archaeology, the Earl of Carnarvon, obtained a concession to dig in the most intensely excavated site in the whole of Egypt: the Valley of the Kings. Gaston Maspero, who signed the authorization, assured Lord Carnarvon and his archaeological aide, Howard Carter, that there could not possibly be anything more to find in the Valley. Carter recalled, however, that the same thing had been said when the American archaeologist Theodore Davis had obtained his concession in 1902. Over the twelve succeeding seasons, Davis had unearthed three important new tombs and found the coffin and mummy of the heretic King Akhnaton. It was certain of Davis' secondary finds that gave Carter the idea that the tomb of Tutankhamen might be in the Valley. A cup buried under a rock, a broken gilded box found in a small rock tomb, and some large earthenware jars containing funerary material – all these finds bore the name Tutankhamen and suggested the existence of his tomb somewhere in the vicinity.

Carter and Carnarvon started digging in 1917 and continued for five seasons with little success. A small deposit of alabaster jars bearing the names of the pharaohs Rameses II and Meremptah were found, but nothing else of note came to light in the entire triangle of their concession. There was some debate whether they should devote a sixth season to the site or move on to a more promising one elsewhere. Finally they decided to put in a final season as there were still some areas where they had not dug.

Immediately below the entrance to the tomb of Rameses VI there were some ancient workmen's huts erected on a foundation of flint boulders, originally to accommodate labourers in the tomb of Rameses. Eventually the only spot left unexcavated was directly underneath the huts, and late in his last season, after Lord Carnarvon had gone back to England, Carter ordered them to be demolished. When the first one was taken down there was revealed beneath it a step cut into the rock. Two days of feverish excavation revealed a stairway leading down beneath an overhanging rock. At the end of it the upper part of a sealed doorway was disclosed. A peephole drilled in the door revealed beyond it a passage filled with rubble. Carter could scarcely control his excitement. The seals on the door indicated that this was the tomb of an important person, and the presence of the huts above it showed that it had not been entered since the days of Rameses VI. Feeling that such a potentially important find should be shared with his sponsor, Carter telegraphed Carnarvon to come from England, and filled in the excavation again to await his arrival. He would have been less in suspense if he had first cleared another few inches down the doorway, for there, quite distinctly, was the seal of Tutankhamen.

Nearly three weeks later Carnarvon arrived from England and the excavation was resumed. It took workmen several days to clear the rubble in the passage beyond the door, and when they had done so a second sealed door was revealed. When a hole big enough to shine a light through was made in this door, the most fantastic sight ever to meet the eyes of an archaeologist was revealed to Carter. In the chamber beyond were a golden throne, golden couches, alabaster vases, statues, animal heads, and gold snakes, as well as a piled-up profusion of boxes and caskets. Only there was no sign of a sarcophagus, and when the excavators broke into the room they found that it was only an antechamber and in two of the walls there were other sealed and plastered doorways.

At this stage further progress was delayed by the fact that the crowded antechamber could not be cleared until its contents had been cataloged and photographed, and in some cases given special preservative treatment because of their fragile state. This work required experts from all over the world, and once again the excavation was filled in until a team capable of doing the job properly could be assembled. Three months passed before one of the sealed doors from the antechamber was breached. Shining his light through the first hole made in the door, and moving it around in all directions, Carter announced to the assembled scientists and officials that he seemed to be looking at a wall of solid gold. When eventually the entire doorway was cleared, Carter and Carnarvon were the first to enter the room beyond, and when they did so they found that the apparent wall of gold was a huge shrine that nearly filled the room. Moving with extreme care to avoid damaging priceless funerary gifts, they went to the eastern end of the shrine. Here there were two great bolted doors, which when opened revealed a second shrine, also with great doors that were sealed as well as bolted. Deciding to leave the seal intact and the pharaoh undisturbed for the time being they then went to the other end of the sepulchral chamber, where they found a low door giving entrance to yet another room, a small one but furnished with greater treasures than had been found elsewhere in the tomb: exquisite figures in gold of guardian gods and goddesses, and miniature shrines with funerary statues of Tutankhamen adorned with emblems of the underworld.

At this stage, after a series of distinguished visitors had seen the tomb, the excavation was closed down again. Two years passed while the Egyptian government made up its mind whether the concession should be extended, and an international commission sat to adjudicate how the finds should be divided. During this time Lord Carnarvon died in a Cairo hotel of an infection caused by a mosquito bite, and the myth of 'the curse of the pharaohs' was born. It was the winter of 1925-26 before investigation of the tomb could be resumed. Returning to the sealed second shrine, Carter entered it only to find within it a third. His own words describe the next stage:

'With suppressed excitement I carefully cut the cord, removed that precious seal, drew back the bolts, and opened the doors, when a fourth shrine was revealed, similar in design and even more brilliant in workmanship than the last . . . An indescribable moment for an archaeologist! What was beneath and what did that fourth shrine contain ? With intense excitement I drew back the bolts of the last and unsealed doors; they slowly swung open, and there, filling the entire area within, effectually barring any further progress, stood an immense yellow quartzite sarcophagus . . . Especially striking were the outstretched hand and wing of a goddess sculptured on the lid of the sarcophagus, as if to ward off an intruder. It symbolised an idea beautiful in conception, and, indeed, seemed an eloquent illustration of the perfect faith and tender solicitude for the well-being of their loved one, that animated the people who dwelt in that land over 30 centuries ago.'

The lid of the sarcophagus weighed over half a ton and hoisting tackle had to be brought into the chamber in order to lift it. First the four shrines had to be carefully dismantled and removed, and as this was being done Carter noticed that each of their 80 component parts was numbered, but some of them had been assembled wrongly, and his feelings of admiration for the original craftsmen and of scorn for the workmen were as if they were his contempo-

Howard Carter and his assistant remove the partition wall between the
Antechamber and Burial Chamber in Tutankhamen's tomb

raries. When at last the heavy lid of the sarcophagus was raised all that could be seen was something bundled in linen cloths. These were removed to reveal a golden effigy of Tutankhamen on the lid of a coffin. This proved to the the lid of the first of three coffins, each one nested within the other, and each decorated with an effigy of the king, wearing and surrounded by symbols of the religion of Osiris. The innermost coffin was made of solid gold and the mummy was covered by a mask of beaten gold portraying the youthful king probably as he had looked in life. The one disappointment of the whole fabulous find was that the actual mummy was in a worse state of preservation than those of the other pharaohs that had been found in the communal tomb, for the embalming substance that had been poured liberally over it had caused it to be carbonised. Unwrapping the linen bindings covering the body was a delicate task. Each turn brought to light some golden amulet, symbol, or magic sign. In all, 143 pieces of jewellery were found among the winding sheets wrapped around the mummy, all of them placed in accordance with ritual procedures prescribed in the *Egyptian Book of the Dead*. The walls of the tomb were richly decorated with hieroglyphs and friezes depicting the dead Pharaoh's soul passing through the trials of the underworld and then ascending into heaven to become one with the god Osiris. Fortunately Egyptologists were, by that time, fully acquainted with these Egyptian afterlife myths through the *Book of the Dead*. The contents of the tomb (not just treasure, but everyday objects and even pots of food and beer – what archaeologists call 'grave goods') were intended to sustain and enrich the dead pharaoh's soul as they had done in life. Nevertheless, many of the odd items found by Carter in Tutankhamen's tomb – like a man shaped-wooden frame filled with Nile silt and seed corn – were clearly for some ritual purpose.

The *Book of Coming Forth by Day*, better known as the *Book of the Dead*, consisted of texts that were buried with all ancient Egyptians who could afford it. It was basically a step-by-step survivor's guide to the afterlife, which offered protection and spells to enable the soul to survive the various periods of the netherworld, together with details of various ceremonies – for example, the weighing of the heart to judge if the deceased deserved eternal life.

The *Book of the Dead* was compiled during the period of the Middle Kingdom (around 2050–1750 BC), but was clearly based on older texts. Such texts – known as the Pyramid Texts – were eventually discovered in several pyramids dating from the 5th and 6th Dynasties (i.e. those immediately following the dynasty which had built the Giza Pyramids) and dated at least four hundred years before the compilation of the *Book of the Dead*.

The Pyramid Texts had been discovered by chance. In 1879, a workman saw a desert jackal disappear into a seemingly insignificant hole beneath the Pyramid of Unas, last pharaoh of the 5th Dynasty (c.2300 BC). Investigating, he saw that it was not a burrow, but a man-made tunnel. If the workman was hoping to find treasure he was disappointed – the pyramid had been sacked long before. Fortunately for Egyptology, however, the walls and ceiling were covered with beautiful and elaborate inscriptions. When translated, they proved to be a cornucopia of religious information. Four other pyramids from the 5th and 6th Dynasties (built over a period of roughly a hundred years) were also found to contain similar inscriptions. Together with the *Book of the Dead*, the Pyramid Texts constituted the religious equivalent of the Rosetta stone:

The ancient Egyptians believed that in the age of Osiris Zep Tepi, (meaning the 'First Time'), the god-pharaoh and his consort Isis had ruled the land of the Nile. They raised their people from barbarism, and taught them the arts of civilisation. But Osiris' brother Set grew jealous of the god's power and murdered him. To prevent him returning from the dead, Set cut Osiris into pieces, then scattered them across Egypt. The grieving Isis succeeded in retrieving the pieces, and reconstructed the body by binding them together again (this is probably the origin of the 'bandaging' of mummies). Osiris returned to life long enough to beget the god Horus on his wife, then went to live in the sky. Horus avenged his father's murder, and Isis eventually joined her husband in the heavens.

The Pyramid Texts made it clear that the constellation of Orion

was in fact Osiris, while the star Sirius was Isis. The eyes of
Horus – one of them damaged in the battle with Set – were associated with the sun and moon.

The texts also shed a great deal of light on the religious beliefs
of the previous dynasty. But, as the Egyptologist Sir Wallis-
Budge pointed out, the confusion of some of the Texts suggests
that the scribes did not fully understand what they were writing.
This seems to indicate that they were based on texts that were far
older – perhaps millennia older – than the Fifth Dynasty.

The association of Osiris with the constellation of Orion led to
a striking discovery concerning the Pyramid of Cheops. In 1964,
an academic paper linked the so-called 'air shafts' – which run
diagonally out of the King's Chamber to the outer walls of the
Pyramid – with the constellation of Orion. The Egyptologist
Alexander Badawy had asked an astronomer, Virginia Trimble,
to calculate the positions of the stars around 2550 BC, at the time
the Pyramid was built.

It should be explained that the stars change their positions in
the sky due to a phenomenon known as the precession of the
equinoxes, which is due to the wobble of the earth's axis. This
wobble causes the earth to spin like a gyrating top, returning to its
original position every 25,992 years. Without this wobble, the
stars would be fixed in their courses; as it is, the positions of the
constellations change like a vast clock, so the position of the
Spring equinox appears to move backwards through the zodiac.
This is why it was necessary for Virginia Trimble to calculate
what the sky looked like at the time the Pyramid was built.

Using these figures, Badawy was able to show that, in 2500 BC,
the southern air shaft in the King's Chamber was aligned on the
constellation of Orion – that is, that someone using the shaft as a
telescope in 2500 BC would have seen the three stars that consti-
tute Orion's 'belt' (Orion is shaped like an hourglass) pass overhead every night.

But why build precisely aligned shafts into a tomb at all?
Badawy pointed-out that one of the titles of a living pharaoh was
'Osiris on Earth'. The Pyramid Texts show that pharaoh's death
ceremonies were partially a re-enactment of the murder and

resurrection of Osiris, with the ultimate aim of sending the pharaoh's soul to become one with Osiris in the sky.

The constellation of Orion is eclipsed for a period of each year by the tilt of the Earth. It disappears beneath the northern horizon, only to reappear 70 days later.

To the ancient Egyptians, this was also a re-enactment of the death and rebirth of the god. Badawy believed that the southern shaft was designed as a spiritual channel: a sort of launch tube to direct the soul of the Pharaoh from his corpse to the re-emerged Orion/Osiris over the southern horizon. In the early 1990s, a Belgian construction engineer called Robert Bauval also became interested in the Great Pyramid's air shafts. Using computer technology he confirmed Badawy's earlier findings, but also made some striking new discoveries, such as that the shaft was aligned on the star Zeta Orionis in Orion's belt, and that the southern shaft of the Queen's Chamber would have pointed to Sirius – the star of the goddess Isis- at the same time.

Studying the Pyramid Texts, Bauval came to believe that he had found the key to some previously obscure sections. For example, the corpse of the pharaoh is sometimes shown with an erect phallus. In the myth, Isis impregnates herself with Horus on the phallus of Osiris. But Bauval also suspected that the Queen's Chamber shaft might played a part in the ceremonial impregnation of the goddess, and that as Sirius/Isis rose from below the horizon after her yearly eclipse, the body of the pharaoh would be positioned in the Queen's Chamber to shoot his spiritual seed along the shaft to 'father' the next pharaoh (Horus). Later, at the new rising of Orion/Osiris, the body of the pharaoh would be carried to the King's Chamber and, in a ceremony referred to in the Pyramid Texts as the 'opening of the mouth', the jaw of the corpse would be struck open by the dead man's son (Horus), freeing the soul to fly up the shaft towards Osiris.

In short, Bauval suggested that the Great Pyramid was not a tomb but a kind of launch-pad.

In 1995, a year after publication of Bauval's *The Orion Mystery*, a German engineer named Rudolf Gantenbrink was commissioned by the Egyptian authorities to de-humidify the

Great Pyramid, whose limestone interior was being damaged by the carbon dioxide in the breath of tourists. Gantenbrink designed a kind of robot tractor, the size of a child's toy, which could explore and photograph the air shafts. This was brought to a halt at a kind of door or portcullis that blocked the southern shaft of the Queen's Chamber. The blockage had metal handles, and a tiny crack at the bottom of the right hand corner. Gantenbrink made the mistake of allowing his discovery to be leaked to the press, and promptly lost his job. At the time of writing (June 1996), Dr Zahi Hawass, the director of the Giza plateau, is organising his own team to investigate what lies behind the door.

Robert Bauval's interest in the connection between the Giza pyramids and the stars of Orion's belt did not originate from a study of the Pyramid Texts, but from a striking insight dating back ten years. In 1982, while visiting the Cairo Museum, he had seen a poster with an aerial photograph of the Giza pyramids. From this he observed the curious alignment of the three pyramids. Each is positioned with its sides facing the four points of the compass. The two largest – the Great Pyramid and the pyramid of Chefren, lie on a diagonal. But the smaller Menkaura Pyramid is off-set a little to the east.

Why was this, wondered Bauval? Menkaura was just as powerful as his two predecessors. Why had he settled for a much smaller monument, and why had he built it out of alignment? The usual explanation for its smaller size was that Menkaura built his pyramid last, and may have had a depleted treasury. As to the off-setting, perhaps the geography of the site had forced him to build there. Neither of these explanations convinced Bauval.

The next year, in November 1983, Bauval was camping in the desert of Saudi Arabia. One night, star gazing at 3 a.m., a friend started to explain to him how sailors find the rising point of Sirius by looking for Orion's belt. The friend pointed out Orion, shaped like an hour-glass, to the right of the Milky Way, which flows across the sky like a river running from north to south. The friend pointed out Orion's belt, and added: 'In fact, the three stars are not perfectly aligned – the smallest is off-set to the east.' He was interrupted at this point as Bauval suddenly shouted: 'I've got it!'

What Bauval had noticed is that the three stars of Orion's belt are aligned exactly like the Giza pyramids. In other words, that the Giza pyramids seemed to 'reflect' the stars of Orion's belt, – the two larger pyramids corresponding to the bright stars of Zeta and Epsilon Orionis, with the Menkaura pyramid as the smaller Delta Orionis. When he later obtained a radio-telescope photograph of Orion's belt and super-imposed it on an aerial photograph of the Giza Pyramids, he found the two matched perfectly. This explains why Bauval was later delighted to discover that the shaft of the King's Chamber in Cheop's Pyramid was aligned specifically on Zeta Orionis: the Pyramid's heavenly counterpart.

Looking at the four other stars of Orion – the outer corners of the hour-glass shape – Bauval noticed that the upper right and lower left points of the constellation corresponded precisely to two pyramids on the ground: respectively, the pyramid at Zawyat al-Aryan and Nebka's Pyramid at Abu Ruwash. All that was needed to prove the theory beyond doubt was two more pyramids corresponding to the other two corners: unfortunately, these do not exist – or, if they ever existed, have long since disappeared beneath the sand.

Bauval also suggests that the ancient Egyptians saw the great concentrated band of stars called the Milky Way as an earthly counterpart of the sacred River Nile – the giver of life in the barren desert. We know from Egyptian texts that they regarded the land of Egypt as an exact reflection of the heavens. So argues Bauval, the building of the Giza pyramids was an attempt to recreate Osiris' heavenly body – the constellation of Orion – on the west bank of the Nile. It even seems possible that the rumour of star-maps that sent Al-Mamun to explore the Great Pyramid was simply a garbled version of the truth: that the pyramids are a star map.

A major mystery remains unsolved. If Egyptian civilisation began around 3000 BC, how did the Egyptians develop the skills revealed in the Giza pyramids in a mere 500 years – skills that modern builders and architects admit they could not match? (A Japanese attempt to build a smaller replica of the Great Pyramid for an exhibition ended in failure.)

According to Bauval, and to his friend Graham Hancock (co-author of a book called *Keeper of Genesis*), the answer is that Egyptian civilisation was not founded around 3000 BC, but thousands of years earlier – perhaps as early as 10,500 BC – by the survivors of another civilisation, who were fleeing from a catastrophe. We shall consider the evidence for this belief in a later chapter.

CHAPTER 3

CLUES IN THE CUNEIFORM

In the early 19th century, as Egyptologists were puzzling over the secrets of the pharaohs, archaeologists in the Middle East were unearthing the buried cities of the Babylonians Assyrians, Armenians and Persians. The key to understanding their past lay in the strange writing called cuneiform, described by one archaeologist as looking 'like bird tracks in wet sand.' The ability to decipher cuneiform, the oldest form of written language, threw open a door on thousands of years of lost history.

In 1840 a remarkable Frenchman became consular agent in the small, hot, dusty town of Mosul in what is now southern Iraq, in the land known as Mesopotamia. Paul Emile Botta was not an archaeologist, but a qualified physician with a deep interest in natural science. He had already travelled once around the world. A professional diplomat with a gift for picking up languages, he soon made many friends among the local Arabs. Gradually his imagination was fired by the ancient history of this forgotten corner of the Turkish empire, and he quickly became known among the Arabs as a man interested in buying antiquities. Botta would go around from hut to hut, asking if they had any old pots or vases for sale, or where they had got the bricks they had used to build an outhouse. He was particularly interested in bricks that had strange markings on them. The news of his interest must have spread because one day an Arab came to him from Khorsabad, some 10 miles away. He said that near his village there was a mound containing thousands of the inscribed bricks and many other things that would greatly interest the Frenchman.

Botta had been in Mosul for a few years at that time, and had learned to be sceptical about the marvels promised him by well-meaning Arab informants. He didn't go himself to investigate the Khorsabad site, but sent two workmen instead. When his men returned to report that they had found not only masses of inscribed bricks but also the walls of an ancient building with carvings and pictures on them, Botta hurried over to see for himself. What he saw convinced him that he had found a palace of one of the old Assyrian kings, and possibly the site of the city of Nineveh itself. He withdrew a team of workmen from Kuyunjik, a site near Mosul where he had had them digging to little avail for a year, and set them to work at Khorsabad. The year was 1843, and with Botta's find Mesopotamian archaeology was born.

The ancient history of the land between the two great rivers, the Tigris and the Euphrates, was at that time known only from references in the Bible. The exact location of the great cities of Nineveh and Babylon, on which the God of the Hebrews had visited his wrath, was quite unknown, and in the early 19th century nobody suspected that the civilisation of the great cities of southern Mesopotamia, of Sumer and Ur, had developed earlier and in some aspects attained higher levels than the Egyptians. For centuries there had been nothing to see in the flat deserts of Mesopotamia except an occasional mysterious mound. In the traditions of the Arabs of the area there were no ancestral memories or legends of the time when the inhabitants of this land had been proud, prosperous, powerful, literate, and cultured. A few travellers in the past had brought back odd trophies from the rubble of the Mesopotamian mounds, but before Botta came to Mosul nobody had excavated in the area.

In Mesopotamia, as in Egypt, the key that gave access to the mysteries of its past was a language. It was a language even more mysterious and difficult, or as one traveller said 'more adverse to the intellect,' than hieroglyphics, because it consisted of abstract geometrical shapes in which a sort of arrow or wedge shape predominated. The language had been called *cuneiform*, from the Latin word *cuneus*, meaning wedge, and for decades before Botta went to Mosul European scholars had been poring over, comparing, and trying to interpret the strange inscriptions found on ruins, on monuments, and on pieces of pottery and clay found both in Mesopotamia and southern Persia. They had achieved a considerable degree of success, thanks largely to the pioneering efforts of a young schoolmaster from Gottingen in Germany named Georg Friedrich Grotefend.

Grotefend undertook to crack the secret of cuneiform lightly, as the result of a wager made when drinking with some friends. He was only an amateur orientalist, and was no specialist in ancient languages, but often problems that confound orthodox methods of solution will yield to the unorthodox. Grotefend's breakthrough was achieved by his trying to find a logical rather than a philological solution to the problem of the cuneiform. Working with copies of some cuneiform inscriptions from the ruins of the royal palace of the ancient Persian city of Persepolis, he noted that a certain group of signs kept being repeated. It was a known fact that the Persian rulers had always begun their proclamations with their names, followed by the words 'great king, king of kings', so Grotefend deduced that the repeated signs represented the word 'king'. The frequency of their repetition suggested that more than one king was named, so he conjectured that the introductory formula might read: 'X, great king, king of kings, son of Z, etc.' If his conjecture was right, he reasoned, there must be three groups of characters that stood for the names of three rulers, who in order of appearance would be son, father, and grandfather. There were a number of such genealogies in ancient Persian history, and Grotefend tested a number of them against the groups of characters that he had isolated as the names. He was able to eliminate some of the genealogical groups for purely logical reasons: that of Cyrus – Cambyses – Cyrus, because all three names began with the same letter and there was no common symbol at the beginning of each name in the cuneiform text; that of Darius – Artaxerxes – Xerxes, because the middle name was too long. Eventually he hit upon a genealogy that fitted the text that he was working with. It was: Xerxes – Darius – Hystaspes. Grotefend was confident that he was right in this because the formula 'great king, king of kings,' was not found in the text after the name Hystaspes, and he knew that Hystaspes had been the founder of the royal line but never a king himself. Thus by sheer reasoning he worked out that his text read: 'Xerxes, great king, king of kings, son of Darius, great king, king of kings, son of Hystaspes.' Many contemporary scholars were sceptical and unconvinced, but Grotefend was later proved to be right.

Before Grotefend achieved his breakthrough in the 1800s, nobody had known for certain that cuneiform was a kind of writing and not just decoration. If it was assumed to be writing, there was no clue as to how it should be read (horizontally or vertically, from left to right or vice versa), or as to whether it was an abstract picture language or a method of phonetic transcription. Grotefend's achievement was not only that he translated a few words of cuneiform, but that he also reasoned out the correct answers to these questions. By establishing the phonetic values of some of the strange characters he showed the way for other scholars to proceed.

Danish, German, French, Irish, and English scholars made contributions to the deciphering of the varieties of the cuneiform in the 50 years following Grotefend's publication of his theories and translation in 1805. Of these, the outstanding contribution was that of the Englishman Henry Rawlinson. A soldier, a diplomat, and a member of Parliament as well as a scholar, Rawlinson brought physical courage as well as intellectual ability to the task of understanding the ancient inscriptions. In 1836, when he was 26 years old, he first became acquainted with Grotefend's work. Earlier he himself had deciphered a number of inscriptions, having tackled the problem in a manner very similar to that employed by Grotefend. Needing more inscriptions to work with, in 1837, while on military service in Persia, Rawlinson undertook the hazardous task of copying the inscription of Darius from the rock face at Behistun.

In the mountains of Kurdistan there is a narrow pass through which the road from Ectabana in Persia to Babylon in Mesopotamia used to pass and which today forms part of the highway from Baghdad to Teheran. Mountains rise sheer from this pass to a height of 4000 feet, and between 200 and 500 feet above ground level there is carved in the rock face an immense relief celebrating the person, exploits, and victories of the mighty King Darius. Beside and beneath these carvings there are fourteen columns of writing in three distinct variations of the cuneiform script – Old Persian, Elamite, and Assyro-Babylonian. The Darius inscriptions were therefore a kind of Rosetta stone of the cuneiform. The problem was that they couldn't be copied in sufficient detail for study unless somebody actually climbed up on to the rock face. This is precisely what Rawlinson decided to do.

The old Persian sculptors who had done the carvings had worked from platforms which had then been cut away, leaving a ledge about 18 inches below the inscriptions. Rawlinson worked from ladders that were propped up on this narrow ledge. He had to have ladders of different lengths in order to copy all the characters, and of course he needed to have his hands free for the work. If we imagine him standing on the high rungs of a nearly vertical ladder with a sheer fall of hundreds of feet behind him, we surely cannot but admire the man's dedication to scholarship. 'In this position I copied all the upper inscriptions,' he later wrote, 'and the interest of the occupation entirely did away with any sense of danger.'

From this ledge, however, he could only get access to the text in Old Persian. The Elamite and Assyro-Babylonian texts were even less accessible, and to get a copy of the latter he had to avail himself of the help of 'a wild Kurdish boy' who climbed up the perpendicular rock face 'in a manner which to a looker-on appeared quite miraculous.' The work was completed without mishap, and Rawlinson was able to present to the specialist scholars of the world a parallel text in three ancient unknown languages. The Old Persian text was the key to the other two, as the Greek of the Rosetta stone was the key to the Egyptian hieroglyphics, and it was Rawlinson, working by the methods that he and Grotefend had independently established, who rendered the first complete translation of the Darius inscription 'I am Darius, the Great King, the King of Persia, the King of the Provinces, the son of Hystaspes, the grandson of Arsames, the Achaemenian. From antiquity are we descended; from antiquity hath our race been kings . . .' Thus began a long, grandly boastful text describing how Darius had, by the grace of the god Ahura Mayda, defeated all his enemies, and particularly those who had rebelled against him at the beginning of his reign. The rebel chiefs, the text announced, had fallen captive to Darius, who had cut off their noses and ears, put out their eyes, exhibited them in public in fetters, and finally crucified them.

Even with the help of the Old Persian text and Rawlinson's translation, the other two languages on the Behistun rock proved difficult to crack. Elamite eventually yielded to the combined efforts of a Dane, Niels Westergaard, an Irishman, Dr Hincks, and an Englishman, Edwin Norris. Norris developed an intriguing theory that the language of the Elamites, a people about whom scarcely anything is known, was related to Finnish! The third text, the Assyro-Babylonian, however, proved the most difficult of the three. This was particularly frustrating because it was the language of all the inscriptions on the buildings, the relics, and the curious clay bricks that had been unearthed in profusion in Mesopotamia since Paul Botta started excavating there in 1843.

The problem was that the Assyro-Babylonian cuneiform was not an alphabetical script, with each symbol representing a sound. It appeared that a single symbol could represent a variety of sounds or meanings, and when a number of symbols were brought together to make a word or phrase the pronunciation of the resultant whole might bear no relation to that of its component parts. For instance, the name of the Assyrian king known in the Bible as Nebuchadnezzar was in fact pronounced Nebukudurriussur, but if the group of characters that spelled the name were pronounced according to their individual phonetic values they rendered the quite different word An – pa – sa – du – sis. Many scholars abandoned the problem as insoluble. Then the lucky find of a batch of clay tablets that together made up part of a kind of dictionary of cuneiform signs encouraged a number of specialists to persist in their efforts. One of these was a brilliant Englishman named William Henry Fox Talbot, later remembered as a pioneer of photography. Fox Talbot carried out a clever ruse that conclusively proved to the world that the apparently impossible task of translating Assyro-Babylonian cuneiform had been accomplished.

Fox Talbot first made his own translation of an Assyrian cylinder. He then sent it in a sealed envelope to the president of the Royal Asiatic Society in London, together with the suggestion that other well-known scholars in the field should be asked to make their translations of the same text. Rawlinson, Dr Hincks, and a French scholar, Jules Oppert, were invited to do so. Each unaware of the others' efforts, they sent their translations to the Society in sealed envelopes. When these were simultaneously opened by a commission of independent judges, and the translations were compared, the sceptics who had been murmuring that other so-called translations were no better than guesswork were silenced for good. Although a few words and phrases were differently interpreted by the four translators, their texts were substantially the same. So the writings in the strange script which someone once said looked like the marks left by birds walking over wet sand, and which were now coming out of Mesopotamia in great numbers, could be read. At last knowledge could be gained of the ancient civilisations that were Western man's cultural ancestors and whose relics had lain for centuries buried beneath the desert sands.

Paul Botta had financed his purchases of antiquities and his archaeological digs from his own pocket, but when his discovery at Khorsabad was announced generous funds were made available from official sources in France to enable him to continue the good work. Gradually his excavations uncovered the remains of what had obviously been a very grand palace, with courtyards, public rooms, and private apartments all splendidly ornamented and decorated. Unfortunately, though, most of the decorations and sculptures quickly disintegrated when they were exposed, and if the French government had not sent out an artist, Eugene Flandin, to work with the excavators and make copies of the

Assyrian reliefs as they came to light, these records of the life and achievement of a lost civilisation would have disappeared. Larger artifacts, however, remained intact, and Botta repaid his sponsors by shipping back to Paris numerous fine large pieces of Assyrian sculpture. The transportation of these trophies, some of which weighed as much as 12 tons, was difficult and hazardous. Wagons with extra-strong axles and wide wheels were needed for the 10-mile journey to the Tigris, and a rough track had to be laid over the route. To reach the port of Basra on the Persian Gulf, the sculptures had to be floated down the river on traditional Mesopotamian rafts buoyed up with inflated skins. A number of Assyrian kings and gods, so recently exhumed from the sand, plunged back into oblivion beneath the tempestuous waters of the Upper Tigris, but Botta continued his efforts undeterred, and the Assyrian rooms in the Louvre today testify to his success.

Transportation was only one of his problems. Another was the Turkish governor of the area, Mehmed Pasha, who believed that the Frenchman was hunting treasure and wanted a substantial portion for himself. Disappointed in this, he summarily banned excavation of the Khorsabad site and refused to allow Arab workmen to work for Botta, justifying his actions by saying that the Frenchman was building a fortress and the excavations were defence entrenchments. Botta countered by going over the pasha's head to his superiors in the Turkish capital of Constantinople and obtaining permission to continue with his work. Mehmed however remained troublesome, and Botta's vexations from this quarter were only ended by the pasha's premature death.

Botta continued to believe that he had discovered Nineveh, and in 1850 he published in five volumes, illustrated by Frandin, his *Monuments de Ninive*. When it became possible to read Assyro-Babylonian cuneiform later in that decade, it was revealed that the palace Botta had excavated was that of the Assyrian king Sargon II of the 8th century BC, and that Khorsabad had formerly been known as Dûr-Sharrukin, or Sargon's Town. It was left to a friend of Botta's, the Englishman Austen Henry Layard, to discover the actual Nineveh. He found the great city, ironically, beneath the great mound at Kuyunjik, the site that Botta had abandoned when he took his team of workmen to Khorsabad.

Layard's name is outstanding in Mesopotamian archaeology. In fact it is virtually synonymous with it just as Petrie's is with Egypt and Schliemann's with Troy. His books, *Early Adventures*, *Nineveh and its Remains*, and *Discoveries in the Ruins of Nineveh and Babylon*, are still highly readable classics of 19th-century travel and archaeological literature. He first travelled in the region at the age of 23 in 1839–40, and in *Early Adventures* he writes eloquently of the urge that inspired the most important achievements of his career in archaeology:

'I now felt an irresistible desire to penetrate to the regions beyond the Euphrates, to which history and tradition point as the birthplace of the wisdom of the West. Most travellers, after a journey through the usually frequented parts of the East, have the same longing to cross the great river, and to explore those lands which are separated on the map from the confines of Syria by a vast blank stretching over Assyria, Babylonia, and Chaldea. With these names are linked great nations and great cities dimly shadowed forth in history; mighty ruins, in the midst of deserts, defying, by their very desolation and lack of definite form the description of the traveller; the remnants of mighty races still roving over the land; the fulfilling and fulfillment of prophecies; the plains to which the Jew and the Gentile alike look as the cradle of their race.'

Of all the 'mighty ruins, in the midst of deserts' that Layard saw on his first journey, the one that most fascinated him was the enormous mound known to be the site of the Biblical city of Nimrud, or Nimrod, which was named after its founder. According to the Bible he was one of the grandsons of Noah. Layard longed to excavate it, but lack of funds prevented him from undertaking any excavations on his own initiative for a further five years. Botta's successes and generous official funding made him envious, and in 1845, although he still had only £60 to finance his venture, he took a river boat down the Tigris to begin his excavations at Nimrud.

This was not a particularly good time or place for such an expedition, for the new Turkish governor proved a tyrant and the desert tribes were in a warlike mood and inclined to vent their feelings on any foreigner. Layard was lucky, however, in gaining the friendship of a tribal sheik named Awad, whose territory included the great mound of Nimrud. Awad took an interest in the Englishman's work and was pleased to supply him with cheap labour. Layard was lucky, too, in getting his excavations off to a successful start. Faced with a virtual mountain, and helped only by six Arabs with picks and shovels, he had no idea where to begin, and when Awad pointed out a piece of yellowish stone sticking out of the ground he told the workmen to start digging there. It was hard work, for after months of drought the earth was packed hard. But Layard swung a pick, too, and his team's labours were soon rewarded. An alabaster slab was uncovered, then a second one attached to it, then eight more. The ten slabs formed a square, with a gap in one corner: the shape and proportions of a room with a door. Layard ordered the men to dig down the faces of the slabs, for these were obviously the tops of the walls of a room, and when they did so some inscriptions were soon revealed, then a finely decorated frieze. Walls so decorated and faced with alabaster could surely belong to nothing less than a royal palace.

Excited by this first find and impatient to know what other treasures the mound might contain, Layard split his team. He took half of them to dig on the other side of the mound, and again his luck, or his sense of divination, was extraordinary. The first pick swung struck stone, and more hours of exhausting labour brought to light an inscription frieze and carvings in relief. Layard declared himself 'well satisfied' with his first day's work at Nimrud; as indeed he must have been, having unearthed the walls of two Assyrian palaces.

On the second day of excavation the first chamber was cleared and some interesting fragments were found among the rubble on the floor: some exquisitely carved flowers, part of a tiny sphinx, a small robed figure, some pieces of porcelain with traces of gilding. Awad, convinced that the Englishman must be looking for treasure, covertly showed Layard some flakes of gold leaf he had found, and was astonished when Layard cheerfully told him that he could keep all the gold he found. The archaeologist's interest in old carvings, inscriptions, and statues was a mystery to the desert Arab, but the lure of gold encouraged him to recruit more helpers, and at the end of five days Layard had excavated a maze of chambers with interestingly decorated and inscribed walls. He had also investigated the most conspicuous feature of the site, the pyramid-like mound that the ancient Greek historian Xenophon had written about, which he found appeared to be only a mass of solid brick. It was in fact one of the tall stepped towers of the typical Mesopotamian temple complex, known as a *ziggurat*. Layard knew that Botta had unearthed a similar mysterious structure at Khorsabad, which had contained no sculptures, and as movable sculptures were the main object of his quest he soon abandoned the investigation and returned to the palaces, where a maze of rooms and passages was gradually excavated.

Many of the rooms boasted fine reliefs, powerful and graphic portrayals of the Assyrians engaged in their most characteristic occupations of fighting, pillaging, and hunting. The first sculptures that he found, however, were disappointingly badly damaged. One of the palaces bore signs of having been destroyed by fire. Weather and vandalism had also taken their toll. But in the other building some fine pieces were eventually found. There were a pair of perfectly preserved winged lions that stood 12 feet tall and had long cuneiform inscriptions between their legs. There were winged bulls, too, and griffin-headed human figures, and sculptured eagles and massive bearded men. And one day, when Layard was temporarily away from the site, two tribesmen came to him and announced excitedly that they had found Nimrud himself. Layard hurried back to the mound, where all the diggers were gathered around a trench from the bottom of which there projected a huge head of blanched stone, crowned with a rounded turban and with triple horns. Layard knew that this superb piece would be the human head of a lion or bull colossus, and that such figures were usually to be found in pairs, flanking an entrance or gateway. He paced out the usual width of such an entrance and ordered his workmen to dig another trench, and sure enough they came upon a duplicate colossal head.

Unfortunately the news that Nimrud himself had been unearthed had reached the Turkish governor in Mosul, and he, uncertain whether Nimrud had been an infidel or one of the faithful and what observances were due to his 'remains,' ordered Layard to suspend digging until this theological problem could be resolved. The order, coming as it did when the work was proceeding apace and exciting discoveries were coming to light daily, meant an intolerable delay, but fortunately very soon afterward there arrived from Constantinople a permit to excavate authorised by the Sultan himself, and Layard was able to complete his first excavation, which turned out to be the palace of King Assurnasirpal II, an Assyrian ruler of the 9th century BC, and to send to Britain a mass of magnificent reliefs and colossal sculptures to provide the British Museum with an Assyrian collection to surpass that of the Louvre in Paris.

In his book, *Nineveh and its Remains*, Layard records a marvellous speech that a reflective Arab sheik made to him one evening after an arduous day's work inching a colossal sculpture of a bull out of a trench prior to conveying it to the Tigris and thence shipping it to England.

'In the name of the Most High,' said the sheik, 'tell me, O Bey, what you are going to do with those stones. So many thousands of purses spent upon such things! Can it be, as you say, that your people learn wisdom from them; or is it, as his reverence the Cadi declares, that they are to go to the palace of your Queen, who, with the rest of the unbelievers, worships these idols? As for wisdom, these figures will not teach you to make better knives, or scissors, or chintzes; and it is in the making of those things that the English show their wisdom. But God is great! God is great! Here are stones which have been buried ever since the time of the holy Noah – peace be with him ! Perhaps they were under ground before the deluge. I have lived on these lands for years. My father, and the father of my father pitched their tents here before me; but they never heard of these figures. For twelve hundred years have the true believers (and, praise be to God ! all true wisdom is with them alone) been settled in this country, and none of them ever heard of a palace under ground. Neither did they who went before them. But lo! here comes a Frank (European) from many days' journey off, and he walks up to the very place, and he takes a stick [illustrating the description at the same time with the point of his spear], and makes a line here, and makes a line there. Here, says he, is the palace; there, says he, is the gate; and he shows us what has been all our lives beneath our feet, without our having known anything about it. Wonderful! Wonderful! Is it by books, is it by magic, is it by your prophets, that you have learnt these things?'

After Nimrud, Layard decided to excavate Botta's old site at Kuyunjik. At the time some people thought that his decision must have been motivated either by sheer perversity or by a malicious hope that another success would confirm his ascendancy over his French friend and rival. A more charitable view would be that he really was, as the sheik implied, a genius as an archaeologist, and had learned at Nimrud to survey the Mesopotamian mounds with an eye for surface clues that told him where to dig. Whatever his motivation, his success was again virtually immediate and one of supreme archaeological importance.

First he had his workmen dig a vertical shaft into the mound until they struck a brick platform 20 feet below the surface. He then had tunnels dug from this platform in various directions, one of which eventually revealed a wall relief and then a gate flanked by winged bulls. Within a month he had opened nine rooms of a building that later turned out, when Rawlinson and Hincks had translated the copious cuneiform inscriptions found on its walls, to be one of the greatest palaces of Nineveh, that of one of the cruellest, greediest, and most powerful of the Assyrian kings mentioned in the Bible: Sennacherib. When the great hall of this palace was cleared there were revealed all around its walls reliefs depicting Sennacherib's conquests in great and realistic detail. Background landscapes and the modes of dress of the people portrayed made possible the identification of the various campaigns recorded, and the extent of Sennacherib's dominion and the ruthlessness with which it was established were conveyed with terrible immediacy. Here was a tyrant who had shown mercy to none, and had boasted of his tyranny and cruelty, but who had also created at Nineveh the most splendid and architecturally sophisticated city of its day and age. The palace reliefs, moreover, gave an account of Sennacherib's war against the kingdom of Judah which was entirely consistent with the account in the Biblical Second Book of Kings. This was a discovery that delighted believers in the historical authenticity of the Bible.

In his book, *The Monuments of Nineveh* (1853), Layard printed some imaginary reconstructions of the city of Nineveh, with its tremendous palaces overlooking the Tigris. The Assyrian kings had built on a colossal scale, and surely could not have conceived that all the buildings they had constructed, and even the very language they spoke and wrote in, would be utterly forgotten and lost to the world for more than 2000 years before curious scholars brought them to light again. The total eclipse of Assyria after it had fallen, and the conditions to which its great cities and palaces were reduced, were an uncanny fulfillment of the terrible promise recorded in the Biblical Book of Zephaniah that the Lord:

'. . . will stretch out his hand against the north, and destroy Assyria; and he will make Nineveh a desolation, a dry waste like the desert.

'Herds shall lie down in the midst of her, all the beasts of the field; the vulture and the hedgehog shall lodge in her capitals; the owl shall hoot in the window, the raven croak on the threshold, for her cedar work will be laid bare.

'This is the exultant city that dwelt secure, that said to herself, "I am and there is none else." What a desolation she has become, a lair for wild beasts !'

The Hebrew prophet has it that the utter destruction of Nineveh was the work of the Lord. If so, the Lord employed for his purpose the combined forces of the Babylonians, the Elamites, and the Syrians, but oddly enough not the Hebrews themselves. The Second Book of Kings records how the king of Judea, Hezekiah, was invited by the king of Babylon to join the coalition against Assyria, and how, on the advice of his chief minister, Isaiah, he declined: an unwise decision, as it turned out, because when Assyria was overthrown Judea became one of the spoils of war and the Jews became vassals of the Babylonians.

Sennacherib himself did not live to see his palace sacked and the wrath of the Lord visited upon his city of Nineveh. He was murdered by his brothers in 680 BC, and succeeded by a son, Esarhaddon, who kept up the family tradition of waging total war. He extended the Assyrian empire into Egypt. A typical inscription of his reads: 'I surrounded Memphis and captured it in half a day with the aid of breaches in the walls, devastating fire, and scaling ladders. I despoiled and ravaged it and caused it to be consumed by fire. The pharaoh Tarku, his queen, the ladies of his harem, Ushanahuru his legitimate son and heir, and his other sons and daughters, his goods and possessions, his horses, his cattle, his sheep, I carried away as spoil to Assyria.'

It was the Assyrian practice to parade a captive king through the streets of Nineveh with a ring through his nose or lips, like a bull. All the male inhabitants of a conquered city were massacred, and often a pyramid of their heads was built, while the young females were first raped and then burnt alive with the children. And these ruthless acts of war were graphically recorded on the walls of the palaces of Nineveh and boasted about in the cuneiform inscriptions. The Assyrians could hardly have expected anything less than total destruction when at last their empire fell to an alliance of their enemies.

It fell in 626 BC, when Assurbanipal was king. This ruler is the most interesting of all the Assyrian kings and one to whom history owes a great debt. He waged a few wars in the early part of his reign, but was basically a peace-loving man and a scholar. His chief fame rests on his having built up, in his palace at Nineveh, a library of 30,000 inscribed clay tablets, a veritable encyclopedia of all the knowledge of his day. The most important result of Layard's excavation of the mound at Kuyunjik was the discovery of this library.

The actual find was made by one of Layard's assistants, Hormuzd Rassan, a native of Mosul who had become a Christian and had an Oxford education. In the palace that Sennacherib had built, Rassan found two rooms which had apparently been added at a later date, and where, miraculously, the scholar-king's library had survived the devastation. The fire that had destroyed the palace had helped preserve many of the tablets by baking them until they were very hard.

Assurbanipal had sent agents all over the immense empire that he ruled on missions to collect or copy ancient texts, and a text of his own records his motive: 'I wrote on tablets, both wrote and read them, and when I had finished with them, I placed them in my library so that I can peruse them for myself or read them aloud to my guests.' There were texts on medicine, on philosophy, on astronomy, on mathematics, and many on magical arts such as divination and exorcism. As the tablets and copies of them were made available to scholars, the cuneiform experts had the time of their lives. One of them, George Smith of London's British Museum, discovered among the tablets that Rassan had sent to the Museum a number that recounted the deeds of an epic hero named Gilgamesh. Smith found the story that he gradually decoded from the cuneiform and assembled into order utterly enthralling, and when he found that the end was missing he went to Kuyunjik to seek among the rubble for the missing tablets – and miraculously found them. The find was doubly sensational, for the tablets that concluded the great Gilgamesh epic contained an account of a great flood very similar to that given in the Old Testament of the Christian Bible, including a prototype Noah named Utnapishtim.

Gilgamesh is great as a work of literature and fascinating as a counterpart of the Genesis Flood story. But arguably the most important discovery to emerge from the library of Assurbanipal was that centuries before the Assyrians and Babylonians there had existed in Mesopotamia another great civilisation from which these later ones had derived. These precursors had apparently been non-Semitic, and also it seemed that they had been the originators of cuneiform writing. In Assurbanipal's day their language had already been defunct, and he had found it 'curious and obscure,' just as European scholars were later to find Assyro-Babylonian to be. It was the Irish scholar Edward Hincks who first observed that the baffling discrepancies between the symbols of cuneiform and the sounds they represented could be explained on the hypothesis that the Assyro-Babylonians had inherited a script and the method of syllabic transcription from another people and roughly adapted it to their own language. The 'dictionaries' found in Assurbanipal's library afforded evidence of the existence of this earlier, non-Semitic, highly literate people, but who they were, where they had originated, and where they had settled were mysteries.

The French cuneiform expert Jules Oppert discovered that the title 'King of Sumer' occurred frequently in their texts, and it was he who called the people of this lost civilisation the Sumerians. At the time the only clue to their existence was in the cuneiform tablets, and not a single ruin or artifact was known to exist. No one suspected that when the skills of the archaeologist and the cryptologist had brought to light the lost world of Sumer, it would prove to be older than Egypt and the originator of most of the arts and crafts that go to make up the activities and contributions characterising what we consider civilisation.

CHAPTER 4

BEFORE BABEL

'And they said go to, let us build us a city and a tower, whose top may reach unto heaven.' Thus the men of Babel brought down the wrath of God in the Book of Genesis; but did such a tower ever exist? At the same time that cuneiform was yielding up its secrets, 19th century archaeologists began to suspect that Babylon was in fact the Biblical city of Babel. Guided only by a few vague phrases from the Old Testament, some determined men set out to uncover the remains of the Babylonian empire – and stumbled upon the forgotten cities of the Sumer and Akkad, the earliest civilisation of the Middle East.

In 1850 two Englishmen, Henry Loftus and Harry Churchill, rode out into the desert of southern Mesopotamia in search of the land of Shinar. Their expedition was inspired by half a sentence in the Book of Genesis: '. . . as they journeyed from the east, they found a plain in the land of Shinar; and they dwelt there.' The vast desert plain of southern Mesopotamia had not attracted many European explorers. The temperature often exceeded 100°F, many of the Arab tribes were far from friendly, and the occasional low mounds of sand and rubble that were the only indications that this land had once been inhabited had never been known to yield anything of value. It took a man led by a dream to venture out into this inhospitable desert, and Henry Loftus was such a man. He dreamed of finding the lost land of Shinar.

Fortunately some of the desert Arabs were friendly and cooperative. As Loftus and Churchill slowly travelled southward they heard rumours that near a place named Warka on the Persian Gulf was the site of an ancient city called Erech, which was another place mentioned in the Bible. When the Englishmen eventually reached the spot they found a huge heap of rubble covering an area some six miles in circumference. They spent three months on the site, and as well as tracing out the contours of the city they collected some clay tablets and pieces of pottery covered with cuneiform inscriptions. Loftus' prize find was a large, unbroken burial urn covered with writing. To carry it back to civilisation he had to hire Arab bearers, who carried it slung between two long poles and insisted on making the journey a funeral march. Nomads they met along the route wailed and threw dust into their hair in mourning for the remains of one who must have departed this world some time between 3000 and 5000 years ago.

Loftus was not a cuneiform scholar, and he did not know what his random collection of inscriptions would mean to scholars. Only when he got back to England did he learn that the name 'Erech' was inscribed on several of his clay tablets and that he had discovered the first of the old Biblical cities that lay beneath the sand of the plains of Shinar, a name which scholars soon found was synonymous with the land of Sumer. In the next 50 years other great cities, now reduced to rubble, were identified: Ur, which the Bible said was the birthplace of Abraham; Eridu, Fara, Lagash, Larsa, Nippur, and Babylon; and, as the sands gave up their secrets, Europe gradually came to realise that it was not the Greeks or Egyptians, but the Sumerians who created the earliest known civilisation, commanding the essential skills to develop an advanced culture. On the now arid plains at the head of the Persian Gulf there had flourished a highly organised civilisation of independent city states, dating from around 4000 BC (1500 years before the building of the Giza Pyramids). Ironically, Biblical scholars' method of dating – generally accepted by the majority of Europeans up to the mid-nineteenth century – placed the creation of the world in the year 4004 BC.

Like the ancient Egyptians, the Sumerians seem to have

evolved rather abruptly from primitive farmers to a fully functional, well-developed civilisation. Leaving no apparent evidence of gradual development they spontaneously developed the skills of writing, building with brick and the construction of arches, mathematics, astronomy and engineering, the use of wheeled transport and the domestication of beasts of burden, and the mining, refining and the working of metals. Their texts show that they had an established code of justice, strong institutions of government and administration, and a basic understanding of democracy. As with the sudden emergence of Egyptian culture, the abrupt flowering of the Sumerian civilisation was quite baffling to the archaeologists who unearthed its relics. The historian Thorkild Jacobsen has commented: 'Overnight, as it were, Mesopotamian civilisation crystallises. The fundamental pattern, the controlling framework within which Mesopotamia is to live its life, formulate its deepest questions, evaluate itself and evaluate the universe, for ages to come, flashes into being, complete in its main features.'

As we saw in chapter 2, the religious myths of a people can shed some light, however uncertain, on the development of their culture. Just as the ancient Egyptians believed the seeds of their civilisation had been given to them by the gods Osiris and Isis, the Sumerians seem to have had their own 'gift of knowledge' legend. A Babylonian priest-historian of the 5th century BC named Berassus recorded an ancient tradition concerning the origins of his civilisation. He said that there had come from the sea we now call the Persian Gulf 'an animal with reason, who was called Oannes' and who appeared to be part-human and part-fish, and that this Oannes had taught men 'to construct houses to found temples, to compile laws, and explained to them the principles of geometrical knowledge.' Agriculture, letters, and science – 'in short . . . everything which could tend to soften manners and humanise mankind' – were taught by this strange being, who at sunset 'would plunge again into the sea, and abide all night in the deep; for he was amphibious.' Berossus said that other beings like Oannes appeared after him and continued the work of instruction. It sounds a very tall tale, but interestingly one of the finds at

Nimrud was a representation of this amphibious creature, Oannes, which confirm Berossus' description of him. It is interesting to note that the shamen of the Central African tribe, called the Dogon, tell a similar tale. In the time of their ancestors, they say, a fish-like people called the Nommo arrived from the sky in a craft that spouted flame and caused a dust storm as it landed; these visitors taught them, among other things, that the star Sirius has an invisible twin. It was only in the mid-twentieth century that Sirius was discovered to be a double-star by western astronomers, whereas there is evidence that Dogon cult of the Nommo extends back for some centuries. (They themselves claim that the Nommo arrived about three thousand years ago.) Beyond a staggering coincidence, how else could the Dogon – a comparatively primitive people know this fact unless told so by somebody who had the knowledge or technological skill of present day astronomers?

In this volume, we shall avoid discussing the theories popularised by Erich von Daniken and his followers: that civilisation was brought to earth by space men in fiery chariots – not because alien contact is inherently improbable, but because there is a simpler explanation for the achievements of past civilisations like the Sumerians, Egyptians and Maya: that their knowledge was a legacy from some far older civilisation that has now been forgotten.

It was skilful engineering that made fertile the land between and around the estuaries of the two great rivers, the Tigris and Euphrates. By means of irrigation the land was made to yield abundant crops, but stone, metals, and hard wood suitable for building were not to be had in the vicinity of the Sumerian cities, and to obtain these commodities, essential to the settled and civilised life, the Sumerians had to become travellers and traders. They built long boats with big square-shaped sails which sailed the Mediterranean to the north and ventured southward down the Gulf and around to the coasts of Africa. A hierarchical society developed, with a ruling class, a priesthood, a merchant class, a class of scholars, and a class of artisans. The profession of scribe was highly honoured and was the gateway to important posts in the administration. There also existed special schools for teaching the craft of the scribe, which was not only well remunerated but also tended to become a family profession. 'Among all mankind's craftsmen,' reads one clay tablet, 'no work is as difficult as the scribal art. It is in accordance with the fate decreed by the god Enlil that a son follow the work of his father.'

The profusion of clay tablets with identical texts that archaeologists have found, obviously produced by trainees practicing their skills, are the products of such schools. That it was only the sons of the wealthy and privileged who were able to have such training is implied by the text of a paternal admonition which has a familiar ring and which also gives an insight into the lives of the working class. The father scolds his son for truancy, and reminds him of his privileged position: 'I, never in my life, did I make you carry reeds to the canebrake. The reed rushes which the young and the little carry, you, never in your life did you carry them. I never said to you, follow my caravans. I never sent you to work to plough my field. I never sent you to work, to dig up my field . . . Go, work and support me, I never in my life said to you.' In this text, inscribed on a clay tablet found at Erech, a father's disappointment thunders across 4000 years – a marvel the Sumerians made possible with their invention of writing.

They wrote on clay tablets because clay was readily available and a handful of it could quickly be slapped into a flat square, written on while still damp, and then baked in the sun. Great expertise and versatility were achieved in the craft, and all aspects of Sumerian life were put on record, from commercial transactions to poetic epics. A tablet unearthed at Nippur, for instance, comprised a physician's prescription for an unknown ailment: 'Sift and knead together, all in one: turtle shell, the sprouting naga-plant, salt (and) mustard; wash (the sick part) with quality beer (and) hot water; scrub (the sick spot) with all of it (the kneaded mixture): after scrubbing, rub with vegetable oil (and) cover with pulverized fir.' The ingredients of the medication may seem strange, but the tone is practical, there is no pseudomagical mumbo jumbo, and the physician clearly has a conception of antiseptic procedure which many European physicians lacked as late in our era as the 19th century. And this was some 2000 years before the Greek, Hippocrates, who is generally credited with being 'the father of medicine'.

There are many surviving tablets that testify to the fact that a system of law was highly developed in Sumer. Several have been found recounting a murder trial known as 'The Case of the Silent Wife'. A temple official named Lu-Inanna had been murdered by a gardener, a barber, and a third, unidentified man. The killers had told the victim's wife, Nin-dada, what they had done, and she had not betrayed them to the authorities. When they were apprehended and brought to trial, Nin-dada was summoned to court, but she declined to testify and remained silent. The case was referred to a higher court, the Citizens' Assembly at Nippur, where a nine-man team of prosecutors demanded that the wife's silence should be construed as complicity in the crime and that she should pay for it with her life. But two assemblymen protested, brought up evidence that the dead man had not provided adequately for his household, and asked: 'A woman whose husband did not support her, after she heard that her husband had been killed, why should she not remain silent? Is it she who killed her husband? The punishment of those who actually killed should suffice.' This plea for justice and clemency prevailed with the Citizens' Assembly and Nin-dada was acquitted. The Sumerians were certainly more enlightened and humane than the later Assyrians, according to whose laws a wife was a man's property and could have her ears, her nose, her nipples, or her breasts cut off for marital offences.

As a source of information about life in ancient Sumer, we have in addition to the inscribed clay tablets a large number of decorated cylinder seals. These were small stone cylinders with designs carved on them, which when rolled over a piece of wet clay made a mark that served to identify the person whose text was inscribed thereon. The seals were personalised, and generally depict something particularly relevant to the owner. Collectively they afford us a fascinating picture of Sumerian domestic, social, economic, and religious life.

The archaeologists who recovered these artifacts from the sands of southern Mesopotamia had to adopt quite different work methods from those employed by men like Botta and Layard. The vigorous wielding of pick and shovel that had achieved sensational results at Khorsabad, Nimrud, and Kuyunjik would only have destroyed the Sumerian artifacts wholesale. The archaeologists who excavated the Sumerian cities had to be more careful and scientific in their approach. There was no rush to this inhospitable area after the announcement of the discovery of Erech by Loftus and Churchill, and it was only toward the end of the 19th century and in the first half of the 20th that the cities of Sumer were systematically investigated. In this work the contributions of two archaeologists were outstanding: the German, Robert Koldeway, who excavated Babylon between 1898 and 1917, and the Englishman, Leonard Woolley, who excavated Ur between 1922 and 1932. As Ur was the older city and an integral part of Sumerian civilisation in its heyday, whereas Babylon flourished later, we will consider Woolley's find first.

Near the mound of rubble that was Ur there was a smaller mound at Ubaid, and it was here that Woolley began his excavations. With luck comparable to Layard's, he almost immediately found the ruins of a temple dating from the First Dynasty of Ur, and within it a tablet with an inscription which when translated read: 'A-anni-pad-da, King of Ur, son of Mes-anni-pad-da, King of Ur, has built this for his lady, Ninhursag.' This tablet enabled Woolley to date the temple and its contents at about 2700 BC, for these kings' names tallied with information on other king lists which had been dated. Ninhursag was known to be a mother goddess. On a frieze found in the temple she was represented by sacred cows that were depicted being milked by priests of the temple.

Woolley's first excavations of the mound of Ur turned up some gold beads, which made him suspect that he might find greater treasures deeper down. With admirable restraint, he deferred serious excavation until he had trained his work force of Arab tribesmen to use tools with care and not to damage their finds. He then tackled a site that he had identified as a cemetery lying within the walls of a temple. Some 1800 graves were investigated, and found to contain nothing but bones; but among them were some deep tunnels, indicating that grave robbers had been at work and that there were other graves deeper down.

Woolley's finding the Royal Tombs of Ur has been compared with Carter's discovery of Tutankhamen's tomb. Although the treasures he unearthed were not so fabulous as the pharaoh's they were magnificent and of even greater interest to historians and archaeologists. They were more than 1000 years older than the Egyptian artifacts. The first find was the tomb of a man whose seal identified him as Mes-kalam-dug, and on whose skull there was a helmet of beaten gold fashioned like a wig with hair that fell in curls at the side and was knotted at the back – a superb specimen of the goldsmith's craft. There were also gold-mounted daggers, a shield inlaid with gold and lapis lazuli, and bowls made of gold, copper, and silver. 'Nothing like these things had ever before come from the soil of Mesopotamia,' said Woolley.

This though was only the beginning. A stone pavement was uncovered, and because the stone must have been imported Woolley surmised that the pavement must lead to a royal tomb. He excavated the length of it and came to a sloping trench where lay five skeletons with headdresses of gold, lapis lazuli, and elaborate bead necklaces. At the end of the row were the remains of a harp across which lay the bones of the gold-crowned harpist, as if she had expired while still playing. All around this area were scattered tumblers and chalices of gold, silver, and copper, and there were the remains of a chariot that had been decorated with gold lions and coloured stones, and also the bones of the animal that had been harnessed to it.

As more of the Royal Tombs were discovered the evidence built up that it had been customary for the royalty of early Sumer to be interred accompanied by a host of attendants, and that these had not been slaves but people (mostly women) of rank who had gone to their deaths bedecked in all their finery and jewellery. In one grave the remains of 63 men and women and 6 oxen were found, in another the skeletons of 68 women and 6 men, and in a third, known as the 'Great Death Pit', there were 74 bodies laid out in tidy rows. The treasures recovered from these graves were not only the personal adornments of the dead, but also some exquisite works of art, mostly animal portraiture, such as the well-known figure of a ram standing with its front feet in the branches of a tree, which Woolley conjectured might be a Sumerian version of Abraham's sacrifice of 'the ram caught in a thicket', for of course Abraham was associated with Ur.

A wealth of information about life in Sumer 5000 years ago was provided by the so-called 'Standard' of Ur, a mosaic panel that was found in one of the tombs. Worked in mother of pearl and mussel shell against a background of lapis lazuli, the mosaic depicts several scenes of everyday life, such as a banquet scene, a procession of soldiers and of fettered prisoners, and a gathering of sacrificial animals. It is not so detailed as the wall paintings in the tomb of the Egyptian landowner, Ti, but it provides some vivid pictures of life in the earliest known era of civilisation.

The Biblical association of Abraham with Ur is problematical. Abraham is supposed to have been the progenitor of both the Jewish and the Arab races, but the early Sumerians were not a Semitic people. Nobody knows for certain where they originally came from, although there is some suggestive evidence that they were associated with another ancient culture which has recently been discovered, that of the Indus valley in India. But by about 1500 BC the Sumerians no longer existed as a people, for their cities had fallen to Semitic conquerors. Their culture and institutions, though, had remained alive and civilised the invaders, who adopted their method of writing and learned their engineering and building techniques and much of their science and lore. Humane Sumerian principles of law were preserved and elaborated by the great Babylonian king, Hammurabi, who reigned from 1792 to 1750 BC. Under Hammurabi the city of Babylon became established as the cultural and political capital of Mesopotamia, eclipsing the Sumerian cities of the southern plain where civilisation had been born.

The sight that most impressed the Greek historian Herodotus when he visited the ancient city of Babylon in about 450 BC, was the great Ziggurat. It was, he said, eight stories high, and there was a path winding around the outside of it by which visitors could ascend to the temple at the top. Within the temple all there was for the visitor to see was a huge and opulently decorated couch with a golden table beside it. It was part of the religion of the Babylonians, Herodotus explained, to have women always recumbent on this couch for the enjoyment of the god Marduk, who would from time to time descend from heaven to have intercourse with her. Furthermore, it was the religious duty of every woman of Babylon to prostitute herself at the temple at least once in her life. Dressed in her finest clothes, she had to sit in the holy enclosure and wait until a man chose her by tossing a silver coin into her lap and uttering the words, 'The goddess Ishtar prosper thee.' It was the woman's religious duty to submit herself, and Herodotus drily remarked that tall and beautiful women invariably performed their duty within hours, whereas some of the ugly ones had to wait years for the opportunity to do so. And the rich, he noted, surrounded themselves with a host of attendants in order to keep away strangers, having made prior arrangements for a suitable partner to accost them.

No other ancient source of historical evidence exists to confirm Herodotus' account of the goings-on at the Babylonian temple. There is, however, ample evidence that the great Ziggurat existed and was one of the wonders of the ancient world. And there are traditions that identify the structure as the tower of Babel mentioned in the Bible.

The story of the building of the tower, as related in the Book of Genesis, goes: 'And they said one to another, go to, let us make bricks and burn them thoroughly. And they had brick for stone, and lime they had for mortar. And they said, go to, let us build a city and a tower, whose top may reach into heaven; and let us make us a name, lest we be scattered abroad upon the face of the whole earth.' As there is no natural stone in southern Mesopotamia, where Babylon was located, the detail about the tower being made of brick argues in favour of the idea that the Babylonian Ziggurat was the tower of Babel. And both the detail about the bricks, and specific mention of the aspiration to reach the heavens, are found in a cuneiform inscription of the Babylonian king Nabopolassar: 'The lord Marduk commanded me concerning Etemenanki, the staged tower of Babylon, which before my time had become dilapidated and ruinous, that I should make its foundations secure in the bosom of the nether world and make its summit like the heavens. I caused bricks to be made . . . I caused streams of bitumen to be brought by the canal Arahtu . . . I deposited in the foundations under the bricks gold, silver, and precious stones from the mountains and from the sea . . . For my Lord Marduk I bowed my neck, I took off my robe – the sign of my royal blood – and on my head I bore bricks and earth. As for Nebuchadnezzar, my first-born son, the beloved of my heart, I made him bear the mortar, the offering of wine and oil, in company with my subjects.' Confirming this account, and the Biblical tradition of the overweening ambition of the builders that incurred God's wrath, there is an inscription of Nebuchadnezzar's which says: 'To raise up the top of Etemenanki that it might rival heaven, I laid to my hand.'

Nebopolassar, who ruled from 626 to 605 BC, stated that in his day the tower was dilapidated and ruinous. It is possible that the original tower went back to the age of the great Sumerian lawgiver Hammurabi and had been destroyed by Sennacherib. We know from cuneiform and graphic records that the Assyrian despot turned his wrath on the city of Babylon in the year 689 BC. His army attacked and took the city, slaughtered every one of its inhabitants, razed its buildings, and finally diverted the waters of the Euphrates to flood the ruins and wash away much of the rubble. But after Nineveh itself suffered a similar fate, Babylon rose again to power and splendour. Nebopolassar and Nebuchadnezzar not only re-built the Ziggurat, but also built around Babylon the most impregnable defensive walls ever seen in the world at that time, the most splendid royal palace, and, according to some ancient historians, an architectural masterpiece worthy to be ranked with the pyramids as one of the seven wonders of the world: the famous Hanging Gardens of Babylon.

By the beginning of the Christian era, however, Babylon was once again a ruined and almost abandoned city, and its architectural and engineering marvels had largely been destroyed. Alexander the Great had conquered it in the 4th century BC, but had died in 323 BC there at the age of 33 as the result of a fever or poisoning. The Greek general under whose rule it then fell, Seleucus Nicator, decided to build a new city some 40 miles to the north, which he called Seleucia and built partly with materials taken from Babylon. For some time Babylon remained of religious importance, and the festival and the shrine of Marduk were preserved, but by the year 50 BC the Roman historian Diodorus Siculus wrote that 'only a small part of the city is now inhabited, and most of the area within its walls is given over to agriculture,' and his contemporary the Greek geographer Strabo wrote that the Ziggurat was destroyed and that only the walls stood as evidence of the former greatness of Babylon.

Brick, of course, does not last as well as stone. By modern times the ravages of weathering had combined with the destruction of ancient conquerors to reduce Babylon to rubble. But after Layard had achieved his spectacular success at Nineveh, for archaeologists the lure of the other great city of the Assyro-Babylon empire was greatly enhanced.

A pioneer English archaeologist, Claudius Rich, had in fact made a preliminary study of the Babylon site in 1811. He only spent 10 days there and employed a small party of workmen, so he could do little more than make a few sketches and measurements, collect some inscribed bricks, and probe about a bit in the rubble. He noted that there was a great square mound which the Arabs called the tower of Babel, but his investigation of it was inevitably cursory and yielded no interesting discoveries. A coffin excavated from it gave off such a stench when it was opened that it was obvious that the mortal remains in it were of no great antiquity. Layard, too, had this unpleasant experience when he briefly investigated the site in 1851, and in a report he wrote that the chances of finding anything of importance in the vast sprawling brick heap did not justify the cost of a thorough excavation, which he estimated at £25,000. The excavation of Babylon was therefore left to the German archaeologist Robert Koldewey, who devoted 15 years, between 1898 to 1917, to the work.

By the 1890s the situation in Mesopotamia was very different from the situation in the days of Botta and Layard. Both the Turkish authorities and the local inhabitants had become aware of the value of the artifacts to be found and excavated in the historic sites. This meant that it was no longer possible to ship masses of sculptures to the museums of Europe, and also that there was a brisk covert trade in antiquities. Many Arab tribesmen had adopted their procurement and sale as a means of livelihood. This situation, combined with the nature of the Babylon site, required a different type of archaeologist from Layard – that is, a man more concerned with the acquisition of knowledge than of treasure, and one not impatient for quick and sensational results but content to work carefully and systematically over a long period of time. Robert Koldewey was just such a man. And as well as possessing the personal qualities and motives for his task, Koldewey also had the advantage of being generously funded. Although the Germans had made great contributions to Assyro-Babylonian scholarship, they had not shared in the early archaeological bonanza. The Koldewey expedition was therefore intended to some extent to make good the omission for the sake of German national prestige. So Koldewey was enabled to engage a work force of more than 200 men to shift and sift the mountains of rubble that were the remains of Babylon.

His first great find was the legendary defensive walls of the city. Everybody had thought that the description of the walls of Babylon given by Herodotus must be exaggerated. The Greek historian had said that one wall was broad enough for two chariots each drawn by four horses to pass each other. Koldewey's excavations showed that this was no exaggeration. To expose the walls was a gargantuan task. At some points rubble as deep as 75 feet or more had to be removed, but when at last a section of the walls was laid bare Koldewey found that the defensive system of Babylon comprised a series of three walls, all made of fired brick. The first wall was 24 feet thick, the second 25 feet thick, and between them was a space of more than 38 feet, which had apparently originally been filled with earth. This would have provided more than enough room for the passage of the two large chariots of Herodotus' description. The space between the middle and the inner walls had been a moat, and the inner wall had been fortified with towers spaced every 160 feet. Koldewey estimated that there had been some 360 such towers and that the circumference of these fortifications had been 10 miles. This latter estimate seemed to contradict Herodotus' statement that Babylon had been some 15 miles square, or a circuit of 60 miles, but if he had included the suburbs, farms, and villages clustered around the city outside the walls he may not have been far wrong. The 10-mile extent of the walls was certainly a phenomenal feat of engineering and a clear testimony to the power and genius of Nebuchadnezzar, who had built them.

Nebuchadnezzar's own account of the fortification of Babylon, found inscribed on a cuneiform tablet, corresponded with Koldewey's findings. 'I caused a mighty wall to circumscribe Babylon,' the king had written. 'I dug its moat; and its escarpments I built out of bitumen and kiln brick. At the edge of the moat I built a powerful wall as high as a hill. I gave it wide gates and set in doors of cedar wood sheathed with copper. So that the enemy, who would [wished] evil, should not threaten the sides of Babylon, I surrounded them with mighty floods as the billows of the sea flood the land . . . I heaped up a heap of earth beside it, and surrounded it with quay walls of brick. This bastion I strengthened cunningly, and of the city of Babylon made a fortress.'

Robert Koldewey was an architect by training, and his primary interest was in the architecture of ancient Babylon. One day his workmen unearthed a curious arched structure at a part of the site identified with the oldest part of the city. This find intrigued him as an architect. It was not only the unique shape, but also the fact that it was made partly of stone and that in the midst of the ruins there was a well with three shafts, that interested Koldewey. Here, he surmised, had stood some very unusual and cunningly contrived artifact. He studied all the ancient descriptions of the city for clues and came to the conclusion that it must have been the elevated park known as the Hanging Gardens of Babylon.

The account that confirmed him in this belief was that of the Roman Diodorus Siculus, and specifically mentioned both the arched, or vaulted, structure that supported the gardens, and the fact that stone was used in the construction. The relevant part of Diodorus' description went: 'The Garden was 100 feet long by

100 wide and built up in tiers so that it resembled a theatre. Vaults had been constructed under the ascending terraces which carried the entire weight of the planted garden; the uppermost vault, which was 75 feet high, was the highest part of the garden, which, at this point, was on the same level as the city walls. The roofs of the vaults which supported the garden were constructed of stone beams some 15 feet long . . .' As according to Diodorus stone was only used at one other place in Babylon, Koldewey felt certain that the structure he had found must be the supports of the fabled Hanging Gardens. The presence of the triple-shafted well also supported the hypothesis. There could have been a chain of leather buckets that passed empty down one shaft and full up the other, carrying water to the highest level where it would be channelled to supply all the gardens. The middle shaft could have been constructed for maintenance purposes.

If Koldewey was right in his conjectures, the Hanging Gardens had been nothing magical, as their traditional name suggested, but rather a kind of terraced park laid out on the roof of a specially designed building. A description by the Jewish historian Josephus appeared to confirm this. Writing about the 'prodigiously large and magnificent palace' that Nebuchadnezzar had built, Josephus said: 'In this palace he erected very high walks, supported by stone pillars; and by planting what was called a pensile (hanging) paradise, and replenishing it with all sorts of trees, he rendered the prospect an exact resemblance of a mountainous country. This he did to please his queen, because she had been brought up in Media, and was fond of a mountainous situation.' There was no doubt that the construction of the Hanging Gardens of Babylon had been an engineering tour de force at the time, but the plausible reality unearthed by the German archaeologist did rather diminish the romance and the mystery of that particular wonder of the world.

In bringing to light the Processional Way of the god Marduk and the Ishtar Gate which spanned it, Koldewey compensated for his revelation of the down-to-earth reality of the Hanging Gardens by giving the world a glimpse of the former grandeur and splendour of Babylon.

The Processional Way was a broad thoroughfare leading from the outer wall of the city to the Gate of Ishtar, which was the main entrance to the inner citadel of Babylon. One of Nebuchadnezzar's inscriptions described it: 'Aibur-shabu, the street of Babylon, I filled with a high fill for the procession of the great lord Marduk, and with Turminabanda stones and Shadu stones, I made this Aibur-shabu, from 'the holy gate' to Ishtar-saki-patebisha, fit for the procession of his godliness, and linked it with those parts which my father had built, and made the way a shining one.' Koldewey's excavation brought to light the street whose construction was so magnificently described. It was nearly 74 feet wide and on each side there were walls 22 feet high, which made the street a kind of gully running into the heart of the city from the perimeter, and therefore a death trap for an invader who tried to enter by that way. Spaced along the walls were enamelled reliefs of lions in bright colours – 120 of them in all. The foundations of the street itself were of brick covered with bitumen and then limestone paving slabs on the underside of each of which was the inscription: 'Nebuchadnezzar, King of Babylon, son of Nabopolassar, King of Babylon, am I. The Bale street I paved with Shadu slabs for the procession of the great lord Marduk. Marduk, lord, grant eternal life.'

Processional gates and triumphal archways were of course common in later Roman and European civic architecture, but the Gate of Ishtar was earlier than any of them and was the best preserved of all Babylonian remains that Koldewey unearthed. Buried beneath tons of rubble, the colourful decorations on the Gate had remained intact for more than 2000 years. And in this bleak and barren waste of clay and brick, the colours of the decorations adorning both the Gate of Ishtar and the Processional Way were a welcome contrast and exciting find. Nebuchadnezzar had inscribed that he had ordered that the gate should be 'made glorious for the amazement of the people' and had had it decorated with enamelled reliefs of nearly 600 bulls and dragons on the brick walls. Koldewey found that many of these reliefs were in a very good state of preservation. Of particular interest were the many representations of the dragon of Babylon, a curious creature with a scaly body, a long neck supporting a horned serpent's head from which projected a split tongue, and with paws on its forelegs and talons on its hind legs. This dragon, known as Sirrush, was known from the Bible to have been a creature sacred to the god Marduk. The multitudes of them enamelled in silver and bronze against a bright blue background on the Gate of Ishtar must have been an impressive sight for the worshippers of Marduk. It is still impressive to the visitor to the ruins of Babylon, although rather fewer than a third of the original number remain. Others have been taken away to museums, particularly to the Berlin Museum, where a reconstruction of the Gate of Ishtar is one of the principal sights.

Bright blue, too, according to Herodotus, was the upper temple of Marduk which crowned the great Ziggurat. There was also a lower temple, he tells us, in which there was a statue of the god seated on a throne with a large table beside him and a footstool in front – all this made of pure gold and weighing 800 talents, that is to say about 26 tons. The name of the temple-tower, Etemenanki, meant 'The House of the Foundations of Heaven and Earth'. In its day it must have been one of the most awesome structures in the world. Standing on the flat plain of Babylon and rising to a height of 300 feet, it was said to be visible from a distance of 60 miles. No less than 58 million bricks had gone into its construction. There could have been no contemporary building comparable to it, and this fact, combined with the fact that ancient descriptions of it tallied with Biblical descriptions of the tower of Babel, indicated that it was indeed the fabled tower that in the Judeo-Christian tradition symbolised man's extreme and culpable ambition. But before Koldewey excavated at Babylon nobody knew for certain whether the great pile of rubble that the Arabs called the tower of Babel really was the Biblical structure.

Of course Koldewey was only able to excavate the foundations, but these proved to be both compatible with the descriptions in the Bible and in Herodotus and consistent with a description of the dimensions of the tower of Babel given on a Babylonian tablet. This tablet was discovered by the English Assyriologist George Smith, disappeared after his premature death in 1876, and turned up mysteriously years later in the Oriental collection of the Louvre in Paris. It stated that the dimensions of the base of the tower of Babel were 300 feet by 300 feet and the height was also 300 feet, and that there had been seven different stages with given distances between them; the top one, the actual temple of Marduk, being 80 feet long, 70 feet wide, and 50 feet high. Koldewey's excavation was of course only able to confirm the dimensions of the base, but that was enough to convince him that here indeed had stood the terraced tower that was sacred to the Babylonians and an object of ridicule and self-righteous indignation to the Jews.

The entire 15 years' work of the German archaeologists, with their 200-strong labour force, did not succeed in producing for the tourist any overwhelming impression of the grandeur of ancient Babylon. On the rubble-strewn site that they left the only impressive structure is the remaining part of the Gate of Ishtar, and the visitor has to use his own imagination to envisage what this great walled city with its magnificent palaces and temples must originally have been like. Koldewey's work, however, is accounted one of the triumphs of archaeology. After Babylon had been ransacked for centuries, first by conquerors and then by opportunist builders for its bricks, and had been reduced to a wasteland of debris and dust, he patiently unearthed what remained of it, which was enough to show that in its age it must have been an architectural phenomenon of a complexity and sophistication unequalled in the world.

Some decades before Koldewey began his work, the poet Wordsworth had written: 'Babylon, Learned and wise, hath perished utterly, Nor leaves her speech one word to aid the sigh, That would lament her.' But the archaeologist and the scholars proved the poet wrong; the first by laying bare the lineaments of the vanished city, and the second by translating the many cuneiform inscriptions found among the rubble, including those of the proud and gifted rulers, Nabopolassar and Nebuchadnezzar, under whose sway Babylon, which even then had a history going back nearly 2000 years, enjoyed a last brief but splendid period of glory before the prophecies of Jeremiah were fulfilled. Babylon, declared Jeremiah, 'shall become a heap, a dwelling-place for dragons, an astonishment and a hissing, without an inhabitant;' and 'the wild beasts of the desert with the wild beasts of the islands shall dwell there, and the owls shall dwell therein; and it shall be no more inhabited for ever.' Strangely enough, in the light of this latter prophecy, when Babylon fell to the Persians in the 4th century BC it was used as a royal game park by the Persian kings.

CHAPTER 5

THE FORGOTTEN EMPIRE
OF THE HITTITES

The Old Testament mentions the Hittites, but offers no further details, leading 19th century historians to conclude that they were a small and unimportant tribe – otherwise, why were they not better documented? By the turn of the century, however, evidence had come to light which suggested the Hittites once rivalled the great empires of Assyria and Egypt. How could the memory of such a powerful race have been lost to history?

In several places in the Old Testament there are brief references to some people called Hittites. They seem to have been living in that part of Palestine where the Hebrew patriarch Abraham and his wife Sarah settled in their old age. When Sarah died, Abraham bought a burying ground from someone called Ephron the Hittite. Abraham's grandson Esau married a Hittite girl. Many generations later, King David seduced Bathsheba, the wife of Uriah the Hittite, one of David's officers. His successor King Solomon included some Hittite women among his numerous wives and concubines. The writer of the First Book of Kings goes on to list them along with Moabites, Ammonites, Edomites, Sidonians, and other 'strange [foreign] women'.

There is nothing in any of the Bible references to suggest that the Hittites (or *Chittim*, as they are called in the original Hebrew) were in any way a remarkable people. They appeared to pose no threat to the Israelites – unlike the powerful Egyptians and the

Assyrians (a people occupying what is now mainly northern Iraq), for example. Yet one reference in the Bible long puzzled scholars. In Chapter Seven of the Second Book of Kings, a Syrian army is laying siege to the Israelite capital, Samaria, whose inhabitants are dying of a famine. During the night, God causes the Syrian soldiers to have a collective hallucination in which they hear the sound of a great army equipped with chariots and horses on the move. They say to each other, 'Lo, the king of Israel hath hired against us the kings of the Hittites, and the kings of the Egyptians to come upon us.' So terrifying is this prospect that the Syrians, leaving their tents, food, and possessions, flee for their lives.

Could it be, scholars wondered, that the Hittites were in fact a powerful nation? Otherwise, why would they be mentioned in the same breath with the Egyptians and cause such alarm? And if they were indeed a powerful nation, then somewhere there must be archaeological evidence of their civilisation. But none had so far emerged.

Of course, there are many inexplicable statements in the Bible. Often a confusing point such as that in the Second Book of Kings turns out to be simply a mis-translation. But in 1822 the Rosetta Stone bearing Greek and Egyptian characters was deciphered and this made it possible for scholars for the first time to read Egyptian hieroglyphics. As the many Egyptian texts and inscriptions were translated, new evidence emerged regarding the Hittites that put the puzzling biblical reference in a new light. Egyptian records contained several references to the 'people of Kheta', which scholars thought might be the same as the 'Chittim' of the Bible. In 1300 BC, Rameses II had fought the 'abominable Kheta' and their allies at Kadesh, in Syria. A huge relief carved on the walls of an Egyptian temple shows the pharaoh and his troops inflicting injuries on their foes, who are depicted as rather unattractive long-haired people wearing heavy clothing. Later in his reign, Rameses made a peace treaty with the Kheta, and this treaty is carved on the wall of one of the temples at Karnak. For some time this was all that could be discovered about the enigmatic Hittites. Then, toward the end of the 1800s, more bits of evidence began to come to light that put scholars on the long path toward the eventual discovery of a forgotten empire.

The way was strewn with examples of mysterious writing. In 1812 in the Syrian city of Hamath, Johann L. Burckhardt, a young Swiss traveller, had spotted a block of basalt set into the corner of a house and inscribed with hieroglyphic characters. Burckhardt described the stone in his book *Travels in Syria and the Holy Land*, noting that the characters 'in no way resembled those of Egypt.' Only a few years later, Burckhardt died, and his discovery of the Hamath stone – which was but one of his many discoveries – was virtually forgotten. His book was not published until 1922.

In the meantime, however, two American travellers found the same stone and several others like it when they visited Hamath in 1870. When they tried to make copies of the inscriptions, the local inhabitants warned them off. The stones, it seemed, were regarded as having miraculous powers, including the ability to cure rheumatism, and the citizens of Hamath did not want foreigners tampering with their effectiveness.

A year later, William Wright, an Irish missionary, finally succeeded in getting a good look at the stones – but only through the intervention of the Turkish governor of Syria. The governor then had the stones removed to the new archaeological museum at Constantinople, after first allowing Wright to examine them and make impressions, which the missionary gave to the British Museum.

About the same time, a stone with the same kind of writing on it was discovered in a mosque at Aleppo, about 100 miles north of Hamath. This stone, too, was credited with healing powers. When European scholars showed interest in the stone the townspeople removed it and hid it – but not before the scholars had made copies.

No one could decipher the strange hieroglyphs, but Archibald Sayce, a British archaeologist, put forward the theory that the picture writing was Hittite. About two years after Sayce proposed this idea, a British Museum team of excavators discovered the long-lost city of Carchemish. It was this city by the Euphrates

River that Assyrian inscriptions dating from around 1100 BC had described as the capital of the 'Land of Hatti' – and the Hatti were yet one more candidate for the identity of the Hittites. Among the foundations of the city they found a number of inscriptions in the same indecipherable picture-writing as had been found at Hamath and Aleppo. On the evidence gathered so far it seemed that if the Hatti and Hittites were the same, then their kingdom had been located in Syria.

Then some surprising new evidence appeared. An English traveller named E. J. Davis reported seeing similar inscriptions carved into the rock in the Taurus Mountains in southern Turkey. The inscriptions themselves were next to some relief carvings that reminded scholar-detectives of other large-scale reliefs found some years earlier north of the Taurus Mountains on the Anatolian Plateau. Suddenly, it no longer seemed so certain that the Hittites' home was in Syria. Might they in fact have come from the bleak, rocky plains of Anatolia? Sayce published another paper entitled 'The Hittites in Asia Minor,' advancing this new theory.

As yet, however, there was no proof. No one knew for certain that the hieroglyphs were Hittite and no one had yet succeeded in deciphering them.

Then in 1887 the search for the Hittites took a new turn. An Egyptian peasant woman digging for fertiliser near the site of an ancient Egyptian city at Tell el Amarna, found some clay tablets inscribed with the wedge-shaped script known as cuneiform writing. Realising that such objects might be valuable, other people began to dig at the site, and within the year some 200 tablets came on the black market in Cairo. The export of antiquities was prohibited by Egyptian law, but some found their way into foreign museums. Examination revealed that they were the archives of the Pharaoh Akhenaten (reigned 1379–1361 BC) whose capital city stood near Tell el Amarna, where the tablets were found.

The 'Amarna letters,' as they came to be called, included correspondence from the leaders of the other nations of Akhenaten's time, such as Babylonia and Assyria. Most of them were written in the Akkadian (Babylonian) language and all of them in cuneiform. Among the tablets were some from the leaders of Syrian and Palestinian states loyal to Egypt, in which they referred to the military activities of the king of Hatti and complained of his aggression – more evidence that the Hittites were a military power. One letter, also written in Akkadian, was from the Hittite king himself, Suppiluliumas. Addressing the pharaoh as an equal, he congratulated him on his accession to the throne. The Hittites were beginning to emerge into the light of history.

The letters referring to the activities of the Hittite army indicated that they were moving southward into Syria and Lebanon, which suggested that the Hittite kingdom itself was located north of the Taurus Mountains.

Although all the Amarna letters were written in the Babylonian cuneiform script, two of them were in an unknown language. Scholars were able to discover only that they were addressed to the king of a place called Arzawa; and so, for want of any other identification, the language was dubbed 'Arzawan'. Yet another unknown people had appeared on the scene.

About 10 years after the discovery of the Amarna tablets, a few tablets written in 'Arzawan' were found near the village of Bogazköy, in northern Turkey. Only recently had the bleak Anatolian plain begun to attract the attention of archaeologists. Before then, they had been fully occupied in excavating the legendary cities of Mesopotamia and the Aegean and the temples and tombs of Egypt. There were, it is true, some intriguing ruins in the area around Bogazköy but as there was no historical evidence that any very advanced civilisation had existed there, there was no good reason to comb this desolate part of the world in search of an ancient civilisation.

The Bogazköy ruins first came to light in the 1830s when Charles Félix-Marie Texier, a Frenchman, discovered the remains of a city 'as large as Athens in its prime', encircled by a wall whose gates were adorned with carvings of lions and a sphinx. Not far away, Texier found a formation of rocks decorated with large reliefs and with hieroglyphics later found to match those discovered at Hamath and Aleppo. By the end of the 1800s, having yielded examples of both the hieroglyphic 'Hittite' and the cuneiform 'Arzawan,' Bogazköy was becoming a place of some interest.

One of the people who found it interesting was Dr Hugo Winckler, an expert in cuneiform at Berlin University. Winckler was familiar with the 'Arzawan' texts from Tell el Amarna, and in 1903 had gone on an expedition to Lebanon to look for more writing in this language. Although this expedition was not successful, it was to lead to a great discovery. Some months after his return to Berlin he received by mail a tablet in 'Arzawan,' sent to him by a Turkish museum official whom he had met on his trip. As soon as possible Winckler hurried to Constantinople, where the museum official, Macridy Bey, told him that the tablet came from Bogazköy.

The two men set out for the remote village – with Winckler, who seems to have been a cantankerous individual, complaining every step of the way of the primitive travelling conditions. The journey was, however, worthwhile. Winckler gathered 34 more cuneiform tablets before the rainy season forced him to discontinue the search.

By the following summer of 1907 he had obtained financial support for the excavation of Bogazköy, and with Macridy Bey and a German assistant he set up operations there. Villagers dug among the ruins in the haphazard way of those days, while Winckler examined and catalogued the hundreds of tablets that they unearthed. Most of the tablets, being in 'Arzawan', were undecipherable. But some were in Akkadian, which Winckler could read easily. One day he was handed an Akkadian tablet that began:

'The covenant of Rameses, Beloved of Amun, Great King of the land of Egypt, hero,

'with Hattusilis, Great King, King of the land of Hatti, his brother, providing for good peace and good brotherhood in the relations of the Great Kingdom between them for ever . . .'

It was confirmation of the peace treaty made after the battle of Kadesh, the same one that was carved in Egyptian hieroglyphics on the temple wall at Karnak.

For Winckler it was an electrifying moment. He held in his hands a letter written to one king from another, a letter of such importance that the recipient would certainly have kept it safely stored in the royal archives. For that, clearly, was what Winckler had discovered: the royal archives and the capital city of the Hittites, called Hattusas.

Of the 10,000 tablets excavated by Winckler's team at Bogazköy, there were enough in Akkandian to enable scholars to begin piecing together the formerly unknown Hittite history. The 'Arzawan' language in which the majority of the tablets were written, was obviously the Hittites' own language. As for the hieroglyphics, there were relatively few of these, and philologists (language experts) were unable at that point to determine their relationship, if any, to the cuneiform Hittite.

The cuneiform language was by no means easy to translate. For several years, the philologists had no success, partly because they assumed that, like Akkadian and the other languages of that part of the ancient world, it was a Semitic language. Then, while examining a Hittite text, Bedřich Hrozný, a Czech scholar, suddenly saw resemblances to German words. Further study revealed grammatical similarities to other Indo-European languages and confirmed one philologist's earlier guess that the two 'Arzawan' letters found at Tell el Amarna were written in an Indo-European tongue. By the 1930s most of the important Hittite texts had been translated.

Wherever the Hittites came from originally, they had evidently moved down into Anatolia by about 1900 BC. We know this from writings left by Assyrian traders. The Assyrians then controlled the trade route leading from Anatolia to Mesopotamia and had established several trading settlements in Anatolia. They kept careful records of their dealings with the native population. Those found at Kultepe (the ancient city of Kanesh) contain a number of Hittite names among those of the Hattite people, who are now called Proto-Hittites.

Confusingly, the people we call Hittites were not, strictly speaking, entitled to the name. The true Hittites were the native Anatolian tribe whose home was the area around Hattusas, from which their own name was derived. The Indo-European invaders, whatever they originally called themselves, simply adopted the name of the original inhabitants.

It seems to have been a relatively peaceful invasion. There is no evidence of any sudden attack on Anatolia or any large-scale violence. The Indo-European migrants must have lived in Anatolia for at least 150 years before they began to build up military power and conquer the land they lived in. Their conquest was made easier by quarrels among the Hattian princes, who were intermittently at war with each other.

The first Hittite monarch to make a name for himself was Anittas, who ruled a city called Kussara and who began to conquer the lands and cities of his Proto-Hittite neighbours. One of these conquered cities, Nesa, he made his new capital; but Hattusas – for some unknown reason – he destroyed and declared accursed. 'But in its place I sowed weeds,' he wrote. 'Whosoever becomes king after me and peoples Hattusas once more, let him be smitten by the weather-god of Heaven!' Ironically, this accursed city was to become the capital of the Hittite kingdom and empire established by Anittas' successors.

There is a documentary gap between the reign of Anittas, who died around 1750 BC, and the next powerful ruler, who is sometimes called Labarnas in Hittite texts but who later called himself Hattusilis, the 'man of Hattusas'. Apparently undaunted by Anittas' curse, he moved the capital to that city, which had an easily defensible site, and then began to expand his kingdom southward and eastward. His adopted son, Mursilis I, launched an ambitious campaign of conquest down into Syria, where he subdued Aleppo, and then drove on into the Euphrates valley. His aim was partly to capture this vital trade route, for Assyria had become a vassal of the Babylonians and was no longer an effective trading power. Mursilis and his army eventually reached the splendid city of Babylon, which they captured and looted. This seems to have been a purely aggressive act, for there is no evidence that the Babylonians posed an immediate threat to the Hittites. It served, however, to give the Hittites an instant reputation as a power to be reckoned with. On the return journey, Mursilis reinforced his reputation by conquering the Hurrians, a then-powerful people through whose kingdom – called Mitanni – he had to pass.

Mursilis had been home for only a few years when he was assassinated by one of his family. For several generations after this the Hittite kingdom was both torn from within by palace intrigues and assassinations and weakened on its borders by attacks from their neighbors, chiefly the Hurrians. Finally, one king, Telepinus (reigned 1525–1500 BC), managed to establish a law of succession that was generally followed throughout subsequent Hittite history. He also succeeded in repulsing the barbarian invaders that threatened the northern and eastern frontiers of his kingdom, and he made a treaty of peace with the kingdom of Kizzuwatna to the west.

The re-emergence of the Hittites as a military power began some 60 years after Telepinus' death. King Tudhaliyas II moved into Syria and destroyed the city of Aleppo, which had defected to the Hurrian camp during the period of Hittite weakness. The Hurrian king of Mitanni responded to this new threat by forming an alliance with Egypt, and once again the Hittite kingdom had to defend itself against attacks from the south.

In the year 1380 BC, King Suppiluliumas I came to the throne. Soon after his accession he began to build an empire. He made a surprise attack on Mitanni and sacked its capital city. He then reconquered the Syrian states that had depended on Mitanni and pushed southward as far as Lebanon, acquiring several states that had been vassals of Egypt. Fortunately for Suppiluliumas, Egypt, under Akhenaten, was preoccupied with religious reform and had no time to fight for petty border states.

Suppiluliumas then set about consolidating his empire by means of a series of diplomatic marriages. Members of his family were married off to the heads of the newly conquered states. Thus ties of family loyalty strengthened the treaties between Hatti and its vassals.

The king was rather suspicious, however, when he received a marriage proposal for one of his sons from the queen of Egypt. The queen was Ankhesenamun, widow of the boy king Tutankhamen, who had succeeded Akhenaten.

'My husband has died,' wrote the young queen, 'and I have no sons, but of you it is said that you have many sons. If you would send me one of your sons, he could become my husband. I will on no account take one of my subjects and make him my husband. I am very much afraid.'

It seems that the queen's grandfather, Ay, who already held considerable power, planned to marry the girl himself and so become pharaoh, as soon as the time allotted for embalming Tutankhamen's body was over. Suppiluliumas knew nothing of this, and he suspected a trap. He sent an envoy to Egypt to investigate. The envoy returned with another message from Ankhesenamun, chiding him for his distrust and repeating her plea for a husband. Without further delay the king dispatched his son Zannanza to Egypt. But the crafty courtier Ay had the Hittite prince assassinated on his arrival, and married the unfortunate Ankhesenamun himself.

Nearly a century later a union did take place between the two royal houses when Rameses II took as his principal wife the Hittite princess Naptera. This marriage took place 13 years after the two nations signed the peace treaty following the Battle of Kadesh – the same treaty that Winckler discovered at Bogazköy.

Although the reliefs at Karnak represent Kadesh as an Egyptian victory, in reality neither side emerged clearly triumphant. The immediate cause of the conflict had been the defection to Egypt of a Hittite buffer state. After the battle, this state, Amurru, returned to the Hittite fold, preserving the status quo.

Although the Hittites were a warlike people, they seem to have been relatively civilised by the standards of the da.y. There is little evidence of their having committed atrocities against their foes, and they ruled their vassal states firmly but diplomatically, trying to win their loyalty rather than terrorising them, as the Assyrians were to do later.

The Hittites appear to have had a strong sense of justice. Although specific information about their legal system is sparse, we do have a document instructing the king's judicial representatives in the conduct of a case. It repeatedly urges them to 'do what is just' and 'administer justice fairly'. However the same document also states that 'if anyone oppose the judgment of the king, his house shall become a ruin. If anyone oppose the judgment of a dignitary his head shall be cut off.'

The Hittites were a religious people and collected a large number of gods, including many from neighboring countries. Teshub, the all-important weather-god, for instance, they adopted from the Hurrians. In common with other ancient peoples, the Hittites also deified their kings, but only after their death. One of the king's responsibilities was to lead the most important of the Hittite religious rituals, the 38-day spring festival. Many of these festivals must have been celebrated at Yazilikaya, the beautiful rock sanctuary near Bogazköy whose walls are inscribed with reliefs depicting the Hittite gods and kings.

The Hittites do not seem to have been a very imaginative people. Their art never reached the degree of sophistication and skill shown by the Egyptians or the Assyrians, for example. Apart from a few myths, their writings consist mainly of religious texts of a tedious, ritualistic character. Of their architecture only foundations remain, giving us a clear idea of floor plans but almost no idea of Hittite structures.

It was in the arts of warfare and diplomacy that the Hittites excelled. They seem to have invented chariots with spoked wheels, which were lighter and more manoeuverable than the disc-wheeled variety, and their swift chariot troops were the main strength of the Hittite army. It was a surprise attack by these charioteers that lost Rameses the initiative at Kadesh and prevented an Egyptian victory.

After Kadesh, the Hittite Empire was to last for another 100 years. Having established a balance of power with Egypt, the Hittites enjoyed fairly amicable relations with that great kingdom. The new threat came from Assyria, which was once again independent and was just beginning its rise to power. Also toward the end of the 13th century, conflicts with western Anatolian states increased, particularly with Arzawa, one of their closest neighbours to the west. To the north the Phrygians, another Indo-European people, were moving down and pressing against the northern frontier. Hittite texts also refer to a people called the Ahhiyawans, who, according to one theory may have been the Achaeans – Homer's name for the Greeks. Further excavations of Hittite sites may turn up evidence in favour of the theory – and perhaps historical support, too, for Homer's account of the war between the Achaeans and the Trojans.

The fall of Troy took place around the year 1200 BC, about the same time that the Hittite Empire collapsed. We do not know exactly how it collapsed – detailed historical information has not been discovered. We do know, however, that throughout the Middle East and the Mediterranean lands, great upheavals were taking place. Egypt was attacked by invaders whom the Egyptians called the 'Sea People'. The Mycenaean civilisation based in southern Greece was destroyed by Dorian invaders moving down from the north. Whatever specific events led to the final extinction of the Hittite Empire, they were part of a pattern of migration and political ferment that affected virtually all of the known world.

According to Greek writings, the Phrygians now became the dominant power in Anatolia. As to the fate of the Hittite people, this is still, to some extent a mystery. Some of them must have moved south into Syria. For here, south of the Taurus Mountains, Hittite culture re-emerged in what we call the Neo-Hittite states. These were a number of more or less independent city-states, a few of which – notably Carchemish – had once been vassals of the Hittite Empire. It is probable that the passage in the Second Book of Kings about the 'kings of the Hittites' is a reference to the rulers of the states, and not to the kings of the Hittite Empire. These petty kings were also the Hittites referred to by the Assyrian king Tiglath-pileser I in a document dating from around 1100 BC.

The extent to which these Neo-Hittite states were related to the Anatolian Hittite Empire is still in doubt. From the evidence it looks as if their language was that of hieroglyphic carvings that Burckhardt and others discovered in Syria during the last century, and not that found on the cuneiform tablets at Bogazköy. Philologists had been trying to decipher the hieroglyphic writing for decades when, in 1947, a bilingual text was discovered. It was found at the ancient town of Karatepe, capital of the Hittite province of Kizzuwatna. A long hieroglyphic inscription on a palace wall was followed by another text in Phoenician. Comparison of the two texts revealed that their content was the same in both cases. Philologists have established that this writing was a dialect of an Indo-European language called Luwian, which resembled cuneiform Hittite in some respects. Although hieroglyphic Hittite was sometimes used by the scribes of Hattusas, examples of this language have more often been found in Syria. Some writers have suggested that it was the people of Kizzuwatna who moved down into Syria from their homeland in the Taurus Mountains and brought Hittite culture, and the hieroglyphic Hittite language, into this area. Unfortunately, few Hittite writings have survived from this period, and we have only the sketchiest outline of the history of these Neo-Hittite states. At Carchemish, excavators discovered hieroglyphics giving a reasonably complete genealogy of the rulers of that state; but most of the little we know of Neo-Hittite history comes from the records of other nations, mainly Assyria. Apparently the Neo-Hittite states enjoyed a certain amount of prosperity, for the increasingly powerful kings of Assyria were able to demand large amounts of gold and silver from them as tribute.

For several centuries Assyrian power waxed and waned, but by the early 9th century BC Assyria had become a formidable aggressor. In 876 the Assyrian king marched his armies through Syria with virtually no resistance from the Hittite rulers, who apparently made no effort to combine against him. A few years later, twelve kings of Palestine and Syria formed an alliance against Assyria, which the Assyrians ruthlessly crushed. Their king boasted that he 'scattered their corpses far and wide ... With my weapons I made their blood to flow down the valleys of the land ... With their bodies I spanned the Orontes as with a bridge.'

For a while the Neo-Hittite states enjoyed some autonomy under Assyrian rule, but in 738 Assyria began annexing these states. By the 7th century they were merely provinces of Assyria. Their language and culture were dying out. The very existence of the great empire of Hattusas, from which they had derived much of their civilisation, was sinking into oblivion.

Today, after more than 70 years of rediscovering the Hittites, we still have many unanswered questions about them. For one thing, some of the statements in the Old Testament referring to Hittites living in Palestine do not tally with what we have learned of Hittite history. When Abraham arrived in Palestine he found living there the 'sons of Heth', whom the writer also calls Hittites. This was around 1700 BC, when the Hittites were just beginning to achieve power in Anatolia and had not started their expansion into Syria. Even at its peak, centuries later, the Hittite Empire never reached into Palestine. It is possible that the people called Hittites in the story of Abraham were really Hattians, the Proto-Hittites who had for some reason wandered far from their Anatolian home and settled in the hills of Palestine. The confusing similarity of the names 'Hattian' and 'Hittite' might account for this puzzling biblical passage.

Later, in Chapter 13 of the Book of Numbers we read that when Moses led the Israelites into the 'land of Canaan' they found Hittites among the tribes that lived in the mountains. Although we do not know the exact dates of the Exodus, it may have occurred as late as the mid-13th century BC. By this time, of course, the Hittite Empire was at its zenith and embraced most of Syria. Yet Palestine was in the Egyptian – not the Hittite – sphere of influence. One Hittite text offers a possible explanation. Written in the time of Suppiluliumas, it states that the 'weather-god of Hatti brought the men of Kurustamma [a northern Hittite state] into the land of Egypt' – a term meaning all the land under Egyptian rule. Exactly why they went there the writer doesn't say, but the British scholar Oliver Gurney, in his book *The Hittites*, suggests that the reference to the weather-god may mean that the move was organised or sanctioned by the Hittite state. The text goes on to say that these people and the 'people of Egypt' then violated an oath they had sworn to the weather-god; whereupon the Hittite king 'invaded the border land of Egypt'. It is possible that these people from Kurustamma settled in the hills of Palestine and that they are the Hittites referred to in Numbers and some of the other parts of the Old Testament. As yet, however, this is only a guess.

Another question that has not been answered is the whereabouts of the original home of the Hittites. It has now been established that they came from the north, but this could include almost anywhere in Europe and Asia. Philologists have pointed out one possible clue: the Hittite language belongs to the 'centum' group of Indo-European languages. These are the language groups, including Greek, Italic, Celtic, and Germanic, that originally used a variant of 'centum' to express the number 100. (The Romance languages still use 'cent,' 'cento,' and so on; and in English the root survives in such words as 'century' and 'centipede'.) The eastern Indo-European languages used variants of 'satem' for 100. This bit of evidence supports the theory held by many scholars that the Hittites originally came from Europe – possibly from the area of the Danube. Other scholars, however, believe that they came into Anatolia through the Caucasus Mountains and were of eastern origin.

There also remains the question of what happened to the Hittites after the collapse of their empire. Although some of them moved into Syria and helped to form the Neo-Hittite states, and some must have remained in Anatolia under the rule of the invaders, it is possible that others may have moved north. In his book *The Hittites, People of a Thousand Gods*, the German writer Johannes Lehmann offers for consideration an intriguing theory relating to this question.

In AD 98 the Roman historian Tacitus wrote in his *Germania* of a warlike people called the Chatti who lived between the Rhine and Weser rivers. In the course of time the name Chatti was altered to Catti, then Hassi, and finally Hessians. Their land was called Hesse. Were the Chatti of whom Tacitus wrote the descendants of the Hittites of Anatolia? The idea seems farfetched. Yet, Lehmann observes, archaeologists have discovered signs of Hittite influence – if not of their actual presence – in Western Europe. Images of a god riding on a bull, the Hittite weather-god, have been dug up at sites all along a path leading from Syria through Anatolia and then into Europe along the Danube and the Rhine, with an offshoot leading into Italy. A few have even been found in Britain. A map showing these sites is included in a book entitled *Altanatolien* by the German scholar Theodor Bossert.

A 1500-mile migration by the Hittites is a long way from being proven, but it is not all that implausible. Other peoples, notably the American Indians, have migrated for thousands of miles. It may be that in the next few years or decades conclusive proof of a Hittite migration to Germany will come to light. The possibility that some of the Hessian mercenaries who took part in the American War of Independence may have been remote descendants of the Hittites would certainly add a strange footnote to history.

CHAPTER 6

THE GOLDEN KINGDOMS

With the fall of Troy and the mysterious disappearance of the Hittites, a power void was created in what is now northern and central Turkey. The Greeks, in the depths of the cultural dark age that followed the Trojan war, jealously watched the new kingdoms that sprang up in Western Anatolia, and told tales of their incredible riches. Over the centuries, the stories of the Phrygian and Lydian kings acquired mythic status. Midas of the golden touch and Croesus, the richest man in the world, were immortalised in fables. Then, in the 20th century, archaeology uncovered the reality that lay behind the tales of a golden age.

To have the 'Midas touch' is generally accounted a blessing. It wasn't such a blessing to Midas himself. According to the ancient legend, Midas was the son of the goddess Cybele by Gordius, the Phrygian king who devised the Gordian knot. He himself in due time became King of Phrygia, and proved a wise and good ruler. He won the favour of the god Dionysus by rescuing the drunken Silenus, the gross old man who had been Dionysus' tutor, from peasants who had tied him up on the banks of the Sangarius. As a reward Dionysus granted Midas a wish. The king wished that everything he touched should be turned to gold. He soon regretted making this wish, though, for he was unable to eat because his food turned to gold. He prayed to Dionysus, who told him to dive into the Pactolus river, which he did, and thereafter the river flowed with gold dust.

This legend is historically interesting because it commemo-rates a civilisation about which very little is known. Phrygia was situated in central Anatolia in what is today Turkey. Modern archaeology has shown that a high civilisation flourished there for several centuries from about the middle of the 8th century BC Archaeologists used to think of this area as one of transit between Europe and Asia. It is only since 1950, when a team of American archaeologists led by Professor Stuart Young of the University of Pennsylvania began excavating the site of the Phrygian capital of Gordium, that historians have realised that there were prosperous ancient civilisations in Anatolia.

Assyrian annals of the 8th century BC speak of a ruler called 'Mita of Mushki' as one of their most powerful enemies in the north. This king has been identified with the one the Greeks called Midas and credited with the foundation of Phrygian civilisation. Many experts today believe that Phrygian culture contributed to the development of early Greek civilisation, for when Phrygian and Greek architecture of the 7th and 8th centuries BC are compared, the Phrygian is seen to be manifestly superior. Phrygian pottery and metal work of the period too is often very fine. As a consider-able number of Phrygian metal objects have been found in and around Greece but no corresponding Greek products of the same period have been unearthed in Phrygia, the case for Phrygian influ-ence on Greek culture would appear to be strong.

The legend of the Midas touch and of the Pactolus flowing with gold dust is believed to be based on the fact that in ancient times the rivers of Anatolia did in fact carry down great quantities of gold and that the prosperity of the region was founded on this happy phenomenon. The Phrygian capital was situated on the river Sangarius, which is today called the Sakarya. Gordium was obviously an important centre, for one of the things that has been unearthed there is a section of a great highway, known as the Royal Road of the Achaemenid Persian emperors. This came from Susa, in what is today southern Iran, crossed the Sangarius at Gordium, and continued to Sardis, the capital of neighbouring Lydia.

When Greek and Persian structures of later periods had been

cleared away, the Gordium archaeologists found ample evidence that the Phrygians had been great architects. There were remains of military, civil, and religious buildings. In one there was found a great hall paved with an intricate mosaic of coloured pebbles, the earliest example of this technique that has ever been discovered. But the richest discoveries were made in the burial mounds just outside the city. The Phrygians had buried important people in tomb-chambers made of timber which were roofed and then covered with tons of earth. The biggest of such burial mounds or *tumuli* found at Gordium was originally-called the 'Tomb of Midas', and was a mound some 170 feet high and 800 feet in diameter. American archaeologists located the burial chamber by drilling down into it from the top of the mound. When they had done this they dug a horizontal tunnel toward it. They found that the chamber of timber had been surrounded by a stone wall and covered with an inner mound of stone rubble in order to bear the tremendous weight of the earth piled above. The wall had to be breached and a good deal of the rubble removed before the archaeologists gained access to the inner chamber. Because these operations weakened the support it was with some apprehension that they finally ventured to enter. They were hardly reassured when they found that part of the roof had already fallen in. They had to construct temporary supports before they could investigate the contents of the chamber.

Just under the spot where the wall had been breached, the Americans found the skeleton of a Phrygian king lying on an immense bed, which had collapsed, but which was covered with twenty rich coverlets. The floor was strewn with bronze vessels that had apparently been on a structure of shelves which had also collapsed. There were ornamented copper cauldrons standing on iron tripods against the walls, which had apparently originally been filled with food and drink. But there were no objects made of gold among the funerary relics. Considering the reputation of the fabled Midas, the American archaeologists found this rather puzzling and disappointing.

There is a second legend associated with this mysterious ruler. It was said that he was once called upon to judge the comparative skills of the god Apollo on the lyre and the satyr Marsyas on the flute. He declared Marsyas the winner, and Apollo vindictively rewarded him with a pair of ass's ears. Midas hid his affliction under his Phrygian cap, and the only person who knew about it was his barber, whom he swore to secrecy. The barber, however, found it very difficult to keep the extraordinary secret to himself, and to gain some relief he dug a hole in the ground and confided it to the earth. But reeds grew from the spot and whenever they were rustled by the wind they could be heard to say, 'King Midas has ass's ears.' Midas, according to the legend, killed himself in desperation by drinking the blood of a bull.

Very often the traditional heroes of one culture are portrayed as devils or buffoons in another, and this preposterous tale is probably a Greek attempt to discredit a foreign ruler whose achievement in establishing Phrygian civilisation was one of the outstanding individual accomplishments of the ancient world. At Gordium the American archaeologists found a terracotta bust of Midas, portraying him with two immense ears, but it was of late date and Greek origin and obviously not a confirmation of the legend but rather a product of it.

The kingdom next to Phrygia to the west, Lydia, began its golden age a little later. It is believed that Midas died in about 695 BC, and that Gyges, the first ruler of the great Mermnad dynasty in Lydia, assumed power in about 687 BC. Since about 1200 BC Lydia had been ruled by a dynasty known as the Heraclids, for they were supposed to be descended from the god-hero Heracles. He had been sold as a slave to Omphale the Queen of Lydia and had then become her lover. The last of the Heraclids, King Candaules, was apparently murdered and usurped by Gyges, and the Greek writers Plato and Herodotus relate different fantastic accounts of how the dynastic change came about.

In Plato's tale, Gyges was a shepherd who fell into a chasm after a thunderstorm and an earthquake, and there found a bronze horse with a dead man inside. There was a gold ring on the dead man's finger. Gyges took it and found that the ring could be manipulated so as to make its wearer invisible. He immediately conceived and carried out a bold plan. He used the magical property of the ring to enable him to gain admission to the queen's bedchamber, became her lover, and then murdered the king and took his place.

Herodotus' account is somewhat less fabulous and makes Candaules' folly as much the cause of his downfall as Gyges' ambition. Gyges, in this story, was originally a courtier and favorite of King Candaules. The king was so proud of the beauty of his wife, Toudo, that he wanted to boast of it to another, and obliged Gyges to play the voyeur so that he could see her naked. Gyges was reluctant to comply, and when he did he was discovered by the queen, who was angry but at the same time flattered and attracted to him, and who gave him a choice between instant death or murdering her husband and taking his place both in her bed and on the throne. He naturally took the latter option, and thus began the great Mermnad dynasty.

These are fantastic tales, but the common factor of Gyges' violent usurpation of Candaules and annexation of his wife are probably historically true. Herodotus' account of events immediately following the coup also rings true. Though Gyges held the reins of power, the Heraclid faction had considerable support and was a threat to the security of his regime. In order to avoid civil war the two sides agreed to put their claims to the arbitration of the Delphic oracle. The oracle declared in favour of Gyges, who showed his gratitude by endowing the Delphic shrine with generous gifts of silver and gold: an act of realpolitik which showed shrewdness in consolidating his power.

Gyges' wealth became legendary. A contemporary Greek poet, Archilochus of Paros, wrote: 'Naught care I for the wealth of Gyges, lord of Sardis.' He may not have cared, but great rulers like the Assyrian Assurbanipal and the Egyptian pharaoh Psammetichus certainly cared for the military and political power that Gyges came to wield through the deployment of his wealth. In his reign of some 35 years he made the Lydian capital of Sardis a city of international importance both politically and socially. Diplomacy and generalship must have been among his accomplishments, but the gold of the Pactolus, the legendary river on which the city of Sardis was situated, was the foundation upon which his prosperity and power were built. It was in his reign that the mining of gold began from the mountains whence the torrent of the Pactolus carried the precious metal down to enrich the sands of Sardis.

If it was personal ambition that drove Gyges to seize the throne of Lydia, that ambition became identified with the national cause during his reign. Though he was reputed eventually to have become a shrewd economist and wise ruler, Gyges began his reign as an aggressive expansionist. Sardis lay about 65 miles inland from the Aegean coast. Between Lydia and the coast there were a number of small Greek city states, such as Miletus, Magnesia, Smyrna, and Colophon. Probably realizing that if Lydia were to prosper commercially it would need access to the sea, Gyges led military campaigns against these coastal Greek city states. At the same time he sent envoys to conciliate the more powerful city states of mainland Greece.and further generous offerings to keep the Delphic oracle well disposed toward him. Although success attended most of his military enterprises, he was not always triumphant. The Roman historian Plutarch retells a story of a shameful Lydian defeat. They had laid siege to the city of Smyrna and sent to its ruler, Philarchus, a demand that the women of Smyrna should be sent out to them. The Smyrneans had just decided to agree to this humiliating condition when a slave girl suggested to Philarchus that instead of sending out their wives and daughters the Smyrneans should dress up slave girls in fine clothes and send them out. This was done, and when the Lydians were exhausted from their dalliance with the slave girls the Smyrneans attacked and overcame them.

The Lydians' love of luxury was famed among the Greeks at a later period, and this story, which Plutarch quoted from a Smyrnean historian, may well be simply propaganda reproduced. The fact that Gyges' troops were no mere pleasure-lovers is suggested by their keeping at bay the wild tribesmen of the north, the Cimmerians, who terrorised the cities of Asia Minor in the 600s BC, seeming to appear suddenly from nowhere, indulge in an orgy of plunder, murder, destruction, and rape, and then disappear as suddenly and mysteriously as they arrived. But when the

Cimmerians fell upon Sardis in 657 BC they met strong and determined opposition and were defeated. The success emboldened Gyges and consolidated his power, and for the remaining 12 years of Gyges' reign Sardis was a proud and prosperous city. But in 645 BC a more massive and ferocious force of Cimmerians attacked, Sardis was sacked, and Gyges himself killed. The ruthlessness of the sacking was indicated by the recent discovery by archaeologists of the skeleton of a little girl killed by the collapse of a burning house.

The Mermnad dynasty consisted of a succession of five kings: Gyges, Ardys, Sadyathes, Alyattes, and Croesus. The Cimmerian conquest proved only a temporary setback for the Lydians. Gyges' son, Ardys, re-established Lydian morale and continued to fight fiercely against the Greek city states of the coast. He also had a fine tomb built to house his father's remains, with a colossal burial mound or tumulus raised above it to commemorate his greatness.

In the 1960s an American archaeological expedition began to investigate the royal cemetery to the north of Sardis. There, among about 100 burial mounds, three are conspicuous by their immense size, and the middle one of these is believed to be the tomb of Gyges. It is about 130 feet high and 650 feet in diameter. When a tunnel was bored into this mound it was discovered that other tunnels had penetrated it, and there were signs that these had been made by tomb robbers in Roman times. The most interesting discovery, though, was of a substantial wall of limestone blocks comprising a circular structure of about 300 feet in diameter erected deep within the tumulus. On a number of these blocks an incised monogram was found. The monogram is cryptic and a number of alternative ways of reading it have been suggested, the most plausible of which is that it spells 'Gugu', which was the name by which Gyges was known in Assyrian records of the period.

Tunnelling was continued beyond the inner wall and reached the centre of the mound, and a number of other exploratory tunnels were dug around the centre, but no actual burial chamber was found. In other Lydian tombs burial chambers have been found situated off-centre, sometimes at a considerable distance, no doubt in order to trick robbers and other intruders, so perhaps King Gyges' skeleton remains undisturbed to this day beneath the great tumulus at Sardis.

The grandeur of Lydia under the Mermnads lasted less than 200 years, and it ended when its civilisation and influence had reached their very height in the fifth generation under King Croesus. This king, whose name has been synonymous with fabulous wealth for 2500 years, succeeded to the throne of Lydia in 560 BC at the age of 35. He began his reign by completing the work that Gyges had started and the other Mermnad rulers had continued: the subjection of the Greek cities of the coast and extension of Lydian sovereignty to the Aegean in the west, the Mediterranean in the south, and the Hellespont in the north. Eastward he subdued all the nations up to the river Halys, and at the height of his power was master of an area about half the size of modern Turkey.

The Pactolus river and the golden mountain of Tmolus continued to disgorge their wealth, Lydia prospered too by trade and Croesus invited philosophers and great men from all over the Greek world to visit Sardis and view its splendours. Legend has it that one of these visitors was Solon, the lawgiver of Athens, a man famed for his wisdom, and that an interesting discussion took place between him and Croesus. After showing Solon around his treasuries, Croesus asked him who he thought was the happiest man he had ever met. Solon answered without hesitation that Tellus of Athens was, because he had lived in a lovely city, had lived to see his sons and grandsons grow to manhood, and had died gloriously and with honour, defending his city.'Who, then, was the second happiest?' asked Croesus, clearly angling for flattery. But Solon calmly answered that he thought perhaps Cleobis and Biton were, because they had enjoyed wealth, health, and public acclaim in their lives and had died in their sleep in the temple of the goddess Hera after sacrificing and feasting. No longer containing his annoyance, the king then demanded of Solon why he took no account of Croesus' own happiness. The Athenian explained that such was the jealousy of the gods, and so subject to change was human life, that it was impossible to call any man happy until his life was done and he had died a happy death. Croesus, according to Herodotus' telling of this story, angrily dismissed Solon from his court and declared that he considered him foolish to take no account of present happiness and success.

In Herodotus' histories it is always difficult to distinguish fact from fable, for many of his tales are obviously told in such a way as to point a moral. Because Herodotus is our main source of knowledge of the life of the last Lydian king, the historical Croesus remains something of a mystery. He presented such a dramatic example of the downfall of the mighty that a philosophically-minded, moralising historian like Herodotus could hardly resist embroidering his narrative. He tells us that after his interview with Solon, the king was disturbed and he had a dream in which he saw his son Atys killed by an iron weapon. Fearing that this was a prophetic dream, Croesus forbade Atys to lead the army, had all iron weapons removed from his apartments, and to compensate Atys and divert his attention he contracted a marriage for him. Some time later Croesus received a request to send Atys and some companions to hunt down a wild boar that was terrorising a region. He was reluctant to do so, and when Atys protested he explained to him about the dream. The young man still insisted on going, and pointed out that as a boar does hot have tusks of iron he would be quite safe. Croesus relented, but as a precaution sent a Phrygian prince, Adrastus, as his bodyguard. When eventually the boar was brought to bay, Adrastus hurled his javelin at it but missed his aim and killed Atys by mistake, thus fulfilling the king's prophetic dream.

This story is so obviously an illustration of Solon's teaching about the unpredictable nature of human fortune that we cannot be certain that Atys ever really existed. Herodotus goes on to say that Croesus spent two years mourning his son's death, and was eventually awakened from his resultant apathy by news of the conquests of Cyrus the Persian. Here Herodotus undoubtedly reports authentic history, for the growing power of Cyrus at this time was a matter of concern not only in Lydia but also in Greece,

Egypt, and Babylon.

In order to determine whether he should make war on Cyrus, and whom he should ally himself with if so, Croesus decided to consult an oracle. But first he conducted a test to find out which of the oracles was likely to be the most reliable. He sent envoys to famous oracles throughout Greece and even to one as far away as Libya, and instructed them simultaneously to ask the oracles, at a certain time 100 days after their departure from Sardis, to specify what King Croesus was doing at that particular moment. When the prearranged time came, Croesus was cutting up a tortoise and a lamb and boiling them in a bronze cauldron. Two of the oracles tested gave the right answer – a remarkable feat of clairvoyance – and one of them was the oracle at Delphi.

Perhaps recalling his ancestor Gyges' happy dealings with the Delphic oracle, Croesus sent sumptuous gifts to Delphi before putting his question. He received the reply that if Croesus made war on the Persians he would destroy a great kingdom, and that he should seek to ally himself to the strongest of the Greek states. Delighted with this response, Croesus sought an alliance first with Athens, and when his overtures failed there, with Sparta, and began to prosecute war against Cyrus, ignoring the counsel of a renowned wise man of Lydia, Sandanis, that the enterprise was not only risky but also no benefits could accrue from success in it, for the Persians were a poor and hardy people.

In the spring of 547 BC Croesus led his army out to challenge Cyrus. He marched beyond the River Halys and subdued part of Cappadocia. Cyrus brought an army of considerably greater numerical strength to oppose him. A day-long battle took place, and though heavy casualties were suffered by both sides neither came off decisively victorious. Cyrus declined to continue the struggle the next day, and Croesus, aware of his numerical inferiority, did not press the matter but withdrew to Lydia, planning to gather a bigger army, with allies from Sparta, Egypt, and Babylon, and to engage Cyrus again the following year. Back in Sardis in October, Croesus sent envoys to ask his allies to send their forces the following spring, and then disbanded those of his own forces that were not Lydians. But Cyrus had spies who brought him news of Croesus' plans and moves, and realising that he would be at a disadvantage the following year he decided to strike while Croesus was unprepared. He descended on Sardis with his large army, and although the crack Lydian troops and cavalry acquitted themselves valiantly they were overwhelmed and Sardis fell to the Persians.

According to Herodotus, when Cyrus had made Croesus captive he had a huge pyre prepared and bound the Lydian king upon it in chains. With the flames rising around him, Croesus remembered Solon's saying that no man could be accounted happy until he had had a happy death, and he called out the name of the great Athenian. Cyrus asked him what he was saying, and Croesus said he was remembering the words of a man whose philosophy all rulers should heed. A brief discourse on the Solonian wisdom by Croesus so impressed Cyrus that he gave orders for the flames to be extinguished, but this proved impossible and Croesus' life was only saved by the intervention of the god Apollo, who sent a storm to put out the flames. Croesus, whose wisdom was now enhanced by his experiences of downfall and deliverance, thereafter became a professional wise man at the court of Cyrus and gave the founder of the Persian empire much sound advice.

An inscription on a Babylonian cylinder of this period probably gives a truer account of events than the philosophical Herodotus. It states simply that 'Cyrus, King of Persia, marched into Lydia, killed its king, took its booty, and put a garrison of his own therein.' So ended the glory of Sardis and the Mermnad dynasty. Its great kings receded into the enigmatic shadows of legend, and its fabulous treasures enriched the ascendant dynasty of Cyrus, the lord of central Asia.

In 1913 archaeologists from Princeton University found at Sardis a tomb in which there were two tombs. One of them contained the bones of an old man and the other those of a girl of about 17 years. The bones disintegrated as soon as they were touched, but in the girl's coffin there remained a profusion of gleaming gold jewelry: headbands about her head where her hair had been, earrings beside the head, a large ring on the finger bone of one hand, gold beads scattered about her feet, and resting on her breastbone a magnificent necklace of intricately wrought gold and superbly fashioned precious stones, a masterpiece of the goldsmith's art. Such artifacts as these, today to be seen in the museum at Istanbul, bear mute witness to the achievements of a vanished kingdom whose rulers' names have come down to us as synonyms for fabulous wealth.

CHAPTER 7

THE MYSTERY OF THE ETRUSCANS

The Romans, the mightiest conquerors known to ancient history, were themselves once the vassals of a people called the Etruscans, whom the Roman historians described as thoroughly wicked and tyrannical. (The story of the rape of Lucretia by the Etruscan king Tarquinius raised indignation in generations of Roman nobles.) When the Romans overthrew their conquerors, they suppressed them with such thoroughness that they destroyed most of the clues to the history of that enigmatic race. Where did this prosperous, creative, luxury-loving people come from when they colonised central Italy about a thousand BC? Their influence on the Romans - and thus of all of subsequent western culture - was great, but their writings remain untranslated, so we have only fragmentary clues to the mystery of the Etruscans.

Before Rome became a republic it was ruled by a dynasty of Etruscan kings. Sextus, the son of one of these kings, became infatuated with a Roman matron named Lucretia. One night when Lucretia's husband was away, Sextus gained entrance to her bedroom and threatened to kilı her if she did not allow him to make love to her. Lucretia declared that she would rather die than betray her husband, to which the inflamed Sextus replied that if she forced him to kill her he would place a murdered naked slave beside her body so as to give the impression that she had been killed while committing adultery. Lucretia was forced to comply. Returning home, Lucretia's husband Collatinus found her in tears. After hearing the cause, he tried to console her, assuring her that she was not dishonoured because she had been taken by force. But Lucretia did not take so lenient a view of her predicament. 'It is for you to see what is due to him. As for me, though I acquit myself of guilt, from punishment I do not discharge myself; nor shall any woman survive her dishonour pleading the example of Lucretia.' And she plunged a knife into her heart. This outrage by the son of a much-hated king was all Collatinus and his friends needed to incite them to rebellion. They carried Lucretia's body to the forum, where they soon attracted a large crowd. Their grief and anger had the desired effect. The Roman people decided to banish the king, Tarquin the Proud, along with his family. When Tarquin returned to Rome from his military camp the gates were shut against him. Sextus was killed by the revolutionaries and the other sons were sent into exile.

Such, in abbreviated form, is the Roman historian Livy's account of how in 510 BC Rome came to shake off Etruscan rule and begin its long road to domination of the known world.

It is doubtful if the rape of Lucretia – if in fact it really happened – was the immediate cause of the Roman revolt. The story has all the earmarks of propaganda: typically licentious Etruscan assaults typically virtuous Roman lady and brings down on himself and his co-oppressors the vengeance of the outraged patriots. It is worth remembering that the story was not written until some 500 years after the city's liberation and that its author was a Roman historian motivated by a desire to present his nation's history in the most favourable light.

True or not, the story is unusual in that it describes the action of an individual Etruscan. For although we now know a great deal about the Etruscan way of life, the people themselves remain elusive. They have faces – the faces painted on the walls of their tombs and sculpted in terracotta – but no identities in any meaningful sense of the word. This is because we have no Etruscan literature. We have not discovered any Etruscan Plato, or Sophocles, or Seneca to comment on the nature of humanity from an Etruscan viewpoint or give expression to Etruscan myths and ideals; there are no accounts of Etruscan heroes or statesmen written by their compatriots. Those examples of Etruscan writing that we possess are for the most part brief tomb inscriptions identifying the deceased and the parents of the deceased, as well as a few short texts, apparently of a religious nature, the longest of which contains about 1500 words.

Not only is the written legacy meagre; it is also largely incomprehensible. As yet, no one has succeeded in translating the Etruscan language. The few Etruscan words whose meanings are known are mainly proper names, including those of the Etruscan gods.

For Etruscan history, we must therefore rely on the often critical writings of their contemporaries and rivals, particularly the Greeks and Romans. We see the growth, zenith, and decline of Etruscan civilisation reflected in a series of distorting mirrors. In their art, however, the Etruscans reveal themselves with a spontaneity and vividness that makes us think we know them very well. The walls of their tombs are covered with detailed representations of Etruscan life. If a picture really were worth 10,000 words, as a Chinese proverb claims, we would need no writing to tell us their story. As it is, we can only piece together fragments and are left, still with a mystery.

Along with their language, the big puzzle about the Etruscans is their origin. Where did they come from? The home of the Etruscan civilisation, called Etruria, was west central Italy, a region that now includes the provinces of Tuscany (a name obviously derived from 'Etruscan') and Umbria. This area had been inhabited for many centuries before the distinctive Etruscan culture appeared in it. The earlier inhabitants (who *may* be the ancestors of the people we call Etruscans) are called Villanovans, because the first excavations revealing their existence were made at the hamlet of Villanova, near Bologna. The Villanovans were skilled in iron-working and pottery and they usually cremated their dead. Yet the ashes of the dead were surrounded with objects presumably needed in the afterlife: jewellery and other accessories, weapons, and household implements.

Villanovan tombs dating from around the 7th century BC show a change both in funeral customs and in the quality of the objects. Cremation begins to be replaced by inhumation – burial of the body. Along with the obviously native-produced objects are some foreign products: vases, pots, statues, and jewellery from Greece, Egypt, Phoenicia, and other Mediterranean lands, some of them made of precious metals. Obviously, the people buried in these tombs were wealthier than their predecessors and were trading with other nations.

It was about this time – from about 750 BC onward – that the Greeks began colonising the southwestern coast of Italy. Hesiod, a Greek poet of the 8th century BC, refers in one of his poems to the 'far famed Tyrrhenians' who occupied the area north of the Greek settlements in Italy. 'Tyrrhenians' is the Greek name for the people we call Etruscans, which brings us to the theory that the Etruscan people originally came from somewhere else. The first person to put this theory in writing was Herodotus, the Greek historian who lived in the 5th century BC. He tells of how, sometime after the Trojan Wars, a great famine occurred in Lydia, a nation located in part of what is now Turkey. As the famine grew more severe, the Lydians tried to ignore their hunger by playing games and eating only every other day. Eventually the king decided that half of the population would have to emigrate. The group chosen by lot to leave the country were led by his son Tyrrhenos. They set out in ships and finally settled in the 'land of the Umbrians' – central Italy. They no longer called themselves Lydians, according to Herodotus, but adopted the name of their prince and called themselves Tyrrhenians.

Actually, the Etruscans called themselves Rasena – a word found in various dialects of Asia Minor – but the Greeks persisted in calling them Tyrrhenians, and the part of the Mediterranean that adjoins the west coast of Italy is still called the Tyrrhenian Sea. Although the Romans accepted the theory of their Lydian origin and often called them Lydians, they also called them Tusci, or Etrusci, from which their modern name is derived.

Most of their contemporaries accepted the theory of the Etruscans' Eastern origin. An opposing view was put forward by

Etruscan mask of Medusa from the 6th Century BC

Lost Worlds

Dionysius of Halicarnassus, a Greek historian living in Rome in the 1st century BC. He observed that the 'Tyrrhenians . . . do not have the same language as the Lydians. . . . They do not worship the same gods as the Lydians; they do not have the same laws. . . . It thus seems to me that those who say that the Etruscans are not a people who came from abroad, but are an indigenous race, are right; to me this seems to follow from the fact that they are a very ancient people which does not resemble any other either in its language or in its customs.'

In the light of modern discoveries neither Herodotus nor Dionysius has an airtight case. If, as Herodotus states, the emigration from Lydia took place around the time of the Trojan Wars (around the beginning of the 12th century BC) this would mean that the 'Tyrrhenians' were settled in Italy at least 500 years before the civilisation we call Etruscan makes its appearance. As it stands, Herodotus' story is roughly analogous to some modern historian's claiming that English settlers colonised North America in the Middle Ages – despite the fact that there is no evidence of their colonisation before the early 17th century. It may be that the Lydian source from which Herodotus took his information had given the wrong date. Or it may be that the Lydian emigrants settled somewhere else – which would create a whole new mystery for some enterprising archaeologist.

Despite the confusing matter of the dates, the basic theory that the Etruscans were an Eastern people is quite plausible. Dionysius' claim that their customs did not resemble those of any foreign people was based on inadequate knowledge. Equipped with detailed studies of the customs, laws, and religions of ancient peoples, the modern historian can see resemblances unknown to a man living in Dionysius' time. The fact is that the Etruscans did resemble some Oriental peoples in many aspects of their civilisation.

One of the most striking similarities was the emphasis in their religion on foretelling the future. The Etruscan religion – in fact every aspect of Etruscan life – was dominated by the pronouncements of the *haruspices*, the priests who studied various natural phenomena and interpreted their significance for the future. They claimed they could tell from the direction and duration of thunder and lightning, for example, which of the gods was sending a message and what sort of message it was. The birth of a deformed child or animal was also regarded as significant. But it was the art of hepatoscopy, the examination of the liver of a sacrificed animal, that was the keystone of Etruscan divination – as it was for the people of Babylonia and other parts of Asia Minor. In fact the practice of telling fortunes from the livers of animals seems to have originated around 2000 BC in Babylonia, one of the most ancient civilisations. Excavations in that part of the world have unearthed many terracotta models of livers engraved with prophecies based on the physical characteristics represented on the model. Etruscan art contains many pictures of priests divining the future from the livers of sacrificed animals. Some of the complexity of the art can be inferred from a bronze model of a liver found at Piacenza in 1877, which was probably used as a teaching model. Its surface is divided into 40 sections, each inscribed with the name of a god or goddess and each corresponding to a division of the sky. The liver of an animal dedicated and sacrificed to the gods was believed to be an image of the Universe and so capable of revealing its aspects at that moment.

This peculiar practice and the overriding importance it assumed both in the ancient Near East and in Etruria is one bit of evidence supporting the theory of the Etruscans' Eastern origin. Among Western peoples divination had no such importance. The Greeks, for example, might consult an oracle for advice on an important matter, but not in the course of conducting the ordinary business of life. Among the Greeks there was nothing corresponding to the *Disciplina Etrusca*, a detailed book of ritual, mostly concerned with divination. The practice of liver divination was virtually unknown. The Romans, whose civilisation was influenced by the Etruscans, adopted these divination practices somewhat half-heartedly, leaving the actual performing of the rites to the expert Etruscan priests. No other people in the Western world were so adept at rites as the Etruscans or so dominated by their religion.

There were, to be sure, some resemblances between Etruscan

religion and those of the Greeks and Romans. Some of their gods and goddesses were the same. The three supreme Etruscan deities, Tinia (the most powerful), Uni, and Menrva, who were worshipped as a trinity in sanctuaries with three halls, were adopted by the Romans as Jupiter, Juno, and Minerva. On the other hand the Etruscans adopted some of the Greek gods, such as Poseidon (called Neptune by the Romans and Nethuns by the Etruscans) and Apollo (Aplu in Etruscan). But the Etruscans' attitude toward their gods differed sharply from that of the Greeks and Romans. The Greeks, especially, regarded their gods as beings more or less like humans but equipped with supernatural powers. They invented stories dramatising the gods' weaknesses and defects. These same myths were often pictured in Etruscan painting – which was strongly influenced by the Greeks in both style and content – but the Etruscans clearly regarded these gods as powerful and mysterious beings who demanded constant devotion.

Another way in which the Etruscan differed from their neighbours was in the status enjoyed by their women. The Greeks and the early Romans kept their women out of sight. Only courtesans attended their banquets; respectable women remained at home with the servants, pursuing useful occupations such as spinning or weaving. Etruscan society was more enlightened in this respect. It was considered perfectly natural for women to accompany their husbands to games, chariot races, and banquets. This custom of dining together was completely misunderstood by the Greeks and the Romans. Theopompus, a Greek writer of the 4th century BC, noted for malicious scandalmongering, described in authoritative detail the lax behavior of the Etruscans:

'The Tyrrhenians possess their women in common; these take great care of their bodies and exercise naked, often along with men. . . . They sit down to table not beside their husbands but beside any of the guests, and they even drink to the health of anyone they please. Moreover they are great wine-bibbers and very beautiful to behold. The Tyrrhenians bring up together all those children that are born to them, heedless of who their father may be. These children live in the same manner as their protectors, passing most of their time in drinking and having commerce with all the women indifferently.' And so on.

Other writers presented a more restrained picture of Etruscan life; but it is difficult to evaluate their accounts in the absence of any comment from the Etruscans themselves. We must turn to the images in Etruscan tombs. There, in the frescoes, we find ample evidence of sensuality, though nothing to support the wilder assertions of Theopompus. Certainly there are signs that the Etruscan woman was considered a worthwhile person. Her sculpted image reclines beside that of her husband on a sarcophagus; tomb inscriptions give the names of both the father and the mother of the deceased. By contrast, among the Greeks and Romans only the father's name was normally given. Among the tombs at Caere (now Cerveteri) is one built solely for a woman and furnished with more than 100 objects – gold ornaments, perfume bottles, and a dinner service – for her use in the afterlife. Such objects are sometimes engraved 'I belong to Larthia' (for example) indicating that women had possessions of their own.

None of these marks of status seems remarkable from a modern viewpoint, but to the Greeks and Romans they must have seemed eccentric, to say the least. Yet in the earlier civilisations of Crete and Mycenae women also attended public games and enjoyed a degree of equality. And in Lydia, the Etruscans' supposed homeland, the mother's name sometimes appears on tomb inscriptions as it does in Etruria.

Perhaps the most persuasive evidence in favour of the migration theory is the Etruscan language. Although its alphabet is similar to the Greek, the language itself does not resemble any of those within the family of languages known as Indo-European, to which Greek and nearly all other ancient and modern European languages belong. It is hard to believe that if the Etruscans had lived in Italy since time immemorial they would have developed a language so radically different from those spoken by their neighbours.

As Dionysius observed, however, their language is not the same as that of the Lydians, another Indo-European tongue, nor does it even resemble it. The same can be said of other languages of Asia Minor. If the Etruscans were emigrants from another land, then there ought to be another group of ancient people – those who remained at home – who spoke the same language. Unless, of course, the population had died and their civilisation been extinguished.

Wherever and however the Etruscans were living before about 700 BC, from that time onward they enjoyed a life of great prosperity. Their land was fruitful and rich in minerals, particularly tin, copper, and iron. It was the mining of these much sought-after metals that gave the Etruscans the wealth to buy and fashion into exquisite ornaments the gold, silver, and ivory of lands to the east and south. The Etruscans had mastered the subtler techniques of jewellery making very early in their history. Their skill in the technique of granulation – decorating the surface of gold jewellery with thousands of tiny gold beads – exceeded that of any other goldsmiths of the ancient world. The formula of the solder they used in this process died with their civilisation and has never been rediscovered.

Of course, we are not one hundred percent sure that it was the Etruscans themselves who did this work. Many of the vases once thought to be Etruscan have since been proved to be of Greek origin. The confusion was caused by the fact that Etruscan potters, from about 700 BC onward, copied Greek styles. Greek craftsmen lived and worked in Etruria and had a strong influence on Etruscan taste. But the Etruscans also borrowed themes from the art of Egypt, Mesopotamia, and Syria. The result is an art full of fabulous beasts – winged horses, sphinxes, and the chimera, a creature incorporating a lion, a goat, and a snake.

The Etruscans were not only skilled craftsmen but also aggressive traders and mariners. Any ideas the Greeks may have had about controlling the western Mediterranean were checked by the Etruscan navy, which quickly gained dominance of the Tyrrhenian Sea and expanded their trade all along the coast of southern Europe and North Africa. They soon came into conflict with the Greeks who had established colonies in France and Spain as well as in Italy. Greek writers of the 6th and 7th centuries BC refer bitterly to the 'piratical Tyrrhenians'. Carthage, too, had ambitions in the Mediterranean, and a three-sided contest began, in which Carthage was ultimately the victor.

On land, the Etruscans extended their sphere of influence to include a large section of the Italian peninsula from the Po valley in the north to Campania in the south. Yet the Etruscans never formed a unified nation. Etruria consisted of a number of independent city-states that were bound by ties of custom, language, and religion. They joined forces temporarily for military purposes – for example, to fight off invading Celts – but their essential disunity later made them vulnerable to the highly organised and disciplined Romans. The Etruscan states were governed first by priest-kings and later by magistrates elected by the ruling class. The only regular occasion on which the heads of states met together was the annual festival of the god Voltumna. Sometimes this religious occasion also served a political purpose; it gave the representatives of the various states an opportunity to discuss matters of general concern and settle any differences between them. The festival was apparently held in some kind of sacred grove in the area around Volsinii (now Bolsena).

If there was a temple there in honour of Voltumna, it has disappeared, along with nearly every other above-ground Etruscan building. This is because the Etruscans built mainly in wood and bricks, using stone only for the foundation. From those foundations that remain we can see the floor plans of their temples and houses. Our ideas of what the structures looked like are derived mainly from their tomb interiors, which they built to resemble homes, and from terracotta decorative elements such as friezes and statues that adorned their temples. The few remaining arches and city walls show Etruscan building techniques applied to the planning of cities.

Like most other aspects of Etruscan life, the foundation of a new city was pervaded with ritual. As always, the omens had first to be read by the priest. These would determine the orientation of the city. Then the founder, equipped with a bronze ploughshare and with part of his toga draped over his head, for reasons that are not clear, would plough a furrow marking the boundary of the city. According to the Romans, who adopted these foundation rites, there were also rules for the orderly geometrical layout of streets and placements of gates and temples. Yet archaeologists have found little evidence in the sites of Etruscan towns of such Roman-style regularity. Here again, the written information about Etruscan customs is secondhand and at least partially misleading. The Etruscan ritual books for the founding of cities have disappeared.

Ironically, it was the Etruscans who made Rome – originally just a group of villages – into an important city, ringed with fortifications and endowed with fine buildings. The Etruscans were noted for their skill in hydraulics, and one of the achievements of the Tarquins was the draining of the forum and the construction of a sewer system. Livy tells how the hated Tarquin the Proud 'caused to be constructed, despite the protestations of the people who found this labour very trying, a great subterranean sewer intended to receive all the filth of the city, a work which our modern magnificence found hard to equal.' This was the famous Cloaca Maxima, which empties into the Tiber and is still in use today.

The legacy of Etruscan rule in Rome included not only engineering techniques, which the Romans were to develop with impressive results, but also certain customs we now think of as typically Roman. One was the triumphal procession, in which the king was preceded by officials bearing the fasces, the rods and axe that were the symbols of unlimited power. Another custom was the gladiatorial combat. Although these gladiatorial fights to the death did not take place on the scale found in the later Roman Empire, they were certainly a well-established Etruscan custom. They grew out of the practice of sacrificing prisoners of war in honour of the Etruscan dead; this custom was then modified so that the prisoners fought each other.

Even after the Romans won independence from the Etruscans, it still took them more than 200 years to defeat their former masters. This gradual, piecemeal conquest was aided by the Etruscans' disunity, their over-reliance on omens – even in conducting a war – and their misfortune in having occasionally to fight off the Celts to the north as well as the Romans to the south. Eventually, however, the last Etruscan stronghold, Volsinii, fell in 280 BC. It came about through a rebellion of the city's slaves –

the people who made possible the luxurious life of the Etruscan aristocrats. Some citizens who managed to escape from the violence in their city appealed to the Roman army for help. The Romans obligingly killed the slaves, offered the surviving aristocrats hospitality, and razed Volsinii to the ground.

Etruscan civilisation did not disappear at once. For another 200 years Etruscan arts and crafts were practiced, though not on the high level of earlier times. Some of the city-states enjoyed a degree of autonomy. Etruscan religious beliefs and practices survived until the fall of the Roman Empire. Every year delegates still gathered to honour Voltumna at his festival. Officially, the Etruscan language had been replaced with Latin, but it continued to be spoken for a few hundred years after the Roman conquest. Some Etruscan cities were deserted and allowed to decay; others were rebuilt by the Romans. Under the earth outside the Etruscan cities lay the cities of the dead, which were soon forgotten.

Throughout the Middle Ages the Etruscans remained a shadowy people, known only to a few scholars who could read what the Greeks and Romans had written about them. In the Renaissance curiosity about these people began to revive. A Dominican friar, Giovanni Nanni, caused a certain amount of excitement in 1498 when he published a collection of fragments attributed to various obscure writers of antiquity. His book included some Etruscan inscriptions which he claimed to have copied on the walls of tombs near his native city of Viterbo (originally an Etruscan town). Although Nanni has long been regarded as a hoaxer, it seems likely that the book's Etruscan fragments are genuine. His translations, which were based on the traditional assumption that all languages were derived from Hebrew, are less reliable.

Interest in Etruscan civilisation was further stimulated by the writings of Thomas Dempster, an exceptionally pugnacious Scotsman who – when he was not engaged in brawls – taught and studied at some of Europe's major universities. His massive work *Seven Books Concerning the Kingdom of Etruria*, included all the existing knowledge of the Etruscans, drawn from classical sources, and Dempster's own interpretations and conclusions.

Although Dempster's scholarship was impressive, the book lacked any firsthand investigation of Etruscan remains. At the time Dempster was writing, the early 1600s, archaeology did not exist.

It was not until the 18th century that excavations began at Volterra, some 40 miles southwest of Florence. One of the most important Etruscan cities, it had a wall five miles in circumference, parts of which are still standing. Outside the wall, the excavators discovered thousands of tombs filled with treasures, which soon found their way into museums and private collections throughout Europe. The Guarnacci Museum at Volterra, founded shortly after the excavations began, houses one of the largest and finest collections of Etruscan art in the world.

As more and more tombs were opened at other sites and more riches were discovered, a new word, 'Etruscomania', was coined to describe the passion for Etruscan art that was sweeping through Europe. At the same time, travellers and scholars were also beginning to discover the art and ruins of ancient Greece, and a certain amount of confusion resulted from the mixture of Greek and native Etruscan artefacts found in Tuscany. A spirited dispute broke out between Giovanni Batista Piranesi, Italian architect and engraver, whose book on Roman architecture claimed that it owed everything to the Etruscans and nothing to the Greeks, and Pierre Jean Mariette, a French connoisseur who replied that the Etruscans were originally Greek and had learned architecture from their forebears. National pride, artistic prejudices, and fragmentary understanding of ancient history combined to make the new field of Etruscology a fertile area for speculation and error.

The haphazard and often destructive approach of the excavators added to the confusion. Some people were interested only in the profitable aspects and salvaged only the items of obvious commercial value. No one bothered to make a careful inventory of the objects found in a tomb, and often humble objects that might have yielded worthwhile information about Etruscan life were thoughtlessly destroyed. Snatched from their context, with no notes of what was found with them, the valuable pieces lost much of their archaeological significance. Many of the wall paintings that reveal so much of Etruscan life were damaged by the smoke of the excavators' torches or simply left to deteriorate.

While the looting continued into the 19th century (one of the arch-looters was Napoleon's brother Lucien, whose estate included the tombs of Vulci), interest grew in the Etruscans themselves. George Dennis, an English explorer, spent six years travelling from one Etruscan site to another, making notes and sketches of what he found. His observations were published in 1848 in two volumes entitled *Cities and Cemeteries of Etruria*. Dennis's achievement was mainly to describe in vivid detail the many sites that had already been discovered, but he also discovered several new Etruscan burial sites. Today, Etruscan remains are still unearthed from time to time. Unfortunately, though, most Etruscan cities lie beneath modern towns, where the density of building rules out much archaeological work. Had serious archaeologists been on the scene in George Dennis's day, before so much urbanisation had taken place, we would certainly know more about the Etruscans than we do now.

The person who arguably did more than anyone else to open people's eyes to the beauty of Etruscan art was D. H. Lawrence, the English novelist. His book *Etruscan Places*, published in 1932, two years after his death, overflows with praise for the lively, sensuous paintings on the walls of the tombs and for the unfettered way of life they depict.

'The naked slaves joyfully stoop to the winejars. Their nakedness is its own clothing, more easy than drapery. The curves of their limbs show pure pleasure in life, a pleasure that goes deeper still in the limbs of the dancers, in the big, long hands thrown out and dancing to the very ends of the fingers, a dance that surges from within, like a current in the sea.'

Lawrence's boundless enthusiasm takes us to the other extreme from those classical writers who could find nothing good to say about the Etruscans. Certainly the paintings surge with life, and the Etruscans obviously delighted in music and dance and sport and in their own bodies. (Although whether slaves did their work 'joyfully' is open to question.) What Lawrence ignored or discounted was the rigid, hierarchical structure of Etruscan society, its occasional cruelty, and the all-pervading demands of the Etruscan religion. To be sure, that religion made few moral demands on the faithful, but having to consult the gods on every occasion must have taken some of the spontaneity out of life.

The Etruscans were, quite literally, a god-fearing people. Paintings in the later tombs depict frightful demons punishing the dead. Aita, a corruption of Hades, the Greek god of the Underworld wears a wolf's skin over his head. The figure of Charun, who carries the dead into the underworld, is not the placid ferryman of the Greeks but a hideous grimacing figure with bluish flesh that reminds the onlooker of bodily decompostion. He carries a club to smash the skulls of the dying in order to finish them off. He is accompanied by Tuchulcha, a repellent creature with the face of a vulture and the ears of a donkey, who clutches snakes in his hand ready to strike.

It may be significant that at the time most of these grisly scenes were painted, Etruria was bit by bit falling into the hands of the Romans. In many religions, particularly those of eastern lands, priests were inclined to attribute political setbacks to inadequate piety on the part of the people and exhort their flock to mend their ways in order to forestall disaster. The frightful demons represented in the paintings may reflect a 'revivalist' phase in the Etruscan religion; or they may simply give visible expression to an increasing pessimism concerning life in this world and the next.

In the faces of some of the later portrait statues one can see traces of an apparent resignation or perhaps world-weariness that presents a sharp contrast to the carefree, smiling faces in earlier tombs. The paintings and statues suggest that a change was occurring in the Etruscan world view – a change that would be natural enough in circumstances of decline and defeat.

Of course, it is possible to interpret the situation the other way around. Perhaps the decline in Etruscan power and the collapse of the city-states before the Roman offensive were originally caused in part by the mentality reflected in the late Etruscan art. Did the fatalism of their religion undermine the initiative and energy shown by the Etruscans in their early days? Or did their life of pleasure begin to cloy, and lead them to a preoccupation with suffering and a passivity in the face of danger?

Endless psychological games can be played on the causes of the Etruscans' decline without ever being able to prove whether the insights are even remotely correct.

One of the frustrations facing scholars is that although, according to Roman writers, the Etruscans did have a literature, that literature has disappeared. Many scholars doubt whether Etruria ever produced much, if any, imaginative writing, but certainly they did write some history and perhaps some religious poetry. Marcus Terrentius Varro, a Roman writer of the first century BC, included some Etruscan texts in his book *The Divine Anliquities*, which dealt with the history, geography, and anthropology of early Italy. This book was still in existence as late as 1320, when Petrarch reported having seen it. Since then it has vanished.

The longest piece of Etruscan writing to have been discovered is a 1500-word text on a piece of linen used to wrap an Egyptian mummy of a young woman. The wrapped mummy was donated to a museum in Zagreb, Croatia, in the mid-1800s and the wrappings removed and displayed separately. Not until 1891 was the mysterious writing identified as Etruscan. Although scholars have still not succeeded in reading it, they are fairly sure that it is a ritual calendar of some sort. It consists of several sections, each of which seems to begin with a date (though this is by no means certain). Also, there are frequent references to 'gods' – one of the few known Etruscan words – and many repetitions, suggesting a kind of ritual response.

Why an Egyptian mummy should be wrapped in an Etruscan manuscript has naturally puzzled the experts. Some have suggested that the young woman was an Etruscan – one of those who fled to Egypt after the Roman conquest – and that the writing had some significance for her. A more likely explanation perhaps is that the embalmer simply used any linen he could lay his hands on, even if it was covered with writing. The text could have reached Alexandria when Etruscans were migrating from their Eastern homeland (if they did make such a journey) or when some of them left Etruria after the conquest. The fact that the linen was torn into strips, breaking the sequence of the lines, and wrapped with the writing inside suggests that its use was accidental.

The seemingly endless task of trying to translate the Etruscan language has engaged the efforts of hundreds of scholars and codebreakers, both amateur and professional. They have approached the task in two basic ways: by comparing it with other languages and by examining a text as one would an encoded message, trying to find clues within the language itself. Neither of these methods has yielded any significant results. The problems can be illustrated with reference to a pair of dice found in an Etruscan tomb at Toscanella more than 100 years ago. Each face of the dice is marked with a word: *Max, ci, zal, śa, θu,* and *huθ.* We know that in ancient times dice were marked with the numbers l through 6, just as they are today, so it seems likely that these six words represent the first six numbers. The words used for numbers in one language are often very similar to those used in a related language. For example: 'une, dos, tres' in Spanish and 'uno, due, tre' in Italian. If a language could be found having similar words for the first six numbers, it might supply meaningful translations for other Etruscan words. But if the words on the Toscanella dice do represent numbers, no one has yet succeeded in finding a language whose number names correspond to them.

Pursuing the possibility that the words are not those of numbers but rather a sentence of some kind, other people have suggested an enormous variety of translations, based on various borrowed words from both Greek and Gothic to produce: 'May these sacred dice fall double sixes.'

The search for a key to the Etruscan language has for many people become an obsession. They may decide, on the basis of a few similarities, that Etruscan is related to Egyptian, or Basque, or Gaelic, for example; and then, using the chosen language as a key, offer translations of the few existing Etruscan texts. The translations are usually somewhat forced and often meaningless, and each tends to meet with a certain amount of derision from those holding different theories.

What the scholars keep hoping to find is an Etruscan 'Rosetta Stone' – a text that is repeated in another, known language. Such a hope is not unreasonable. When Rome began ruling Etruria the government must have sometimes had occasion to issue statements not only in the official language but also in the language of the Etruscan people. A bi-lingual text of even a few hundred words would give us not only the meanings of those Etruscan words in that particular text but also clues, through roots, prefixes, and suffixes, to many other Etruscan words and to the structure of its grammar.

A certain amount of excitement followed the discovery, in 1964, of three gold tablets, one inscribed in Punic – the language of the Carthaginians – and the other two in Etruscan. The three tablets were found lying together between the sites of two Etruscan temples at Santa Severa on the Tyrrhenian Sea. Professor Massimo Pallottino, the leader of the excavation, and his associates set to work on the three texts, which together contained about 90 words. The Punic text consisted of the dedication of a temple to the goddess Astarte offered by the king of the Etruscan city of Cisra, which had stood on that site. It raises a number of questions about the relationship between the Etruscans and their occasional allies the Carthaginians and about the role of Astarte, chief goddess of the Carthaginians, in Etruscan religion. It is worth noting that Astarte, the goddess of fertility, was also worshiped in Lydia and that in that country her cult, noted for its orgiastic rites, also involved prostitution. One of the charges brought against the Etruscans by the Greeks and Romans was that their young women acquired their dowries by prostituting themselves. Was the dedication of a temple to Astarte a kind of ecumenical-diplomatic gesture made by the Etruscan king to the Carthaginians ? Had he simply been converted to her cult? Or did his action have deeper roots, to be found in an Eastern homeland?

As for the Etruscan texts, they were disappointing. Although they do seem to contain information similar to that on the Punic tablet, careful examination has shown that neither is a literal translation. Once again the Etruscans have proved inscrutable.

Still, the archaeologists, scholars, and codebreakers keep on digging and pouring over Etruscan texts, hoping to find a key that will unlock the mystery of this baffling language and perhaps reveal the origins of these fascinating people.

CHAPTER 8

THE SECRETS OF THE STANDING STONES

While the Egyptians were building the pyramids, and the Babylonians were constructing the Hanging Gardens, the Neolithic farmers of northern Europe were erecting circles or rows of standing stones. Until the beginning of the 20th century, cultured opinion held that they were Druidic temples, dating from about 600 BC and dedicated to human sacrifice. When an astronomer, Sir Norman Lockyer, first announced his opinion that they were intended as giant calculating machines, he was dismissed as a fantasist. It is only in recent times that computer analysis of the heavens has shown that Lockyer was correct, and that – as the Scottish engineer Alexander Thom put it – the builders of the megaliths were 'Stone Age Einsteins'.

One summer evening in 1934, after a hard day's sailing up the west coast of Scotland, an Oxford University professor took his boat into Loch Roag on the Isle of Lewis to find an anchorage for the night. A full moon was rising over the hills, and silhouetted against it was a most impressive sight: the tall standing stones of Callanish, the ancient monument that has been called the Scottish equivalent of Stonehenge.

Professor Alexander Thom went ashore, and, standing in the middle of the mysterious stone circle, he noticed that according to the pole star the structure was aligned due north-south. This observation fascinated him, for he knew that in the days when the stone circle was constructed there was no pole star because its constellation hadn't reached its present position. He wondered whether the alignment was a chance occurrence or had been deliberately planned. If it was deliberate it would probably be found at other megalithic sites. Thom decided to check whether it was, and thus began 30 years of painstaking study, involving survey work at no fewer than 450 sites in remote spots in the British Isles, which led to the publication in 1967 of his book *Megalithic Sites in Britain*, and in 1971 of *Megalithic Lunar Observations*. It also led to a revolution in thinking about European prehistory. It had previously been assumed that barbarians had inhabited Western Europe in prehistoric times, when civilisation had first arisen in the Middle East. Thom's findings demanded a radical change of this view. 'I'm an engineer,' he wrote, and indeed his professorship was in engineering. 'I'm certain these people were too—and proud of it.'

By 'these people' Thom meant the megalith builders. The word *megalith* comes from two Greek words meaning simply 'large stone', and its adjective is used for a variety of structures from single standing stones known as *menhirs*, to structures in which three standing stones support an immense capstone, known as *dolmens* or *cromlechs*, and to piles of rough stones burying a tomb or serving as a memorial or landmark, known as cairns, and of course stone circles. Professor Glyn Daniel of Cambridge has estimated that there must be between 40,000 and 50,000 megalithic tombs or temples in Western Europe. The question of who built them has given rise to at least as much speculation and controversy as any other question in archaeology.

The phenomenon is not exclusive to Western Europe, but it is peculiarly concentrated there, particularly in the form of menhirs and stone circles. The practice of building tombs of stone – and dolmens are thought to have been tombs – is a natural development from cave burial. As such it might be expected to occur spontaneously in different parts of the world. But the erection of single standing stones, or avenues or circles of them, is a practice that at first consideration appears rather pointless. As the French archaeologist Professor P. R. Giot wrote of the standing stones:

'Whether isolated or in groups, they remain enshrouded in mystery. This is no doubt why their study has, unjustifiably, been comparatively neglected. . . . With the very limited evidence at his disposal, the interpretation of single menhirs is one of the archaeologist's nightmares.'

The mystery is deepened when we think of the labour involved. All other archaeological evidence bears witness to the fact that the inhabitants of Western Europe at the time when the megaliths were erected were neolithic farmers living in small communities who possessed only the most primitive tools and technology. Professor Richard Atkinson, the Englishman who excavated around Stonehenge, estimated that the transport of the 81 sarsen stones from Avebury, some 15 miles away, would have taken 1500 men working continuously for 5.5 years. And the construction of nearby Silbury Hill (which is not a megalith but is of the same period) he reckoned would have taken 18 million man-hours. In the 1830s a capstone from a megalithic tomb near Saumur in France was moved to serve as a bridge. It took 18 pairs of oxen and enormous rollers, each consisting of four oak tree trunks lashed together, to shift it. The great stone known as the Grand Menhir Brisé in Brittany, which now lies broken on the ground, weighed about 380 tons and stood 60 feet high. In the famous nearby avenues of menhirs at Carnac there are no fewer than 3000 great stones. The labour involved in erecting them, and the thousands of other stones and stone structures in Brittany and the British Isles, was prodigious. The idea that they were erected by giants or magicians long prevailed, and a form of it has even been seriously proposed by a present-day British writer on the subject, John Michell. But if we do not allow ourselves flights of fancy about supernatural engineering we must assume that the megaliths were erected by manpower. The question of why such prodigious manpower was put to such a purpose then becomes one of the most intriguing puzzles that enigmatic relics of the ancient world pose for modern man.

John Aubrey, the celebrated 17th-century English antiquarian and diarist, was out hunting with some friends just after Christmas, 1648 when they came to the village of Avebury. There

Aubrey experienced a revelation. He realised that he was standing in the middle of an immense prehistoric temple. Where others saw, and for centuries had seen, only a lot of old stones and a few mounds, Aubrey saw evidence of a grand design. The design stands out quite clearly on a modern aerial photograph, even though today there are far fewer stones at Avebury than there were in Aubrey's day, thanks to the efforts of such men as the 18th-century farmer known as 'Stone-Killer Robinson'. He devised a means of breaking them up by toppling them into fiery pits and administering a dash of cold water and a hammer blow.

The Avebury circle is so large that the medieval village has grown up within it. It was its size that had hidden it from view and made its component stones seem a mere random assembly. Stonehenge, however, could not be ignored. Standing on the open Salisbury Plain, its great stones clustered in an obviously man-made design, it invited speculation about the men who had built it. The 12th-century English historian Geoffrey of Monmouth had written that it was built about AD 470 as a memorial to 460 ancient British chieftains massacred by Hengist the Saxon. His view prevailed, for lack of a more authoritative one, until the 17th century, when British royalty began to take an interest in Stonehenge. King James I of England visited it, and had his architect Inigo Jones make drawings showing its original construction. Jones expressed the opinion that it had been built by the Romans in the first or second century AD in honour of the god Coelus, and that it could not possibly have been built by the 'savage and barbarous' early Britons. They, he said, would have been quite incapable of achieving such 'stately structures, or such remarkable works as Stonehenge.' John Aubrey was less scornful of the early Britons, or of their priests, the Druids. When asked by King Charles II to survey the site and write an account of it, he stated that its history went back beyond Saxon and Roman times. Referring to both Avebury and Stonehenge, he wrote that since the Druids were 'the most eminent order of priests among the Britons, it is most likely that these monuments were the temples of the priests of the most eminent order, the Druids, and it is strongly to be presumed that they are as ancient as those days.'

Aubrey's view was taken up and elaborated in the next century by Dr William Stukeley, whose book, *Stonehenge, a Temple restored to the British Druids*, was extremely influential. It inspired so much other fanciful literature about Druids and their practices that the popular view has prevailed down to our day that Stonehenge was erected by Druids for purposes of ritual sacrifice and sun worship. The discovery that it might have been used to predict eclipses has been, as it were, added to this view by proposing that the possession of such an expertise would have enabled the Druidic priesthood to manipulate ignorant people by demonstrating apparent magical powers over the heavenly bodies. We know about the historical existence of Druids from references in the writings of Julius Caesar. Possibly Stonehenge and other monuments throughout Britain were used by them, but they certainly did not erect the megaliths, and Stonehenge was built much earlier than 460 BC, as Stukeley had conjectured.

Archaeology as a scientific study could not make much progress until the late 19th century. Then the mind of Western man gradually became emancipated from the Biblical version of prehistory as it had been interpreted by Archbishop Ussher of Armagh, Ireland, whose calculation that Man had been created on 23 October, 404 BC had been adopted as dogma by the Church. When the findings of geology, and of fossil remains testifying to human life on earth thousands of years ago, combined with evolution theory to overthrow this dogma, the way was open for a scientific study of prehistory. The most obvious area for the pursuit of this study was the Near and Middle East, for there relics were conspicuous, varied, and well preserved. Moreover there were traditions and written records to guide archaeological field work and to help interpret its findings. Western Europe, by comparison, was unspectacular and unpromising. Its enigmatic clusters of rough stones, its great mounds and chambered tombs, could not be related to contemporary historical or literary records, and their existence was not obviously inconsistent with the idea that the people who built them were superstitious barbarians. The Swedish archaeologist Oscar Montelius expressed the prevailing view when he wrote in 1908: 'At a time when the people of

Europe were, so to speak, without any civilisation whatsoever, the Orient and particularly the Euphrates region and the Nile were already in enjoyment of a flourishing culture.'

This view led to the idea known as the theory of *diffusionism*. This suggested that civilisation had first arisen in Mesopotamia and Egypt about 3000 BC and that aspects of it had gradually spread westward. Archaeological findings appeared to support this view. For example, it was possible to trace the spread of the practice of burial in chambered tombs from the Aegean via Malta, Spain, Portugal and France, to Britain and Scandinavia. And as the British archaeologist Sir Mortimer Wheeler wrote in 1925: 'The general analogy between the *mastabas* (of Egypt) and many types of chambered tomb is too close to be altogether accidental.' Evidence of the achievements distinctive of high civilisations, such as sculpture, fine metalwork, and sophisticated decorative art and design, was not to be found among the relics of Western European prehistory.

The conclusion that 'megalithic culture' was derived from, but greatly inferior to, the high civilisations of Mesopotamia, Egypt, and the Aegean was a natural one to make. It is only quite recently that it has been proved to be untenable and the diffusionist theory in its simple form has now been discredited.

The discovery in 1949, by the American chemist Willard Libby, of a means of dating prehistoric relics by measuring the amount of radioactive carbon-14 they contain, signalled a revolution in archaeology. At first the radiocarbon dating technique seemed to confirm established ideas, and the few anomalies it threw up could be ignored. Some archaeologists were sceptical of its reliability. They pointed out for instance that although we know that the building of the Great Pyramid was begun about 2600 BC, the radiocarbon technique of dating yielded the result 2200 BC. It was not until 1967 that the reliability of the technique was established beyond dispute. Then, not only was the error in dating the Great Pyramid explained, but at the same time prevailing ideas about the relative antiquity of Near, Middle Eastern, and Atlantic European artifacts were confounded.

In California there grows a tree known as the bristlecone pine.

Some of these trees are 5000 years old, and, as they grow one ring on their trunks each year, their age can be precisely known. In 1967 Professor Hans Suess conceived the idea of taking tree-ring samples and comparing their known calendrical ages with the ages yielded by radiocarbon dating. If the latter technique were accurate, the ages should of course correspond. It turned out that they didn't correspond, but that the discrepancy between the two dates was a factor that varied predictably, becoming larger the further back in time. This meant that the old radio carbon dates were wrong, and that, in order to correct them, dates of around 1000 BC had to be pushed back by 200 years and at about 3000 BC by nearly 1000 years. This meant that, when the original radio-carbon data for the Great Pyramid was corrected, the new date coincided with the known historical date. But when megalithic sites were radiocarbon dated they proved to be considerably older than the eastern civilisations that they were supposed to be derived from. Megalithic chambered tombs turned out to date from 4500-4000 BC, long before the building of the Egyptian *mastabas* and of the round tombs found around the Aegean. And the first construction at Stonehenge itself was found to be at least contemporary with, and probably earlier than, the Great Pyramid of Cheops. The signs were that an indigenous culture had evolved independently in Western Europe in prehistoric times.

The year 1967 was an exciting year for students of European prehistory. In addition to the evidence of the unsuspected antiq-uity of megalithic artifacts afforded by the new dating estimates, there came evidence of their unimagined mathematical and geometrical properties. For that year Professor Thom published his *Megalithic Sites in Britain*.

For years following his first insight at Callanish, Thom, assisted at first by his sons and later by his grandsons, had carried surveying equipment to remote megalithic sites and taken careful measurements. As he completed an increasing number of surveys, it became clear that the sites had been chosen and the stones located by men who had a knowledge of astronomy as well as of geometry and mathematics. They had also possessed sophis-ticated techniques and equipment. 'Some sites,' he wrote, 'for example Avebury, were set out with an accuracy approaching 1 in 1000. Only an experienced surveyor with good equipment is likely to attain this sort of accuracy. The differences in tension applied to an ordinary measuring tape by different individuals can produce variations in length of this amount or even more.'

Thom's main discovery was the 'megalithic yard,' the unit of measurement used by the prehistoric builders. This unit, the equivalent of 2.72 feet, together with another unit that was precisely 2.5 times the megalithic yard and which he called the 'megalithic rod', Thom found to be a constant feature of the dimensions of all the stone circles he surveyed. The radii and circumferences of the structures, as well as the distances between individual stones, were found to be always multiples of the megalithic yard. Thom's surveys revealed that a majority of the structures were not exact circles. Some were egg-shaped, some elliptical, some flattened on one side, and some elongated. But whatever its shape the circumference and radius of each stone 'circle' was measurable in whole numbers of megalithic yards. And always the accuracy was uncanny. It was inconceivable that this accuracy was due to chance. Thom made his discovery when surveying sites in Scotland, which being more remote are generally more intact than those further south. But as his studies progressed he found that all megalithic sites from Brittany, France to the Orkneys, the islands off northern Scotland, were all laid out according to a consistent principle of measurement. He concluded that there must have been a prehistoric culture on the European coast of the Atlantic Ocean of considerable sophistication and with some kind of central administration. For if the measuring instruments used in the construction of the megaliths were not officially standardised and issued, but were obtained by each local community copying from its neighbour's, there would certainly be a greater degree of localised error and variation than was in fact found.

When Thom first announced his findings, most archaeologists were sceptical and some were positively hostile. His findings were of course irreconcilable with the picture of Neolithic man and his culture in northwest Europe that had emerged from decades of orthodox archaeological research. But *Megalithic Sites in Britain* was such a scholarly and exhaustive study, so unsensational in its presentation and impeccable in its mathematics, that its findings could not be dismissed as nonsense. An independent mathematician, Professor David Kendall of the Statistical Laboratory at the University of Cambridge, subjected Thom's figures to a series of tests using a computer. Kendall reached the conclusion that there was no more than a one percent chance that the dimensions of the stone circles could have been achieved without the common unit of the megalithic yard. Thom was vindicated and historians had to start revising their ideas.

The revision demanded by the new evidence was not a minor one. One fact that had to be taken into account in it was that the megalith builders had understood the principle of Euclidean geometry 2000 years before Euclid, who lived in about 300 BC. Within the stone 'circles' Thom discovered geometrical figures formed by key features which were measured in whole numbers of megalithic yards. Of all possible triangles there are a limited number with sides measurable in whole numbers. We call them Pythagorean triangles, but the megalith builders had apparently had them all worked out long before Pythagoras. At Avebury, for instance, Thom found that 'the basis of the design is a 3,4,5 triangle set out in units of exactly 25 MY (megalithic yards) so that all the resulting shapes come out in multiples of 5 or 10.' At Woodhenge, another site on Salisbury Plain, there are five concentric circles with perimeters measuring exactly 40, 60, 80, 140, and 160 MY, and with internal dimensions based on the Pythagorean triangle 12, 35, 37. At Stonehenge there is an outer ring known as the Aubrey Holes (after John Aubrey, who first drew attention to them), and the holes numbered 56, 7, and 28 define the points of a perfect Pythagorean right-angled triangle with sides of 40, 96, and 104 MY, as does every other corresponding set. Thom found comparable symmetries between features in all the megalithic sites he surveyed, and concluded that the megalith builders had been experienced and clever geometers and mathematicians. It appeared that they had varied the shapes of their stone 'circles' by way of experimenting with different geometrical figures, and setting and solving for themselves a number of geometrical problems.

It was surely inconceivable, though, that the tremendous physical effort involved in erecting the megaliths should have been invested in mere intellectual exercises, or even in laying down demonstrations of, or 'teaching machines' for, mathematical and geometrical principles for the benefit of future generations. Clearly, there must be more to them than that. And of course there was. There was the knowledge of astronomy that their siting and construction testified to.

It was the Englishman William Stukeley in the 18th century who first observed that Stonehenge is aligned to the midsummer sunrise. In 1901 Sir Norman Lockyer, director of the Solar Physics Laboratory at South Kensington, London, published a book showing that Stonehenge and many other similar monuments were aligned on many of the stars as well as on the sun. Then in the 1920s Admiral Boyd Summerville surveyed 90 sites and announced that 'In every instance . . . orientation of one kind or another has been found.' So when Thom began his work he had guidelines and precedents for considering the megaliths as devices for calendrical calculation and astronomical observation. It was well known that by taking sight-lines from particular marked positions in stone circles to natural or man-made features of the landscape, precise observations could be made, for instance of the sun at the solstices and equinoxes. These annual phenomena perhaps require a little explanation. The solstice occurs twice a year in northwest Europe, once in summer when the sun reaches its maximum distance from the equator on about June 21, and once when it reaches the tropic of Capricorn to begin its journey back again around December 21. The equinox also occurs twice a year, when the sun crosses the equator, making the night equal in length to the day. These equinoxes occur about March 21 and September 23 of each year. But the full extent of the megalith builders' astronomical knowledge was not known, and it astonished Thom himself when he found unequivocal evidence of it.

The cycle of the sun's positions throughout the year is simple

The Standing Stones at Callanish

and constant, but the moon is quite a different matter. In fact its cyclic pattern cannot even be understood without taking into account a period of 18.6 years. Over this period it first rises and sets in extreme northerly and southerly positions. Then it moves inward from these extreme positions for a period of 9.3 years and outwards toward them again for a second 9.3-year period. Astronomers call the extreme positions reached by the moon every 9.3 years its major and minor 'standstills'. For a few days on either side of these standstills it is possible to observe a small perturbation of the moon's orbit, generally known as the moon's 'wobble', which is caused by the gravitational attraction of the sun. It was thought that this phenomenon had first been observed at the end of the 16th century of our era, but Thom discovered clear evidence that the megalith builders had known about it. Evidence that they possessed this knowledge lay not only in their great observational exactitude and subtlety, but also their ability to predict eclipses. For it is when the moon's perturbation is at its greatest that eclipses occur.

The size and location of the fallen Grand Menhir Brisé near Carnac in Brittany, France had always been a mystery. Thom's survey of the region revealed that its purpose had been to pinpoint to within a fraction of a degree the moon's major and minor standstills and the exact amount of its perturbation. The megalith served as a foresight marker for the points of rising and setting of the moon at the extremes of its 18.6-year cycle. The eight different points that an observer would occupy in order to use the megalith in this way, one of which was as far as ten miles away from it, were predicted by Thom. At four of these sites prehistoric markers in the form of mounds or stones were found.

The power to predict is the main criterion that science demands a hypothesis should satisfy. Thom's predictions in this case and several others greatly enhanced the credibility of his astonishing disclosures. For instance, at Kintraw in Argyll, Scotland, there is a single tall standing stone in a field. Thom predicted that this stone would align with a point on the horizon between two mountain peaks where the sun would have set at the mid-winter solstice, and he indicated a point on a steep slope at a distance from the stone which would have been the observation point from which this alignment was obtained. Excavations were carried out at the point he indicated. The archaeologists were astonished to find an artificial platform of rubble with two massive boulders situated at one end where the observation point would have been. With such evidence, the astronomical theory of the function of the megaliths became virtually irrefutable.

Thom was not alone. There were other distinguished professors canvassing the astronomical theory in the 1960s. Gerald Hawkins, professor of astronomy at Boston University, Massachusetts, studied Stonehenge with the help of a computer. Hawkins came up with evidence that alignments of distinctive features of the Stonehenge complex pointed to all major astronomical events. He also observed that the number 56 is almost exactly three times the 18.6 years of the moon's cycle, and showed how the 56 so-called 'Aubrey Holes' at Stonehenge could be used to predict eclipses. England's most famous astronomer, Professor Sir Fred Hoyle, supported Hawkins' theories. He restated the basic and most fundamental problem posed by the megaliths as a whole when he wrote that the construction of Stonehenge demanded 'a level of intellectual attainment orders of magnitude higher than the standard to be expected from a community of primitive farmers.'

So we still come back to the original mystery, the original question: who were the megalith builders? The archaeological evidence shows that without doubt the standing stones of northwest Europe were erected at a time when the lands were inhabited by uncivilised Stone Age farmers. The properties which we can now see that the megalithic structures possess must have been beyond the comprehension of such people, and therefore we have to assume that there existed in their midst an intellectual elite, or priesthood, which coordinated its efforts over centuries. Their object was to achieve the knowledge and establish the traditions that it did, and to do so it commanded the services of a substantial labour force. Such an elite, supported by tribute and taxes paid by the farming communities that made up the population, is known to have existed in other parts of the world, such as among the

Maya people of Central America. In his book on the megalith builders, Dr Euan MacKie of the University of Glasgow, Scotland, has argued that we may in fact have archaeological evidence of the existence of an intellectual elite in Western Europe in Neolithic times which has hitherto been otherwise and wrongly interpreted.

In the winter of 1850 a tremendous storm lashed the Orkney Isles. On the western coast of the largest island it washed away some sand dunes to reveal the stone foundations of an ancient building. Later excavation of this site showed that it was a complex of buildings, some of which appeared to have been built for individual occupation and others for communal use. There were signs that a disaster had occurred there at the time when it was inhabited, and which had resulted in its abandonment. Some pottery found on the site was flat-based and decorated with deep grooves and abstract reliefs, unlike anything found anywhere else, and archaeologists long assumed that Skara Brae, as the site was called, was an isolated Neolithic farmers' village. A similar settlement, with the same type of pottery, was found on another Orkney island, Rousay, in the 1930s, and in the same decade Grooved Ware pottery, as it became known, was found at Clacton in Essex, which exploded the myth that it was a unique Orkneyan artifact. More Grooved Ware was found when Woodhenge on Salisbury Plain was excavated in the 1960s and other sites in southern England have since yielded more examples, particularly the site known as Durrington Walls, also on Salisbury Plain. Radiocarbon dating showed that the settlements at Durrington Walls and at Skara Brae had flourished at the same time, and the similarity of their artifacts suggested that Skara Brae had been something more than an isolated farming settlement. An ingenious study of the food refuse – in the form of animal bones – of the settlement at Durrington Walls, and a comparison of it with the refuse from another Neolithic site, the nearby Windmill Hill causewayed camp, has shown that the Durrington Walls inhabitants enjoyed a different diet from that of the ordinary members of a Neolithic community, an interesting discovery which strongly suggests that they were members of an elite class.

At Stenness, near Skara Brae, there is a stone circle, and at Quanterness, also nearby, a chambered cairn has been found. Dr MacKie has suggested that the three sites are related, and that his theory explains another mystery posed by megalithic remains. This is the question of who was buried in the great chambered tombs. It used to be assumed that these were the burial places of whole Neolithic communities. But as radiocarbon dating has shown that burials in particular places were spread over very long periods of time, the probability is that the few hundred occupants of these tombs found throughout the British Isles were a very select group. Therefore it seems likely that they were, in fact, members of a kind of intellectual theocracy, a class of priest-architect-designer-astronomers who were the megalith builders themselves.

Here again, we are faced with the paradox of a primitive society of hunter-farmers whose scientific knowledge seems to exceed their cultural development – Alexander Thom spoke of 'Stone Age Einsteins', and admitted that their intelligence was at least equal to his own. Unfortunately, unlike the Egyptians and Sumerians, the megalith builders left no written records, so we have no idea of why primitive farmers needed such detailed knowledge of the heavens. It cannot have been simply for the purpose of planting crops – this hardly requires a detailed knowledge of the 19 year lunar cycle. All we know is that an elite class of priest/technicians organised the building of stone circles of incredible geometrical complexity.

Egyptian records also make it clear that a similar, elite class of priest/technicians oversaw the building of the great Nile Valley monuments. Their own legends claim that their knowledge was passed down from the gods who ruled Egypt in the remote epoch called 'the First Time'. But an unconventional Egyptologist named Schwaller de Lubicz has claimed that the Sphinx had been built millennia before the date usually ascribed to it (2500 BC) by survivors from a far older civilisation that had been destroyed in a violent cataclysm – the civilisation that Plato called Atlantis. We will study this thesis more closely in later chapters.

CHAPTER 9

MURDER IN THE PEAT BOGS

Police forensic scientists are occasionally called upon to inspect the bodies of murder victims that are decades old, but in 1952 Danish experts were asked to conduct an autopsy on a corpse well over a thousand years old: perfectly preserved in an ancient peat bog. Searching the records, investigators discovered that over the years numerous other ancient bodies had been dug from peat bogs across Europe. The evidence pointed to hundreds, perhaps thousands of ritual murders, taking place over centuries. Why and by whom were these people killed? The oldest murder hunt in history had at last begun.

It was a late April day in the quiet Danish countryside. Men from the nearby village of Grauballe toiled in a drained bog, cutting slabs of fibrous brown peat. For thousands of years peat had served their ancestors as a fuel for heating homes and cooking food. Suddenly one cutter's spade crunched into something hard. As he began clearing peat from the obstruction, his glance fell on a brown human head with short hair. Below the head, a neck and shoulders peeped from the peat. The horrified men stopped work and gazed at the corpse. A breeze sighing through the birches around Nebelgård Fen and the peaceful nearby hills seemed to make the apparition only more incongruously gruesome.

At first sight the men had found the victim of a recent murder – committed perhaps that same year of 1952. Or could the corpse date from a more remote past? Several feet of undisturbed peat had formed over the body since its disposal.

Someone called in the local doctor, an amateur archaeologist. He suspected the corpse to be ancient and notified the Museum of Prehistory at Aarhus, the county capital. Soon the prehistorian Dr Peter Glob was on his way. Dr Glob, who later set down his findings in *The Bog People*, first published in Denmark in 1965, and is today Director of the National Museum in Copenhagen, stepped down into the pit and examined the body. He judged that the Grauballe man lay in an old peat working filled in by maybe as much as 2000 years of bog deposits. He decided to delay disinterment until he could arrange to transport the body safely back to the country museum for proper study. This proved surprisingly simple. Men drove a metal roofing sheet through the peat, under the corpse. Then they lifted the body still in its peat cocoon. Many helpers heaved the great load onto a truck which gingerly drove the 25 miles to Aarhus.

There, a small army of experts began exploring the body from the bog. They established that it had lain chest down, in a twisted posture, with left leg and arm outstretched and right leg and arm drawn upward. They found that the weight of peat pressing down upon it had somewhat flattened the body. Also, they discovered that bog chemicals had begun dissolving bones away. But the skin of head, torso, and limbs remained miraculously intact. So did some of the internal organs.

There was nothing else – no clothing, no personal possession – from which to establish the individual's identity. At least, so the archaeologists thought. But when they briefly placed the body on display, some of the spellbound public had different ideas. Among the visitors was a farmer's wife from the Grauballe area itself. The old woman claimed the corpse to be that of a peat cutter who had vanished late in the 1880s. There followed a newspaper story describing how she had even recognised 'Red Christian's' face as it lay in the museum. People grew sceptical. Was this indeed the world's oldest known well-preserved body, as the scientists suggested? Could any corpse ripened by nearly two milleniums survive with hair and fingernails intact and even stubble on the chin ? Surely it seemed far likelier that the Museum of Prehistory's prize exhibit was no more than a drunk drowned by falling in a bog sometime in living memory.

The scientists' belief that here lay a lifelike Iron Age man remained unshaken. They had good reasons to be confident. First, there was the dark brown colour of the skin, which past experience told them had been literally tanned by soaking for centuries in bog water starved of oxygen but rich in tannin and soil-acids – a sure defence against bacterial decay. This would explain not only the skin's survival but also the signs of bone destruction – a long-term effect of immersion in soil-acid that is highly concentrated.

The second proof of the bog man's antiquity came in prehistoric pollens found in peat at the level where his body lay. These pollens showed he had lived and died at a time when heather, clover, bird's foot trefoil, and other wild plants flourished nearby. They grew on old farmlands abandoned when soil exhaustion had cut crop yields. The plants were known to have thrived in Denmark in the first four centuries of the Christian era.

But what put Grauballe man's date beyond all reasonable doubt was the carbon contained in his body. Scientists took away bits of liver and muscle and measured their C14 (radioactive carbon) content with a special Geiger counter. The amount of C14 in organ tissue drops off slowly at a known rate after death. The reading for the Grauballe man showed conclusively that he had died within a century (on either side) of AD 310. When the press published these findings the former sceptics fell silent.

Meanwhile, the Iron Age body had been yielding other secrets. Deformed by the overlying peat and damaged by the peat cutters, head and neck nonetheless provided clear proof of how the Grauballe man had died. Repeated knife blows had ripped his neck from ear to ear, severing the gullet. Puckered forehead, screwed up eyes and mouth half open in a cry spoke of the victim's fear and agony as he perished. X-rays revealed more damage, this time to bones. Two leg bones were broken, and the skull was fractured, though experts could not say whether these injuries had occurred before or after death. Early signs of rheumatoid arthritis and the condition of the teeth showed that the man had been aged at least 30 when he died

Cause of and age at death had been determined. There was also even evidence to show at what time of year the bog man had been murdered. This came from remarkable finds in his intestines. Analysis of substances found in the digestive tract showed that just before death the man had eaten a vegetarian meal containing more than 60 kinds of food plants, chiefly seeds of uncultivated species. He had probably swallowed the mixture in some kind of gruel. There were no leaves, or fruits that ripen in summer and autumn. It seemed, then, that the Grauballe man had consumed his frugal last meal in winter or early spring.

The question of who this Danish bog man was remained open. Had he had a recent criminal record, finding his identity would have proved simple. Police laboratory tests revealed fingerprints as plain as those of most living men, and line patterns on part of the right hand plainer still. As it was, all that the fingerprints proved was that these were not a toilworn peasant's hands. Their owner had done no heavy manual work for at least some months before he died. They suggest he had held a special status in society, perhaps as priest or chieftain.

Impressive though they were, these findings left unanswered some tantalising questions. Who was he? Why was he killed? Why had his body been thrown in a bog? These mysteries surrounding the Grauballe man in fact formed just part of a much larger puzzle. For the prehistorians knew he was by no means the sole victim of an Iron Age killing to be done away with in this fashion.

Only two years before his discovery, peat cutters had found another well-preserved ancient body, this time in Tollund Fen, a few hours' walk west from the Grauballe man's bog burial. Tollund Fen is larger than Nebelgård Fen; it grew from an ancient lake slowly choked by vegetation. A steep sunken track leads down to the bog past dark firs and pale, shimmering aspens.

Out in the fen, farm workers were harvesting fuel for the winter. It was spring, and around them rose the evocative, bleating lovecalls of snipe. Then, as at Nebelgard Fen two years later, a macabre find marred the rural tranquillity. The cutters found themselves staring down at a body lying in a peat cutting about three feet below the surface of the bog. They called the police. But Peter Glob also hastened to the scene. This time there was little doubt of the bog man's antiquity. For one thing he wore an ancient type of leather cap made of eight pieces of skin sewn together and held on with a hide chinstrap. Also he lay just above a layer of 'dog's flesh', as Danes call a reddish peat layer formed by a particular kind of moss early on in the Iron Age. Like the Grauballe man, the Tollund man had been placed in an old peat working. But he had died much earlier: about 2000 years ago.

This makes the preservation of his head truly astonishing. No other head 2000 years old has remained so well preserved. The left side of the face was somewhat creased, but the right side – the side that had been lying downward – could have belonged to a living, breathing individual. Its serene, intelligent expression suggested a gentle, thoughtful, even noble personality. Each pore, each furrow, each wrinkle of experience around the eyes reinforced the illusion that Tollund man was still alive. So, too, did the day's growth of bristle visible on chin and upper lip. The calmly closed eyes and the tranquil expression on the mouth suggested that the corpse was merely asleep. The body's peaceful, curled-up attitude conveyed the same impression.

At first glance you would think that death had occurred naturally, and unsuspected. But a plaited leather noose around the neck told a different story. Later, pathologists' reports suggested that death had come by hanging and not by simple strangulation.

A further life was doomed when people took away the body to be studied. To do this, the Danes built a massive crate around the slab of peat enshrining the Tollund man. Then helpers manhandled the load, weighing nearly a ton, onto a horse-drawn cart. The work overstrained one individual's heart and he collapsed and died. The bog had yielded an old corpse but claimed a new life in return.

Like the Grauballe man, the Tollund man himself proved to contain few clues to suggest how and why he had been killed. Apart from his cap he wore no more than a leather belt. His gut revealed nothing but the relics of a last meal, again of seeds eaten in winter. Here, then, lay another Iron Age man who had met a violent end. Was he murder victim, human sacrifice, or executed criminal?

Both these famous finds have been at least in part preserved. Scientists soaked Tollund man's head for six months in water containing acetic acid and formalin. During the next six months they switched to alcohol and toluol; then to toluol and paraffin; finally to toluol and heated wax. A year after the preservation processes began, the head had shrunk a little but kept its shape superbly. Today visitors can meet this Iron Age man face to face in Silkeborg Museum about six miles from Tollund Fen.

The Grauballe man fared even better: scientists decided to save his entire body by completing the natural process of preservation already far advanced by 1600 years of bog submersion. Nineteen months' soaking in an oak bath containing tannic acid came first, then a month in distilled water containing Turkish red oil. Next came impregnation with lanolin and other substances. Lastly parts of the body received injections of collodion. The Grauballe man was now ready to go on public show in his own special room in the Museum of Prehistory at Aarhus.

These bog men found in the early 1950s were the first to be salvaged with such care, but not the first to be found. From time immemorial, tanned, well-preserved corpses had, as it were, popped up from Danish bogs to startle peat diggers. More than 150 such bodies are known to have sprung from the fens in the last two centuries alone.

But before archaeology found its feet, people had no idea how old many of these were. They simply shunned the corpses as devils, or gave them Christian reburial. Serious study of these bog corpses is rather a novel development. This means that we have lost a great deal of evidence. Nonetheless enough survives to enlarge the picture provided by the Tollund and Grauballe men and to provide more clues to their deaths and disposal.

The decade before their discovery yielded three finds in one Danish bog alone. This is less surprising when we remember that the Danes stepped up peat cutting for fuel in and just after World

War II. This time the location was Borremose (Borre Fen), a great flat expanse of low land in north-central Denmark. In 1946 peat cutters came on a small well-preserved man about six feet deep in soft peat. Research showed that some 2000 years ago someone had thrown his corpse into an already ancient and birch-overgrown peat working. Tanning had turned his skin to black leather, but one eyeball was still yellowish white. Several details will be already familiar from what you read earlier. For instance, a day's stubble covered the lower part of his face. His hands showed no trace of hard manual work. His intestines contained a vegetarian meal consisting of weed and other seeds that would have been eaten in winter. He had died from hanging or strangling. The death weapon in this case was a hemp rope with a slip knot. There was also bone damage, and the man had been naked. But in some ways this find differed from those of the Tollund and Grauballe men. Two sheepskin capes, one with a collar, lay rolled by the Borre Fen man's feet, and beneath his head lay a fragment of cloth. Then, too, a birch branch about three feet long had been placed on his body.

A year later the second Borre Fen body emerged, less than a mile northeast of the first. It lay face down in yet another old peat working. But this time the corpse was that of a woman, with long hair dyed red-brown by the bog water. A shawl, blanket, and bits of cloth covered the lower part of her naked body, which rested on a birch-bark sheet. Bronze and amber ornaments fixed to a leather strap had hung from her neck. The skull had been pulverised and the right leg broken. Nearby lay the tiny bones of an infant, also a clay pot that helped archaeologists determine that both had died about the same time as the Borre Fen man. Short sticks had been placed over the woman.

The third Borre Fen body turned up in 1948, less than a mile south of the first. This, too, bore the same approximate date as the others. Like the second find, the corpse was female. Her plump body lay face down, under a belted blanket used as a skirt. Someone had smashed her face and partly scalped her.

Women as well as men, then, had ended up in bogs in Iron Age Denmark. Brutal battering seems to have killed the two Borre Fen women, while strangling or throat-cutting had done away with all three men so far described. Was this chance, or part of a pattern ? If part of a pattern, what was its meaning? And why had someone placed sticks near two of the corpses?

The answers to some of these questions begin to emerge as we probe back through time. In 1942 a young woman curled up 'like a question mark' was extracted from a 'dog's flesh' peat layer in Bred Fen, east of Borre Fen. Her hair was plaited and coiled high on her head beneath a little woollen bonnet. Other relics led her discoverers to think that someone had dumped her into the bog naked and trussed but uninjured, maybe to drown.

The same year yielded an early middle-aged man, from Søgard Fen in central Denmark. He lay on a bed of downy bog-cotton flowers, with sandals and a cap, and wrapped – not dressed – in three leather capes, one fewer than those found with a bog body at Karlbyneder in eastern Denmark, in the early 1900s.

Four years previously a bog man with a curious hair style had appeared, a mere stone's throw from where Tollund man's body was later recovered. He wore his hair pulled into a knot at the left side of the back of the head. Someone had strangled or hanged him with a leather strap and wrapped him in skins before dropping him into the bog.

The grisly trail of bog body finds leads us back through the 19th century. It grows fainter the farther we leave behind mass literacy, telephones, cars, and cameras, which between them ensure that scientists learn of, reach, and visually record the latest bog body before it rots or someone reburies it as just another unknown corpse.

This last is what happened to a supposed murder victim discovered in 1893 at Rørbaek in northern Denmark. The bog man was reinterred, but rediscovered by chance when a plough struck the coffin 70 years later. By then, though, only bones and hair remained of what, a lifetime earlier, had been a well-preserved body. Better luck had come in 1892 when a bog man with hair, shoes, and some clothing was photographed where he lay, in a bog just north of Tollund Fen. The photograph – the first of any Danish bog man – still survives.

Although most bodies were lost to posterity, people sometimes preserved durable objects discovered with the corpses. Glass beads and a bronze pin forming part of a neck decoration, 1700 years old, survive from a woman's body found in 1843 on the Danish island of Falster.

Denmark's National Museum also has a check skirt, horn comb, and other articles discovered in 1879 with an early Iron Age woman. She lay in Huldre Bog in East Jutland, with a willow stake on her breast. Branches and stakes survive too from the 19th-century find of 'Queen Gunhild' – whose supposed corpse was discovered in central Denmark. Old tales told how her political enemies had had the 10th-century Norse queen savaged and drowned in a bog. Scientists soon demolished the 'Queen Gunhild' attribution. But, significantly, we know from ancient tradition that people pinned down dead witches with stakes to stop their ghosts walking. This could help to explain the finds of sticks near this corpse and those of some other Iron Age bodies.

Sticks, clothes, and personal ornaments make up almost all of the few surviving relics of 19th-century bog body finds. But we also have valuable written accounts going back to the late 18th century. Thus we know that in 1797 southwest Denmark produced a short, stocky corpse with curly red hair. Two leather capes rested on top of him and three hazel sticks lay beside his body. We have a much more detailed account of a bog man found in 1773. He lay naked with hands placed as though tied behind him. His throat had been cut to the bone, and the killers had laid twigs or sticks on his carcass.

The researcher who counted 150 bodies known from Danish bogs also studied the same phenomenon in other countries. He credited what are now East and West Germany with a still larger number and listed over 70 from the British Isles, 50 from the Netherlands, and 20 from Norway and Sweden. Europe's grand known total he put at 700 – more than three-quarters of them from northwestern Europe. Some represent victims of recent accidents or murders, and soldiers and airmen killed in the world wars. A very few go back 5000 years or more to the Stone Age. But most were Iron Age men and women, largely from the millenium beginning about 500 BC.

County Down, Ireland, produced the first detailed account of a find outside Denmark. In 1780 a peat cutter found a small female skeleton at the base of a small mountain bog. Hair, clothing, and ornaménts suggested a woman of rank, perhaps a Danish noble-woman from the time of the Viking invasions. This century Galway yielded a fine 400-year-old corpse with clothing and stomach contents intact. But such finds generally lack the hall-marks of the brutal murders described for Iron Age Denmark. It is as we move east from Ireland across northwestern Europe that signs of this practice increase.

Several bog bodies have cropped up west of the River Ems. They include the double discovery in 1904 of a naked man and woman at Werdingerveen in the Dutch province of Drenthe. Of the man, only the skin (with signs of a wound near the heart) had survived. The woman's skin and hair were a gleaming brown. Assen Museum preserves the remains of this find.

Perhaps the richest non-Danish source of Iron Age bog people is the Schleswig-Holstein region just south of Denmark's present boundary with West Germany. From here, in 1640, came the first bog body to be recorded. In 1790 peat cutters at Bunsok came on a corpse caged by poles and sticks. More than 80 years later, a near-naked man with a skull fracture emerged from Rendswühren Fen near Kiel. He became the subject for the world's first bog-body photograph, and people preserved him − in a fashion − by smoking. His skeleton, with its taut shroud of shrivelled skin, survives in a Schleswig museum. Here, too, lies the tanned skin of the Damendorf man − minus the skeleton, which had entirely dissolved.

The Eckernförde region that produced him has been the source of many other discoveries. Among the most striking of these was a naked, 14-year-old girl with bandaged eyes, who had seemingly been drowned in a shallow peat pit. A heavy stone weighed down her body. Bone studies showed she had suffered from malnutri-tion in the cold, damp winters of nearly 1900 years ago. Less than a month after peat workers discovered her corpse in May 1952, the same Windeby bog revealed a man's body hardly any distance away. He had been pinned down with forked branches and hazel wand had been used to choke him to death.

As a last Schleswig-Holstein example we may mention an even more gruesome object from near Osterby. This was the severed head of a man with long, greying hair, drawn together on the right-hand side and ingeniously tied in an elaborate knot. This reminds us of the 1938 Tollund Fen find.

The bog bodies themselves, then, reveal certain patterns, but not what these signify. To grasp who these Iron Age people were and how they had lived and died we must enlist the aid of other sources of information. One is the collection of archaeological finds of clothes, tools, and buildings made and used near the bogs while these were reaping their macabre harvest. Our other aid consists of contemporary Latin writings, especially by the Roman historian Cornelius Tacitus. Archaeology has proved Tacitus to be a cautious and broadly reliable writer. Tacitus in his work *Germania* briefly describes the Germanic tribes that held northern Europe in his day. It therefore embraces the very people, places, and time that concern us.

Prehistorians now believe that the Iron Age Germanic peoples derived largely from the Battle Axe people – speakers of Indo-European tongues who migrated from southern Russia more than 4000 years ago, penetrating into east, central, and parts of northern Europe. Intermarriage between the newcomers and established Europeans produced the Germanic tribes. Those of the southern Baltic area built a rich Bronze Age culture largely based on trade in Baltic amber with the wealthy Mediterranean civilisations. Some families seemingly grew rich and powerful from a monopoly of bronze.

About 500 BC all this was changing. Celts drove a wedge between the northerners and their southern markets. From Celts, though, the Germanic peoples learned to make cheap, serviceable tools from abundant iron. With trade hamstrung and bronze devalued, the ruling class in and near Denmark lost wealth. Meanwhile the northern climate worsened. Cold, wet weather ushered in the Iron Age. Winning a living from the land became difficult. For these reasons the old class structure probably broke down and a poor, more egalitarian society of hardy, sturdy fisherfolk and farmers was left to grapple for its living with a hostile land and sea.

What did these people look like? Tacitus tells us that the Germanic peoples were tall and strongly built, with fierce blue eyes and reddish hair. But bog body finds reveal that this picture is oversimple. Some adults were short by modern standards. A poor winter diet left traces of malnutrition. Also, teeth suffered harsh wear from grit in flour produced by grinding grain with stone implements.

Most men went clean-shaven. Women often had bobbed hair. Bog body finds of both sexes normally reveal reddish, peat-stained hair. But the severed greying head from Osterby had had blond hair. Peter Glob describes 'Queen Gunhild's' hair as dark brown, and the Grauballe man had probably been dark-haired as well.

The two finds of heads with curiously knotted hair tally with description by Tacitus of the Swabian knot known also from ancient sculptures. Invented by the Swabian tribe and copied by their Germanic brothers, this hair style lent extra height to its wearers and thus made them appear more frightening in battle.

Germanic men dressed simply. Men found in the bogs were usually naked, covered only with one or more short skin shoulder capes. Julius Caesar encountered Germanic warriors inadequately clad like this, and Tacitus wrote that most German men wore just a cloak or cape pinned by a brooch or thorn. They spent days by their fires in nothing else – no mean survival feat if performed in the cold, wet winters of the early Iron Age. Only the rich, said Tacitus, wore underclothes. These were long and skintight. But bog finds show that at least some early Iron Age men had coats, leggings, shoes, and caps. Tunics and trousers seemingly came later. But the naked, belted corpse of Tollund man may well have worn a linen suit of flax or nettle fibre, long since dissolved by soil-acids.

We know much more about what the women wore. Tacitus

describes low-cut, sleeveless, linen outer garments with a purple pattern. Roman sculptures show similar clothing. Best of all, two fine sets of Early Iron Age clothing survive from eastern Denmark. One was a long, woven, sleeveless gown gathered at the shoulders by brooches, and with a fold to serve as a hood – a style brought in from Greece where women were using similar dresses when the wearer of this one was dropped in a Danish bog 2400 years ago. The other costume comprised a plaid skirt woven from wools of contrasting browns, a shawl with a bird's bone pin, and two furry skin capes. Some women also wore caps. But bog bodies generally lacked ornaments.

From the Roman historian Tacitus we learn that Germanic tribes lived in farming villages of houses detached, not abutting according to the Roman practice. He noted: 'Every man leaves an open space around his house, perhaps as a precaution against the risk of fire.'

The remains of just such an Iron Age village have come to light at Borre Fen in northern Denmark. This small, moated settlement of 20 turf-walled houses, maybe roofed with thatch, stood on an island in the marsh, guarded by an earth wall and a wooden fence. Each morning, the men probably crossed the marsh by causeway to the fields and pastures where they tended cattle and toiled to grow grain on family plots. Meanwhile, back at home, the women threshed and ground grain; baked bread; made cheese and beer; moulded and baked clay pots; and wove cloth on simple looms. At night, men literally drove cattle and other livestock indoors, where the creatures' body heat combined with peat fires to ward off the damp, penetrating cold. Then the peasants supped off porridge, cheese, possibly some meat, washed down by an alcoholic liquor made from grain.

We can well imagine that at times like this men drank heavily and gambled to forget their day's drudgery. 'Drinking bouts lasting all day and night are not considered in any way disgraceful,' wrote Tacitus.

When crops failed and starvation loomed, whole bands of Northmen roamed far afield, seeking plunder where they could. Indeed in 113 BC the Cimbri and Teutonic tribes from all over northern Denmark rampaged south deep into Europe, invading France and Spain. Their troops repeatedly crushed Roman armies until they were annihilated in northern Italy. Such exploits led Tacitus to see warfare as the favourite mode of life among these hardy, brave barbarians.

In reality, most Northmen were usually peasants, working desperately hard to win enough food from the land to tide them through the winter. Small wonder that the tribes inhabiting Denmark and the northern part of Germany did their utmost to appease their chief deity – Nerthus, an earth mother goddess who made crops grow and animals bear young in spring.

Probably the Iron Age Danes inherited their cult from Middle Eastern people who revered the same deity under such names as Ishtar and Astarte. In each case, the goddess supposedly assured summer plenty, but only if you offered her some sacrifice. And it had to be the right sacrifice, made in the right place, at the right time of year, in the right way, by the right person.

Tacitus again holds clues to what went on. Of Nerthus' worshippers he wrote: 'They believe that she takes part in human affairs, riding in a chariot among her people. On an island of the sea stands an inviolate grove, in which, veiled with a cloth, is a chariot that none but the priest may touch. The priest can feel the presence of the goddess in this holy of holies, and attends her with deepest reverence as her chariot is drawn along by cows. Then follow days of rejoicing and merrymaking in every place that she condescends to visit and sojourn in. No one goes to war, no one takes up arms; every iron object is locked away. Then, and then only, are peace and quiet known and welcomed, until the goddess, when she has had enough of the society of men, is restored to her sacred precinct by the priest. After that the chariot, the vestments, and (believe it if you will) the goddess herself are cleansed in a secluded lake. The service is performed by slaves who are immediately afterwards drowned in the lake. Thus mystery begets terror and a pious reluctance to ask what that sight can be which is seen only by men doomed to die.'

In slightly garbled form, Tacitus thus describes a typical ancient Indo-European fertility rite symbolising the holy spring marriage of sky and earth from which would flow a fruitful summer. First, the god and goddess Journeyed by wagon in procession around the countryside. The goddess was possibly abstract or an image hidden in the cart. The god, her husband, would have been a priest or some other specially selected man. Wherever they passed, people acclaimed their holy union. But its consummation came with a ceremonial climax – a man's life offered to the goddess. Who but her husband would have been most fitting for this sacrifice?

Many finds help us to piece together such a picture. Danish bogs have yielded numerous Iron Age carts, tossed in, piecemeal, as sacrifices, notably in northern Zealand, the large island east of mainland Denmark. From here came two superbly ornamented wagons each with a single seat of honour, arguably for the goddess or her image.

Proof that many bodies belonged to sacrificial victims include the nooses around the necks of the Tollund man and other bog men. Several such ropes remind us strongly of the bronze torques separately tossed in bogs as sacrificial offerings. Moreover torques feature as necklets on a Bronze Age image of the naked goddess, and on goddess heads depicted on the Gundestrup cauldron. This famous Celtic work of art was offered up to Nerthus in a Danish bog close to the Iron Age village of Borre Fen from where three of the bog bodies mentioned earlier derived. Then, too, there is an early Iron Age illustration of the twisted neck ring scratched upon a disc-shaped stone around the embracing figures of a man and woman. A giant ear of corn behind the woman identifies her with a force that makes plants grow. The twisted neck ring, then, was the hallmark of the goddess of fertility. Strangling someone with a twisted rope meant consecrating him or her to Nerthus.

The curiously varied seed meals eaten by the Tollund and Grauballe men may have represented special sacrificial meals, not just a lack of protein at the end of winter. The timing of their deaths is right for spring sacrifices. Then, too, the delicate, unworn hands of several victims suggests that these were priests or at least no ordinary peasants.

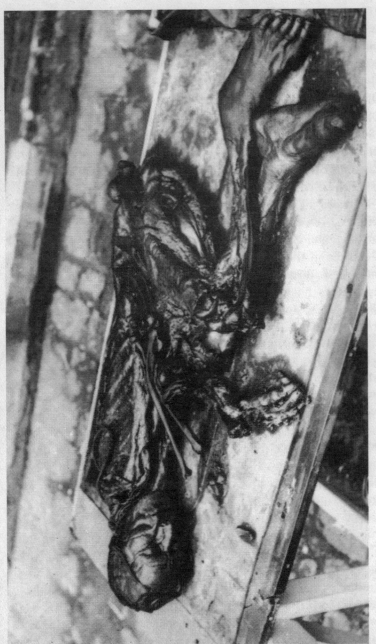

The body of the Tollund Man found in Aarhus, Denmark

That theirs were no simple burials we know, too, from the fact that early Iron Age Danes normally cremated bodies, while later Iron Age peoples buried dead, but furnished them with tools and ornaments. Most bog burials lacked either.

Lastly, people chose bogs for sacrifices because these wooded hollows were landmarks in a tree-denuded landscape. 'Their holy places are woods and groves,' says Tacitus.

Sometimes, apparently, the victim was not preordained but picked by chance. Tacitus describes how the Germanics cast lots with chips of wood – a forceful reminder of the debarked slips of wood beneath one Borre Fen woman's body.

But were all the Iron Age bog bodies simply offered up as sacrifices, or did some die for other reasons? Slit throats, drowning, and decapitation perhaps suggests no more than local differences in the killing methods used. But Tacitus explained some such deaths otherwise. Describing Germanic capital punishments he wrote: 'Traitors and deserters are hanged on trees, cowards, shirkers, and sodomites are pressed down under a wicker hurdle into the slimy mud of a bog.' The idea was for state offenders to suffer public punishments, while 'deeds of shame' were buried out of sight. Elsewhere Tacitus describes how husbands punished unfaithful wives by shaving off their hair and driving them naked through the street. The bog bodies – unclad, some shorn, some pinned down by branches – indeed awaken echoes of these practices.

Nonetheless, the circumstantial evidence is strong that Tollund man and many more bog people had died as sacrificial bride-grooms of the goddess Nerthus to ensure that crops would grow and men would thrive through the year ahead.

Folk memories of these barbaric rites had faded by the early 1900s. But people in one Danish parish recalled a curious spring custom. Sir James Frazer describes it in *The Golden Bough*. A little girl was crowned with flowers and dressed as a bride, with a little boy as her groom. With 'outriders' on hobbyhorses, they journeyed in procession from one farmhouse to another. At each farmhouse people gave the couple gifts of food. Farmers' wives arranged a wedding feast and we read that 'the children danced merrily in clogs on the stamped clay floor till the sun rose and the birds began to sing.'

Iron Age ceremonies linked with ritual murder persisted, then, even into our own Industrial Age. Christian children performed them in innocence, for the bogs had long ceased to claim bodies.

CHAPTER 10

THE FOOTPRINTS OF
KING ARTHUR

Was King Arthur a myth invented by medieval court romancers or did he really rule over Dark Age Britain? In the chaotic centuries that followed the collapse of the Roman occupation, few Britons had the time or education to write their history. If a Great King had existed, his memory might indeed survive only in the legends committed to memory by the bards. Nevertheless, as we saw in the chapter on stone circles, archaeologists do not always need to rely on written records to ferret-out the truth behind a legend. Twentieth century study of Dark Age sites has shed a new light on the 'Once and Future King'.

'He drew his sword Caliburn, called upon the name of the Blessed Virgin, and rushed forward at full speed into the thickest ranks of the enemy. Every man whom he struck, calling upon God as he did so, he killed at a single blow. He did not slacken his onslaught until he had dispatched four hundred and seventy men with his sword Caliburn. When the Britons saw this, they poured after him in close formation dealing death on every side. . .'

King Arthur's defeat of Saxon invaders in southwest England is full of a superhuman heroism typical of the book it comes from: Geoffrey of Monmouth's *History of the Kings of Britain*. It was this 12th-century mixture of fantasy and fact that gave us the Arthurian legend as we know it today.

Behind the legend stands the dim figure of a 5th-century British warrior who may have led Romanised, Christian, Celtic peoples in a last great stand against barbarian Anglo-Saxon invaders. From Denmark and Germany wave upon wave of these militant migrants had invaded England after Roman rule collapsed there in about AD 400. In the hands of historians, poets, and romancers, Arthur grew from a little-known war leader to a great national hero whose exploits shone forth from an otherwise obscure, gloomy corner of British history. Arthur's deeds inspired pride in their nation's remote but glorious past among future generations of British readers – including the English, against whose Anglo-Saxon ancestors Arthur had traditionally fought. The man and his legend still hold a strange fascination.

But did he ever live? Do the tales woven around him enshrine a man or a myth? Recent studies of old texts and sites linked with the Arthurian legend lead some scholars to answer 'yes' to both questions; others remain sceptical. To explore the question of Arthur's identity, let us first see something of how the tales told about him took shape.

The oldest-known written evidence of Arthur consists of scanty references in early medieval copies by monks of much older manuscripts, most of them handed down by word of mouth. Three manuscripts are especially important. The first is a copy of a mid-6th-century Latin work by a monk named Gildas – a tedious and largely inaccurate writer who mentions a British defeat of the Saxons at the siege of Mount Badon. Gildas credits no individual leader with this victory, which apparently halted for a while the Saxon advance across England. The second source, the 10th-century *Welsh Annals*, firmly links Arthur's name with the Battle of Badon. They refer, too, to 'the strife of Camlann in which Arthur and Medraut (Modred) perished.' Such annals were based on yearly entries kept by monks in the Dark Ages to help them reckon the dates of Church feast days. They are often reliable guides to actual people and events. But because their starting points were often arbitrary, putting accurate dates to the events they describe is sometimes difficult.

The third early source is a *History of the Britons* compiled in the early 800s in North Wales by Nennius, a cleric translating already ancient Welsh tales into Latin. Nennius calls Arthur the Britons' *dux bellorum* (commander-in-chief), not king, at Mount Badon. Nennius goes on to list 11 more battles in which Arthur fought, based it seems on an old Welsh poem. Much of his account appears authentic, but Nennius also describes 'marvels', including Arthur's son's grave which apparently altered in length each time Nennius measured it. Already, it seems, we are crossing the border from fact to fantasy.

By the time Nennius wrote his *History*, Welsh legends had firmly enshrined Arthur as a Celtic hero overcoming giants, witches, and monsters. Written in the 10th century, the poem *The Spoils of Annwn* features Arthur's overseas quest to the land of the dead for a magic cauldron – the prototype, perhaps, for the Holy Grail, a vessel that figures in later Arthurian legend. Celtic tales, too, told of heroes like Gwalchmai and Llenlleawc, patterns for the Arthurian knights Gawain and Lancelot. Arthur's wife Guinevere first appeared in Celtic form, as Gwenhwyfar. But what is lacking is any real proof that such characters did indeed exist.

By 1100 Arthurian tales told in Wales had also reached France and beyond. In Italy, a doorway at Modena Cathedral actually featured a sculpture showing Guinevere rescued by Arthur, Gawain, and Kay.

It was in the 12th century that Arthur's adventures began to assume their familiar literary shape. In 1125 an English chronicler named William of Malmesbury called for an authentic account of the man then hailed as Britain's national hero. He hoped that an authenticated biography and the discovery of Arthur's unknown burial place would discredit such fantasies as the legend that Arthur would one day return. Written about 1135, Geoffrey of Monmouth's lively *History of the Kings of Britain* claimed to be just such a factual account. However, the book was a stew concocted from old Celtic legends and histories and spiced by the writer's own vivid imagination.

Geoffrey tells how Merlin the magician helped the British king Uther Pendragon seduce Igerna, the wife of the Duke of Cornwall. From this union Arthur was born at Tintagel Castle.

Crowned king at the age of 15, Arthur subdued much of Europe with his knights and his sword Caliburn (also called Excalibur). He set up court at Caerleon in Wales. At Camblam Arthur killed his rebellious son Modred, the fruit of an incestuous liaison, but was himself mortally wounded and taken to the Isle of Avalon to be tended. Brave, generous, and chivalrous, and with a mysterious beginning and ending, Geoffrey's Arthur emerged as a world figure, appealing hugely to the medieval love of chivalry, adventure, and mystery.

Subsequent writers embellished the story. In 1155 Robert Wace's French translation of Geoffrey's history anticipates the wounded Arthur's return from Avalon, and mentions for the first time the now famous Round Table. Less than half a century later Layamon's English version of Wace explained the table as a device to stop precedence quarrels among Arthur's knights. It also had Arthur shipped to Avalon by Morgan, a fairy queen. The tale that the boy Arthur won Britain's crown by drawing a sword from a stone emerged in the early 1200s, in Robert de Borron's *Merlin*.

Meanwhile other legends inspired the late 12th-century French romancer Chrétien de Troyes to write long poems about the amours and wondrous adventures – including the quest for the Holy Grail – of the chivalrous knights of Arthur's court at Camelot. Chrétien demoted Arthur himself to an impotent figurehead, whose wife was seduced by Lancelot.

Arthurian stories snowballed during the Middle Ages. They found their richest expression in Sir Thomas Malory's 15th century English *Morte d'Arthur* (Death of Arthur). This work sets its last poignant scene in Glastonbury, Somerset, renowned as the Arthurian Avalon long before Malory wrote.

Plainly, much of the matter in most of these Arthurian stories is fiction – so much in fact that some people believe that historians simply invented Arthur to plug a gap in Britain's national history. But at least Arthurian legend was based on old Celtic tales of remembered events: some lost, others garbled during the centuries of retelling before men wrote them down.

Some scholars seeking to sift fact from folklore believe old documents do prove that Arthur lived. But sceptics find many of their arguments tortuous and unconvincing. For instance, whole theories have been underpinned by a medieval scribe's supposed misspelling of a single word.

At least, the Arthurians maintain, we have the names of actual places linked with Arthur's name. Several stand out: Tintagel, where he was apparently born; Camelot and Caerleon, where he held court; Glastonbury, where he died. Then there are the thirteen battle sites listed in Nennius and the Welsh annals.

These sites, Arthurian scholars supposed, might hold archaeological clues helping to prove that the hero had once truly lived, reigned, and fought.

In some cases the first difficulty was finding a site to fit its place name. Tintagel at least posed no such problem. Geoffrey of Monmouth, who first linked Tintagel with Arthur, described a castle standing high on a coast and surrounded by sea except for a rocky isthmus joining its rock to the mainland. This description exactly fits a particular headland in North Cornwall. The headland formed part of the manor of Bossinney, listed in 1086 in *Domesday Book. Domesday Book* mentioned no headland castle, but archaeological studies begun in the 1800s revealed traces of ancient fortification, as well as later works. You can still see the huge bank that once commanded the landward approaches to the headland. A deep ditch fronts the bank and a palisade once crowned it. To reach the headland, people had to thread their way along a narrow passage between the ditch end and a steep sided rock. On the peninsula itself there are traces of a great stone hall and a small chapel comprising simply nave and chancel. There were also no doubt smaller, wooden buildings which have long since disappeared. Disappointingly, however, it turned out that this stronghold was built at least 600 years later than Arthurian times. Carved stonework discovered there in the 1800s suggests a date of about 1150 for the complex. That makes it the undoubted remains of a castle built by Henry I's illegitimate son Reginald soon after 1141 when Henry created him Earl of Cornwall. Significantly, Earl Reginald's half-brother Earl Robert of Gloucester was Geoffrey of Monmouth's patron. Almost certainly, then, Geoffrey located Arthur's birth at Tintagel to flatter the royal family whose patronage he valued. It is true Geoffrey first wrote his account of Arthur before the medieval castle had been built, but that version of his history has disappeared. Geoffrey probably produced the surviving version in about 1145, adding Tintagel as a topical – and tactful – afterthought.

If Tintagel was indeed first fortified as late as the 1140s, then it hardly seemed likely that Arthur could have been born there. But evidence that there were stone buildings on the site as early as the 400s supports the claim of the Aurthurians.

Excavations in 1933–34, conducted by Dr C. Ralegh Radford, unearthed not only medieval ruins, but traces of no less than eight earlier structures, all protected by the same bank and ditch that the medieval builders later reinforced. Radford believed that the remains were that of a Early Christian monastery and labelled the buildings accordingly: the monk's cells, the sacristy, the library and so forth. This interpretation of the Tintagel ruins remained the generally accepted version for over fifty years, leading many scholars to completely discount the site as a possible birthplace for Arthur – after all, how many births would have taken place in a monastery?

Then, in 1983, a brush fire on the opposite side of the promontory from the castle removed a layer of turf and revealed the remains of about fifty small rectangular huts, all dating back to the earlier period of inhabitation. Further investigation led the discovery of other ancient building remains on previously unexcavated areas of the site. Far from being a small, isolated monastery, as Dr Radford had imagined, it seemed the Tintagel headland was well populated for Celtic times. Dr Radford himself found evidence of extensive trading associated with the early Tintagel settlement. French stone mortars for grinding food, fragments of olive oil jars from the eastern Mediterranean and pieces of Samian crockery – as used by the Romans of the period – littered the site. In retrospect, it is surprising that he could have been so certain that Tintagel was simply a monastery.

Recent archaeological work headed by Professor Charles

Thomas has thrown up a very different theory to Radford's. Thomas suggests that there may never have been a Celtic monastery on the Tintagel promontory. A footprint has been found, carved into solid rock, pointing across to the Early Christian chapel and the contemporary burial mounds around it. It has been noted that Celtic kings were known to have revered their ancestors in ceremonies in which they also associated themselves with the land – perhaps by placing a foot on a sacred spot.

Today, the general consensus in archaeological circles is that the Tintagel headland was the summer home of an important chieftain in the fifth century AD. There he traded Cornish tin with Mediterranean merchants and held court among his nobility. (Tintagel was probably too cold and windswept to be used as a home all year round). The size of the fifth century site, Thomas says, and the obvious evidence of extensive trading rule out Dr Radford's monastery theory. If Professor Thomas is right, it is no longer impossible for King Arthur to have been born at Tintagel.

Locating the place where Arthur is reputed to have been born proved a good deal easier than the next task – that is, establishing just where the shadowy monarch held court. Where was that world-famous Camelot? Caerleon, Winchester, and London have all been named by medieval writers. Caerleon does indeed contain impressive ruins, but they were Roman, and the so-called 'Round Table' there is in fact what remains of a Roman amphitheatre. Winchester Castle contains a massive circular table of ancient oak. Could this be the vital clue? Unfortunately, radiocarbon dating carried out in the 1970s demonstrated that the timber was after all of medieval date. The explanation is that from the 13th century growing interest in Arthuriana resulted in numerous courtly entertainments called Round Tables, where men and women imitated the feasts, dances, and jousting that they imagined had enlivened Arthur's court. In 1348, for example, England's Edward III instigated the Order of the Garter partly to revive the traditions of Arthurian knighthood. Later still, England's Tudor kings claimed Arthur as an ancestor (they were after all partly Welsh, which was something) and indeed a painted Tudor rose appears in the centre of Winchester's Round Table.

Camelot's claim to be the seat of Arthur's rule is not made easier by the fact that there is no town or city in England or Wales of that name. Chrétien de Troyes was vague about its setting. Malory – evidently influenced by the Table there – equated Camelot with Winchester. Other writers claimed that Camelot could still be seen in Wales – a reference, some think, to Caerleon's (or maybe Caerwent's) ancient Roman walls.

In 1542 an antiquarian named John Leland suggested another possibility. He wrote: 'At South Cadbury stands Camallate, sometime a famous town or castle. The people can tell nothing there but that they have heard say that Arthur much resorted to Camallate.' No one can be certain why Leland placed Camelot at South Cadbury in Somerset, in southwest England. It may have been, as he wrote, that the local people simply believed that it had been there. Perhaps a combination of local place-names and geographical features influenced him. He certainly corrupted the 'Camel' of two local villages called Queen Camel and West Camel into 'Camallate'. He may well have been impressed with nearby Cadbury Hill, a steep-sided limestone peak some 500 feet high which dominates the surrounding countryside. Crowning the hill is South Cadbury Castle. No castle stood here in Leland's time, for the banks and ditches, now largely wooded, that ring the hill are the remains of an Iron Age fort built on the summit before the Romans came to Britain in 55 BC.

In Leland's time, it seems, a good deal of largely unrecorded legend was gathering about the hill. Later written tradition locates Arthur's palace on the level summit; forges a subterranean link between two hillside wells; and holds that the hill is hollow and that Arthur and his knights lay asleep inside, to emerge in time of national need.

Whatever Cadbury Hill's Arthurian connections might have been, its Iron Age fort alone suggested this to be a site worth investigation. Accordingly, for one reason or another, archaeologists have been burrowing in the hill on and off since the late 19th century.

In 1890, South Cadbury's rector reported opening a hut-dwelling on the summit and discovering a flagstone that –

contrary to workers' expectations – did not lead to King Arthur's cave. Twenty-three years later a somewhat sketchy but better documented dig revealed pottery attributed to late Celtic times. But justification for large-scale excavation emerged only in the 1950s when ploughing turned up surface finds including scraps of Tintagel-type pottery and a piece of glass from Dark Age France. It was not much. But it was enough to convince Ralegh Radford, that South Cadbury Castle had indeed been Camelot. Moreover in 1955 an aerial photographic survey revealed dark patches on the pale, cultivated summit – crop-marks betraying extensive areas of ancient soil disturbance. Interest in a major excavation now gained momentum.

In 1965 leading archaeologists and Arthurian scholars formed the Camelot Research Committee which found enough money to finance a trial dig in 1966, under Leslie Alcock, an authority on the archaeology of Dark Age Britain. What followed proved so fruitful that the project ran on to 1970.

The first problem was deciding where to work. The 18-acre summit was too big to excavate entirely. The team thus set out to find those areas most likely to reward investigation. Surveyors drew up a contour plan, and the archaeologists used a banjo-shaped metal detector to criss-cross the hilltop in a search for buried metal objects. At the same time, local variations in the soil's electrical conductivity showed up the sites of old, filled-in post-holes where upright building supports had once stood.

The first season's digging hinted at a long but remote history of habitation. Neolithic, Bronze Age, and Iron Age peoples had all left their mark upon the hill. More importantly for the Camelot Research Committee, so had Celtic peoples of Arthurian times. The personal possessions found seemed unexciting: a small misshapen iron knife and fragments of Tintagel-type pottery. Significantly, though, these fragments came from each of the three trial sites. This suggested extensive Dark Age occupation by a relatively wealthy group. But what most excited some archaeologists were the remains of a Dark Age defensive wall and other structures uncovered during the five seasons' work.

Trenches cut across the inner defensive rampart revealed seven phases of building and rebuilding between pre-Roman and medieval times. One rampart in particular produced the kind of evidence that enabled scholars to say with certainty that it had been a barrier erected in Arthurian times by Celts, presumably against the Saxons. It survived as a rather low narrow mound of rubble, but in places it was plain that the outer surface had been faced by stones, with gaps once filled by posts supports for a timber breastwork built above the rubble mound. Moreover alignments of the stones inside the core revealed that the walls had consisted of a timber framework held in place by rubble heaped up on the beams. Presumably defenders would have stood, protected by the breastwork, on a wooden platform placed above the stonework. The fort's Celtic builders had evidently lacked the Romans' skill in dressing stones and bonding them with mortar. Instead, they plundered dressed stones from nearby Roman ruins, and in particular a temple standing on a hill. They then built their drystone wall somewhat in the fashion of the pre-Roman Britons. Unsophisticated, maybe, but impressive nonetheless, for their defence extended some 1200 yards, surrounding the entire surface of the hilltop. Leslie Alcock felt that the sheer size of the area enclosed implied that South Cadbury had acted as a base for an army large by late Celtic British standards – possibly created from the independent Celtic kingdoms' small fighting forces, gathered at this strategically important site to halt the Saxons' attacks on southwestern Britain.

Tell-tale soil stains derived from rotted timbers reinforce this picture of military strength by helping archaeologists to visualise the impressive gate tower that commanded the southwest entrance to the fort. We must imagine here a narrow wooden passage led into the wall, closed by two pairs of doors and capped by a protected lookout platform raised above the general level of the rampart.

Late on in the excavations another exciting find appeared. Pits and post-holes confusingly covered the summit centre – burrowings spread out over several centuries. From this confusion, close study extracted a pattern made up of rows of post-holes. In Arthurian times these holes had evidently held posts supporting a timber hall over 60 feet long and half as wide, with a screen near one end separating one-third from the rest. Wooden posts had apparently helped to support a thatched roof laid on a wooden framework. In this primitive hall the camp's commander-in-chief had almost certainly held counsel and issued commands. Arthur himself, perhaps?

This barnlike building is a far cry from the splendid palaces in which writers describe Arthur holding court. But the real Camelot – if it ever existed – may well have been more like a 'Wild West' frontier fort than a sophisticated city.

Twelve miles northwest from Cadbury Hill the steep-sided mass of Glastonbury Tor rises above the fields of the north Somerset plain. In Arthurian times the hill was a peninsula flanked by shallow sea and marsh. Antique lettering on some modern maps identifies Glastonbury Tor as the Isle of Avalon, where the mortally wounded Arthur was traditionally carried. Here, too, the legend states that he died and his body was buried low down on the hill's western flank. Reports of Arthur's links with Glastonbury date from about 1150, when Caradoc of Llancarfan wrote a *Life of St Gildas*. Caradoc describes how the Abbot of Glastonbury helped Arthur rescue Guinevere from King Melwas, her abductor: But people seem to have connected Glastonbury with Avalon in the 1190s. By then, the monks of Glastonbury Abbey claimed to have found the bones of Arthur and Guinevere buried near the abbey church's Lady Chapel. Gerald of Wales, who visited the abbey soon afterward, claimed that he saw the bones. He also mentioned a golden lock of hair that turned to powder when seized from the grave.

Thirty years later, Ralph of Coggeshall described the exhumation. But the least fanciful account – based largely on oral tradition – appeared a century later. This was by Adam of Domerham, a Glastonbury monk. On two important points accounts agreed: a lead cross had marked the grave, and the grave had been sited between two ancient pyramids. Otherwise the versions differed tantalisingly. A 'hollowed oak' had held the bodies, claimed Gerald; Ralph referred to a sarcophagus. Ralph wrote that the Latin text upon the cross had read: 'Here lies the famous King

Arthur, in the Isle of Avalon buried.' Gerald phrased the inscription differently and included a mention of Guinevere. To honour their famous find the monks installed them in a superbly carved double tomb within the abbey church. Adam of Domerham's account tells what happened next. At Easter 1278, King Edward I watched while the tomb was opened and the bones removed. Arthur's were 'of great size' and Guinevere's 'of marvellous beauty'. Edward ceremonially laid the bones in caskets, minus the skulls which were removed for public veneration. The tomb containing the caskets was then resited before the high altar.

During the Reformation, religious zealots smashed the tomb, and no one knows what happened to the bones. Researchers came across the tomb's foundations in 1931 in the ruined abbey. Traces of the original burial persisted, too. John Leland saw what was claimed to be the cross after 1540. An engraving of it features in William Camden's *Britannia* early in the 1600s. The cross apparently survived at Wells until the 18th century and then simply vanished.

However, in 1962 archaeologists discovered what could have been the very grave from which the medieval monks had lifted Arthur's bones. Digging into the old cemetery south of the site of Glastonbury's Lady Chapel they found traces of a broad pit that may have held the base of a massive cross. Some three yards south of this lay fragments of an ancient mausoleum. Cross and mausoleum were probably the 'pyramids' already mentioned. Writing early in the 12th century, William of Malmesbury had implied that both were really crosses, built up in several stages.

Between the two, archaeologists found a large hole had been dug and filled in about 1190. Proof of that date were distinctive stone chips lying in the hole – waste struck from masonry by the chisels of masons constructing the nearby Lady Chapel in the 1180s.

Here, then was Arthur's grave. Or was it? Sceptics claim that the 12th-century monks had forged both grave and antique lettering upon the cross. They had the motive: they badly needed cash to make good fire damage done in 1184. By claiming to hold

Arthur's bones they would attract pilgrims – and donations – to Glastonbury.

However, supporters of the monks' account claim that the cross, although post-Arthurian, really did predate the medieval exhumation. They argue that St Dunstan, then Abbot of Glastonbury, could have had it made about 945 when he removed old grave markers in the course of building up the level of the cemetery. From Arthur's burial, so this theory goes, St Dunstan took away a stone slab bearing a simple 6th-century inscription and replaced it with the cross – a more elaborate memorial in keeping with Arthur's growing reputation. Disappointingly, no Arthurian period pottery turned up at Glastonbury Abbey. But a dig on the top of nearby Glastonbury Tor bared scraps of amphoras, old hearths, and other proofs of Dark Age settlement. Who the settlers were, however, remains a mystery.

So far we have looked at the evidence for Arthur's supposed birthplace, his capital, and the place where he was buried. The other sites associated with his name are chiefly battlefields. Dark Age battles were generally fought at strategically important river crossings. Those linked with Arthur's name suggest he campaigned all over Britain. Of the thirteen battles named in early works, twelve are victories from the old Welsh list reported in Nennius' *History of the Britons*; the 13th and last is the final 'Camlann' cited in the *Welsh Annals*. Unfortunately Nennius does not say who Arthur conquered and it is hard to find the sites described. His first battle took place at the mouth of the River Glein. There were two English rivers called Glen but there were doubtless more before the Anglo-Saxons changed their names. So we have no idea where Arthur fought his first battle.

Nennius sites the next four battles on the River Dubglas in a district named as Linnuis. Some scholars suggest that Linnuis was one of two Roman sites called Lindum. The more likely of the two would place the battle in a Scottish valley called Glen Douglas near Loch Lomond. There, Arthur could have fought against the Scottish kingdom of Dalriada though four times seems improbable. Another explanation is that Linnuis is a scribe's misspelling of *lininuis*, a word supposedly derived from

Lindinienses, the name of a tribal group living near two 'Dubglas' rivers that cross the north Dorset Downs of southern England. Leslie Alcock argues that this would be a likely area for Arthur to engage Saxons advancing from the east.

The 6th, 8th, and 10th battles named by Nennius fit no known place names. But the 7th was 'the battle of the Caledonian Forest' (the 'wood of Celidon'). This must mean a battle fought in Scotland, which the Romans called 'Caledonia'. Just where it happened and who Arthur fought there we cannot say.

The 9th battle occurred in the 'city of the legion' which scholars identify as either Chester or Caerleon. Arthur reputedly won his 10th victory at Agned. Geoffrey of Monmouth equates Agned with Edinburgh. The hill there called Arthur's Seat does hold traces of a Dark Age fort. But some old manuscripts name the battle site as Breguoin or Breguein – names that set the scholars scurrying off to places in England.

The last two battles were the crucial ones for Arthur. Mount Badon seems to have represented Arthur's greatest triumph. Here, he felled 960 men, single-handed, in one day, Nennius declares, in true heroic mein. The *Welsh Annals* imply that the whole battle lasted three days and nights, during which Arthur 'carried the cross of our Lord Jesus Christ on his shoulders.' Gildas calls the struggle a siege. Moreover, he makes it plain that Badon was a British, Christian victory against the invading Saxon heathens. The date of Badon is debatable – AD 490 or 518 appear the likeliest contenders. The place is also uncertain. It could have been one of the five Badburys (named from an Old English word for Badda's fort – Badda being possibly some legendary Saxon hero). Bath in Avon (or rather, a nearby hill) is another possibility because 'Badon' would have been pronounced 'Bathon' in the old British tongue.

This brings us to the last struggle – the 'Camlann' of the *Welsh Annals* and Geoffrey of Monmouth's 'Camlam'. It was this evidently civil strife (variously dated 510 and 539) in which Arthur was killed and which apparently left the British kingdoms divided against their common Anglo-Saxon foes. The names of the Cornish River Camel and Somerset Cam have helped to make each popular as the likely battle site. Slaughterbridge near Camelford in Cornwall does have an old memorial stone called 'Arthur's tomb'. But place-name experts identify Camlann with Camboglanna, a Roman fort in northwest England and a likely site for civil war between two British armies.

The uncertainty surrounding Arthur's battle sites has led some scholars to dismiss the whole list as legendary. Others think that Arthur's name became attached to battles fought by several warriors. Others declare that he was a purely northern figure, and that all southern so-called Arthurian sites are spurious. Evidence for this theory comes largely from a sentence in Aneurin's 6th-century *Y Gododdin*. Describing the mighty warrior Gwawrddur, Aneurin wrote: 'He glutted black ravens on the wall of the fort' though he was not Arthur.' In other words, in battle Gwawrddur was as valiant as Arthur, slaughtering enough enemies to gorge the birds that feed on carrion. Traditionalists claim this shows that the Arthur of Tintagel and Camelot was already venerated as a national hero by the 9th century when *Y Gododdin* was probably first written down.

This chapter has merely nibbled at the mystery surrounding King Arthur. What underlying truths, if any, have we managed to expose? Certainly not the Arthur of medieval chivalry and splendour. Arthur was more probably commander-in-chief of a British force that briefly stemmed the westward-flowing Anglo-Saxon flood. He may possibly have been an obscure Scottish chieftain's son. One fact is certain: the only datable evidence for Arthur lies in archaeology and old manuscripts. The first provides no mention of his name. The second is scanty, ambiguous, and unreliable.

CHAPTER 11

THE FORGOTTEN AMERICANS

Up until 1961, most people would have named Christopher Columbus as the first European to discover America. But it was in that year that excavations at a site in Newfoundland permanently changed our view of American history and dislodged Columbus as the first white American. By 1992, the 500th anniversary of his first landing, the celebrations of Columbus' epic voyage were being overshadowed by the arguments as to just how many other people had beaten him to it. Who were these forgotten adventurers and why has the news of their great discovery remained hidden for so long?

For weeks the three Spanish ships had been sailing with no glimpse of land. Hour by hour, day by day, a persistent wind pushed them westward, away from the Canary Islands where they had stocked up with provisions.

It was late September in 1492 and the 90 seamen aboard the *Nina*, the *Pinta*, and the *Santa Maria* grew understandably scared. They believed no one had ever sailed for so long in one direction without sighting land. Scholars had long before established the idea that the world was round. But no one had actually circled the globe or shown that land indeed rimmed the western Atlantic. For all the crews knew, nothing but trackless ocean lay ahead. They wondered how long their Italian-born admiral Christopher Columbus would persist in his plan to reach the Indies from the east, in order to bypass the Moslems controlling the Asian route to this rich trading region. Already, the seamen surmised, they might have sailed too far to return in the teeth of a wind that was chasing them ever farther from home.

Unrest was fuelled by the discomfort of shipboard life. Few had bunks to sleep on. The dull, inadequate food began to run low. Faults showed up in their frail wooden craft – none as large as many a modern seagoing yacht.

Men began secretly grumbling. Complaints led to plots to oust a commander evidently bent on sacrificing his crew to what now seemed a monomaniac's fantasy. It took all of Columbus' skills as a commander to prevent discontent erupting in mutiny. He kept control by a judicious mixture of threat and promise – threat of punishment for dissidents, and promise of a big cash reward for the first man to sight land.

After more than a fortnight at sea, one of the two Pinzon brothers captaining the *Nina* and the *Pinta* suddenly cried 'Land, land!' to Columbus aboard the nearby *Santa Maria*. Pinzon had glimpsed an island-like shape in the distance. Night fell as the ships set course for his haven. But morning revealed no more than storm clouds mimicking land. This was just one of several false sightings.

After more than three weeks, Columbus knew he had spanned more than 2000 miles, but he kept this great distance a secret to avoid scaring his men. However, seagulls began to show up, and after nearly four weeks on the ocean the crews glimpsed flocks of land birds. The birds were probably on their southward autumn migration from North America to the Caribbean area. Columbus took heart and steered southwest after the birds, judging that they would be unlikely to stray far from land. By October 8 the numbers of birds increased and the air grew fresh and fragrant, reminding the men of Seville in the spring. Three days later came the first clear proofs that land lay at hand. The crew of the flagship Santa Maria noticed a green branch. Next, men from the Pinta fished up a carved stick. People on board the Nina discovered a thorn branch with berries on it. That night Columbus thought he glimpsed a light in the distance, and claimed and later received the reward. But it was 2 a.m. on October 12 before Rodrigo de

Triana aboard the *Pinta* glimpsed land in the moonlight. It proved no more than a small green island, peopled by black-haired, olive-skinned natives, whom Columbus mistakenly took to be Asian Indians. Later that day Columbus set foot here on San Salvador (Watlings Island) in the Bahamas.

In spite of his subsequent landfalls in Central and South America, Columbus always believed he had reached the fringe of East Asia. It was only when Spanish and other voyagers had mapped and colonised the Americas that Columbus gained fame as the discoverer of a brand new continent.

But did he really discover it? He was plainly not the first man in the Americas. The Amerindians' ancestors had peopled both continents long before. How far back is disputed. Some prehistorians put their arrival about 30,000 years ago; others even earlier. All agree, however, that these Stone Age explorers came in on foot across a land bridge once linking Siberia with Alaska. From North America's northwestern tip, hunters probed south, and when the Europeans arrived they found Amerindians in every habitable corner of the Americas. But the inflow of people from Asia was stemmed as ice caps melted some 10,000 years ago and meltwater raised ocean levels, submerging the Bering Land Bridge between Asia and North America. Archaeological evidence shows that the Bering Strait thus created proved no barrier to the Eskimos' maritime ancestors. But the civilised world once thought no one had made the long sea crossing from the east, until Columbus anchored off the Bahamas. However, old records, recent research, and voyages made in reconstructions of early ships now suggest that Columbus was only the last of a long line of European voyagers who sailed west across the Atlantic, discovering and rediscovering America.

In the late 1970s close study of old Bristol customs records revealed that ships from this west British port may have been secretly fishing off Newfoundland and even trading with the local Indians as early as 1479 – that is, 13 years before Columbus discovered the Bahamas. Officially the ships were trading with Ireland. But they took too long about it. One of the ships, for instance, completed a return voyage in 115 days, during which time another vessel completed three round trips to Ireland.

These vessels officially plied at a loss persistently enough to make their trading figures suspect. Above all the nature of their cargoes changed. Before 1479 many exported cloths, iron, salt, wine, and vinegar. From 1479 they switched to cloth and dyeing substances, condemned wine (used for pickling fish), and honey. Their imports altered strikingly, too. Instead of linen, Irish oak, salmon, and other articles of obviously Irish origin, the ships brought back salted and pickled fish, and timber. It seems unlikely that these could have come from mainland Europe, for almost anywhere there the Bristol seamen would have met hostile monopolies. The historian who analysed these figures suggested that the Bristol shipmen were really taking stores to a depot in Newfoundland where they caught fish in the rich offshore waters, then landed to mend damaged ships, and also to trade cloth for furs with local Indians. Naturally enough, they would have kept their commercially valuable discovery a closely guarded secret. Unfortunately for this theory, no traces of any such depot have so far turned up.

Intriguingly enough, though, the chief sponsor of John Cabot's voyage to mainland North America in 1497 was a leading Bristol citizen, called Richard Amerycke. In 1896 a local antiquary, Alfred Hudd, claimed that America had been named in Amerycke's honour and not, as customarily believed, for the contemporary Italian explorer Amerigo Vespucci. But America's 'Amerigo' origin is much the better authenticated.

Standing at the eastern threshold of the North Atlantic, the British Isles have produced several rivals to Columbus. Some have had support from unexpected quarters. In 1962 the Russian geographer Samuel Varshavsky suggested that the adventurous Carmelite friar Nicholas of Lynne had anticipated Columbus by more than a century, arriving in America soon after 1360. The evidence is slim indeed.

The Welsh advance claims for their own Prince Madoc, who predated Nicholas by almost two centuries. Old writings depict Madoc as a son of Owain Gwynedd, a powerful ruler of North

Wales. Not much is known about him. Indeed, only considerable study has separated Madoc the voyager from nine other Madocs. He emerges from legend as a big, bold, handsome, landless, sealoving adventurer. The chance find in an English sale-room of old port records dating from 1166–1183 links his name with the ship *Gwennan Gorn* (Horn Gwennan) which also figures in the Madoc legend.

Early accounts suggest that Madoc set forth with about 30 men in one or two ships – presumably tubby, square-sailed vessels with single masts, such as appear on old ports' seals. Among fanciful references to Madoc's 'magic unsinkable ship', we find more credible references to his use of a lodestone as a primitive ship's compass and the fact that he fastened his ship's timbers with horn nails rather than iron nails which would have produced false compass readings.

The port record discovered in England gives Madoc's point of departure as Aber-Kerric-Guignon. Tradition identifies this with Rhos-on-Sea in North Wales, where a rocky beach seemingly marks the remains of the old stone pier on the former rivermouth from which Madoc allegedly set forth on the first of two long westward voyages. His motive for travel seemed twofold: civil disturbance at home and the urge to seek land rumoured to lie in the west. Where he sailed and what he saw are clouded by fantasy and distorted by British post-Columbian writers seeking to prove their country's prior claim to have discovered America. However, a significant early account, evidently written before 1240, was produced by someone called Willem the Minstrel. Willem tells how Madoc discovered a 'treacherous garden in the sea' – perhaps the great weedy tract of the Sargasso Sea met by Columbus. Some have supposed that 'one of the isles of Llion' that Willem describes was Bermuda or somewhere in the Bahamas. According to Willem, Madoc returned from his first voyage to fit out another, which some authors believe set out from the island of Lundy in the Bristol Channel.

Proof that Madoc indeed founded at least one colony in North America apparently came to light after Welshmen began settling there in the 17th century. A Welsh clergyman wrote that he was travelling overland from Carolina to Virginia in 1666 when he was captured by Welsh-speaking Indians. Later came various reports of Welsh-speaking Indians claiming Welsh ancestry. Then explorers allegedly discovered white-skinned, fair-haired Indians deep inside North America. These were the Mandans of the Missouri River area. They reputedly made Welsh-type coracles, and people claimed that their words for coracle, paddle, and many other objects strikingly resembled the Welsh equivalents. In 1837 smallpox effectively destroyed the tribe and its traditions were lost.

Meanwhile, more hints on its 'Welsh' origin emerged, notably a letter written in 1810 by John Sevier, 'founder of Tennessee'. Sevier claimed that an old Cherokee chief had told him of indianised whites descended from Welsh colonists. These had landed at Mobile Bay near the mouth of the Alabama River, then travelled north, the chief had declared. This could have happened long after Columbus discovered America. But a Spanish chart of 1519 labels the Mobile Bay area Tierra de los Gales (Land of the Welsh), linking the Welsh with America before they had any business to be there – unless perhaps the Madoc tradition is true. Borne by the winds and currents, Madoc could well have fetched up on this northern shore of the Gulf of Mexico about the year 1170. But there is no indisputable proof that he did.

One thing is certain: Madoc lived long after Europe's first undoubted voyagers to set foot in North America. In about 1070 the German monk Adam of Bremen wrote an ecclesiastical history. In it he describes the Norse discovery of Vinland – a distant isle where grapes and wheat grew wild. Adam had obtained his information in Denmark, but the discoverers of what we now know to have been part of North America were actually of Norwegian origin. Proof largely lies in the old Icelandic sagas – family histories at first passed on by word of mouth, but eventually written down. Many scholars dismissed these ancient tales as mere folklore until in 1837 a Danish historian showed that they had a factual basis.

Coupled with archaeological finds, the sagas give us amazing insight into exploration of the North Atlantic 1000 years ago. At that time most ships were frail and largely lacked effective navigation aids. No wonder most seamen seldom sailed far out of sight of land. Norse adventurers, though, were made of sterner stuff than most. Roving in their long, lean, sharp-prowed, square-sailed Viking ships, Norse emigrants had settled Iceland before 900 AD. Briefly outlawed from Iceland, in 981 Erik the Red sailed west to Greenland, where he soon set up a colony upon the southwest coast. In about 986 the Norwegian merchant Bjarni Herjolfsson sailed off to join the colonists, but rough weather blew him off course and into dense fog where he drifted for days. At last the fog lifted and he glimpsed an unfamiliar, wooded coast ahead. Bjarni reckoned he had overshot Greenland and found land to the south. Rather than risk attack by natives, he altered course to the north. Days later another stretch of tree-clad shore appeared. Later still, Bjarni reached a harsh, rocky, icy landfall. He sailed on, eventually reaching the very fjord in Greenland where the original Norwegian colonists had landed.

Norse colonists flourished for centuries in Greenland, but in that treeless land they always lacked wood. Thus Bjarni's story of forests to the southeast excited speculation. About the year 1001, Leif Eriksson (Leif, son of Erik the Red) hired Bjarni's vessel and took 25 men on what proved a successful voyage of rediscovery. Bjarni's rocky shore Leif christened Helluland (Flat Rock Land); the next, Markland (Forest Land); and the third and southernmost, Vinland (Wineland), from the grapes he found there.

The sagas describe this last landfall in astonishing detail. We learn that Leif sailed his ship between an offshore island and a cape jutting northward from the nearby mainland. He landed where a river flowed from a lake. Salmon teemed in both. Wild wheat and 'grapes' flourished nearby, and grass grew through the frost-free winter, which had longer days than in Greenland or Iceland. Leif and his crew built sturdy houses and wintered there.

Next spring Leif sailed back to Greenland, but then his fellow Norsemen took up the challenge. Thorvald reached Vinland but died in a fight with Indians, whom the Norsemen called 'Skraelings'. However, Thorvald's followers spent two years ashore before retracing their journey.

About AD 1006 Thorfinn Karlsefni took people and cattle, meaning to colonise Vinland. They too built houses and Thorfinn's wife bore him a son – the first recorded European child to start life in the New World. The first winter proved harsh, and only a stranded whale saved the pioneers from starving. However, the local Indians seemed friendly, bartering furs for milk and red cloth. Then quarrels erupted. Two Norsemen died in the fighting. Outnumbered, Karlsefni pulled out.

Leif's sister Freydis led a separate bid to colonise Vinland. There were other attempts, but all foundered. By about 1400 worsening climate destroyed the Greenland colony too, removing a vital stepping stone on the Norsemen's northern route to America. Only their sagas survived to tell how a New World had been found and lost.

But what part of this continent had the Vikings actually discovered? They vividly described the places they saw, but lacked the navigation tools needed to pinpoint their position. For decades archaeologists searched unsuccessfully for traces of Norse settlements in North America. Such evidence was essential to prove the sagas' story. In 1898 the so-called Kensington Rune Stone turned up in Minnesota, but its 'old' Scandinavian inscriptions proved fakes. In 1965 Yale University disclosed a map depicting Vinland, supposedly drawn in about 1440. For years even experts were fooled. Then ink tests unmasked the Vinland Map as a modern hoax.

Meanwhile, a Norwegian archaeologist had made a meaningful find. With the old sagas as his chief travel guides, Helge Ingstad set out in 1960 to look for signs of lost Norse settlement along the northeast coast of North America. Walking, flying, travelling by bus, he scoured the seaboard from Rhode Island northward. Ingstad knew that two days' northward sailing had separated Bjarni's glimpses of two wooded shores and that three more had brought Bjarni to a glaciated coast. In all, Bjarni had spent nine days sailing to Greenland from what had probably been Vinland. Ingstad knew, too, the time Leif Eriksson had required to retrace Bjarni's voyage in the opposite direction. By marrying this information with the pattern of ocean winds and currents in the area and by calculating the likely rates of sail for Viking craft, Ingstad believed that he could find the places so clearly described in the sagas. His travels convinced him that cold Baffin Island had been Bjarni's Helluland. He thought Labrador's white beaches backed by forests matched Leif Eriksson's account of Markland. From there Leif Eriksson had needed a mere two days to get to Vinland. Ingstad felt that the Norseman's destination must have been Newfoundland – fish-rich, grassy, forested, and mild in winter.

Because Newfoundland's climate is unsuitable for grapes, many archaeologists have refused to recognise Newfoundland as Leif's Vinland. One explorer who retraced Leif's voyage by boat in 1966 favoured Massachusetts as the likely site. There, far south of Newfoundland, wild grapes abound beside Nantucket Sound. But Ingstad noticed that some Viking voyagers had reported picking grapes in winter somewhere north of Vinland. Ingstad argued that the Vikings' grapes had not been grapes at all, but the juicy red squash-berries from which Newfoundlanders make wine today. On the other hand, maybe 'Vinland' could be a simple mistake, based on the misreading of one letter in an old Scandinavian word. If so, the Norsemen had christened it 'Grassland' – a likely name for an island with good grazing.

Either way, Ingstad clung unshakably to his conviction that he need hunt for Vinland no farther south than Newfoundland. Accordingly he visited fishing villages there. He was searching for old ruins near a shore facing an island flanked by a cape, and backed by meadows and forest, with a river that flowed to the sea from a lake. His persistence paid off. At last he met someone who had heard of something likely at L'Anse aux Meadows ('Meadow Bay'). George Decker, a leading local personality, directed Ingstad to the site, where he found a river flowing from a small lake. It wound through low-lying land and emptied in a bay. Nearby stood an island, and a northward jutting cape. Far off lay the shore of Labrador. Inland grew grasses, berried bushes, and coniferous woodland. The waters around teemed with fish. Ingstad found he could trap fish in man-made tidal pools as the Norsemen had done. Here, too, darkness fell about 4.30 on midwinter day. It all matched the sagas' Vinland like a dream.

But there was more to come. Inshore a low rise bore the fuzzy outlines of old tumbled buildings. Surely here, if anywhere, lay the remains of homes fashioned by the New World's first European visitors.

Beginning in 1961, years of summer-season excavation followed. They revealed no less than eight structures. The largest had been a house 70 feet long, 55 feet broad, and subdivided into six rooms, mostly small. Floors had consisted of beaten clay, walls of turf, and grassy sods had waterproofed the roof. There were signs of ancient hearths and holes for cooking in. A separate structure turned out to be a smithy. There were also signs of a steam bath – a kind of primitive sauna.

The buildings resembled known medieval Norse houses. A brooch and part of a Norse spindle confirmed this supposition. Radiocarbon tests of wood from the ruins gave the significant date of about AD 1000. Only a few dozen people had lived here, and then only briefly, before fire had burned down their homes. It had been a small, poor settlement. No on-site relics linked it directly with Leif Eriksson. But it was undeniably Norse and predated Columbus' voyage by nearly 500 years. The finds at L'Anse aux Meadows brilliantly justified Ingstad's theory and rewrote North American history.

If the Newfoundland discoveries solved one mystery, they only pointed up another. For old Norse writings suggest that white men had preceded Northmen to North America. Near Vinland supposedly lay *Hvitramannaland* ('Land of the White Men'), also called *Irland-ed-Mikla* ('Ireland the Great'). Also two Skraelings (American Indians) reportedly told Vikings they had seen men dressed in white, shouting and carrying poles with cloths attached. The Vikings believed this description fitted the Irish, whose priests dressed in white and may have carried banners in a religious procession.

This account appears to support claims that the Irish had found America before the Vikings. Such claims rest on an epic voyage narrated in the *Navigatio Brendani*, or 'Voyage of St Brendan', first written down about AD 870 but probably far older. More than 120 Latin versions survive, and there are many others. With surprising consistency, they describe how a 6th-century Irish saint sailed west into the Atlantic with a select band of companions, variously put at from 14 to 150. They sought a fabled Paradise. After seven years of adventures, St Brendan arrived there to find a beautiful land luxuriantly covered in plants. The narrative left its location vague. But St Brendan's Island, as this paradise came to be called, made a major impression upon Europe's mapmakers.

A Catalonian chart of 1375 put it just west of southern Ireland. Other mapmakers took it to be one of the 'Fortunate Isles', of antiquity. Accordingly the Hereford chart of the 13th century located it among the Canary Islands. Various 14th- and 15th-century maps give its name to Madeira. But as the eastern Atlantic became better known, mapmakers began pushing the island farther west into that ocean. By the early 1800s the Atlantic was well known enough for most people to dismiss the whole story as a myth. Yet soon there were scholars suggesting that St Brendan's landfall had been no less than America. They cited the Viking 'evidence' and declared that the plants and creatures described in the *Navigatio* tallied with America's. Then, too, Brendan had reportedly guessed his 'island' paradise must be a continent because he failed to reach its limits. A weedy sea that trapped Brendan's boat until his men rowed themselves clear sounded suspiciously like the Sargasso Sea. This suggested that Brendan had maybe reached the Bahamas by the southerly route that Columbus followed much later.

But would Irish monks have risked a daring exploratory voyage some 1400 years ago? They possessed only small, open, rather unmanageable sailing boats; a sketchy notion of geography; and little more than sun, stars, and birds as guides. Undoubtedly they did sail far to find secluded islands where they founded monasteries. They built beehive homes and boatlike oratories on the forbidding Great Skellig island, eight miles off the coast of western Ireland. Sailing northward, they passed the Shetlands and reached the Faroe Islands where Vikings found them living in the 8th century. In 825 an Irish monk reporting a 30-year-old account of Iceland, mentioned the summer glow from the Arctic midnight sun, and pack ice north of Iceland. Thus Irish monks voyaged freely between North Atlantic island stepping stones before the Vikings. Could they, like the Vikings, have sailed the northern route to North America?

The British sailor-writer Tim Severin believed so, and thought this route more likely than any suggested southern crossing. To prove his point, in 1976 he set out on a voyage in what he felt must be the long-vanished wake of St Brendan's vessel. Appropriately, Severin named his craft the *Brendan*. He built it in the image of its predecessor, basing his design on old chronicles and the living tradition of the Irish curragh – a long type of open boat still used by Irish fishermen. The result was a whalelike craft 36 feet long, with an outer skin of 49 tanned oxhides, joined by 20,000 flaxen threads, and drawn across a 'wicker-work' ash-lath frame lashed together by two miles of leather thongs. Tarpaulins stretched between the gunwales to keep out storm waves gave Brendan the appearance of a giant kayak. Two square flaxen sails emblazoned with red Celtic crosses provided the driving power.

Because modern curraghs are rowing boats, and have tarred canvas coverings, no one knew quite how the oxhide sailing ship Brendan might handle, or if she would remain afloat. Even big modern trawlers have sunk in North Atlantic storms. Severin prudently set sail in spring, when winds were likeliest to aid an east-west transatlantic crossing via the northern island stepping stones, for he knew his square-sailed boat, unlike a modern yacht, would make no progress in a headwind. From St Brendan's supposed starting point at Brandon Creek in southwest Ireland, Severin coasted north past the Aran Islands and Iona to the Isle of Lewis, then on to reach the Faroes. Meanwhile the crew grew hardened to their primitive mariners' conditions: cramped quarters, monotonous food, and the stench from a leather hull, waterproofed with wool grease. Incidentally, warm southern waters would have dissolved the grease and sunk the vessel, a fact that made a northern route for St Brendan's voyage that much more likely. The men learned of both the *Brendan*'s strengths and limitations. Only six days out, the craft impressively weathered a gale. But storms and calms later meant that she spent more than a week covering the last 100 miles to the Faroes. Above all, though, her flexible hull held and kept out water. Two months after setting forth, the Brendan proudly sailed into the harbor of Reykjavic, the capital of Iceland.

It was now late July. Contrary winds and threatened autumn gales forced Severin's crew ashore for winter. Next May they resumed their voyage – their target, Newfoundland. This second leg proved nearly fatal. In late May mountainous seas swamped the cabin. The crew survived – thanks to pumping and an oxhide shelter hastily rigged across the gap that had let in the water. Worse followed a month later. The *Brendan* had cleared southern Greenland when she ran into a huge field of ice floes. Two vast slabs ground together, nipping the *Brendan* and punching a hole in the hull. Again only pumping and a leather patch sewn over the puncture saved the crew from an ice-water death. At last, in July 1977, and six weeks and 3500 miles out from Iceland, the *Brendan* touched shore in Newfoundland.

This voyage by a boat of ancient design brilliantly proved that St Brendan *could* have reached America. Moreover the *Brendan*'s route helped throw new light on some of his adventures. The *Navigatio* describes a narrow channel separating a 'Paradise of Birds' from an 'Island of Sheep'. The word Faroe in fact means 'Island of Sheep' and the Brendan's journey through the Faroes took it past Mykines Island whose cliffs spewed seabirds like confetti. The *Navigatio* also vividly describes an 'Island of Smiths' whose hostile savages hurled molten slag at the passing Irish vessel, and seemed to set the isle ablaze by stoking up their furnaces. The account fits Iceland, with its frequent volcanic activity.

The 'Great Fish Jasconius' of the *Navigatio* could only be a whale. At different stages in their voyage the *Brendan*'s crew glimpsed no less than five species of these giant creatures, some attracted to their odoriferous, whale-shaped craft. The legend also described St Brendan's encounter with a 'thick white cloud' and a crystal column – identifiable respectively as fog and an iceberg. Vessels coasting from Greenland down to Labrador often meet these hazards. Severin saw both. At one time his crew were grabbing hold of floes to urge the *Brendan* through the pack ice – an improvised technique recalling how St Brendan's monks traditionally forced their vessel through a marble 'net' to get a close glimpse of an iceberg.

Plainly the *Navigatio* is partly fiction. No one today believes its tale of fish surfacing to hear the saint say Mass. The numbers it gives are often symbolic: 3 for the Holy Trinity, 12 for Christ's Apostles, and so on. But much compels belief. Between the years AD 570 and AD 870 several Irish curraghs probably reached North America. The *Navigatio* may represent a confused compendium of the discoveries of those navigators who managed to return.

Even as Severin was sailing the *Brendan* to Newfoundland, scholars there were poring over local 'proofs' that Irish or maybe other Celts had sailed in long ago. The clues were merely scratches in the rocks – but marks that some experts consider had been purposefully made. Slow-growing lichens had so well encrusted some that these at least seemed ancient. Similar scratches have turned up elsewhere in eastern North America. A casual observer would dismiss most as the random doodling of Red Indians or as furrows gouged by modern ploughs or rasped by stones embedded in the base of moving ice. However, certain students of old writing systems believe the scratches to be ogam – an ancient Celtic form of writing where straight lines differing in number, length, and angle stood for different letters. What appeared to be traces of this script convinced some scholars that early Irish priests had set their mark upon New England's rocks.

In 1976 Barry Fell in his book *America BC* went even further. Summarising his hypothesis, *The Times* of London declared Fell believed that New England rocks enshrined the speech of Celts who had lived in Spain and Ireland 3000 years ago. From this, Fell theorised that Celtic mariners had reached America and intermarried with Red Indians some 1500 years before St Brendan's legendary transatlantic voyage. Among supporting evidence for this idea, Fell drew attention to New England's mysterious 'root cellars' – stores for keeping root crops through the winter.

Many archaeologists dismiss Fell's theories as, to quote one critic, fruits of 'the maniacal fringes of archaeology'. They think that 17th-century European colonists made the stone-roofed caves that Fell refers to. But Fell argues that root cellars were unknown in the colonists, European homelands. Moreover he declared that some New England root cellars bore traces of old writings.

Admittedly the largest of such structures are not easy to explain away as food stores. Strangest of all are 22 'cells' composed of uncemented granite slabs that sprawl across Mystery Hill, a New Hampshire hillside 40 miles north of Boston. The major features include a flat-topped four-ton 'Sacrificial Stone,' rimmed by a rock-hewn gutter. Below the stone a passage leads into a long, Y-shaped, more than man-high chamber from which a resonant shaft rises eight feet to the Sacrificial Stone. One theory suggests this was a speaking tube that eerily conveyed the voice of a priest hidden in the chamber to devotees around the Sacrificial Stone above. These big, uncemented stone building blocks and crude roofing recall Europe's ancient megalithic structures. Yet as one scholar said, 'The big things are too little, the small things so big.' The site impressed him with disorder and naivete. Maybe we have here a relatively recent fake or folly rather than an ancient monument influenced by European Bronze Age builders.

Mystery Hill is only one of many alleged circumstantial proofs of Old World voyagers that have been unearthed in North America. Some are blatant forgeries. But others merit careful study. A startling account of these appeared in 1971 in *Before Columbus* by Cyrus H. Gordon of Massachusetts' Brandeis University. Professor Gordon defends the authenticity of artifacts that others have dismissed as spurious, or wrongly dated. To Gordon, evidence abounds of early Old World contacts with the New. Research convinced this specialist in the ancient cultures of the Mediterranean and Middle East that Vermont's one-roomed stone structures roofed by loaf-shaped megaliths resembled a 4000-year-old Maltese temple. He implies that both were built by Bronze Age mariners who had evolved a world-wide culture. Pottery from Japan appeared in Ecuador 5000 years ago, declares Gordon. He believes that a sculptured head recovered from within a Pre-Columbian pyramid in Mexico was a Roman work of art fashioned 1800 years ago. He cites a hoard of Roman and Arabic coins more than 1000 years old discovered off Venezuela as proof of a Moorish Pre-Columbian transatlantic voyage. Gordon also suggests that Portugal's Coimbra map of 1424 genuinely features areas of North America.

Most dramatic of all, perhaps, Professor Gordon claims genuine antiquity for two inscriptions found in North America. One involves lines and circles scratched into a stone found near Fort Benning, Georgia, in 1966. Manfred Metcalf, who discovered the stone, declared that he was looking for slabs to build a barbecue pit when he found the stone in the crumbling wall of a 19th-century mill. Men had built the mill before Sir Arthur Evans found the first Minoan inscriptions at Knossos in the early 1900s. Yet the Metcalf Stone's inscriptions also seemed to be Minoan – possibly a Cretan inventory of around 1500 BC. Professor Gordon remarks that there were also parallels between Cretan and Mayan writing. He suggests, too, that the 'feathered headdress' and other objects pictured on the so-called Phaistos Disc from ancient Crete had counterparts in Aztec glyphs. Gordon suggests that back in Bronze Age times there must have been some cultural connection between seafarers of the eastern Mediterranean and the Amerindians.

Hebrew coins dating from Bar-Kokhba's anti-Roman revolt (AD 132–135) have reportedly turned up at three Kentucky sites since 1932. Unfortunately none of these finds resulted from methodical excavation by archaeologists. However, back in 1891 a United States Bureau of Ethnology report had actually published a Hebrew inscription found at Bat Creek in nearby Tennessee. Intriguingly, remarks Gordon, this inscription was printed upside down. The discoverer had wrongly thought the writing to be Cherokee. This is not surprising, because archaeologists found the stone lying under the skull of a dead chief buried with his wife and seven attendants in a mound that had been undisturbed for centuries. Not until 1964 did someone try to read the writing right way up. The result was no more than a cryptic Canaanite fragment. But scholars recognised the word 'Judea' and the letter forms suggested a date about AD 100. This stone and the Bar-Kokhba coins convinced Professor Gordon that Hebrew refugees from Roman rule had somehow sailed to North America in the 2nd century AD.

Bristol merchants, Welsh princes, Norse colonists, Irish monks, Celtic sailors – this chapter has examined the claims and evidence for most of the men and women who probably crossed the Atlantic from Europe to North America before Columbus got there. There are numerous other claims. In 1970 the Norwegian explorer Thor Heyerdahl sailed from Morocco to Barbados in a flimsy reconstruction of the reed boats of ancient Egypt. The successful voyage of his *Ra II* makes it conceivable that it was after all the Egyptians, many centuries before Christ, who first made the transatlantic crossing. Nor did all these early explorers travel from Europe. Chinese inscriptions have been found on Pre-Columbian objects, and in 1962 a Chinese claim was made that a Buddhist monk with five companions sailed across the Pacific to Mexico from China via the Kurile and Aleutian Islands in AD 459.

The existing transoceanic Pacific and Atlantic currents make any or all of these journeys possible. We can never know who really first discovered America. Whoever he was, it is clear that his name was not Columbus. Whoever he was, Columbus belittled his achievement, because the Italian sailed there and back and *published* his discoveries. Only then, we may believe, did Old World peoples finally impose their rule and culture upon the New World.

CHAPTER 12

WHERE WAS THE KINGDOM OF PRESTER JOHN?

Medieval Europe was alive with rumours. A great Christian king – called Prester (priest) John – had written to the Pope describing a wondrous, far eastern kingdom. Prester John had also offered his vast and partly magical army towards Christendom's holy war against the infidel Moors. Then came news that Muslim armies were being crushed by a mighty force from the east. Many were convinced that Prester John was on his way and celebrated in the streets. It was only when the decidedly non-Christian armies of Ghenghis Khan tore their way through the Muslim world and stormed into Europe that the illusion was cruelly shattered. Yet the myth of Prester John survived, and popes and kings continued to send men to try and discover his magical kingdom.

When Bishop Otto of Freising in Bavaria met Bishop Hugh of Jabala in Syria near Rome in the year 1145, the Syrian bishop had a most extraordinary tale to tell. A few years earlier, said Bishop Hugh, a Christian priest-king from somewhere east of Persia had won a series of shattering victories against the Samiardi, two brothers one of whom was king of the Medes, the other of the Persians. He had seized their capital of Egbattana, now the city of Hamadan in what is now Iran, and had then gone on to crush a combined army of Medes, Persians, and Assyrians in a three-day battle. The mysterious priest-king had then set out with his army to help the Church of Jerusalem, where at that time Crusading knights from Europe were isolated in a Moslem-dominated and hostile part of the Middle East. Finding his path barred by the River Tigris, the king had headed north, upstream. For years he waited for the river to freeze over so that he could march his army across. But the Tigris had not frozen over. At last, the disappointed priest-king gave up his plan to join forces with the Europeans, and returned home.

Bishop Otto learned that this monarch was known as 'Presbyter Iohannes' – that is, Priest, or Prester, John. John was supposedly descended from the Magi of the New Testament and he ruled their subject peoples 'in glory and prosperity'.

For European Christians living at the time of the Crusades this story had a special significance. It suggested that beyond Europe's Moslem enemies lay a Christian kingdom – strong, militant, and sympathetic to the cause of the Crusades. Not surprisingly, the story fascinated its German hearer.

Bishop Otto had no cause to disbelieve the story. He knew that Moslem powers ruled most of southwest Asia. But he knew too that Christian communities had sprung up there before the Moslems came to power, and still flourished. Modern historians have shown that Christianity somehow crossed the mountains and deserts of central Asia, and had briefly thrived in China in the 8th century. But unlike the Roman Catholic and Greek Orthodox Christians of the West, these Asian Christians were Nestorians. Named after a doctrine supposedly put forward by Nestorius, a 5th-century Patriarch of Constantinople, Nestorians believed that Christ's divine and human natures were separate, not identical as Western churches hold. This heresy was one reason why Western Christians knew so little about what went on among the Christians of the East. There were other reasons. Lack of trade and Moslem hostility in Africa and Asia had left medieval Christian Europe largely unaware of other lands and peoples. The Crusades opened a small window on the Eastern world, but little more than rumours of what lay beyond the Holy Land travelled westward. These rumours dealt mostly with monsters, infidels, and wealth beyond belief.

Bishop Otto was better read, better travelled, and more sceptical than most of his contemporaries, but Bishop Hugh's extraordinary tale of Prester John impressed him so much that the Bavarian bishop incorporated it in a chronicle that he was then writing. That is where modern scholars found Bishop Hugh's account of an incident which some believe sparked off the quest that followed: a centuries-long search by Europeans for Prester John and his successors.

Historians have found that facts support Hugh's story, but that the real events and characters were not those Hugh described. His brothers 'Samiardi' were actually one individual – the Seljuk Turkish Sultan Sanjar. The conqueror of Sanjar's Moslem army was not Prester John but a Mongol Khan named Ye-lu-ta-shih of the Kara Khitai tribe. The scholar Gustav Oppert has tried deriving the name Prester John from Ye-lu-tashih's title *Gur Khan* via a supposed Syriac mistranslation *Yuhanan*, the Syriac for 'John'. But there is no real evidence to support this bit of verbal juggling. Moreover, it seems unlikely that Ye-lu-ta-shih had been a Christian, let alone a priestly Christian king. In his book on Prester John, the American scholar Vsevolod Slessarev points out that this Mongol's contemporaries described him either as a believer in the Persian-based faith called Manichaeism or as a Buddhist. Slessarev suggests that Ye-lu-ta-shih was probably a Buddhist, because Buddhism would have influenced the Mongol's Chinese education. Finally, the battle of 1141 in which Ye-lu-ta-shih had crushed the greatest Moslem soldier of his day occurred nowhere near the city now called Hamadan, but east of Samarkand, in central Asia.

So far Prester John may seem vague and shadowy. But the 12th century also produced the priest-king in more definite form. This form is an extraordinary letter supposedly sent by Prester John to the Byzantine Emperor Manuel I. Some versions of the letter addressed it jointly to Manuel and his counterpart in Western Europe, the German Holy Roman Emperor Frederick Barbarossa. We don't know when the letter first appeared. The 13th-century French chronicler Alberic of Trois Fontaines put the date at about 1165, but Alberic's evidence is often unreliable. All we can say with certainty is that the original letter was addressed to Manuel, who reigned between 1143 and 1180.

This letter provided answers to many of the questions that must have puzzled Bishop Otto. From contemporary copies of it now in museums in London, Paris, and Vienna we learn something of Prester John himself. We learn too of the people and the lands he ruled, and of their natural and unnatural wonders.

The writer began by introducing himself as 'John, Priest by the Almighty power of God and the Strength of Our Lord Jesus Christ, King of Kings and Lord of Lords.' He greeted Manuel who he understood admired Prester John, and had wished to send John gifts. Prester John himself would now send gifts to Manuel. But he wanted to make sure that Manuel held the true faith. People regarded Manuel as a god, but Prester John knew that Manuel was mortal and subject to human infirmities. Manuel would be welcome to visit Prester John. John would place him in high office and load him with treasures should Manuel decide to return to Byzantium.

The writer then explained that Prester John surpassed everyone in virtue, wealth, and power. Much of the rest of the letter spells out the details of his splendour and humility. We learn for example that 70 kings acknowledged John as overlord. Seven kings, 62 dukes, and 265 counts and marquises served at John's dinner table every month in rotation. Twelve archbishops sat on his right at table and 20 bishops on his left. A patriarch acted as his house steward and his cup-bearer was an archbishop and king. Supreme ruler over all these dignitaries, John nonetheless humbly contented himself with the low ecclesiastical rank of priest and on his journeys he rode with a plain wooden cross carried before him.

His wealth lay in the abundant natural resources of his kingdom. Milk and honey flowed freely, and emeralds, sapphires, topazes, and many other precious stones abounded in the River Indus. 'For gold, silver, precious stones, animals of every kind . . . we believe there is not our equal under heaven.' John's palace demonstrated this wealth with its rare woods, fireproof ebony roof, sardonyx palace gates, crystal windows, and tables of gold for courtiers and of emeralds for the emperor himself.

But John's empire embraced wonders beyond mere wealth. Upon a plain stood a hollow stone containing water that cured any Christian bathing in it, whatever his disease. There were other marvels, too, which multiplied with the many versions of the letter that appeared and circulated in the Middle Ages. We read of hares as big as sheep; birds that carried whole oxen to their nests to feed their young; horned, four-eyed men; dog-headed men; Amazons; pygmies; centaurs; unicorns; the Phoenix; gold-digging ants; and salamanders that entered fire and spun threads from which fine silks were woven.

The letter gives us some idea of where these miracles abounded. From his capital at Susa in Persia John ruled 'the three Indias.' This vague realm was often subdivided into Nearer, Middle, and Farther India. These places apparently correspond with what we now call northern India, Ethiopia, and southern India, for medieval Europeans considered that all Africa east of the Nile formed part of Asia, and that no sea separated Ethiopia from India.

In this rich empire, poverty, envy, avarice, theft, and lying were unknown, and peace and justice flourished. Prester John was warlike in the service of the Cross. He could muster 140,000 mounted troops and 1,400,000 infantry. With this army he planned to march to Jerusalem and punish the Christians' Moslem enemies.

No one now believes the letter to be genuine. Scholarly detective work revealed that its author had lifted much of his material from existing medieval sources – among them tales of Alexander the Great, a Latin work on gems, and contemporary accounts of the wonders of the East. Moreover, at the time the letter was written, there was no splendid, thriving capital at Susa. This old Persian city lay half in ruins.

The letter's borrowings, errors, and use of language suggest to most historians that the writer was probably a West European acquainted with the Near East and hostile to the Greeks of the Byzantine Empire. What exactly made him write a hoax letter? Some scholars have suggested that the author had a moral aim: to stress the virtues of Prester John's imaginary Christian kingdom as an object lesson to the West, where Holy Roman Church and Holy Roman Empire were in a state of conflict. The writer may also have hoped to raise the flagging spirits of the Christian crusaders by hinting at a powerful ally to the east. But many think his letter just an exercise in literary composition. Whoever he was and whatever his motive, this hoaxer had an immense influence upon the history of Africa and Asia. For the great age of European exploration and empire-building largely began with the hunt for the fabled Land of Prester John described in the letter.

However, the first, abortive mission may have had another origin. In September 1177 Pope Alexander III wrote a letter to 'John, illustrious and magnificent King of the Indians'. From a surviving copy of the text, we learn that the Pope had heard of John's Christian faith and eagerness to conform to Roman Catholic orthodoxy. The Pope stressed as a major source of his information not the extraordinary letter but his own physician Philip, a travelled man who had visited John's kingdom or somewhere near it. Happy to help John, Alexander now sent him Philip as a messenger. He asked John to respond by sending envoys. We do not know what happened to Philip or even where he went. We can however guess at his destination. Professor Charles Beckingham, a British authority on African and Asian history, has shown that Pope Alexander's reference to Indians might have meant Georgians, Nubians or Ethiopians but certainly not inhabitants of the Indian subcontinent. Closer study convinced Beckingham that Philip's likeliest goal had been Ethiopia.

In 1221, though, came news of an event that once more focused Europe's eyes on Asia as the home of Prester John. From Bishop Jacques de Vitry and Cardinal Pelagius – both with a crusading army in Egypt – came letters describing a recent defeat of Moslem forces by 'King David'. Spice and gem importers trading with the Holy Land from farther east had spread the tale. They reported that Samarkand and other eastern Moslem cities had already fallen to this king, whose troops now marched upon Baghdad. Many people speculated that David must be Prester John's son or maybe grandson. De Vitry even thought that David was Prester John himself.

For De Vitry's crusading force, embroiled in what proved a disastrous campaign, the rumour of a Christian victory may well have been the result of wishful thinking. We now know that the warrior king whose Asian campaign inspired the rumour was a ruthless and most un-Christian Mongol empire-builder named Genghis Khan. But Mongol victories did more than help spread rumors of the legendary Prester John. They made it possible for Christian travellers to go in search of him. This was because under Mongol rule, one power for the first time unified all central Asia and even welcomed Christian travellers. Most came as missionaries or traders, but the land of Prester John was clearly one of their objectives.

In 1245 a Franciscan friar named John de Carpini rode 3000 miles in less than four months to reach the Mongol Khan's camp deep in what is now Mongolia. In 1253, William of Rubruck, another Franciscan, followed in Carpini's footsteps. Then in about 1270 the famous Venetian traveller Marco Polo passed through central Asia on his way to China. Rubruck and Polo both heard tales that put Prester John in a new light. They learned of a battle in which Genghis Khan had killed his Mongol Christian overlord Ung, or Ung Khan. It seems quite likely that there had been such a Christian Mongol ruler. A 13th-century Syrian chronicler called Gregory Abulfaraj recorded a letter of AD 1009 describing the conversion to Nestorian Christianity of a king of the Mongol Kerait tribe. Abulfaraj claimed that the Kerait ruler of around AD 1200 held the title *Ung Khan* which Abulfaraj interpreted to mean 'King John'. Some modern scholars have identified Ung Khan with 'Prester John'. But Ung Khan – or more accurately Wang Khan – was a Chinese title not conferred upon the Kerait king until 1190 at the earliest, long after references to Prester John appeared in Western Europe.

However there was more than one candidate for the title Prester John. For instance, Rubruck favoured a former Mongol king whose Chinese name Ta-Yang-Khan means 'Great King John'. Marco Polo reported that Prester John still reigned in the country of the Keraits, but as a vassal of the Great Khan. Other travellers came up with other candidates. About 1326 Friar Odoric of

Pordenone made a great trek across Asia in which he claimed to have visited a land still ruled by Prester John, but Odoric declared that 'not one-hundredth part is true that is told of him.'

Some travellers went farther. Finding no Christian king or wealthy kingdom in the heart of Asia, they began to wonder whether Prester John reigned there at all. One such sceptic was Jordanus de Severac. This Dominican friar visited India about the time that Odoric was crossing central Asia. De Severac found no trace of Prester John in India, but heard that a Christian monarch, presumably a descendant with the title 'Prester John', lived in Ethiopia – in other words, in what remained of John's old empire of the three Indias, recorded in the letter sent by Prester John to the Byzantine emperor. To Christians now catching up on world affairs, it seemed likely that Mongol conquests had driven John into this obscure 'middle' region of his empire. De Severac fleshed out the new hypothesis with a fanciful account of vassal kings and wild beasts. Once more European estimates of Prester John rode high. Anything seemed possible in Ethiopia, a land as little known to Europeans of the 14th century as Mongolia had been a century or so before. From Ethiopian pilgrims to Jerusalem, West Europeans at least knew that Ethiopia had a Christian king. They knew he sometimes fought the Moslem powers that blocked European travel to his country. In addition, rumours suggested that the Nile rose in Ethiopia, and that Prester John could, if he wished, divert this river, so reducing Moslem Egypt to a desert.

Understandably, European Christians felt such a monarch well worth cultivating as a possible ally. But first they had to find his kingdom. Curiously enough the nation that sought him most persistently was Portugal, the kingdom at the westernmost end of Europe and farthest from Ethiopia. The Portuguese leader who launched this search was Prince Henry the Navigator – a scholar with a burning spirit of adventure. Henry's conquest of the rich Moorish port of Ceuta in North Africa in 1415 fully opened the young prince's eyes to the wealth shipped westward from India by Moslem Arab merchants. What Henry found in Ceuta helped fire the prince with ambition. He would bypass the Arab-speaking

middlemen and their hostile Moslem lands, and reach the riches
of the East directly. At the same time he would find and make an
alliance with Prester John, whose kingdom lay somewhere on the
way to India, where the spices came from. Together they would
crush their Moslem enemies.

Hostile Moslems barred overland routes between Europe and
India, and Italians monopolised east Mediterranean trade. Henry
had to find another route, so he gathered around him scholars,
travellers, and even Moslem prisoners. From them he acquired
much-needed information. Then he sent sailors south down the
coast of West Africa to find a sea route to the East.

Henry's ambitions probably gained fresh impetus in 1452
when an ambassador from Prester John supposedly arrived in
Portugal. This report seems unsubstantiated, though other records
tell of Ethiopian ambassadors to Spain and Italy about this time.
In 1455 a Genoese in Portugal wrote a letter claiming that Prester
John lived six days' travel inland from the coast of Gambia. This
was the first text to attempt to localise the Ethiopian monarch.
Five years later Henry died, his aims unrealized. However, his
ships had probed far south, and after Henry's death King João II
kept up the search for India and Prester John.

The breakthrough came in 1488 when storms hurled
Bartolomeu Dias' frail caravels around the southern tip of Africa.
But this was only part of a two-pronged Portuguese expedition.
King João was already looking for another route to Prester John.
Travellers had told him that 750 miles west of the African
kingdom of Benin, in what is now Guinea, lived the immensely
powerful King Ogané. We now know that Ogané was probably
the king of Ife, another West African state, but João believed the
man was Prester John. Maps suggested that his kingdom must lie
south of Egypt. Accordingly, João sent two monks to reach John
overland via Jerusalem which then lay in Moslem hands. Unable
to speak Arabic, the monks got no farther.

Stubbornly, João tried again, this time sending two lay adventurers who spoke fluent Arabic. Pero da Covilham, previously a
diplomat and spy, and his companion Afonso de Paiva left
Portugal and headed east early in May 1487, just three months

before Bartolomeu Dias headed south on his historic voyage. The emissaries carried with them a letter to Prester John, a map on which to mark his kingdom when they found it, and 400 *cruzados* in cash and letter of credit. Disguised as dealers in honey, the couple daringly cut adrift from Christendom and mingled with its Moslem enemies. They arrived in Cairo, then, wearing Moslem dress, pressed on to Aden. There they parted. Afonso de Paiva was to go direct to Ethiopia and Prester John, Pero da Covilham to sail by Arab dhow to India to trace the rich export trade in spices to its source. Both planned to meet in Cairo and return home.

The scheme misfired. Pero da Covilham succeeded in the first part of his mission. He reached Cannanore, where ginger came from, and Calicut – a port where half-naked men rode elephants, built thatched huts, and shipped pepper from the palm-fringed shore. After visiting East Africa, Da Covilham returned to Cairo only to find that Afonso de Paiva had died there. We shall never know whether or not Afonso's mission to Ethiopia had succeeded.

Pero da Covilham prepared to take ship home to Portugal and his long-neglected wife. He never arrived. Two Jews brought a secret message from King João insisting that he should return only after making every effort possible to track down Prester John. Obediently the weary traveller retraced his Red Sea journey. Da Covilham landed at Zeila in what is now northwest Somalia and in 1494 reached the court of Prester John, or rather, of the Ethiopian emperor, Alexander. But Alexander soon died, and his successor refused Da Covilham permission to leave the country. There he spent his last years, made comfortable by a black wife and lands provided by his captors.

Portugal was not to be in ignorance of 'Prester John' for much longer, once Dias and Vasco da Gama between them had opened up the sea route to East Africa. In 1506 two Portuguese with a Tunisian Moor as guide sailed around Africa, landed at Guardafui on the very tip of the Horn of Africa, and set off inland to Ethiopia. None ever reappeared in Portugal, but two of them at least reached Ethiopia. We know this from a letter written to the king of Portugal by the Ethiopian regent, Helena. Carried by messenger, this letter reached Afonso de Albuquerque, by then Portugal's forceful governor in India in 1512. Albuquerque forwarded the letter and its messenger to Portugal. When they arrived in 1514 King Manuel gave both a rapturous reception, and planned a formal embassy to Ethiopia. Unbelievably, six years passed through naval bungling before the embassy arrived at the Red Sea port of Massawa – then just a mosque and a few stone buildings. A small, mixed group of ambassadors set off into the interior. They included a doctor, painter, organist, fencer, several craftsmen, and a chaplain – Padre Francisco Alvares. Alvares' account of what followed finally revealed the kingdom of Prester John to Portugal. It proved a nation very different from the empire of medieval legend.

From Massawa the party headed inland to the provincial capital of Debaroa, a route that took them up steep mountain paths and out onto a high plateau with fertile fields. Travelling by mule and camel, the ambassadors pressed on through Tigre Province. Here they marvelled at tiny chapels carved into the sides of almost sheer-sided peaks and at local dark-skinned women wearing little more than beads.

For five months, the party travelled through a mountain kingdom of humble villages and wealthy churches, but no towns. At last they met the object of their quest: Lebna Dengel Dawit, whose name they simplified to 'David'. Disappointingly they found that the Abyssinians entitled him not Prester John but simply 'emperor'. Disappointingly, too, his palace proved to be a tent, his capital a mere camp. For the emperor and his court were constantly on tour around the country as affairs of state or wars demanded. More disconcerting still, the man seemed greedy. Instead of showering his visitors with gifts in the spirit of the legendary Prester John, the Emperor of Ethiopia at first demanded gifts from them. He particularly wanted pepper, because spices served as money in this kingdom. But the emperor was certainly Christian, and, if not himself a priest, at least an influence on Church affairs. 'David' maintained the custom of annual rebaptism by total immersion – a practice started by his grandfather against the wishes of the Patriarch of Abyssinia. The emperor dressed in an imperial style befitting Prester John, as the Portuguese discovered on the only time he deigned to show himself. They saw a young man coloured like a russet apple, richly dressed, holding a silver cross, and with a gold and silver crown upon his head. Eventually, too, he showed something of the mythical Prester John's generosity, presenting gifts of gold and silver to the embassy when at last they departed after an enforced stay of several years. The Portuguese reached Lisbon in 1527, more than a century after Henry the Navigator had initiated the hunt for Prester John in Africa.

The ambassadors dispelled the myth that Ethiopia's emperor was rich and powerful. But had they really tracked down the original Prester John's descendant? Some writers have thought so, and that the 'John' of Prester John came from the Ethiopian phrase *Zan hoy* ('My King'), misheard as Gianni by Italian merchants-visiting Jerusalem or Alexandria, hence 'Jean' in French and 'John' in English. But there are strong doubts that Ethiopians addressed their emperor as *Zan hoy* before the 16th century.

In any case, a closer look at early references to Prester John brings us once more back to Asia as the legend's likely starting point. Dr Slessarev's study of Bishop Hugh's account – the oldest known reference to the priest-king John – suggested that a real-life Mongol general had somehow got mixed up with a legendary figure holding an emerald sceptre and related to the Magi. These latter items hint at links with legends of St Thomas, the Apostle, who is believed to have preached the Gospel in India in the 1st century AD, and to have died a martyr there. One story of his martyrdom involves an Indian king's rich but pious son called Vizan (John). The story tells how Thomas converted Vizan and ordained him deacon. When Thomas died Vizan became one of Thomas' two spiritual successors and leaders of the Church in India. Could the legend of a priest-king Prester John have sprung from such a source? Slessarev believes that it could.

Other scholars have dug far deeper back in time to find the Prester's origins. A French historian, Professor Georges

Florovsky, traced the name 'Presbyter John' as far back as St John's epistles. The name, Florovsky felt, became the basis of the myth. The legend of the all-powerful priest-king had simply taken shape and changed according to the spirit of the different ages that had passed it on.

CHAPTER 13

THE MEN OF ZIMBABWE

*It is rare for questions of racism to infect the scientific delib-
eration of archaeologists. Nevertheless, when impressive
ruins were discovered in Rhodesia they were immediately
claimed as the work of white men, despite the palpable
improbability of such a proposition. Zimbabwe – which gave
its name to Southern Rhodesia after independence – was
linked by white colonial settlers with the fabled city of
Ophir; source of the Biblical King Solomon's African gold.
Yet, even though the reasoning of investigators was clearly
swayed by racist bigotry, should we automatically reject
their conclusions? As we have seen, initially improbable
explanations can ultimately be proved true in the world of
archaeology. What was the skin colour of the men of
Zimbabwe?*

On a high plateau in southwestern Zimbabwe, Africa, lies a
sprawling stone complex covering some 60 acres that for many
years has been the subject of mystery and romance. Speculation
about the origins of the giant stone walls and roofless buildings
has ranged from the possibility that they were once in the land of
Ophir – the land that provided the gold for King Solomon's
Temple in Jerusalem, to the possibility that it was once the city of
the legendary Prester John – the priest-King who was supposed to
have ruled somewhere in Africa or Asia in the 12th century.

The first Europeans to hear of the imposing stone buildings –
known as Zimbabwe or Symbaoe – were the Portuguese, who, by

the end of the 1400s, had established a chain of trading posts along Africa's east coast. Their ambitions in Africa had been kindled by Arab stories of gold. But although some gold had been mined and traded for goods from the Orient, the amount that passed through Portuguese hands was much less than they had been led to expect. The land from which the gold came was a confederacy of states ruled by a leader called the Mwene Mutapa (or Benemotapa, in Portuguese writings), which meant 'Ravager of the Lands' or 'Master Pillager'. Stories abounded of the Mwene Mutapa's wealth and power and of some great buildings made of stone that were located in the southern part of his territories. A description of these buildings and of the mines in the surrounding areas was included in a book written by a Portuguese, João de Barros, and published in 1552.

In the midst of a plain, he wrote, 'is a square fortress, masonry within and without, built of stones of marvellous size, and there appears to be no mortar joining them. The wall is more than twenty-five spans in width, and the height is not so great considering the width. . . . This edifice is almost surrounded by hills, upon which are others resembling it in the fashioning of stone and the absence of mortar, and one of them is a tower more than twelve fathoms high.

'The natives of the country call all these edifices Symbaoe, which according to their language signifies court, for every place where the Benemotapa may be is so called. . . .

'In the opinion of the Moors who saw it, it is very ancient and was built there to keep possession of the mines. . . .

'Considering the facts of the matter, it would seem that some prince who had possession of the mines ordered it to be built as a sign thereof . . . and as these edifices are very similar to some which are found in the land of Prester John at a place called Acaxumo, which was a municipal city of the Queen of Sheba, which Ptolemy calls Axuma, it would seem that the prince who was lord of that state also owned these mines and therefore ordered these edifices to be raised there. . . .'

Neither de Barros nor any other Portuguese colonist ever saw 'Symbaoe'. His account is based on reports by the Swahili traders and, like many secondhand reports, it contains some factual errors: the main building, for example, is elliptical, not square. It does, however, offer a correct translation of the name. Although 'Zimbabwe' comes from words in the Mashona language that could mean 'houses of stone', it is more probably derived from those meaning 'venerated houses' – that is, those occupied by the chief. The complex of buildings described by de Barros is the largest of many 'zimbabwes' in southern Africa.

It was de Barros' report that helped to perpetuate the legend that the buildings were ancient – dating back to Old Testament times – and that they had been built by a foreign people. The story persisted, accepted as fact, for the next 400 years.

Because the natives who came in contact with the Portuguese lived in simple mud huts, the idea that the buildings might have been built by the local inhabitants was quickly dismissed. The local population seemed to have no idea when, or by whom, the buildings were constructed. 'The walls were built when stones were soft', they told a later explorer. So both the Christian Portuguese and the Moslem Swahili traders linked Zimbabwe with their own familiar legends of lost kingdoms. João dos Santos, a Portuguese missionary, wrote in a book published in 1609:

'The natives of these lands, especially some aged Moors [Swahilis], assert that they have a tradition from their ancestors that these houses [Zimbabwe] were anciently a factory of the Queen of Sheba, and that from this place a great quantity of gold was brought to her. . . . Others say that these are the ruins of the factory of Solomon, where he had his factors who procured a great quantity of gold from these lands . . . not deciding this question, I state that the mountain of Fura or Afura may be the region of Ophir, whence gold was brought to Jerusalem. . . .'

The First Book of Kings in the Bible tells how Solomon arranged with Hiram, King of Tyre, to have gold and other riches brought to him from Ophir. Hiram's navy 'came to Ophir, and fetched from thence gold, four hundred and twenty talents, and brought it to King Solomon.'

The Portuguese believed that they had at last located the mysterious land of Ophir. Other Europeans were quick to take up the idea. Books by Italian, French, Dutch, and English geographers perpetuated the ideas of de Barros and dos Santos. Milton's *Paradise Lost* refers to Sofala (an Arab African port) as 'Sofala thought Ophir'. The Dutch, who settled around the Cape of Good Hope in 1652, made several attempts to find the stone buildings of 'Ophir' but without success.

Not until the late 19th century did a European set eyes on Zimbabwe. Adam Renders, a German-American hunter, reached it in 1868, having heard of the ruins from a man who had never succeeded in finding them, a German missionary named Merensky. Renders left no record of his discoveries, but a few years later he showed the ruins to Carl Mauch, a German geologist, who wrote detailed descriptions of what he found there.

What Mauch found was a group of ruins extending over some 60 acres of a valley and a nearby hill, constructed of blocks of granite fitted together without mortar. The largest of these ruins called the Elliptical Building – sometimes the Temple – is a huge enclosure whose outer wall measures more than 800 feet in circumference. This wall is, in places, 14 feet thick and up to 32 feet high, and its upper edge is decorated with a chevron-patterned frieze. Within the enclosure are several smaller enclosures and passageways and a solid round tower, 18 feet in diameter and 30 feet high, known as the Conical Tower.

Overlooking the valley is a 300-foot-high hill whose summit is crowned by the Hill Ruins. The walls of these ruins curve in and out among the great boulders to form a pattern of natural and man-made structures in which one seems to grow out of the other. In fact, the granite blocks used to construct Zimbabwe did, in a sense 'grow out' of the hills. Years of alternate heating and cooling of the rocks caused their surfaces to split and shed thin layers of rock some three to seven inches thick, which would then slide down the hillside to collect at the bottom as scree. The builders of Zimbabwe collected and cut these slabs into manageable pieces and fitted them tightly together. The quality of the masonry varies, but the best work is regularly coursed and is wider at the base than at the top, which makes these walls very strong.

Between the Hill Ruins and the Elliptical Building are a number of smaller enclosures known as the Valley Ruins. Many of the walls in these ruins have large gaps that were once filled with circular dwellings made of *daga*, a kind of gravelly clay that was also used to pave the enclosures. Traces of daga still exist in most of the Zimbabwe ruins, though none of the huts have survived.

Following the discovery of Zimbabwe many attempts were made to compare its buildings with other buildings in Mediterranean and Middle Eastern lands that might have influenced its construction. The Elliptical Building, for example, was compared to the temple of Haram Bilqis ('Sacred enclosure of the Queen of Sheba') in a part of the Yemen that traditionally belonged to the biblical queen. The temple does have an irregular elliptical courtyard, but the temple itself is rectangular and symmetrical – whereas there are no straight lines anywhere in Zimbabwe.

Mauch and those who followed him were convinced that the ruins were ancient and that the work was of a foreign culture. In a doorway of the Elliptical Building he found some wood that he identified – wrongly – as cedar and which he claimed could not have come from anywhere else but the Lebanon. Mauch gave a further boost to the Solomon and Sheba theory in an article that was published in a geographical magazine.

By 1890, after Mauch's visit to the Ruins, the whole area occupied by the Mashona, or Shona, people – and which included the Zimbabwe ruins – began to be settled by the British South Africa Company, whose director was Cecil Rhodes. The Company's primary interest was the area's gold deposits, but the ruins of Zimbabwe soon attracted considerable attention. In his book *Great Zimbabwe*, the Rhodesian archaeologist and author Peter Garlake observed that the ruins 'quickly became a symbol of the essential rightness and justice of colonisation and gave the subservience of the Shona an age-old precedent if not biblical sanction. Thus, on Rhodes' first visit to the Ruins, the local Karanga chiefs were told that 'the Great Master had come to see the ancient temple which once upon a time belonged to white men'.'

Rhodes appointed Theodore Bent, a British traveller and anti-quarian, to make a thorough investigation of the ruins. Being particularly interested in Mediterranean culture, Bent looked first of all for signs of it at Zimbabwe, but he soon rejected the idea that the ruins had a Phoenician origin: 'from my own personal experience of Phoenician ruins I cannot say that the Zimbabwe ruins bear the slightest resemblance whatsoever.' He was disap-pointed to find, in excavating the site, that nearly all the objects dug up were African, and that the few pieces of imported glass and porcelain were only a few hundred years old. At one point, he confided to a guide, 'I have not much faith in the antiquity of these ruins, I think they are native. . . .' Yet he continued to search for signs of an ancient foreign culture, and when he discovered some soapstone monoliths carved in the shape of birds in one of the Hill Ruin enclosures, he believed he had found the sign he was looking for. Nothing resembling these had ever been found in Africa south of the Sahara, but they did bear slight resemblances to objects in some Middle Eastern civilisations. Bent also found some similarities between Zimbabwe architecture and that of Arabia, but he never established any clear connection between the two cultures. In the course of his work he visited some of the other stone ruins in Rhodesia, but without any more success. Nevertheless, his book *The Ruined Cities of Mashonaland*, published in 1892, stimulated great interest in these mysterious structures.

In the meantime, the lust for gold was threatening to destroy them. A company called Rhodesia Ancient Ruins Limited was formed with the express purpose of digging for buried treasure among the country's ruins. Although Zimbabwe itself was exempted, at Rhodes' request, a certain amount of unauthorised digging nevertheless went on there. Other sites were badly damaged. In 1901 legislation was passed protecting the sites, and the Rhodesia Ancient Ruins Company was closed down.

The protection was short-lived, however. More damage was soon to be inflicted, this time in the name of scientific inquiry. A journalist named Richard Hall, who had written a book entitled *Ancient Ruins of Rhodesia*, was, in 1902, appointed Curator of the

Zimbabwe ruins. Although his stated responsibility was 'the preservation of the building', Hall began to excavate the site in search of material supporting the ancient origin theory.

He went at his task with enthusiasm, removing stones, undergrowth and even trees within the enclosures, and digging up layer upon layer of archaeological deposits – which in places were 12 feet deep. Much of this material he dismissed as 'the filth and decadence of the Kaffir occupation'. So thoroughly did Hall do his work that later excavators of Zimbabwe have had difficulty finding undisturbed deposits to examine.

Untrained in archaeology, Hall had no idea of how to classify his finds according to the techniques of stratigraphy – the method of carefully examining layers of earth and debris to establish the comparative dates of the objects found in them. He had already classified the ruins into four types and periods: (1) Sabaean (Arabian) of between 2000 and 1100 BC; (2) Phoenician, dating up to the beginning of the Christian era; (3) a transition period; and (4) a 'decadent period,' which he attributed to the native population. The objects he turned up while excavating he assigned to these various periods simply on the basis of quality of workmanship.

Hall's work at Zimbabwe drew sharp criticism from archaeologists outside the country, and after two years he was dismissed. However, he had made extensive notes on his discoveries, and in 1905 he published another book incorporating this material, entitled *Great Zimbabwe*.

Within a year the assumptions of Hall, Bent, Rhodes, and others were to be sharply challenged. The British Association for the Advancement of Science appointed a young archaeologist named David Randall MacIver – a pupil of Sir Flinders Petrie, the famous English Egyptologist – to examine and report on Zimbabwe and other Rhodesian ruins at the Association's next meeting that same year. The title of the book MacIver produced, *Mediaeval Rhodesia*, gave away his thesis: that the ruins were not ancient but only a few centuries old. In his Conclusions, MacIver tersely summed up his findings. In 'not one' of the seven sites he investigated 'has any object been obtained by myself or by others before me which can be shown to be more ancient than the four-teenth or fifteenth century AD. In the architecture . . . there is not one trace of Oriental or European style of any period whatever.' Putting it positively he stated: '(1) That imported articles, of which the date is well known in the country of their origin, are contemporary with the Rhodesian buildings in which they are found, and that these buildings are therefore mediaeval and post-mediaeval. (2) That the character of the dwellings contained within the stone ruins, and forming an integral part of them, is unmistakably African. (3) That the arts and manufactures exem-plified by objects found within these dwellings are typically African, except when the objects are imports of well-known mediaeval or post-mediaeval date.'

In the short time available MacIver could not make a thorough examination of the sites. However, he did study in detail some of Hall's excavations in the Elliptical Building. In enclosure 15, for example, he found that the objects in the lowest layer beneath a stone and cement floor, were virtually identical to those in the upper layers. The bits of pottery found in the trench were exactly like modern native pottery.

At the time MacIver was working, the technique of radio-carbon dating had not yet been invented, so he had to rely on foreign objects whose dates could be established by referring to known stylistic periods. MacIver himself did not find any imported objects within the Elliptical Building that could be so dated, so he relied on Hall's recorded finds of what he wrongly termed 'Nankin' china and Arabian glass and on his own discov-eries of similar wares at other sites. The Elliptical Building, he concluded, was not earlier than the 14th or 15th century.

Not surprisingly, MacIver's report was greeted with approval by his fellow archaeologists and roundly condemned by the white settlers of southern Africa. Hall, who MacIver had sharply criti-cised, replied in 1909 with a book entitled *Prehistoric Rhodesia*, in which he vehemently reiterated his original arguments and in turn criticised MacIver.

The controversy continued for some years without any fresh evidence. Then in 1929 the British Association again sponsored a study of the ruins. The archaeologist appointed was Gertrude Caton-Thompson. Over a period of six months, Miss Caton-Thompson made an intensive study of one of the Valley Ruins and also examined other buildings at Zimbabwe and at other sites. Her report, published in book form under the title *Zimbabwe Culture*, provided the most detailed information yet obtained. In essence it confirmed MacIver's findings; but like MacIver, Miss Caton-Thompson was hampered by a lack of datable foreign objects with which to date the buildings. Under the floor of the Maund Ruin, in the valley, she found some tiny glass beads. An expert was able to demonstrate that they did not come from any pre-Roman Middle Eastern culture but could not positively identify them, apart from an educated guess that they dated from the 9th to 10th century AD. Miss Caton-Thompson cautiously suggested that Zimbabwe might have been built several centuries before MacIver's dates, but she concluded that 'examination of all the existing evidence . . . still can produce not one single item that is not in accordance with the claim of Bantu origin and mediaeval date.' As for the Portuguese statements that the Africans disclaimed any knowledge of the building of the ruins, this 'does no more than show how little the native's mistrust of questions has changed from that day to this.'

By the time the next serious examination of the ruins took place, in 1958, archaeological knowledge had greatly increased and techniques had improved. Most significant, perhaps, was the development of radiocarbon dating, which now made it possible to determine the age of objects containing organic substances (allowing a certain margin of error). In 1950, for example, radiocarbon dating of two pieces of wood found in a doorway of the Elliptical Building established dates of AD 590 (plus or minus 120 years) and AD 710 (plus or minus 80 years) for the samples. This meant that the building must have been constructed sometime after AD 470; but it did not provide a latest date for its construction. For one thing, the wood – an exceptionally durable species – might have already been used in a previous building.

The 1958 excavation was directed toward establishing a 'ceramic sequence' at Zimbabwe and was conducted by the

Rhodesian Inspector of Monuments, Keith Robinson, and later by a fellow archaeologist Roger Summers. Analysis of organic material found among layers of pottery in the Hill Ruins and the Elliptical Building produced dates ranging from around AD 320 to around AD 1380.

Today, the various theories of an 'ancient' Zimbabwe have been effectively demolished, though they continue to have a romantic appeal for some people. Apart from their assumption of racial superiority, theories that the Phoenicians or the Arabs built Zimbabwe have a more understandable feature of offering a link with the known. Until recently, native African history was passed down from generation to generation by word of mouth – a method by its very nature prone to error. The history of the people who built and lived in Zimbabwe may be just as full of drama as that of the Phoenicians, but we shall probably never know it. Without a written language, the history has been largely lost. Attempts to reconstruct it are like putting together a jigsaw puzzle in which some of the pieces seem to come from different puzzles and some are completely missing. Artefacts, native legends, and the writings of explorers must be assembled and moved around in varying combinations until a recognizable picture emerges. Even then, the picture will contain many gaps.

The first people to live in the area around Zimbabwe were Late Stone Age hunters. The exact date is unknown but they had firmly settled in by the time a new group of people moved into the area in the 3rd or 4th century AD. The newcomers were an Iron Age tribe, who may have been a Bantu-speaking people originally from central Africa. Their migration into the Zimbabwe area was part of a large population movement that took place about this time.

Apparently the Stone Age hunters and the Iron Age peasant farmers managed to live together fairly peacefully. Fragments of pottery produced by the newcomers have been found among Stone Age deposits and Stone Age eggshell ornaments among Iron Age deposits, which may indicate that trade was taking place between the two groups. Most Iron Age sites in southern Africa contain glass beads and seashells, indicating that the people also traded with the people on the coast.

Soon after settling in Rhodesia the Iron Age people discovered gold. Some of the gold lay on the surface and could be obtained easily by panning for it in the rivers; later, having discovered its value in trade, the people began to mine the hills for it. Skeletons of accident victims found in old mine shafts show that the miners were women and girls, whose smaller size enabled them to negotiate the narrow passageways. Some of them have Bushman characteristics, another indication of close contact between the two peoples.

The early farmers and miners did not build Zimbabwe. So far as can be seen they did not build in stone at all but lived in huts made of poles and daga. Their occupation of the site of Zimbabwe seems to have been fairly brief, perhaps a century or less. A Hill Ruins section dug by Keith Robinson in 1958 revealed the existence, above a layer of early Iron Age pottery, of a thick layer of sand and quartz fragments that must have been washed down by rainfall over several centuries.

Sometime around AD 1000 new groups of people moved into the Zimbabwe area. Black and plain pottery, quite unlike the red and decorated pottery of the former inhabitants, and the bones of cattle suddenly make their appearance. Clay models of cattle – an indication that the new people regarded animals highly – have also been found in the Zimbabwe area. Most significant, some of the new people began building in stone. The first of these stone buildings has not yet been identified but among the many ruins remaining in Mashonaland, several have sections of poorly coursed wall similar to those found in parts of Zimbabwe, which suggests that they were built at roughly the same time. Further to the west, the people of what is called the Leopard's Kopje ('hill') culture also-built in stone, but in a different style, consisting mainly of stone terraces, rather than walled enclosures.

The people who built Zimbabwe have not, so far, been positively identified. In *Great Zimbabwe*, Peter Garlake suggests that they may have been the Mbire. According to African tradition the Mbire were the first of the Mashona people, and it was they – again according to tradition – who introduced into Zimbabwe the worship of Mwari, the Mashona supreme god. Some scholars believe that the Mbire arrived at Zimbabwe early in the 14th century. By that time, however, Zimbabwe was already established. Garlake points out that as no 'basic cultural change' can be seen in Zimbabwe's development at this time, it seems likely that the Mbire arrived earlier, perhaps in the 11th century.

In any case, sometime around the late 12th or early 13th century, the community living around Zimbabwe – like other communities in the region – began developing into specialized classes – roughly equivalent to peasant, artisan, and governing elite. The elite were able to command the services of the labour force in the construction of stone buildings. It is possible that the first building took place on the Hill – at any rate the Hill Ruins include the oldest walls remaining in Zimbabwe. One of the enclosures on the Hill contained living quarters, an estimated 14 daga huts. Another enclosure appears to have been used for rituals; it has remains of some platforms and had yielded a number of soapstone monoliths, eight of them carved in the shape of birds. Some experts have suggested that these birds represent dead chiefs who, in the Mashonaland religion, intercede with Mwari on behalf of his worshippers.

The hilltop site had a potential defensive advantage, but this may not have influenced the builders. Few other Mashonaland ruins are built on hills, and the later Zimbabwe buildings lie in the valley. Only the Elliptical Building is large enough to have served as a fortress, and it lacks any of the features common to fortified buildings in other cultures, such as battlements and protected entrances.

The stone buildings of Zimbabwe and of the other sites housed only a small fraction of the total population: the ruling class. Garlake estimates that the enclosures at Zimbabwe may have housed between 100 and 200 adults. Hundreds more would have lived in open daga huts outside. These were the farmers, stonemasons, and other craftsmen who supported the aristocracy.

Building in the valley must have begun around the late 13th and early 14th century. At this time gold production increased, in response to increased demand from the Arab coastal towns and from markets across the Indian Ocean. The expansion of trade brought great affluence to the Arab towns and to Zimbabwe. Its location – near the rich gold deposits of Matabeleland and in a river valley that gave relatively easy access to the coast – facilitated its rise to prominence. Excavations in the Valley Ruins and in the Elliptical Building have produced many luxury objects, including ornaments of gold, copper, and bronze produced by native craftsmen, as well as imported items – glass beads and ceramics. During R. N. Hall's two years of excavating at Zimbabwe he found some £4000 worth of gold objects. The wealth must have been concentrated among the ruling elite, but at least their wealth provided work for the rest of the population. The crafts of spinning and weaving were introduced, probably through contact with the coastal towns. Building techniques were refined.

The construction of the Elliptical Building was begun sometime during the 14th century and finished in the early 15th century, when Zimbabwe's power was at its zenith. A noticeable improvement in building technique can be traced in it. Some of the walls are made of irregular blocks of stone placed with little attempt at coursing; in other places – particularly the Conical Tower and the eastern end of the outer wall – the stones are well matched and placed in regular courses.

The building evidently served as the chief's palace. It is by far the largest of the Rhodesian ruins and clearly indicates the importance of the Zimbabwe ruler. Its most striking feature, the Conical Tower, may symbolise a grain bin – grain being a common form of tribute paid to some African chiefs – and so also symbolise the Zimbabwe ruler's authority over lesser chieftains.

The decline of Zimbabwe set in soon after it had reached the peak of its prosperity. Tradition tells of a salt shortage at the Mbire capital (which we can assume was Zimbabwe) sometime around the mid-15th century. As Garlake points out, such a shortage of an essential part of diet which was extensively traded can be seen 'as symbolic of both a depletion of food supplied and a disruption of trade.' It is possible that the land around Zimbabwe had become exhausted after several centuries of intensive farming. Perhaps there was also some interruption in trade, or a dispute of some kind between Zimbabwe and one of its subject communities. In any case, something more than a shortage of salt would certainly have been required to induce the ruler and his people to leave Zimbabwe – which is what happened.

According to tradition, the Mbire ruler, whose name was Nyatsimba Mutota, sent emissaries north in search of salt. They finally found salt deposits some 300 miles north, in the valley of the Zambezi River. Mutota then moved into this area, conquered its Karanga inhabitants, and established a new seat of government. After this act of conquest Mutoba adopted the title Mwene Mutapa 'Ravager of the Lands' or 'Master Pillager'. From his new capital, in what is called the Dande area, Mutota established new trade routes to the east. He extended his domains to include part of Matabeleland, called Guruhuswa, over which he placed one of his relatives named Changamire. His other southern province, Mbire – which included Zimbabwe – he placed under another relative, Torwa. Part of de Barros' secondhand description of 'Symbaoe' states that some of the Mwene Mutapa's wives lived there, cared for by a court official. However, as Zimbabwe and the new capital were some 300 miles apart, this seems unlikely – unless the wives had outlived their usefulness.

Although Portuguese and Arab accounts of the Mwene Mutapa's capital describe his living in splendour in 'sumptuous apartments', it is unlikely that his buildings were anything like as fine as those at Zimbabwe. No one seems certain exactly where his capital was (though one Portuguese report mentions an unidentifiable place called 'Zunbanhy'); it may be that he moved from one 'zimbabwe' to another. In the Dande area stone was in shorter supply than in the south, and the craft of masonry seems to have suffered a decline under succeeding Mwene Mutapas.

Moreover, the Mwene Mutapas' empire itself was short-lived. They did not have the same monopoly of trade that their predecessors at Zimbabwe had enjoyed. And when the Portuguese began to penetrate the area and set up trading posts in the early 17th century, they could deal directly with the Mwene Mutapa's subjects, which greatly undermined his authority.

Zimbabwe ruins

Sometime in the 16th century, during the reign of the third Mwene Mutapa, both Guruhuswa and Mbire broke away from the empire and became independent states. Because Guruhuswa was a rich gold-producing area, its breakaway was a significant loss to the empire. After this, Mwene Mutapa's power declined and Guruhuswa's power increased. The dominant people in this area were the Rozwi, and their king was called the Mambo. The Rozwi kingdom shared several features with the Mwene Mutapa's empire. They, too, worshiped Mwari, and their Mambo, like the Mwene Mutapa, had priestly functions as well as military and economic ones. In fact, the Rozwi seem to have had some kind of special religious status among the Mashona peoples. The Rozwi also built in stone, and some of the most interesting and decorative of the Rhodesian ruins, such as those at Naletale and Dhlo Dhlo, were built by the Rozwi during the 17th and 18th centuries. Some writers have even suggested that some of the later work at Zimbabwe was done by the Rozwi.

Having conquered Mbire, the Rozwi included Zimbabwe among their domains. Although, according to Garlake, they 'never settled or built' there, they 'seem to have recognized its spiritual pre-eminence and visited it for special ceremonies as long as they were able.' The Mambo, who was specially venerated and kept hidden from the gaze of common people, must have found the great Elliptical Building and the sacred Eastern Enclosure on the hill suitably imposing for his presence.

The Rozwi kingdom came to an end only a few decades before the Europeans finally found Zimbabwe. Hordes of savage Ngoni from Zululand swept through the area during the 1830s. They massacred the Mambo and many of his people, and they sacked Zimbabwe. When Mauch arrived at Zimbabwe in 1871, he found the area inhabited by some Karanga under a chief named Mugabe, who disclaimed any knowledge of the buildings, origin or purpose. However Mauch also found a man who was from a tribe related to the Rozwi. His people, he told Mauch, had kept alive the traditions of Zimbabwe, and his own father, a priest, had conducted sacrifices there. Later, Hall found recent deposits of cattle bones in the Elliptical Building, confirmation that sacrifices had taken place. In 1904, during the period of Hall's excavations, the last sacrifice, of some goats, took place at Zimbabwe in the course of a rainmaking ceremony.

Perhaps the strangest aspect of the whole Zimbabwe story is that at the very time the Portuguese were sending back to Europe stories that ancient Ophir had been found, a few hundred miles away from their settlements a living culture was building more 'zimbabwes'. It would be interesting to know how the Rozwi Mambo or the Mwene Mutapa would have reacted to the news that the invaders were attributing their works to people who lived 2000 years earlier and 3000 miles away. Perhaps with a contemptuous smile.

CHAPTER 14

TRAVELLERS ON THE SILK ROAD

For hundreds of years, two of the greatest empires in the world traded with each other while knowing virtually nothing about their partner. Rome in the west sent vast amounts of gold into Asia and in return received precious Chinese silk. Their mutual ignorance was maintained by the bleak and inhospitable stretch of territory that separated them – few travellers ever survived long enough to travel the Silk Road from end to end. Out of practical necessity, goods were relayed from city to city, passing through the hands dozens of owners before they reached the far end of the caravan route. These people of the Silk Road maintained one of the richest trade routes in the history of the world but, with its decay, their wonderfully mixed culture of east and west swiftly disappeared.

It had once been a quiet country lane, curving between rush fences. Even now rustling dead leaves from the poplar and fruit trees that had once flourished on either side, desiccated by the harsh desert wind, were caught at the foot of the fences. Between the fences the wind had swept parts of the ground clear, so that pieces of charcoal and pottery – debris left by the last inhabitants – were clearly visible. A black and white fox terrier crossed and recrossed the roadway, sniffing with interest. His owner, a small, methodical man, poked curiously with his walking stick at withered tree stumps which had once been peach, apricot, plum, and mulberry trees. Straightening up, he looked around at his surroundings thoughtfully. Once this had been a pleasant rural orchard with ripe fruit hanging among green leaves. But the last of that fruit had been picked 16 centuries before, and during the intervening years the wind and sand of the Taklamakan Desert, in the heart of central Asia, had torn at both the orchard and the big house nearby until only timber posts, rush fences, and shrivelled stumps remained. Sir Aurel Stein, a noted British archaeologist, called to his dog and turned back to the house where his diggers were working. It was then a bitterly cold day in January 1901. The house had been abandoned to the desert sometime around 300 AD.

All around him, heaped in smooth, wind-shaped dunes, lay the yellow sand. Here and there a bleached tree trunk protruded. A mound surmounted by rows of timber posts marked where the house had once stood and indicated what the ground level had been before centuries of erosion wore it down into undulating dunes. It was the sort of desert any schoolchild would visualise, endless sand, endless sun, and a silence broken only by the roar of the buran – the violent windstorm which abruptly sweeps out of nowhere, tormenting the desert traveller with a lacerating rush of flying sand that tears at exposed flesh, blows under clothing, and penetrates the most carefully sealed containers. This was pure, uninhabitable desert. No nomad tribes wandered from well to well across it, because in the heart of the desert there are no wells. Only at the edges, where oases have developed near mountain-fed rivers, can man survive.

The house had been part of such an oasis, known as Niya. Niya had once formed a patch of brilliant green in the yellow sand; it had been a resting and watering spot for the weary traders and travellers of the camel caravans that followed the Silk Road – the trade route that connected China and the West. It was nearly midway between Lop to the east and Khotan to the west on the arm of the road that bypassed the Taklamakan to the south. Documents found in the excavated houses indicated the official business transacted there: payments and requisitions made, labourers listed, orders for safe conduct or arrests issued, and so forth. It must have been a bustling place when the caravans were passing through, heading west laden with bright silks and east-bound carrying jade, wool, and precious stones, but most of all gold – Roman gold to pay for Chinese silk, a continual drain of Roman wealth into Asia. With the noise of the animals, the gabble of voices, and the creaking and groaning of carts, Niya must have been a sharp contrast for the travellers to the enveloping silence of the desert track.

Another arm of the Silk Road skirted the Taklamakan, but to the north. On either route, more than 800 long miles had to be covered by caravans moving slowly from one oasis well to another. The wells carried evocative names such as One Cup Well, where the bitter water accumulated so slowly that the first driver to reach it could water his animals, but the person following him had to wait until more trickled between the stones at the bottom of the well; Gates of Sand, the last well before a long waterless stretch of track; and Inexhaustible Spring Halt, where the traveller could drink long and deeply of fresh, sweet water after eight stages in which only bitter water was available.

All the thousands who over the centuries travelled the desert road had one thing in common: all of them were thirsty. Never was there enough water to satisfy the body's relentless demand for moisture, and what there was frequently was bitter or brackish. Walking or riding, under the glaring hot daytime sun or the freezing cold of night, each traveller knew the feeling of cracked lips and dry throat and found his thoughts during the long marches turning more and more often to water, the feel, the sound, and the shimmering wetness of water.

Enclosing this great desert basin are the most immense mountains on earth. To the south lie the Kunlun Shan range of Tibet, Karakorum, Himalayas (which include Mount Everest), and the Hindu Kush, which converge on the Pamirs, the mountain gateway lying just west of the Taklamakan. To the north are the Tien Shan mountains. Marco Polo called the Pamirs 'the roof of the world', taking that name from the Kirgiz shepherds who fattened their flocks on the remote mountain plateaus. From the Pamirs the road descended following the Oxus River (now called

Amu Darya), bearing ever westward across what we know now as the Southern, Russian Confederated States, Iran, and Iraq, and then split into two branches, one dipping southward toward Egypt, the other crossing through Syria and Turkey to ships sailing for Rome. Few men made the entire trip from the Jade Gate of the Great Wall of China all the way to Rome. The goods travelled in stages, each caravan transferring its cargo to the next at the main stopping places on the road. Each trader took his profit, and thus the price of the silk rapidly escalated. It took a year for silk to reach Rome, and by then its price had been doubled and redoubled several times.

Oddly enough, the man who first opened up the way from China to the West had no particular interest in introducing silk to outsiders. His name was Chang Ch'ien, and he was a military officer during the reign of the Han emperor Wu Ti, who ruled from 141 to 87 BC. The Chinese were then being challenged by the Hsiung-nu (the early Huns), who were menacing China's Great Wall frontier. Wu Ti wanted to develop tribal alliances among the people living west of the Great Wall, so Chang Ch'ien was sent to make contact with the Yueh-Chih, a tribe which had been driven from its traditional homeland on China's north-western border by the Hsiung-nu. Wu Ti hoped they would be willing to return to their original territory under Chinese protection and that together they might crush their common enemy.

Chang Ch'ien set out accompanied by about 100 men, including a Hsiung-nu slave, Kan-fu, who had presumably been captured in a border skirmish. The entire party was seized almost immediately by the Huns, and Chang Ch'ien was forced to remain in their hands for over 10 years. His captivity does not seem to have been overly rigorous: he was given a Hsiung-nu wife, who bore him a son. Finally, a Chinese historian records, when 'he had lived in Hsiung-nu territory for some time and was less closely watched than at first', he managed to escape with his barbarian wife and Kan-fu. They made their way west, encountering other friendly tribes, and at last found the Yüeh-Chih, who had settled in Bactria (now northern Afghanistan).

Chang Ch'ien was greeted with respect, but he quickly discovered that circumstances had changed. The old king had died, and his son found Bactria a rich and fertile place. The Chinese were now too far away to bother about, and the new king had no particular wish to avenge his father's death. He did not intend to return, either. Accepting the failure of his mission, Chang Ch'ien tried to go back by a southerly route, but he was again captured by the Hsiung-nu. This time Chang Ch'ien was able after only a year to slip away with his wife and Kan-fu and return to China. He had been gone for 12 years.

In spite of his failure with the Yueh-Chih, the emperor Wu Ti welcomed him back with honour. Chang Ch'ien was made a palace counsellor, and the former slave Kan-fu was given the title 'Lord Who Carries Out His Mission'. They had returned with unique information about the peoples and unknown territories to the west. Chang Ch'ien had discovered that silk, used within China for more than 2000 years, was highly prized by foreign 'barbarians' – and he had pioneered a trade route. Rulers of the central Asian kingdoms and leaders of nomadic tribes to the west of the Great Wall quickly appreciated that a silk trade would be profitable and therefore worth protecting, and the Silk Road came into existence.

Of course, it was never what we now think of as a road. In most places it was merely a track, barely perceptible except to those who were familiar with the route. But within a few years of Chang Ch'ien's journey, caravans of mules and camels were journeying from northwest China to the West. The silk they brought to Rome became the height of fashion, a symbol of wealth and position, and thus a necessity for aristocratic ladies. Gauzy, semi-transparent silk clothed the nobility, and its suppliers built up thriving businesses. Seneca wrote, 'I see silken clothes that in no degree afford protection either to the body or modesty, of the wearer, and clad in which no woman could honestly swear she is not naked.'

Some goods travelled the other way, but the balance of trade was always in favour of the self-sufficient Chinese, who considered themselves uniquely civilised and did not believe any imports from the barbarians beyond their borders were necessary.

Gold, however, was always useful, so gold from the Roman treasury flowed out to China. So great a drain was the cost of silk on the Roman economy, that official measures were taken to restrict the import of silk along with other expensive and exotic goods. The emperor Marcus Aurelius tried to cut back the increasing Roman addiction to silk by refusing to wear it himself and forbidding his wife to do so, but little came of his gesture of renunciation (or his wife's: all the other noble Roman ladies continued to drape themselves in silken luxury).

In 166 AD, when war with Parthia (now a territory divided between Iran and Iraq) had disrupted the western sections of the road, some Roman merchants succeeded in reaching China by sea in an attempt to bypass both the dangers and the proliferating middlemen of the overland route. But the sea route was hazardous and uncertain, considering the frailty of the vessels, and the pirates of the coasts were as ruthless as the bandits of the interior. The price of silk remained high, and no regular sea trade was established. The Silk Road was still the only practical route to China.

More than luxury goods travelled over the road. Gossip and rumours, idle chatter and extravagant reports of the wonders to be encountered further on, enlivened conversation in the towns and stopping places along the route. Travelling artists and artisans carried with them the styles with which they were familiar, thus producing a rich blend of cultural influences. Ideas travelled the road as well. Buddhism was spreading during the same centuries as the infant religion of Christianity moved outward from Judea. In both the East and West the established order was crumbling. In China the Han empire collapsed, fatally shaken by successive peasant rebellions, and the country disintegrated into a quarrelsome collection of kingdoms whose frontiers constantly shifted. In the West the Roman empire fell into pieces under the onslaught of barbarian invaders from the north.

Both civilisations were open to new ideas. Buddhism spread north and westward from India into Bactria and Parthia and then followed the Silk Road east, through the oasis towns of the desert, into China. There Indian Buddhism was absorbed and made

Chinese. Knowing themselves to be far from the sources of their faith, Chinese Buddhists began to make pilgrimages – even as Christian pilgrims, far to the west, travelled to the holy places of their religion.

The earliest on record is that of the Chinese monk Fa-Hsien, who set out westward in the last year of the 4th century to study Buddhist doctrine in India. Travelling with three companions, he followed the Silk Road as far as Kashgar and left such clear accounts of the towns and monasteries on the way that Sir Aurel Stein was able to use his writings as a guide 1500 years later for locating promising archaeological sites. Then the pilgrims turned southward through the precipitous cliffs and gorges of the region where the massive Kunlun and Himalaya mountain ranges meet. It took them six years to reach central India, and a further six years were spent in study and travel – they went as far as Ceylon (Sri Lanka) – before they returned to China by sea.

The missionaries and pilgrims added another colourful thread to the continually shifting tapestry of the Silk Road. During these centuries, however, the road dwindled in importance. Without the stability of central government, the irrigation canals which sustained some of the towns were allowed to run dry, and without water the settlements quickly reverted to lifeless desert. It was during this period that Niya was abandoned. Wave after wave of nomadic horsemen swept in to raid towns in the territories the road traversed. Frequently the invaders would settle and discover the pleasures of peace and relative prosperity, before being invaded in their turn by the next wave of covetous nomads. During these periods of turmoil and disorder, often lasting for many years, trading centres would be either destroyed by ruthless invaders or abandoned by their inhabitants. But the silk trade was sufficiently valuable to insure that some caravans were always kept moving.

In 540 Justinian – ruler of the eastern half of what had been the Roman empire – made another attempt to stop the drain of Roman gold into China. He fixed the price of silk at a level he considered appropriate. But the Persians, who by then controlled the long length of the Silk Road that stretched westward from the Pamirs and sold the silk directly to the Romans, were not impressed. They simply refused to deal at the Roman figure. Faced with the possibility of being unable to obtain any silk at all, the Romans decided to smuggle the secret of silk cultivation out of China so that they would be able to produce it themselves.

By this time the Western world had some idea of how silk was produced, although even the most knowledgeable were vague about the details. It had not always been so. Pliny, the learned natural historian who lived from 23 to 79 AD, wrote that silk was a pale floss that grew on leaves. Later some had become aware that it was spun by insects, but as late as 380 AD Pliny's theory was still considered generally accurate.

The story of how the secret of silk – and the first silkworms – reached the West has become surrounded by a variety of colourful legends. Procopius, the 6th-century historian, wrote that certain monks who had been living in India came to Justinian and told him that silk was produced by caterpillars. They offered, for a sufficient reward, to go into China and bring back some silkworm eggs. These eggs, once smuggled out to the West, could be hatched by covering them with dung, which produced sufficient heat for incubation. Justinian agreed, and the monks left Byzantium only to reappear after many long months with a supply of eggs. (Another version of the story specifies that they presented him with precisely 550 eggs.) The eggs were duly hatched, the caterpillars were fed on mulberry leaves, they spun their silken cocoons, and silk culture was duly established in Roman territory.

Theophanes, another 6th-century historian living in Byzantium, claimed it was a Persian who smuggled the eggs out of China concealed in a walking stick and brought them safely to Byzantium. When Sir Aurel Stein was excavating at Khotan, one of the oasis towns on the arm of the Silk Road bypassing the Taklamakan to the south, he uncovered a painted tablet showing a Chinese princess. According to some sources she was the first to smuggle silkworm eggs out of China and established a silk production centre at Khotan itself – and the town was indeed a silk centre from the 6th century onward. On the tablet one of her attendants points to the diadem worn by the noble lady, under which the eggs were concealed.

But whoever it was – monk, Persian, or princess – it seems certain that the Chinese monopoly was broken during the 6th century and with it much of the power of the kingdoms along the Silk Road. They became progressively less able to pay for protection for the traders, and inevitably the rapacious nomad tribes, their subsidies dwindling, turned to plunder. The Turks threatened the eastern provinces of Byzantium as well as southern Russia; the Arabs, new masters of the Middle East, created a wedge between East and West, becoming familiar with both, while cutting off China and what had been Rome from further contact with or knowledge of each other.

In China, however, the long years of disunity and internecine warfare were drawing to a close. When the T'ang dynasty began in 618, a young Buddhist monk named Hsüan-Tsang was studying in a monastery at Sian, the Chinese city at the end of the Silk Road. He was only 15 years old but was already recognized by his fellow monks as wise and learned far beyond his years. Disturbed by constant disputes on matters of theology, Hsüan-Tsang conceived the bold plan of going to India – he would bring back a library of sacred books and first-hand interpretations of the points most under discussion at the time. He sent a petition to the newly installed emperor asking to leave China by the northwest frontier, but permission was denied: central Asia was still in a state of turmoil. Hsüan-Tsang was determined to begin his pilgrimage nonetheless.

Until he left Lanchow on the Silk Road to Sinkiang, Hsüan-Tsang was disobeying no order, but from that point on he had to travel secretly. His journey demanded great physical courage and spiritual dedication, for it was quite possible that both the journey and his life would be ended at any moment by murderous bandits, false guides, or the terrifying natural hazards of desert and mountains. Abandoned by one guide, he found his own way by following the tracks of camels and other pack animals which were faintly discernible in the yellow sand. At one point he stumbled along for five long days without water. At another, totally lost, he could only attempt to orient himself by the line of his own shadow.

At long last he reached Turfan, then a powerful city on the northern arm of the old Silk Road, where the ruler greeted him respectfully and supplied him with an escort of men to accompany him on the next stage of his journey. He continued through Kucha, the next main trading centre, to the ice-bound Tien Shan mountains north of the Pamirs. His crossing of the mountain range was fraught with hardship, and thirteen of his men perished. He then reached the Great Khan of the western Turks, who arranged for his onward journey to Gandhara, an ancient region of India whose main city is now Peshawar in Pakistan and which was then a great centre of Buddhist worship and learning. Even then the Journey was not easy. He crossed the Oxus into Bactria, came through the Khyber Pass, and then crossed the gorges of the Indus, using rope bridges that swung sickeningly over chasms and roads that clung to the very edges of precipices.

Eventually he reached India, where he travelled around gradually assembling the books which were to become the foundation of authoritative Buddhist teaching in China. When at length he was ready to return to his home monastery he went by way of the Pamirs and Kashgar. His former protector, the ruler of Turfan, was by this time dead, so he took the southern arm of the Silk Road around the Taklamakan. Again he found royal support: the king of Khotan came out to meet him and escort him into his city. Beyond Khotan the passage across the desert was a frightening experience – Hsüan-Tsang wrote feelingly of 'drifting sand without water or vegetation, burning hot and the haunt of poisonous fiends and imps.'

In spite of his obvious disobedience – which by this time was 16 years in the past – the emperor gave him an honourable reception at court when he reached China. When he asked the monk about that long-ago defiance, Hsüan-Tsang replied tactfully, 'I did indeed request your gracious permit three times over, but, receiving no favourable answer and knowing myself to be so insignificant a subject, I could not suppose that you even knew of my request.' The emperor graciously accepted this elegant evasion, and Hsüan-Tsang retired to his monastery. There he revised and enlarged the record of his long years of pilgrimage, which also saw the decline of the Silk Road. He wrote of abandoned towns and deserted temples and provided clear descriptions of the still-powerful cities and their rulers along the route. He had made careful note of the estimated distances between towns and stopping places; he reported the weather, the names and sizes of settlements, and the customs, clothing, and character of the people he encountered. Much of what he wrote was overlaid with superstition and fable, but the factual basis was sound, and the work of Hsüan-Tsang remains an eerily accurate guide to the geography of central Asia and an invaluable record of the life, politics, industries, and religion of its people.

The 9th and 10th centuries marked the decline and dissolution of the T'ang dynasty, which ended in a welter of blood. China was not reunified until 50 years later, in 960 AD, under the Sung dynasty. Weaker than the T'ang had been, the Sung was under continual attack from barbarians. Her wealth and civilisation were a rich lure to the nomadic tribes of the sparse, ill-watered grasslands of the Gobi desert. The northern provinces had already fallen: in 937 the Kitan tribes took northern China, founded the Liao dynasty, and gave their name, anglicised as Cathay, to the country. They were succeeded by the Juchen of Manchuria, who established the Chin dynasty which ruled northern China from 1125 while the Sung controlled the south. This pattern might have continued for centuries but for the birth around 1162 of one of the most influential men in human history: a Mongol chieftain's son who grew up to become the ruthless and barbarous conqueror, Genghis Khan.

Genghis Khan was a military and political genius, and Asia and the eastern reaches of Europe literally ran red with the blood spilled by his ravaging horsemen. He welded together the scattered tribes of Mongol nomads into a massive, invincible army and then flung that army at the world. His first victim was the unfortunate Chin dynasty – by 1215 most of the Chin cities were under Mongol control. He turned west when a Muslim sultan in Persia committed the fatal error of murdering several hundred

Mongol merchants who had travelled along the Silk Road to trade. At Herat in present-day Afghanistan, only one of the hundreds of cities devastated, the vengeful warriors with Genghis Khan at their head carried on their looting and destruction for a full week, and when they swept west to further conquest, 1.5 million corpses lay rotting in the ruins behind them.

By the time Genghis Khan died in 1227 his forces had overwhelmed the Muslim states of central Asia and were ravaging Russia. His successors penetrated as far west as modern East Germany, Czechoslovakia, and Yugoslavia – and they only stopped there when a dispute arose over the succession upon the death in 1241 of Ogotai Khan, the son and heir of Genghis. The Mongol horsemen had proved themselves invincible against the weak and divided Europe of the early Middle Ages.

Cut off from the East by the Arab presence, Europe had had no inkling of the Mongols' spectacular rise to power until, as if by sorcery, the terrible hordes appeared on its eastern flank. Then, when total destruction appeared imminent, their progress (equally inexplicably) was halted and the threat withdrawn. Christian Europeans, still largely ignorant of the danger they had so narrowly escaped, made a few attempts to learn something about the Mongols from missionary envoys. One interesting fact very soon became obvious – the Mongols favoured trade more strongly than most Chinese dynasties – so the old trading routes began to be revived.

The devastation of the Mongol invasion had been appalling, but in its wake came the advantages of central control by a strong power. The cities along the old Silk Road once again sheltered and supplied caravans moving between East and West. The Chinese no longer held a monopoly on silk production, but their silks were still exquisite and greatly in demand in the West. With the silk came porcelain, spices, and precious jewels. In return the Chinese wanted Western glass, dyes, lead, and woollens. The oasis towns along the edge of the Taklamakan desert stirred back into life, military posts were re-established to protect travelling merchants, and regular police patrols controlled the activities of bandits. In the more fertile areas trees were planted along the roads so that people could find their way more easily. It was during this period that the saying arose that it was safe for a maiden to walk the roads with a golden tray on her head.

Given this promising state of affairs, it is hardly surprising that two Venetian merchants, Nicolò and Maffeo Polo, set out eastward in 1260. They did not begin with the precise intention of reaching Cathay: they had spent several years trading in Constantinople and when unrest threatened they had moved further east in stages, fully intending to return to Venice as soon as it was safe to do so. They had gone as far as Bokhara when they received an amazing invitation from the Great Khan himself – Kublai Khan, who was then lord of all the Mongols but had taken the eastern section of his vast empire to rule himself. Kublai Khan, having heard of the presence in Bokhara of two men from the far west who by then had mastered the Mongol language, invited the Polos to come to his capital.

The Venetians were not slow to grasp the opportunity. They reached the court of Kublai Khan in 1266, travelling in relative comfort along the northern arm of the old Silk Road. They were greeted with courtesy and graciousness, and the khan questioned them closely about the West's political organisation and religion. Clearly interested by their replies, Kublai Khan decided with the approval of his nobles, to use the Polo brothers to take a letter to the Pope requesting him to send 100 learned men to present the case for Christianity to Kublai's court and his people. He supplied the brothers with the Mongol equivalent of a passport for their journey – a golden tablet bearing his seal, which declared that the bearers were his personal envoys.

Even protected by the golden tablet it took them three years to reach Venice. When they arrived there in 1269, they discovered that the Pope had recently died and his successor had not yet been elected. They waited for two years, but still no choice had been made. Fearful of waiting longer lest the Great Khan be displeased with them, the Polo brothers decided to set off regardless – but this time they took with them Nicolo's young son Marco. Born after his father's first departure from Venice, Marco was then 17 years old.

The three Polos went first to Acre in what is now Israel, then the gateway port to the East. There they discussed their problem with the resident papal legate, who sympathised but was unable to do much officially. After the Polos had set out on their way eastward the legate himself was elected pope and became Gregory X, and he called the Polos back and gave them letters and gifts for the Great Khan. The learned men requested by Kublai seem to have been in short supply, because Gregory sent only two, and those two may have been learned but they were certainly not brave. At the first rumour of danger they handed over to the Polos all their privileges, papers, and letters and fled back to Acre.

The Polos continued, carrying with them the golden tablet of the Great Khan. They apparently passed through what is now Turkey and then worked their way down to Hormuz on the Persian Gulf with the idea of continuing their journey by sea. After one look at the flimsy, unseaworthy boats in which they would have had to travel, they changed their minds and returned northward through what is now Iran to the Pamirs. Marco Polo believed these mountains to be the highest in the world, and he remarked with wonder that fire did not burn so brightly there, nor did food cook as easily.

From there they followed the familiar trail of the Silk Road through Kashgar, Yarkand (where Marco Polo noticed the prevalence of the condition of goiter, which he suggested was due to the quality of the drinking water), Khotan, Lop (Niya, between them, had long since been covered by sand), and the sparse oases and wells along the edge of the desert. Their caravan, like so many others, inched along the yellow dunes continually watching for signs of water and never finding enough. Indeed, Marco Polo was told that it was unwise to travel with more than 50 people as there was not sufficient water to supply a larger group. At last the Polos and their caravan reached the end of their journey across the plains, mountains, and deserts of Asia – the summer palace of the Great Khan. It had taken three and a half years.

Marco Polo found great favour with Kublai Khan, and the three Polos spent the next 17 years with him. Marco became a trusted civil servant and travelled widely throughout the empire. He covered greater distances and saw more of the world than any European had ever done. At last an opportunity arose for them to return to the West and the three Polos went home, by sea this time, accompanying a Mongol princess who was to be married to a Persian khan. At Hormuz the princess was duly handed over, and the Polos then made their way overland by way of Constantinople to Venice, to family and friends, to fame, and to disbelief.

It was Marco Polo's account of the geography and wonders of the East – as told to a writer in a Genoese prison where both were incarcerated years later – which brought to European attention the existence of a fabulously rich and sophisticated society, a spectacular Cathay hitherto the subject only of vague rumours. So unprecedented was his report that for many it was literally unbelievable. Marco Polo became known as *Il Milione* – the teller of a million tall tales. It took the passage of centuries and the reports of countless others to establish that most of what he reported was absolutely true. He always insisted that he did not write half of what he saw.

What the Polos had no way of knowing was that what they had seen was the brilliant high noon of the Mongol empire. The empire lasted less than a century, and the Ming dynasty which overthrew it was anti-foreign. The trade routes again became the prey of raiding bandits. Merchants and pilgrims could no longer travel in safety, and trade with the Far East faltered and died. In the West ordinary people forgot Marco Polo and the world he had revealed, while princes and navigators tried to find a new route to the riches of Cathay. Ship design was slowly improved, navigation far from shore developed into more of a science and less of a guess, and captains and pilots began to creep down the coast of Africa and then – daringly – westward into the uncharted ocean searching for a sea route to Asia.

Lying forgotten behind their ring of mountains were the cities which had for so long seen the riches of East and West carried past by the slow-moving caravans. Little by little the desert reclaimed them, until in the end there were only small, ragged villages where great cities ruled by great kings had been. The road itself carried only local trade. Finally, after many centuries, came the archaeologist Sir Aurel Stein, who poked with his stick and carefully uncovered traces of the bustling world that had once existed where only silent sand dunes lay.

Over the centuries since Chang Ch'ien first pioneered the route, the fortunes of the old Silk Road have waxed and waned. Stein reported with satisfaction in 1906 that some parts of the route Hsüan-Tsang and Marco Polo had followed were gradually being opened up again, and traders were passing through yearly. During World War II parts of the northern arm of the road were paved in order to transport munitions from the Siberian railhead. The ancient road was still the most direct route.

The old Silk Road and its merchants belong to the past. East-West encounters now take place in different settings, different places. Only tattered relics remain: in an ancient burial ground in the Lop salt desert, stretching east from the Taklamakan, Stein found scraps of fabric. Pieces of brightly coloured patterned silk lay beside fragments of exquisitely worked wool tapestries in the Greek style. For all those centuries these bits of East and West have lain in the forgotten desert side by side, silent witnesses to the mingling of cultures that once took place along the old Silk Road.

CHAPTER 15

THE INACCESSIBLE LAND

We tend to think of lost civilisations as being buried in the distant past. It seems odd to consider one that has been engulfed during the twentieth century. The isolated nation of Tibet has long been sheltered from destruction by its surrounding wall of Himalayan mountains. Now, following the Red Chinese occupation, the Tibetan culture is being systematically eradicated. The mountains have been defor-ested regardless of ecologic cost, while the cities have been filled with Chinese colonists. On the other hand, it could be argued that the Chinese have transported Tibet into the twentieth century although at the cost of the destruction of a unique way of life.

The Dalai Lama was dead. Monks searching for his new incarna-tion fanned out over the countryside and discreetly consulted with local oracles both within and beyond the political boundaries of Tibet itself. In accordance with tradition a regent was assigned to rule until the new Dalai Lama (priest-king) had reached his majority. The regent went to the mystical lake of Lhamo Latso, two or three days' journey southeast of the capital city of Lhasa. The first Dalai Lama was said to have had a vision in which he was told that his patron goddess, the guardian of this sacred lake, would always watch over his successors. So now this particular regent travelled through the mountains to the lake far above the tree line, where the barren ground slopes down to the water's edge and only an occasional boulder breaks through the delicate dusting of snow. On reaching the lake the regent sat and quietly stared into its clear depths, waiting. Deep beneath the surface was a kind of shimmering. It cleared, and on the surface of the water a reflection appeared. It was not a reflection of the mountain peaks surrounding Lhamo Latso – instead it was a typical landscape of eastern Tibet near the Chinese border. The waters shimmered again and, when they cleared, a picture formed of a typical peasant homestead with a stone wall around it. The wall was broken by a gate which led into an inner courtyard, and in the courtyard was a mottled brown and white dog.

On his return to Lhasa the regent was unsurprised to hear that one of the search parties, headed by a revered abbot, had found the reincarnated Dalai Lama in eastern Tibet, at a homestead surrounded by a stone wall and guarded by a brown and white dog. The little boy was only four years old but had instantly recognised the abbot, who was disguised as a servant. The boy had surprised everyone – not least his family – by proving himself knowledgeable in the official court language, which nobody in his remote village had ever heard before. The child was shown two sets of prayer beads, one of which had belonged to the previous Dalai Lama. He immediately snatched at that set, claiming that it was his and asking how the abbot had acquired it.

The signs and omens all seemed favorable; the child seemed quick and bright. But other candidates had also been produced by other teams of searchers, and in a matter of such importance no chances could be taken. A lottery, consecrated by a special ceremony, was held in which a number of names were carefully entered on fluttering pieces of paper. When one was drawn it bore the name of the four-year-old child from Tsinghai province, China.

This was in 1939. He was enthroned in 1940, but 20 years later Bstan-'dzin-rgya-mtsho took off his splendid robes, left his gold-encrusted private apartments, and, disguised as a simple monk, escaped from Lhasa and the ruling Chinese Communist forces across the border into India. There he has remained ever since with a group of followers, waiting to return to his people and his native land.

Tibet has always been a mysterious and hidden land – perhaps never more so than today, when it is firmly included within Chinese territorial boundaries, and the mountain passes are efficiently guarded by Chinese military units who permit no traffic except with China itself. Tibet's first line of defence against a predatory world has always been geographic. The narrow river valleys which shelter nearly all its people, lie within a formidable circle of mountains. The Himalaya range curves around to the south (Mount Everest itself is on the Tibetan-Nepalese border), and the Kunlun range guards the north. Just south of the Kunlun mountains is a high, rocky plain called Chang Thang, which accounts for nearly half the area of Tibet. But Chang Thang is barren, with virtually no rain or snow, and it is inhabited only by scattered nomadic herdsmen who move their flocks of sheep from one sparse grazing area to another. Between Chang Thang and the long lowland valleys of southern Tibet lie still more mountains. The first Tibetans settled in the protected valleys that slope down to the Tsangpo river. They were probably nomadic people from central Asia who over the centuries made their way through the high mountain passes.

In about the 5th century AD the small local groups were united by a single dynamic chief, Songtsen Gampo, who is generally considered the first Tibetan king. A man of varied and unexpected talents, Songtsen Gampo managed to extend Tibetan influence northeast toward China. Alarmed, the Chinese sent him an ambassador, of whom Songtsen Gampo demanded a Chinese princess as a wife. When the Chinese refused he led his armies to the very frontiers of what was then China, past the brackish lake Koko Nor and toward the Great Wall itself. The Chinese emperor capitulated and a princess, Wen Cheng, was dispatched to Tibet.

Wen Cheng brought more than prestige to the Tibetan court. She was a Buddhist, and she brought with her to Lhasa her priests and teachers and an enormous statue of the Buddha made of a mysterious alloy of gold, silver, and bronze which was said to have been miraculously created. (It is still in Tibet, in the temple built to honour the princess' arrival.) Buddhism had already reached Tibet from India, but strengthened by Wen Cheng and another Buddhist royal wife, a Nepalese princess, it began to have a noticeable impact on the traditional Tibetan shamanistic faith known as Bon. Over the centuries imported Buddhism and indigenous Bon formed a singular amalgam to produce the distinctive Tibetan Buddhism sometimes called Lamaism.

In Tibet, Buddhism was securely rooted in royal patronage; in Europe Christianity was similarly propagated and firmly established by emperors who were converted to the faith. Between the 10th and the 15th centuries social and cultural developments in Tibet and Europe were broadly similar: in both, the hierarchy of the church played a pervasive role in secular affairs, and religion shaped the everyday life of ordinary people. But in Europe the 15th century saw the beginnings of the Renaissance and the regeneration of knowledge in practically every sphere of human activity. There was no Renaissance in Tibet. The best way to minimise the intrusion of Tibet's more powerful neighbours was to remain aloof; the best way to remain distinctively Tibetan was to remain a backwater. Locked behind formidable mountains Tibet chose to go its own way.

Life centred around the monasteries. Much of the arable land was owned by the communities of monks (although it was actually farmed by their tenants), and roughly a fifth of the population were attached to monasteries. A huge gulf separated the nobility, which provided the civil service, and the peasants. Every lay official had a monastic counterpart. The most powerful monasteries – those with great houses, vast lands, and traditional prerogatives – wielded enormous influence. Most were ruled by abbots who were often believed to be incarnate lamas descended from the original founders of the monasteries.

This concept was based on the Buddhist belief that for a monk the highest ideal is to achieve the possibility of permanent release from life's sufferings (roughly the state called Nirvana) and then to renounce it in order to return to life for the benefit of others. Sometimes this return becomes a regular and recognizable series of rebirths in human form, as for the Dalai Lama. The abbot of an ordinary monastery, however, is considered to be a lesser level of incarnation. The Dalai Lama is believed to be a living incarnation of Buddha in his aspect of Changchub Sempa, the patron deity of Tibet. The present Dalai Lama is the fourteenth: the first Dalai Lama to be recognized as such was Bsod-nams-rgya-mtsho, the third hierarch of the Yellow Hat sect, who lived in the 16th century. His two predecessors were then also retrospectively declared to have been the Dalai Lama.

By the time of the third Dalai Lama the balance of power in Tibet had shifted decisively from the monarchy toward the great monastic establishments. Political events had aided this development: the Tibetans had escaped the terrible ravages of the hordes of Genghis Khan during his westward march by meeting his representatives at their border and there accepting Mongol overlordship. In return, the Buddhist Mongols accepted Tibetan lamas as their religious teachers, evolving a patron/priest relationship which strengthened the power of the lamas at home as well.

It was about the time of the third Dalai Lama that stories of a strange land locked country behind the mountains began to drift down to the Portuguese Jesuit missionaries, then busy establishing the first Christian outposts in India and China. For centuries a series of rumours had gone around Europe of a Christian king – Prester John – who was supposed to rule a fabulously wealthy Christian kingdom somewhere in the East. In fact, when the first reports of the Mongol advance across Asia reached Christendom, some hoped that the Mongols might in fact be the forces of Prester John, waging a holy war against Islam. When it became painfully clear that the Mongols did not intend to spare the eastern Christian lands any more than they had the lands of the unbelievers, such optimism was regretfully abandoned, but the idea of a hidden Christian kingdom persisted. Therefore, when the Jesuits in India heard of this place called Tibet, where priests wore black robes, never married, and performed rites which sounded very similar to baptism, confession, and communion, the Europeans were tantalised by the idea that behind those mountains might be the lost Christian colony.

The most determined was Antonio de Andrade, a Portuguese priest who was working in northern India in the early 1620s. When he encountered a Hindu pilgrim caravan in Delhi about to depart for a holy shrine near the Tibetan border, Andrade disguised himself as a Hindu and, with a similarly disguised lay brother, Manuel Marques, joined the pilgrims. It was an arduous journey, and the difficulties increased as they moved higher into the mountains. The caravan crept up a narrow path which sometimes became a mere ledge only inches wide, when they were forced to cling to the edge of a cliff hundreds of feet above a roaring river.

When they reached the Hindu shrine the two Jesuits paused only long enough to observe the sacred hot springs. While the rest of the pilgrim caravan worshipped, the Jesuits pressed on to the Tibetan border. Travelling without the protection of a caravan, tormented by snow-blindness and cold so bitter that Andrade lost part of one finger and only discovered it when he noticed the stump bleeding profusely, they finally crossed the Mana Pass into Tibet. They were the first Europeans to reach the hidden land.

They found themselves in the small Tibetan state of Guge, in the town of Tsaparang, far to the west of Lhasa. Although Andrade was disappointed in his hopes of discovering fellow Christians – he described the local lamas as 'souls bred in laziness' – he found the local ruler surprisingly receptive to his message. Although the Jesuits had to return to India almost immediately before the pass was closed by autumn snows, Andrade promised to return the next year. A local war delayed him, though, and it was not until 1624 that Andrade was able to reach Tsaparang again, where he opened a mission. The ruler himself paid for a permanent church a year later, which was built next to his palace for 'the lamas of the West'.

The mission thrived for several years, but shortly after Andrade left in 1630, to become Jesuit superior at Goa, the local lamas overthrew the impressionable ruler, sacked the church, virtually imprisoned the Jesuits in residence, and sold their converts into slavery. When Andrade heard of the catastrophe he dispatched another priest to Tsaparang, but, although he was successful in winning the release of the Christian slaves, the local people were too frightened of the lamas to respond to the remaining missionaries. The Tsaparang mission was abandoned altogether in 1635.

It was nearly 30 years before other Europeans reached Tibet, and when they did they came from China. By the 1650s Dutch merchants had broken the previous Portuguese monopoly on trade with Asia, and the sea routes to China had become increasingly hazardous for Portuguese ships. Faced with the problem of maintaining contact with their headquarters in Rome, in 1661 the Jesuit mission in Peking sent two young priests to discover an overland route to Europe. Although both John Grueber, an Austrian, and Albert d'Orville, a Belgian, were trained geographers, like all Europeans they knew very little about central Asia. It seemed that a route through Tibet to India might shorten a journey known to be long and dangerous, and so after leaving China by way of Hsi-ning, a frontier city on the Great Wall, they turned southwest toward Tibet. Beyond the Wall was the desert; beyond that, mountains and high barren plains; and beyond that, towering mountain ranges guarded Tibet itself. It took them three months of continuous travel – long days of riding, long nights of fitful sleep, during which they were always watching for the bandits who might sweep down upon a caravan – to reach Lhasa.

Their most striking initial impression was of the improbable Potala hill, which rises abruptly at the edge of Lhasa and is crowned by an enormous palace, the residence of the Dalai Lama. The palace was newly built when Grueber and d'Orville reached Lhasa. It was the work of a remarkable individual, the fifth Dalai Lama, who is still known to his people as the Great Fifth. In secular matters he was a skilled military leader and politician who completed the final unification of all the small states of Tibet under a single government and then managed to thread his way through both Mongol and Chinese political manoeuvers to emerge successfully as the sole secular ruler of an independent Tibet. As a religious leader he was no less overwhelming. He reorganised monastic life so that his own reform Yellow Hat sect was clearly in the ascendant, although the traditionalist Red Hats continued to follow their beliefs unmolested, and he centralised the control of both religious and secular life under his own leadership. Wishing to honour his tutor, the fifth Dalai Lama declared him an incarnate lama as well and ordained him Panchen Lama. His seat was at Shigatset and his position was second only to that of the Dalai Lama himself. From that time onward, when the Panchen Lama died, a search was instigated to find his new incarnation in the same way as for the successor to the Dalai Lama. One of the two hierarchs would always perform the initiation for the other.

When Grueber and d'Orville reached Lhasa, Tibet was basking in power, security, and new-found internal unity. The Jesuits were fascinated, if often appalled, by Tibetan life. They found the obeisance shown to the Dalai Lama particularly shocking: such reverence, they felt, was due only to the Catholic pope. Like other visitors through the centuries, they remarked on the brilliance of the courtiers and the lack of personal cleanliness of ordinary Tibetans, a characteristic which has been explained as an adaptation to the high altitude, where ultraviolet rays attack skin not protected by a rich layer of natural oils and accompanying grime. Whatever the reason, both the grubbiness and the pervasive aroma of yak butter have often been noted. Grueber and d'Orville were, however, greatly impressed by the richness of the Potala. Like their Jesuit predecessors, they were struck by the similarities between Christianity and Tibetan Buddhism, but unlike Andrade they did not linger to establish a mission. Their duty was to find an overland route to Europe, and after a short rest stay they continued south to Nepal. In 1662 at Agra, in India, d'Orville died, exhausted by his travels. Grueber pressed on, and he finally did reach Rome.

Their route was clearly too difficult to be used regularly, though, and no other missionaries followed in their footsteps through Lhasa. But the Jesuits in Goa still cherished the dream of a permanent mission there, and in 1715, over 50 years after Grueber and d'Orville's visit, another pair of missionaries set out northward from Delhi to the mountain ramparts of Tibet.

Their names were Emanuel Freyre and Ippolito Desideri, and they were an ill-matched pair. Freyre, a Portuguese Jesuit in his late 50s, was crotchety, sour, and less than enthusiastic about leaving his work of 20 years in the Indian plains. His companion was a young Italian priest, 30 years of age, who volunteered for the mission while still in Europe. Although Freyre was the elder and nominal leader, Desideri was clearly the driving force.

Desideri had come out to India specifically for his Tibetan mission, and he joined Freyre in Delhi. Rather than follow Andrade's gruelling route, they decided to enter Tibet by way of Kashmir, a longer but somewhat easier approach. Even so, Desideri compared their climb through the mountains to a march up 'staircases piled one on top of another', made of ice 'resembling marble in hardness.' Freyre seems to have been timid by nature, and he viewed most of their hardships as personal affronts. No sooner had they reached Leh in Ladakh (now a district of Kashmir but then considered part of Tibet itself), where Desideri had intended to set up the first mission, than Freyre insisted that he would return to India even if he had to go alone. Rather than return the way they had come, Freyre proposed to find an alternative route through eastern Tibet. Unwilling to let his elderly companion struggle back on his own, Desideri reluctantly left Leh with him.

The two made their way with considerable difficulty to the edge of the barren Chang Thang plain. There they were able to join a caravan bound for Lhasa – the captain of which was a charming Mongol princess. She was the first aspect of Tibet that old Freyre approved of, and his report of the journey is full of her kindness. She even saved his life. Freyre, apparently travelling at the back of the caravan, discovered that his horse was dying from the altitude and looked up to find himself alone in the bitterly cold darkness. The princess (alerted by Desideri, who had belatedly realised his companion had fallen behind) sent riders back to search for him. They found him huddled for warmth next to the belly of his dead horse, weak from exposure but vigorously indignant. The old priest was bundled up and brought to the camp where the solicitous princess nursed his weary body and soothed his aggrieved spirit. Shortly afterward the caravan entered Lhasa, and within a few days Freyre, after a dour look around, left for Nepal on his way back to India. Desideri cannot have regretted seeing him go.

Desideri himself was fascinated with Lhasa. After Freyre left he was the only European in the city – a Capuchin mission had been established in 1708, but the friars had been withdrawn four years later. He found the political situation in Tibet very complicated. The Great Fifth Dalai Lama had died, but his grand vizier (suspected to be his bastard son) had managed to hide the fact of his death for several years. The search for the sixth Dalai Lama therefore did not begin until nine years after his presumed birth, and the boy was not finally identified until he was at least 12 years old. Whether because of his late entry into monastic discipline or because he was simply unsuitable, the sixth Dalai Lama did not work out as expected, and he was never ordained a monk. A poet of considerable gifts, his most notable and spectacular characteristic was his love of women. Before the coming of the Chinese in 1951, some brothels in Lhasa were still painted yellow in proud memory of the time when the sixth Dalai Lama had visited them himself.

In spite of his unorthodox behaviour he was loved by his people – he is still spoken of as the 'Merry One' – but the long gap between the death of the Great Fifth and the sixth's assumption of power had permitted a Mongol prince, Latsang, to install himself as king and assume secular supremacy with the backing of the Chinese Manchu emperor. The Yellow Hats resented the king's power, and in this situation the king found the popularity of the 'Merry Sixth' a thorn in his side.

What happened next, like so much in Tibet, is ambiguous and subject to several interpretations. Latsang apparently sent the Merry Sixth on a journey to China and arranged that an assassination would be attempted at Litang, just short of the Chinese border. On the other hand, some Tibetans believe the sixth Dalai Lama simply chose to disappear at Litang and spent the rest of his life as a holy beggar. In any case, Latsang declared him dead and – without following any of the traditional rules for finding a new incarnation – boldly produced a 25-year-old monk as the new Dalai Lama, a 'true sixth' to replace the dissolute pretender. The enraged Tibetans (particularly the Yellow Hat lamas) adamantly refused to accept his candidate and, using their usual methods, discovered a new incarnation, a seventh Dalai Lama, near Litang itself. Latsang countered this move by having the Chinese kidnap the child and take him into China.

It was at this point that Desideri arrived in Lhasa. Obviously more used to kings than Dalai Lamas, Desideri was impressed by Latsang, who listened to his message sympathetically and granted him permission to establish a mission. The priest had high hopes that Latsang himself would accept Christianity, and he learned Tibetan so that he could produce a long treatise which he hoped would convert the king. The king read it and then made a proposition: Desideri would take part in a public debate with leading lamas in which Christianity and Buddhism could be publicly compared. To prepare for this, he suggested, Desideri should enter a Tibetan monastery and learn the dogma and traditions of his opponents. Desideri eagerly accepted.

The proposition was made primarily for diplomatic purposes. Latsang had other, more pressing problems, and whereas he felt it unwise to offend a foreigner of unknown influence, he was not particularly concerned about religious debate. His Yellow Hat opponents had sought outside aid from the Dzungar Mongols, who lived in the northern part of what is now Sinkiang province in China. While Desideri watched, fascinated but helpless, from his monastery, the Mongols, supported by many Tibetan monks, stormed through the mountain ramparts at Lhasa, where they seized the Potala and killed Latsang before he could escape from the city.

When the Yellow Hats and their Mongol allies had triumphed an unpleasant interval followed, during which the Mongols looted Lhasa and the Yellow Hats fell upon their Red Hat rivals. Desideri, associated with the former king, was in considerable danger and fled to a monastery several days' journey from the capital. Meanwhile the Chinese, disinclined to accept calmly an extension of Mongol power which might contribute to a unification of the Mongols – and thus a direct threat to China itself – took a hand. Before his death Latsang had appealed to the Chinese emperor for aid, who dispatched an army. But bad logistical planning and the rigours of the desert crossing broke the strength of the Chinese forces, and the survivors were encircled and massacred by the Mongols. The emperor promptly sent a much larger force to avenge the first, and in the vanguard was the young seventh Dalai Lama, included in order to convince the Tibetan people that the Chinese wanted to restore the old order and drive out the alien Mongols.

As the Chinese advanced, orders were given under the name of the Dalai Lama that all Tibetan men over the age of 12 should join the invading force (even Desideri in his monastery was drafted, but he was exempted at the last moment). After four days of battle with the ferocious Mongols, who were unable to retreat but scorned surrender, the Chinese were triumphant. As promised, the Dalai Lama was restored to his throne and the alien Mongols were evicted – but in their place were installed two Chinese *ambans*, or political residents, who were to remain in Lhasa, backed by a permanent Chinese military garrison, to protect the emperor's interests.

Desideri himself was unable to stay in Tibet. In Rome the Tibetan mission was assigned to the Capuchin order, which claimed priority on the basis of its previous mission. In 1721 Desideri reluctantly left for India, and the Capuchins re-established their mission. It was tolerated for 20 years by the suspicious lamas (and even more wary Chinese) for the medical work they performed, but increasing hostility forced the dwindling mission to close in 1745. For Europeans, the door to mysterious Tibet swung firmly shut.

Before Manchu authority had been established in Lhasa, Tibet's mysteries had been protected by her inaccessibility: if an enterprising foreigner succeeded in conquering her guardian mountains – as did Andrade and the others – he was greeted with courtesy and polite interest. Now Tibet's isolation became a matter of policy. Below on the plains of India, first the Portuguese and then the British were making their influence strongly felt. The Chinese, wary of any encroachment on their territory, saw the Himalayan mountains of Tibet as the outermost ring of their own defence, which they were unlikely to open to any interloper. Under normal circumstances the Chinese ambans did not intervene in Tibetan affairs, but implicit in their presence was the threat of Manchu power, and any dealings with foreigners immediately attracted their suspicious attention.

This the British discovered when, in 1774, the East India Company sent a young Scot named George Bogle to Tibet to investigate the possibility of opening trade. By the time of Bogle's visit the seventh Dalai Lama had died, and since his successor chose to lead a contemplative life, all administrative power was left to his regent (under the watchful eyes of the ambans). Most of Bogle's dealings, therefore, were with the sixth Panchen Lama, who was a vigorous person with sufficient autonomy to deal directly with Bogle up to a point. The Panchen Lama himself apparently favoured trade, or at least some contact with the British, but his freedom of action was circumscribed by the Chinese in Lhasa. He clearly liked Bogle, who seems to have been a personable young man, and during the six months that Bogle remained in Tibet a warm friendship grew up between the two. But the authorities in Lhasa never relented, and in the end Bogle left Tibet and his friend the Panchen Lama without a trade agreement.

One result of his stay there, however, was a lively set of progress reports which he sent to his superiors in India. Bogle's descriptions of Tibet show him to have been a keen observer with a willingness to comprehend the Tibetan motives for customs which appeared extremely bizarre. Earlier visitors had reported their macabre method of disposing of the dead: bodies were taken to a nearby mountain where they were cut into small pieces to be devoured by birds and wild beasts. Bogle commented that, because there was little wood in the country, cremation (practiced in other Buddhist areas) was impractical. He was even prepared to explain the Tibetan aversion to washing, on the grounds that getting wet was 'uncomfortable in this cold climate'. He remarked on the Tibetan custom of polyandry, in which several brothers married the same woman, but he apparently did not recognise it as a way of keeping property together. All the brothers and their wife lived on the land they inherited from their parents, and if one brother chose to leave and take a wife of his own he lost his rights to any of his father's land. Bogle called the system 'women's revenge'.

Despite Bogle's charm and intelligence, however, the Chinese remained implacably opposed to any Tibetan association with the British. Other envoys continued to try in successive years, but the response continued to be negative.

In 1845 two French missionaries, Evarist Huc and Joseph Gabet, reached Tibet from China disguised as lamas. They arrived at Kumbum, a Buddhist sanctuary in northeastern Tibet, where they abandoned their disguise, and from there they proceeded to Lhasa. There they were viewed with suspicion but were taken to the regent (the Dalai Lama at the time was a young child), who was quite taken with the foreigners and their modern marvels. The regent was particularly fascinated by a microscope, which made a louse plucked from the silk robes of a lama appear as big as a rat. Nevertheless the Chinese were as disapproving as ever, and rather than provoke a crisis between the regent and the ambans the two missionaries took their leave.

But Tibet was too important strategically to be left alone. Manchu power was on the wane in central Asia, and both Russia and Great Britain were eager to fill the vacuum; each suspected the ambitions of the other. The British, at work on their Great Trigonometrical Survey of India during the entire 19th century, managed to infiltrate Tibet with specially trained native surveyors known as *pundits*. They were taught to walk in exactly measured paces and to use various surveying instruments, which were ingeniously disguised and hidden in their belongings. The pundits were given code names and were sent out to survey the forbidden territory. In a narrow sense their activities were not political: the only mysteries they set out to expose were geographical. The Tibetans, however, viewed their work as acts of straightforward espionage, and the fate of a captured pundit was not a pleasant one. Those who succeeded did so brilliantly.

One of the most notable was code-named Krishna, or A.K., who performed the magnificent feat of marching from Kashmir, through Lhasa and across Chang Thang, to the Chinese frontier at Tunharang. He finally appeared at the Survey office in Darjeeling five years later. Neither his pace-counting, for which he used the Survey's specially adapted prayer beads, nor his calculations of position ever faltered in all that time, so that after walking 2800 miles across the highest mountain terrain in the world, he was only 9.5 miles south and 2.5 miles west of his own estimated position.

While the British were mapping Tibet with the information brought back by the pundits, the Russians were probing her northern frontiers. The noted geographer Nikolai Przhevalski made four attempts to reach Lhasa between 1871 and 1885 but each time was turned back by the wary Tibetans. Russia's most successful attempt to influence Tibet was made by a Buriat Mongol from southeastern Siberia named Arguan Dorjiev, who had worked for the czar before going to Tibet. In 1885 Dorjiev, who had been trained as a Buddhist monk, became the tutor and companion of the young thirteenth Dalai Lama, and he managed to persuade his student that the czar was actually a Buddhist at heart. He further convinced the young man that only Russia was in a position to defend Tibet from the pressures of Britain on the one hand and China on the other. By 1902 the Dalai Lama was thinking of visiting St Petersburg, and plans were being drawn up to link Tibet to Russia with a branch of the Trans-Siberian Railroad.

This was more than the British would tolerate. In 1903 Lord Curzon, the aggressive viceroy of British India, sent a military mission to Lhasa to force the Dalai Lama to renounce his Russian affiliations. The expedition was to be a last thrust of British imperial power. Francis Younghusband, the young British officer who was chosen to head the mission, was both direct and unyielding, and when the Tibetans refused to negotiate with him at Lhasa his army mowed down their soldiers with rifles. The British marched into Lhasa on August 2, 1904. The Dalai Lama fled into Mongolia with his tutor, so it was his resentful regent, disillusioned that the Russians had not come to his aid, who capitulated to the British.

Ironically, Younghusband and Curzon had gained more than the British wanted. There was no practical way to maintain communication links to India for a permanent garrison in Tibet, and in any case such British dominion over Tibet would upset the delicate central Asian balance of power. Therefore Britain agreed with Russia that China would have full sovereignty over the kingdom, since its collapsing Manchu dynasty presented no threat to anyone. By 1907 the treaty had been signed by Russia and Britain, and the great powers turned their attention elsewhere.

The embittered Tibetans, handed around like a bag of laundry, held their peace. In 1910 the Dalai Lama returned to Lhasa; in 1912, a year after the Republican Revolution swept the Manchu dynasty out of power, Tibet declared its independence. The thirteenth Dalai Lama ruled until his death in 1933; in 1939 his successor, the fourteenth, was proclaimed; and in 1951 the Chinese Communists came, and nothing was the same again.

What is Tibet like now? It is difficult to know. There is no shortage of reports – they range from searing tales of oppression from Tibetan refugees, most of whom had belonged to the monasteries or the nobility, to uplifting accounts of the emancipation of subjugated peasants from Chinese sympathisers who have been permitted to visit the new Tibet. The reality, as usual probably lies between the two extremes. Even the original reason for the Chinese invasion (or, as the Communists claim, the Chinese reappearance) is debatable. Pro-Western commentators claim that China wished to secure her own southern border, as she had tried to do for centuries; pro-Chinese observers claim that Tibet had always been part of China, and that because American agitators were threatening to detach Tibet entirely, Mao Tse-tung resolved to liberate the area from the dangers of foreign influence.

Tibetan armies were then either defeated or 'won over by the extraordinarily good behaviour of the Red armies', depending upon the viewpoint. In 1959 an uprising was attempted, and the Dalai Lama, who until then had co-operated with the Chinese, had to flee to India. Since then, Tibet has been deliberately and systematically incorporated into the Chinese nation. Buddhism, for so many centuries the central pattern of life, has been replaced by Communism and the thoughts of Chairman Mao. Some of the peasants, who for centuries were subject to the monasteries, undoubtedly feel that life has improved. Others may experience much of the same personal misery under their new masters, but bereft of the religion that once sustained them. A considerable number of Chinese now live in Tibet – it is impossible to say exactly how many, as there are no statistics – and they are attempting to raise the Tibetan standard of living. Roads have been built; peasants are becoming factory workers; literacy rates are rising. It is claimed that the Chinese are teaching the young Tibetans to wash – not even the Red Guards can induce the older people to bathe.

From his exile in India the fourteenth Dalai Lama has declared a new constitution for Tibet which would correct some of the worst abuses of monastic power. Since, as his predecessors discovered in the past, the outside world shows little enthusiasm for coming to Tibet's aid except in order to promote outside interests, it seems unlikely that the Dalai Lama will ever be in a position to implement his reforms. A whole generation of Tibetans has now grown up under Communism; whether they would welcome a return to religious rule is certainly open to question. For centuries the secluded land of Tibet has been a puzzle to those outside its frontiers. Behind the 'bamboo wall' it is now more of an enigma than ever.

CHAPTER 16

THE GOD-KINGS OF
THE KHMERS

*Anyone who has read Rudyard Kipling's Jungle Book will
have imagined the ruined splendour of a city consumed by
the jungle. Just such a sight met the eyes of a French
explorer in 1858, although not in India, but in far eastern
Cambodia. The Indian connection remained however, since
the Khmers, who built the beautiful city of Angkor, filled it
with temples to Hindu gods and images of the Indian
Buddha. Indeed, the Khmer kings claimed to be both living
gods and Buddhas incarnate. It was strange therefore, that
the belief in Buddhism ultimately led to the downfall of the
god-kings of the Khmer empire.*

Henri Mouhot, a French naturalist, stood in astonishment at the
sight before him. Rising up through the thick vegetation of the
Cambodian jungle, amid tree-trunks, wild orchids, and scam-
pering monkeys, and festooned with vines and lichen, stood a
magnificent temple. It is easy to imagine Mouhot's astonishment, for the temple he had accidentally discovered that day in
1858 was Angkor Wat, the largest religious building in the
world. 'Grander than anything left to us by Greece or Rome,' he
later wrote of it. The natives seemed to be as awestruck as he
was. When he asked them who had built this enormous temple,
they replied, 'It is the work of giants,' or 'It built itself.'

What Mouhot had discovered while looking for the tributaries
of the Mekong River was more than one temple, however. He

had come upon a whole city of temples. Literally hundreds of them lie imprisoned in the dense, encroaching forest that has grown over them, unchecked, for five centuries. Some of their walls have collapsed, and some of their details have eroded. Even so, the temples of Angkor are among the most astonishing sights the world has to offer. The breathtaking extravagance of these buildings, their seemingly innumerable towers and maze-like corridors, encrusted with elaborate sculptures seem to over-whelm the visitor.

Angkor Wat is the best-preserved of the temples and covers an area larger than Vatican City. This colossal structure is crowned by five towers, each in the shape of a huge lotus-bud. Its corri-dors are lined with literally miles of beautifully carved panels, depicting scenes from Hindu mythology and from the history of the people who built Angkor. Some 2000 statues of temple dancers adorn the walls of Angkor Wat. Their curvaceous bodies and sensuous, yet enigmatic smiles recur throughout Angkor, helping to give a human aspect to this deserted city.

Mouhot was not in fact the first European to set eyes on Angkor. A Portuguese missionary had discovered it in the mid-6th century and had written of the 'forest of huge and terrifying ruins of palaces, halls and temples' – and of a size, he declared, which would be unbelievable if he had not seen them. 'Unbelievable,' in fact, summed up the general reaction to his story (although one man not only believed in the existence of the ruins but also wrote a short book in which he suggested that they might be the remains of the lost continent of Atlantis). During the 17th century several more firsthand reports of the lost city were produced by European missionaries, but again without much response.

Mouhot's account, in his book *Voyages dans l'Indo-Chine, Cambodge et Laos*, was so vivid and detailed that his readers were convinced. Moreover, as the French were at that time begin-ning to colonise that area of Southeast Asia, known as Indochina, they took a special interest in his discovery, Several expeditions to Angkor were organised, and when Cambodia became a French protectorate in 1863, the daunting task of restoration was begun.

Sadly, Henri Mouhot died of a tropical fever before any of this was accomplished and before the history of Angkor could be revealed. He had spent the last two years of his life exploring these ruins, which, he wrote, were 'the only remaining signs, alas, of a lost race, whose very name, like those of the great men, rulers, and artists who adorned it, seems destined to remain forever hidden among the rubbish and dust. . . .'

From the evidence gathered by archaeologists and other scholars we now know that Angkor was the capital of an empire ruled by a people who called themselves Khmers – a name that is preferred by modern Cambodians. The Khmer empire lasted from about the 9th century AD to the 15th, and at the height of its power included all of modern Cambodia, eastern Thailand, Vietnam, and Laos. In 1431 the Thais invaded Angkor and sacked it. The defeated Khmers abandoned their city, and their civilisation vanished.

The history of the Khmers has been pieced together from the inscriptions on their temples, and from the writings of foreign historians – mainly Chinese. Khmer documents and letters were written on palm leaves and animal skins and have not survived. We have no trouble visualising what those Khmers looked like. They are physically very real to us and smile down from the many temple walls. Yet at the same time they are remote, because they have left virtually no record of their ideas.

The foundations of the Khmer Empire were laid sometime during the 1st century AD when Indian traders and missionaries began colonising Southeast Asia. The Indians not only established ports along the coast but also introduced their language, Sanskrit, their religions, Hinduism and Buddhism, and their art and literature to the people of this area. Several kingdoms incorporating both Indian and native cultures grew up along the coast. One of these kingdoms, located around the Mekong delta, was called Funan by the Chinese. According to one tradition its ruling family was descended from a young Indian sailor named Kaundinya who was blown off course and driven toward the coast of Indochina, where he encountered the beautiful Queen Willowleaf, ruler of the country, sailing toward him in a canoe.

He foiled her attempt to seize his boat and, using his magical powers, sank her canoe. Although it was an inauspicious start their relationship later developed into love, and they married and founded the dynasty of Funan.

Most of what we know about Funan comes from the reports of Chinese diplomats. They found it a prosperous nation, fertile, and enjoying a thriving foreign trade. The population included a large number of Indian craftsmen, who built and decorated the temples that the people of Funan dedicated to the Hindu gods and to Buddha. Early in Funan's history, the worship of Shiva, the Hindu god of destruction and reproduction whose symbol was the *linga,* or phallus, became the official religion.

The rulers of Funan extended their jurisdiction over neighbouring states, and by the middle of the 3rd century their empire reached from the Indian Ocean to the South China Sea. One of their northern tributary states was Chenla (as the Chinese called it), home of the Khmers. They called their land Kambujadeśa (Cambodia), meaning the land of the descendants of Karnbu, a mythical priest who founded a royal house. During the 6th century the king of Chenla decided to take advantage of the growing decadence of Funan and attack it. After a series of terrible floods had left Funan extremely vulnerable, the Khmers easily conquered it. They took over not only Funan itself but also most of its empire.

From the mid-500s to the end of the 700s was, for the most part, a time of internal and external conflicts for the Chenla empire. There were frequent wars with the Chams, who lived in what is now South Vietnam; and eventually, for some time during the latter part of the 7th century, Chenla became a satellite of the powerful kingdom of Java.

The first of the great Khmer kings probably owed his position to the support of Java, which had deposed his predecessor. Soon after attaining the throne, Jayavarman II declared – and won – his country's independence from Java. He established a strong central government, unifying the country, and moved the capital inland, where it would be less vulnerable to attack. The site he chose was a mountain near the Great Lake in the area called

Angkor. The lake was teeming with fish, which would provide food for the large Khmer army as well as for the great numbers of slaves and other workers who were to build his city. The forests were full of game, and the high rainfall and the periodic flooding of the land made it very fertile. Another natural asset was the extensive deposits of sandstone, which Jayavarman and his descendants would use to construct great temples to the greater glory of their gods – which they identified with themselves.

The most significant aspect of Khmer life and culture was the cult of the god-king. This cult – called *devaraja* in Sanskrit – was established by Jayavarman II at the same time that he proclaimed his country's independence. A learned brahman performed a ritual in which he declared that the Khmers were freed from Javanese overlordship because their king was divine. He was endowed with the creative energy of Shiva. Therefore the linga, which had long been worshipped as the symbol of Shiva, was now to be equally worshipped as the symbol of the king.

The devaraja cult met with some resistance among orthodox Hindus, but Jayavarman suppressed it with a combination of strong-arm tactics against his opponents and clever propaganda that convinced the masses that their own wellbeing depended on their faithfully following the cult. His methods were successful. Not only he, but each of his successors as well, was accepted as a god.

Of course, the Khmers were not the only people to deify their monarchs. Many ancient peoples believed their kings to be divine. What set the Khmer devaraja cult apart was that it identified the king with an existing god – usually Shiva, but sometimes Vishnu, the protector god. The other god of the Hindu trinity, Brahma, was less highly venerated. Among the Khmers the worship of the god-king assumed an overriding importance. An army of priests devoted themselves to the worship of the royal linga. Naturally, this venerated object had to be suitably housed, and so began the custom of each king building a temple in his own honour. The temple also served as the king's tomb after his death.

The temple that housed the royal linga was regarded by the Khmers as the centre of the world. For them, each new royal temple became Mount Meru, which, according to Hindu mythology, stood at the centre of the Universe and united the earth with the heavens. A French writer on Angkor, George Caedes, explains the connection between the mythical mountain and the temple: 'Just as Mount Meru was supposed to penetrate to the celestial vault and to carry the lowest layer of the heavens on its peak, in the same way the central temple of the city established the liaison between men and gods through the mediation of the god on earth, who was the king.'

Some of the Khmer temples were built on mountains; others were built in the form of stepped pyramids to suggest mountains; still others, such as Angkor Wat, had a raised central section crowned with towers representing peaks. The word 'phnom', which appears in the names of many temples and in the name of Cambodia's capital, Phnom Penh, means 'mountain' in the Khmer language.

Scholarship appears to have been highly regarded at Angkor and learned men often held debates there. Unfortunately, though, their words and thoughts have vanished and it is to Khmer art that present-day scholars turn to get some idea of Khmer beliefs. The carved panels in the temples are a rich pictorial source of Khmer theology and mythology. One of the favourite themes of the sculptors is the Churning of the Sea of Milk. This curious legend, which is of Indian origin, tells how Vishnu, in the form of a tortoise, descends to the bottom of the cosmic Sea of Milk and supports a mountain on his back. A giant snake, or *naga*, is coiled around the mountain and pulled forward and backward by a team of gods on one side of the sea, a team of demons on the other. The churning action produced ambrosia, the food of the gods and a symbol of all that is good in life – health, wealth, and happiness.

In one of the outer corridors of Angkor Wat there is a series of carved panels showing 32 different kinds of hell awaiting those who have sinned in various ways. There is, for example, a Hell of Broken Bones for those who have damaged property, a Hell of Boiling in a Kettle for those who embezzle the king's money or steal from priests, and an extremely unpleasant Hell of Worms for those who offend parents, friends, priests, or gods. The obvious corrective intent of these carved reliefs suggests that this part of the temple was open to the public. Only priests and royalty could enter the more sacred parts of Khmer temples.

The great Jayavarman II moved his capital several times before settling at a place he called Hariharalaya. It was the first of several cities that would be built in the Angkor area over the next 400 years. Very little remains of the secular buildings erected in the reign of Jayavarman II, who died in 850. In fact, apart from the numerous temples and some bridges and roads, no buildings remain even from the later days of Angkor, for the simple reason that all buildings other than temples were made of wood. Even the royal palace was a wooden building, admittedly a richly decorated one. Archaeological work has revealed traces of four palaces, built between 1000 and 1350.

The king who built Angkor Wat was Suryavarman II, who reigned from 1113 to around 1150, and who is regarded as one of the greatest of the Khmer kings. Suryavarman seized the throne from the previous, weak ruler, and he soon showed that he was made of stronger stuff. His military conquests are celebrated in lavish detail on the walls of Angkor Wat. Hundreds of foot soldiers and officers mounted on horses and elephants and accompanied by musicians are carved parading past the king. Another relief vividly depicts a battle between the Khmers and the Chams.

Toward the end of his reign Suryavarman was less successful in battle, but his building program accelerated, transforming the capital, Yasodharapura, into a city of great splendour. Temples were erected one after another, not only by the king but also by members of the aristocracy, who vied with each other in their extravagance. Quantity was matched by quality. The reign of Suryavarman saw the flowering of Khmer art – above all in his temple of Angkor Wat, in which he was worshipped as Vishnu. In this masterpiece, says the Czech writer Miloslav Krasa, 'the art of the Khmers crystalised into its purest form, majestic in its vastness, exquisite in its minutest detail. . . .'

A British writer on Khmer art, Geoffrey Gorer, has suggested that the tranquil sensuality found in many of the reliefs can be traced to the effects of opium. Drug-taking was common among the Khmers of all classes – opium mainly among the court, and various other narcotics among the rest of the population. In the beautiful carvings of temple dancers at Angkor Gorer sees evidence of the state of mind of the opium-taker: 'These . . . flower-garlanded sylphs re-appear endlessly on every wall of nearly every temple; smiling enigmatically . . . seen with such sensual admiration but with no desire . . . in hieratic dancing poses, kindly and formal and inhuman.'

Where did the wealth come from to support all this magnificence? Much of it resulted from the great fertility of the land, which was increased by a more important – if less imposing – building program, that of an irrigation system. Cambodia's rainy season lasts from November to May. By storing the excess water in great reservoirs, called *barays*, and then systematically flooding the rice fields during the dry season the Khmers were able to get three harvests a year from the same land – more than enough to feed the population. There were several of these barays, one of which was over five miles long and a mile across.

The land produced other crops besides rice. One was cotton, which the Khmers wove into fine cloth, some of which they exported. There was also a rich supply of minerals. Chinese travelers in Cambodia wrote of the country's gold, silver, copper, and tin; some of these may have been obtained through trade, however. The network of rivers that crossed the country and the excellent system of roads built by some of the Khmer kings facilitated trade and helped to make Cambodia the richest nation in Southeast Asia.

The construction of the temples and the roads and irrigation system could be accomplished relatively cheaply, as most of the heavy work was done by slave labour. Some of the workers were members of the poorest class who were conscripted for the job; others were drawn from the huge population of slaves.

For all its prosperity and magnificence, the Khmer empire was

Ruins at Ankor Wat

seldom very secure. A few years after the death of Suryavarman
II the peasants and slaves in the provinces revolted. The revolt
began with the murder of a few tax collectors, then quickly
spread and within a few weeks the rebels had reached the capital.
The rebellion was put down with ferocity. The army swept
through the country massacring slaves and peasants by the thousands, until the government – alarmed at the reduction of the
work force – brought the reprisals to a close with a public execution in which the ring-leaders were buried alive.

Several years after the revolt, civil war broke out and a
usurper seized the throne. With Angkor in a weak, divided state,
its old enemies, the Chams, invaded. But they failed to take the
capital and were forced to flee by the Khmers' formidable Royal
Regiment of Elephants. A few years later, in 1177, the Chams
tried again, this time with a surprise attack by ship. They caught
the Khmers unprepared and swarmed into the city where they
indulged in an orgy of looting, destruction, rape, and murder.
After a few days most of them departed, leaving an occupation
force in the devastated city.

Then the Chams made a serious mistake. Living in exile in
Champa at the time was Suryavarman II's son, who had left
Angkor on his father's death rather than contest the claim of a
usurper. The exile, Jayavarman, was a Buddhist. Although
Buddhism had been tolerated throughout the history of Angkor,
its teachings against bloodshed were directly opposed to official
policy. Jayavarman would not use force to gain the throne, but
he now saw an opportunity to gain it peacefully. The Chams, no
doubt believing that he would serve admirably as a puppet,
allowed him to return to his country.

The intended puppet turned out to be the greatest ruler in
Khmer history, Jayavarman VII. The suffix '-varman', borne by
all Khmer kings, is Sanskrit for 'protector'. Jayavarman was
more than a protector; he was his country's avenger. On
returning to his ruined country he immediately took steps to
restore its prosperity and its military strength. Whatever pacifist
scruples he may have had as a Buddhist he now put aside. He
raised a huge army and navy and drove the Chams out of the

country. A few years later his army invaded Champa – pillaging, burning, and butchering as the Chams had done at Angkor. It took several years of fighting to subdue Champa completely, but eventually it was reduced to the status of a province within the Khmer empire.

Able-bodied Chams were brought back to Angkor, where they were forced to repair the damaged temples and to build Jayavarman's new city, Angkor Thom.

If the reign of Suryavarman II was the high point of Khmer culture, that of Jayavarman VII was by far its most extravagant. The new king was obsessed with building. For 40 years the Khmers and the foreign slaves worked feverishly to satisfy the king's insatiable demand for more temples, more libraries, more monasteries. Thousands of them died in the process. The French writer John Audric speculates that Jayavarman 'never completely recovered from the shock of seeing his flattened capital and after that only by the construction of more and more buildings, more massive and sacred than ever, could he efface it from his memory.'

Although a Buddhist, he eagerly adopted the god-king status established by his Hindu predecessors, declaring that he was the living Buddha. At the centre of Angkor Thom he built the great temple of the Bayon, the god-king's spiritual home. It is an overwhelming building, dark and forbidding. In the days of the Khmers the moat surrounding it was filled – as was the custom – with crocodiles. Today the crocodiles have gone, but the visitor is still made uneasy by the constant sensation of being watched. Pierre Loti, a Frenchman who visited Angkor early in this century, described the experience: 'I stared up at the tree-covered towers which dwarfed me, when suddenly my blood curdled, for I saw an enormous face looking down on me, and then another face over on another wall, then three, then five, then ten, appearing from every direction, and all had the same faint smile.'

There are, in fact, some 200 of these faces on the towers of the Bayon, each eight feet high. They represent Jayavarman VII as the Buddha.

Despite his megalomania, Jayavarman seems to have had the rudiments of a social conscience. He had no pity for the mainly foreign workers who died while constructing his buildings, but he did have some compassion for the sick. He built 102 hospitals, locating them throughout the country. They were linked by a new network of roads that radiated out from Angkor Thom. The roads were built of stone and raised above the ground to offer safe travel in times of flood. At intervals along the roads Jayavarman built rest houses – 121 of them – for the convenience of travellers. Both rest houses and hospitals were attached to temples or small shrines, and in the foundation stones of the religious buildings archaeologists have found inscriptions detailing the organisation of the secular building alongside. For example, one hospital employed 32 staff, including two doctors, two cooks, six water-heaters and medicine-grinders, and two storekeepers who distributed the medicines. Ingredients used included nutmeg, cardoman, sesame, and vinegar.

Details such as these go a small way toward giving us a picture of daily life among the Khmers. Unexpectedly, it is the walls of the gloomy Bayon that give us such a lively view of life among the ordinary Khmers. Whereas the reliefs that decorated earlier Khmer temples depicted religious or mythological subjects or the triumphs of the god-king, most of the Bayon reliefs are devoted to scenes of ordinary life. They show men and women at work: fishing, cooking meals, planting, and taking their produce to market. People are shown playing games, dancing, and betting on fighting cocks. A woman is shown about to give birth, with the midwife standing by. Inevitably, there are also numerous battle scenes, but these are rendered more attractive by the backgrounds of graceful foliage and by the fish that swim among the fighting galley ships.

Unfortunately, the great frenzy of building under Jayavarman VII seems to have left the Khmers literally exhausted. There is evidence of haste and carelessness in the construction of many of the temples. Many are in a poorer condition than earlier structures. Many were left unfinished. The civilisation of the Khmers was to last for another two centuries following the death of

Jayavarman VII in 1218, but they were never again to build on a scale even remotely approaching that of the Buddha-king – or, indeed, of his predecessors.

A vivid picture of life in Angkor in the late 13th century has come down to us from Chou Ta-kuan, the Chinese envoy from Peking. Chou Ta-kuan lived in Angkor for a year, observing and reporting to his emperor on conditions in the Khmer capital. Although he regarded its inhabitants as barbarians – not being Chinese – he found certain things to admire, and his report, entitled *Memoirs of the Customs of Cambodia*, is probably fairly accurate. He describes Angkor Thom in great detail and seems impressed by its luxury. The golden towers about the city, he notes, are probably what strike foreign visitors most, and help prompt the title 'rich and noble Cambodia'. One such golden tower was over the private apartment of the royal residence. The great lake about a mile and a quarter from the walled town contained a stone tower in its centre in which a stone Buddha reclined with water flowing continuously from his navel.

He also describes Khmer festivals and pageantry, including a splendid procession of the king and his retinue through the streets of Angkor in which the procession, led by cavalry was followed by hundreds of standards and pennants. A massed procession of musicians came next and there were more bands at the intervals along the route. Behind the musicians large numbers of dancing girls glided by, each wearing flowers in her hair and carrying tall, lighted candles. After them came palace maidens in their hundreds, carrying gold and silver vessels, trays of precious stones, ropes of pearls, and splendid ornaments.

Behind them marched the king's bodyguard, composed exclusively of women, described by Chou Ta-kuan as tall and good looking Amazons. After these came the nobility, riding on elephants and shaded by red parasols; then the king's wives and concubines – some riding on elephants, some in chariots, and some on litters protected with gilded sunshades. Finally – the king himself, riding on an elephant with gilded tusks. He stood upright under a red and gold canopy and was adorned with jewels. In his hand he carried the sacred golden sword, the symbol of his divine authority.

Differences in status among Khmer officials were marked by variations in their trappings. The highest dignitaries in the land had gold shafts to their palanquins and four parasols with gold handles, reports Chou Ta-kuan. Those immediately below them in office had the same palanquin, but only one or two parasols. Lesser dignitaries had silver shafts on their palanquins, or simply a silver-handled parasol. The parasols, with long fringes hanging down to the ground, were made of red Chinese taffeta.

The aristocracy lived in houses with tiled roofs. The middle and lower classes were not allowed to use tiles; their roofs were thatched. Clothing – of which the Khmers wore very little – was also strictly regulated according to class, with bright and intricate patterns being worn only by the upper classes. The common people possessed no furniture, and they cooked their meals with one clay pot, a clay pan for the sauce, and halved coconut shells for ladles.

Even the lower classes, however, owned slaves. Middle-class families might have 10 to 20, and only the poorest of the poor had none. They were held in the greatest contempt, and it was forbidden to have sexual intercourse with them. A foreign guest who did so was ostracised.

Chou Ta-kuan has much to say about the sexual customs of the Khmers, some of it disapproving. Young girls were deflowered between the ages of seven and eleven by a priest, who performed the service by hand, following – in the case of rich families – an elaborate banquet. After the ritual, the girl was free to do as she wished. Wives reserved the right to be unfaithful to their husbands if the husband went away for more than 10 days or so. As in most cultures, there was prostitution. Groups of women loitered in the main square, and Chou Ta-kuan observes that their main targets were Chinese men, because they were generous.

But Khmer women engaged in other business as well. It was they, Chou Ta-kuan noted with amazement, who did the trading in the marketplace. The Chinese, themselves, when they took a wife on settling in Angkor, looked on her business aptitude as one of her more desirable qualities. Some women also held political offices, and some enjoyed high reputations as scholars.

At the time Chou Ta-kuan was living in Angkor the country was still producing three, or even four rice harvests a year. The economy was prosperous. Evidently the irrigation system, which had been allowed to deteriorate in the years following the death of Jayavarman VII, was once again in good working order.

There were, however, other signs of decline. Warfare, particularly against the Thais, was demanding a disproportionate part of the nation's resources. During Chou Ta-kuan's stay he reported rumours that every able-bodied man was being forced to fight in the war against Thailand.

Another sign – although Chou Ta-kuan does not mention it – was that no new temples were being constructed. None had been built since the great burst of building activity under Jayavarman VII, and in a civilisation that had delighted in extravagant architecture, the change was significant.

One possible cause of the lack of building was the spread of Hinayana Buddhism. Jayavarman VII and his followers practiced Mahayana Buddhism, an elaborate and ritualistic form of the religion that a worldly, luxurious court could accept. Hinayana Buddhism, with its simplicity, humility, and renunciation of earthly desires, was opposed to such a pleasure-centred life. In his report Chou Ta-kuan observed that there were, in the streets of Angkor, thousands of Buddhist monks carrying their begging bowls. This form of Buddhism had not appeared in Angkor until the end of the 13th century, when Chou Ta-kuan was writing. It appealed strongly to the common people, offering them a way to become resigned to suffering and to achieve inner peace. At the same time, it undermined the allegiance of the people to the cult of the god-king, even though he identified himself with the Buddha. The new religion taught that the Buddha himself had never claimed to be a god. Kings should give up their riches, as the royal prince Buddha had done, and live simply. By the end of the 14th century, Hinayana Buddhism had become the religion of nearly the entire population, including some of the aristocracy. Once this situation had come to pass, the whole force behind the Khmer civilisation, the power and authority of the god-king, simply withered away.

It is impossible to reconstruct exactly the course of the Khmers' downfall, though some factors that contributed to it have been pieced together. For example, we know that around the beginning of the 15th century there were power struggles within the royal family and that several times the ruling king was deposed for another member of his family. Such events had occurred many times in the past, but now there was no strong leader to command allegiance – let alone the worship accorded earlier kings.

Possibly because of ineffective leadership and possibly because the new religion undermined the will to produce, the Khmers let their irrigation system deteriorate. The rice harvests declined sharply, and without this economic base, the country faced ruin.

It may be that a great flood precipitated the fall of Angkor. A Buddhist legend tells of a flood that supposedly occurred because the king drowned his chaplain's son in the Great Lake for having offended his own son. The naga-king, or snake-god, then caused the lake to overflow the surrounding countryside and destroy Angkor Thom. Apart from the fanciful cause, the story may be true. Even today, the flooding of the Mekong River and its tributaries forces the water level of the Great Lake, which is part of the Mekong River system, to rise and overflow the land. In the 15th century the shore of the lake may have been much nearer Angkor and a flooding of the lake potentially more harmful.

The death blow to Angkor was delivered by the Thais. Eastern Thailand had once been under Khmer domination, but as the Khmers declined they had gained in power and had started invading Cambodia's northern and eastern provinces. In the late 1200s they were already formidable foes, requiring a massive expenditure of Khmer manpower. From 1350 onward the Thais and the Khmers were almost continuously at war. In 1388 the Thais succeeded in taking Angkor Thom. They were aided by conspirators within the government who wanted to bring an end to the *devaraja* cult, which the king and his closest supporters were attempting to revive. The victorious Thais installed a puppet king on the throne and then made the mistake of withdrawing their forces too soon. Within a short time the Thai puppet king had been assassinated and a Khmer king installed in his place.

The internal strife and the weakened economy had left Angkor extremely vulnerable. In 1431 the Thai armies attacked Angkor again. In contrast to their previous restrained behaviour, they now rampaged through the city, looting and destroying. Some of the invaders had a genuine respect for Khmer culture, however, and they took back to their own country many of its ideas and customs, as well as artists who were required to lend their skills to the building of the Thai capital, Ayudhya. They also took with them the beautiful temple dancers, who enjoyed great popularity in Thailand after having been more adequately clothed, in accordance with Thai custom. The tradition of Khmer dancing has survived the centuries, preserved for many years by the Thai conquerors, and modern Cambodian dancers wear the elaborate costumes imposed on them long ago by an alien culture.

Sometime after the destruction of Angkor Thom by the Thais, the Khmers abandoned the city. Exactly what happened has long been a subject for speculation. Records are extremely sparse. However, recent scholarship has discovered that the exodus was a gradual one, and that the king and court remained in the city for a year or two after most of the population had fled. Apparently they made some attempts to get the irrigation system working again, but they lacked the resources for such a daunting task. Malaria swept through the country, and there may have been more floods. Seeing the ineffectiveness of the ruling class, the slaves once again revolted and swarmed through Angkor, looting and burning what was left of it. The government managed to pull itself together in order to deal with the slaves in the customary manner. But the situation was hopeless. Finally, the king ordered the evacuation of Angkor and retreated into the hills.

From that time until the French arrived in the 1800s, Cambodia's history was a succession of civil wars, assassinations, and foreign invasions. The Khmer kings ruled from several places in their stripped-down country, desperately trying to keep their thrones and to keep their neighbours at bay. The nation that had once been the richest and most powerful in Southeast Asia had lost all semblance of glory, or even of self-respect. And while it struggled to survive, the ruined capital of Angkor stood in the jungle, overgrown with weeds, and forgotten.

CHAPTER 17

THE LAST REFUGE
OF THE INCA

When the Spaniards invaded the New World, they expected to encounter primitives living in mud huts, and were astonished by the sheer sophistication of the cities of the Aztecs and the Incas. Their brutal treatment of the natives of Central and South America has led even Spanish historians to deplore their savagery, greed and treachery. The Incas – named after their holy ruler, the son of the sun – were among the final victims of this treachery, and their last surviving king was forced to seek refuge on an almost inaccessible mountain top, in a city whose origin is still a mystery.

It was cold. The mountain mist hung heavily over the stone terraces, and the woman on the stairway shivered slightly and drew her white woollen shawl closer around herself. In the early morning the entire stone city seemed grey. Not until the dawn lightened further would the green of the garden terraces soften the severity of stone against stone.

Above the city rose the precipitous cliffs of the two mountain peaks, one to the north, the other to the south. Between them lay the city itself, clinging to the ridge which dropped off sharply on either side. It was a natural fortress, well guarded against any unauthorised intrusion. All around were spectacular mountain vistas and breathtaking views of the splendour of the Andes in which the city perched preposterously.

The woman looked at none of this. She had lived among these

mountains since childhood, and if the austere magnificence had ever compelled her attention it did so no longer. The mountains were simply there, as the cold morning mist and the unyielding stone beneath her sandals were there. She reached the top of the stone staircase, turned into an open doorway, and vanished into the dark interior. She was a Mama Cuna, a Chosen Woman who supervised and taught her younger companions, and she had neither the leisure nor the inclination to admire the scenery. A new day was beginning, and there was work to do. The new emperor – the Inca – was in the city, somehow dispossessed of his traditional capital, Cuzco, where the 'bearded ones' were suddenly in command. Everything was strange; all the rules that had seemed fixed and sure for generations were now upset. In the midst of the confusion the daily pattern of life stubbornly continued, as if people believed that if they repeated what was known and familiar the nightmare would pass: sanity and stability would return. Thus the Mama Cuna made her way through the city in the early dawn, following her accustomed path as if none of the murder or madness in the valleys below had ever happened.

Nevertheless the days of the city were numbered. At some date not long after, though it was never conquered, the city was to be abandoned. The Spanish never knew of its existence, hidden as it was within its mountain barriers. But for some reason – which we may never know – orders must have been given to leave the city. The gold and silver, the beautiful fine woollens woven by the Chosen Women, the pottery, and the sacred mummies of dead Incas were all taken out of the fortress city. Whether any of the Chosen Women remained behind is not known.

The city remained wrapped in mountain mists and silence, and slowly the jungle crept in through the fortifications and gradually covered the stone steps. The thatched roofs decayed and collapsed. From time to time descendants of the Inca people, by then reduced to scraping out a miserable existence under Spanish colonial rule, probably climbed the mountains to search the burial sites for treasure. But nothing remained of much value: broken pottery was a poor reward for an exhausting climb. Over the centuries the city was forgotten, and now no one even knows its name. It is simply called after the mountain peak which towers over it – Machu Picchu.

Not until this century was it rediscovered. The Spanish had tightened their grip on the land of the Incas, and the once proud land became a colony of the Spanish throne. But all the gold of Peru was not sufficient to sustain an over-extended empire, and in time Spain's power waned and the Republic of Peru was established. In 1911 an American historian and explorer, Hiram Bingham, heard stories of interesting ruins in the Urubamba valley north of Cuzco. The way up from the valley was long and hard (the Inca road leading to the city gate had long ago been destroyed by rockfalls and covered over by jungle), but scattered Inca ruins offered tantalising promise of what might lie ahead.

After nearly a month of steady climbing, through increasing heat and humidity, Bingham mounted a last ridge and saw before him a great flight of beautifully constructed stone terraces. Past the terraces were houses made of the finest Inca stonework. There was what might have been a royal mausoleum, and, at the top of a ledge, a graceful semicircular building followed the natural curvature of the surrounding rock. Everywhere he looked were walls of white granite ashlars fitting perfectly together without mortar, in the traditional Inca style. Even covered as they were with mosses and vines, bamboo thickets and trees, the ruins were spectacular. For Bingham – and for everyone else since his time who has come upon the magnificence of the ruined city – the questions well up instantly: what was this city ? How was it so successfully hidden ? What sort of people were capable of building such incredibly fine buildings on the shoulder of the Andes?

The answers remain wrapped in mystery. In 1527 Francisco Pizarro first set foot on the shore of what is now Peru at Tumbes, then the northernmost coastal city under the control of the Incas. Over the centuries since then soldiers, priests, historians, and archaeologists have recorded what they saw and remembered about the Inca empire, but their information suffers from two essential difficulties. The first is that no outsider ever saw the empire at its most powerful; when the Spanish arrived it was in the midst of an unprecedented political crisis. But the second difficulty is even more crucial – the Incas, like other South American Indians, had no written language. Inca history is entirely a matter of remembering tales passed by word of mouth. By the time the brutal Spanish conquest was complete, few official rememberers' were left.

But even in the days of their glory the Incas were very careful about what they chose to have remembered. The central premise of Inca history was that the children of the sun, Manco Capac and his sister-wife Mama Occlo, were created on the Isle of the Sun in Lake Titicaca and set out from there to teach the arts of civilisation to a barbarous world. This idea, that the Incas were the pioneers of advanced culture in previously primitive surroundings, we now know to be untrue. The Incas actually built their remarkable civilisation on well-established cultural foundations. The fact is that the Incas (or rather the people who called their kings Incas – we do not know what they called themselves) were almost certainly one of a number of small tribes living near Lake Titicaca who fought their way northward to a fertile valley where they established what became their imperial capital of Cuzco. Archaeological evidence suggests that initially the Inca people were no different from their neighbours. Like them, they cultivated potatoes and maize; like them they used only stone tools; and like them they relied on the llama, which had been domesticated for centuries. What appears to have been uniquely their own was a genius for organisation.

The Incas distinguished themselves by the society they established, in which the individual was a disciplined cog in a massive governmental machine. Each person had his or her place and duty, and people who were unable to provide for themselves were supplied with necessities. Conquered tribes were firmly and benevolently incorporated within the Inca framework; their individual histories were suppressed and forgotten as they became identified with Inca power. Inca warriors were valiant and for the most part victorious, but the Inca arts of peace are what still compel our attention.

The basis of political organisation was the *ayllu*, or tribal division. The ayllu was small and tightly knit so that the accomplishments or shame of any member reflected directly upon the entire ayllu. The ayllu held land, crops, and animals in common, and under normal circumstances most individuals were born, lived out their lives, and died within the confines of their ayllu. Only marriage altered membership in that one could not take a husband or wife from within the same ayllu, and upon marriage a woman left her father's ayllu to join that of her husband. Marriage was only partially a personal affair, because if a man had not selected a wife by the time he was 20 years of age a marriage would be arranged for him by an official during a periodic visit.

For women, however, marriage into another ayllu was not the only possibility. Young girls were carefully watched and, by the time they were eight or ten years old, those who possessed unusual beauty or grace or showed particular talent in weaving were called to the attention of the visiting officials, who sent them to become Chosen Women or *aclla cuna* (Virgins of the Sun). The young Chosen Women were closely supervised, and they were taught exquisite spinning and weaving and the rituals of the sun (the god and father of the Incas). Chosen Women dressed in fine white woollens and were rigidly segregated from the rest of society. Some were of noble birth, but within the order there were no gradations in status.

Chosen Women fulfilled several functions. Some remained virgin priestesses all their lives; a very few were selected for the infrequent human sacrifices to the sun; and the most beautiful became concubines of the Inca, earthly representative of the sun. Others were given by the Inca as wives to favoured generals or conquered chiefs. A Chosen Woman who remained in a convent, unmarried, became a Mama Cuna with the duty of passing on her skills to the younger girls. As many as 15,000 Chosen Women lived in sacred enclosures around the empire. The pattern of their lives behind the high stone walls remains a mystery: the bleak rows of cells of the Inca ruins suggest that it was austere. Certainly the fate of a Chosen Woman who was discovered in a sexual liaison was harsh – she was buried alive, her lover was strangled, and his ayllu was razed to the ground; the site was then sown with stones. There could be no mercy for a woman who dared to be unfaithful to the sun god, or for a man who infringed the rights of the Inca.

The ruling authorities were those the Spanish called 'Big Ears' who were all born into the original Inca tribes. Their caste was indicated by their earrings, because the children of the nobility had their ears pierced, and the holes were gradually enlarged until an egg could pass through them. Adults wore the characteristic Inca earrings – rounded bejewelled golden disks. The privileged men of this class were allowed several wives and concubines, elaborate clothing, and extensive estates. But the aristocracy worked hard as the administrators of the state. Idleness in all ranks was punishable by death.

Below these aristocrats born to their station were those who were Incas by privilege. They were not born into the royal ayllus but had in some cases risen through ability. At its peak, the Inca empire was expanding too rapidly to be governed solely by the small ruling caste, and inevitably outsiders became necessary. Other Incas by privilege, who were called curacas, were sons of conquered chieftains. Once vanquished, tribal chiefs were often re-established as rulers while their sons were sent to Cuzco to be impressed by Inca grandeur and trained in Inca ways. They dressed as Incas, had their ears pierced for Inca earrings, and often selected their wives from among the Chosen Women. When they returned to their native territories they were part of Inca power and carried important responsibilities. Most significant, they were bound to the Inca empire – their one-time enemy – with bonds of loyalty for favours received. Their old positions were enlarged and magnified by the glory of the Inca empire.

The key to the Inca system was the realisation that military victory was only the beginning of conquest, that only with a contented and productive population could the empire continue to expand. If a community near the frontier was found to be restive, the population was simply moved in its entirety to an area closer to Cuzco, where the people could be awed by Inca splendour and government officials could keep a close eye on them. The ayllu which had occupied that territory exchanged it for the frontier area thus vacated. Simultaneously, potential troublemakers were thus brought under close watch and a loyal outpost was established. Like many Inca policies, this was sensible, efficient, and totally unconcerned with individual preference.

To record the affairs of this far-reaching government an ingenious system was developed. Lacking any written alphabet, administrative officials employed the *quipu*, a linked group of knotted cords of many colours. The colour denoted the subject while the knots indicated numbers in a decimal system. Although the Incas had no writing and never developed the wheel, it is interesting that they were among the few peoples in the history of civilisation to understand the concept of zero. The quipu itself was a simple and ingenious device meant to aid the memory of skilled interpreters, whose job it was to translate the knots into information. The connotations of the quipu were standardised and were taught to Inca aristocrats as well as to professional interpreters. A noble may not have had to use a quipu himself, but ideally he should always be able to check the calculations of his accountants. Not only did the colours of the wool threads have meaning, but the methods of tying the knots or twisting the threads and the distances between the knots were also significant. Initially sceptical, the Spanish were gradually impressed by the skills of the quipu readers, but unfortunately their conquest marked the end of them. Zealous Catholic priests, believing them to be books of the devil, destroyed the archives of knotted cords which recorded the history of the Inca empire, and as the quipu interpreters gradually died off, their knowledge was no longer handed down. Now the quipus are mute and lifeless, random pieces of string in museum cases, and their meaning is forever shrouded in oblivion.

Without historical evidence, therefore, any dates in Inca history – with the momentous exception of 1527, the year Francisco Pizarro landed – remain educated guesses. It seems likely that the Inca people first emerged as distinct from the surrounding Andean tribes around the 12th century, so in traditional Inca terms this would be the date for the semi-legendary Manco Capac. For the next two to three centuries the Incas established themselves in the Cuzco valley. By the 14th century the Incas had begun to expand outward, first south and north and then in all directions. The great Inca Pachacutec had conquered all of what is now Peru by approximately 1466; his successors extended the frontiers to include Chile (in 1492 – the same year that Columbus arrived in the Caribbean islands) and parts of Colombia (in 1498 – coinciding with Columbus' discovery of the South American mainland).

By 1500 the Inca conquest was complete, and the empire was at its largest. In Cuzco the Inca presided over a magnificent court. He ate off plates of gold and silver, held by his Chosen Women; his clothes were of finest soft vicuna wool, and he wore each garment only once, after which it was destroyed. His nobles were self-assured and competent. Government control was pervasive, leaving no one needy, hungry, or without shelter. Money did not exist – the Incas valued gold purely for its glittering beauty – and taxes were paid by days of labour, from which the aristocracy was excused. But the nobles had their own administrative responsibilities, and death was the penalty for assignments uncompleted.

Inca roads ran the length and breadth of the empire, and bridges of fibre cables spanned the gorges and rivers. The roads were not meant for ordinary coming and going – people could not leave the land of their ayllu without specific permission – but for the travelling officials and, most importantly, for armies on their way to war. As there was no wheeled traffic, the roads were built in steps when the grade was too steep for comfort and safety. Considerable speed was possible for the trained couriers: fish fresh from the ocean reached the Inca's table in Cuzco, 130 miles away, the same day it was caught.

Gold mined from swift-running mountain streams was carried along the Inca roads to skilled goldsmiths who crafted the gleaming metal into exquisite objects. For the Incas gold was 'the sweat of the sun', and all gold and silver belonged to the Inca himself; as the sun's representative he was entrusted with its safekeeping. It was shaped into magnificent ceremonial objects or jewellery and was used to decorate buildings. One great golden sheet covered the end wall of a building which illustrated the sun and moon among the stars and an outline of the history of creation. Like all the other beautiful objects the Spanish seized, it was melted down for easier shipment to Spain, but its glory was remembered in Indian tradition.

Of all their accomplishments, it was in building that the Incas most excelled. Proof of their mastery still stands centuries after the builders completed their work. Massive polygonal blocks lie so close together that it is impossible to insert the point of a knife between them. Using only stone and bronze tools, they constructed buildings so sound that they have survived despite all the quakes and tremors that have beset this earthquake-prone region. Spanish colonial buildings have collapsed, but their Inca foundations have outlasted them.

But the seeds of destruction were sprouting both within the empire and beyond its boundaries. In 1513 Vasco Nuñez de Balboa saw the Pacific, and the Incas began to hear the first vague rumours of 'bearded ones'. Nearly 10 years later the Spanish in Central America first heard of the Land of Gold to the south, and they began their inexorable approach, drawn by the golden lure. In 1527 Pizarro arrived at Tumbes with 13 men on a preliminary reconnaissance, and he took some Indians away with him to be trained as interpreters in anticipation of his return. Reports of these remarkable happenings were immediately forwarded to Cuzco, but the administrators there had other pressing concerns. A terrifying epidemic raged (which may have been acquired from the Europeans in the north), and Huayna Capac, the eleventh Inca, was dying in Quito, which he had established as a base during his campaigns in what is now Ecuador.

With the Inca's death the problem of the succession became acute. Under normal circumstances the procedure was quite straightforward: the reigning Inca selected the most competent of his sons by his *coya*, his empress and principal wife, who was also according to tradition his sister. However, Huayna had spent many years in the north and wished to leave part of his empire to Atahualpa, his son by a princess of Quito of whom he was particularly fond. The major part of the empire – all of it, in fact, except for the new additions he himself had made by his northern conquests – he left to his legitimate heir Huascar, who lived in Cuzco.

The division was unprecedented and calamitous. Civil war inevitably broke out between the half-brothers, and battlegrounds were heaped with bloody carcasses before Atahualpa (an experienced general who had fought with his father) eventually triumphed. Huascar and all his offspring were massacred by his brother's victorious forces. Even his unborn children were ripped from the wombs of their dying mothers. The empire reeked with blood and vengeance as Atahualpa made his way toward Cuzco, a once proud city which had finally been forced to yield to an outsider.

It was at this point, on May 13, 1532, that Pizarro returned to Peru with 106 foot soldiers and 62 men on horseback. Atahualpa was resting before his entrance into Cuzco at Cajamarca, a sulphur spa high in the Andes, where he was recovering from a leg wound received during the war. Pizarro set out from Tumbes, where he left a garrison, for the natural harbour at the mouth of the Chira river, where he founded the settlement of San Miguel. Here he was told about the five-year-long civil war. It was obvious even to an outsider that the deep divisions it had caused had not yet begun to heal, and Pizarro, who had come to conquer, was elated to discover a crack of vulnerability in the massive empire he was about to challenge.

Atahualpa, for his part, was interested but unconcerned by the progress of these curious strangers. He knew that they were few while his own forces were tremendous. Pizarro, once he knew where the Inca was to be found, began the 350-mile journey to Cajamarca. The Spanish soldiers sweated across the coastal desert in their heavy armour and gasped for oxygen as they climbed the precipitous heights. They walked along narrow roadways overhung by massive fortresses, and yet they suffered only random attacks. The Spanish crept across suspension bridges that drooped ominously in the middle and swung disconcertingly in the wind, and yet no one took advantage of their exposed position. Atahualpa, secure in his invincibility, ordered no move against them but simply had them watched. As they neared

Cajamarca he sent out one of his nobles to invite the white men to enter the city as his guests.

As the Spanish clattered through the streets of Cajamarca on November 15, 1532, they found the town strangely quiet: there was no one to greet them. At last Pizarro sent his brother Hernando, with Hernando de Soto, to seek out the Inca while Francisco waited to make a dignified approach. The Spaniards found the Inca seated on a golden stool surrounded by his noblest They were impressed by his regal calm, and Hernando Pizarro invited him to come and dine with his brother. At first Atahualpa made no reply, but when the request was repeated in more courteous terms he spoke. He was fasting that day, he said, but he would come the following day. As they were leaving, Hernando de Soto tried a flourish of Spanish horsemanship. Mounted, he wheeled and galloped toward the sitting monarch before drawing up so sharply (according to the Indian chronicles) that Atahualpa could feel the horse's breath on his face. The surrounding nobles involuntarily flinched, but Atahualpa, who had never even seen a horse before, sat impassive and dignified.

The next day the Inca and his nobles came to meet the Spanish. As guests, unarmed, they walked into a carefully planned ambush. A friar came out to meet the Inca and demanded that Atahualpa declare his allegiance to the Catholic church. Annoyed at the impudence of this insignificant man, Atahualpa tossed the Bible he offered to the ground and pointed to the sun, saying, 'My god still lives.' At this Pizarro gave a prearranged signal, and the Spanish soldiers and cavalry charged the unarmed Indians. After only 30 minutes the proud force of retainers was dead, and Atahualpa was Pizarro's prisoner. As one of those who took part in the battle later commented, 'As the Indians were unarmed they were defeated without danger to any Christian.'

With the Inca held captive, the clockwork efficiency of the Inca empire was stopped short. It was run by a totally centralised administration, and now that centre was powerless. The shock waves reverberated across the vast communication network of Inca roads as officials waited for someone to tell them what to do, as they had always been told before. But there was no one to give the orders. Atahualpa tried to exploit the inexplicable Spanish passion for gold in a bid for freedom. He promised to fill the room in which he was kept in Cajamarca with gold to a point as high as he could reach. The room was 22 feet long by 17 feet wide, and the mark of the Inca's reach about 7 feet high. Runners travelled all over the empire collecting precious objects of the finest craftsmanship to meet the ransom. The room was filled as agreed, but the Spanish dared not free Atahualpa, since they were still so very few against so many. Pizarro, over the protests of Hernando de Soto and his own brother Hernando, finally decided on judicial murder. Atahualpa was accused of treason (trying to raise a force to overthrow the Spaniards), incest (because of his legal marriage to his sister), and of usurpation of the Inca throne rightfully belonging to his dead half-brother Huascar. Predictably enough, he was sentenced to death and executed. The gold ransom was melted down into ingots and shipped to Spain.

With the Inca dead, Pizarro marched on Cuzco. The city – already savaged by Atahualpa's men after the fall of Huascar – was systematically looted and its inhabitants tortured, raped, and murdered. The Inca people had been trained for generations in unquestioning obedience: now this obedience was interpreted as cowardice by the Spanish, who had no mercy. The complex machinery of government that had controlled irrigation, organised agriculture, and maintained the roads and services was allowed to collapse in disarray. Those Indians who survived the first brutal attacks waited dumbly for whatever the unfeeling heavens might unleash upon them next.

After the execution of Atahualpa, Pizarro cast about for a successor and found a young son of Huayna Capac. His name was Manco Capac, and he had escaped the occupation of Cuzco by Atahualpa's men by retreating over the Andes to the east. Pizarro declared that Manco Capac would be the new Inca. He was installed with an impoverished attempt at the traditional ceremony, but crowned or not, Manco Inca and all in Cuzco knew that he was solely a puppet of the Spanish.

Beneath the façade of obedience to his Spanish masters, however, Manco Inca was plotting and organising. In the spring

Inca ruin of the Lost City at Machu Picchu

of 1536 his opportunity came. Playing on the Spanish greed for gold, he had requested that he be allowed to celebrate the April harvest in his traditional lands north of the capital, where at the same time he could hunt for some of his father's fabulous gold treasure which had disappeared from the city and which the Spanish coveted. Using those lines of communication permitted by the Spanish for the puppet government, supporters of Manco Inca had meanwhile organised an army. With the Inca safely out of the city, the secret army attacked Cuzco during Easter week. Spanish communications were severed between Cuzco and the coast, and Spanish settlers in the countryside were seized and beheaded.

For over a year the Inca's forces kept the city under siege. The Spanish counterattacked furiously, relying upon allies among the Inca's subject peoples, who grasped this opportunity to revenge themselves upon their former masters. At last, in 1537, the Inca forces met the Spanish in battle on the plains near Lima, the new capital established by Pizarro. As guerrillas attacking from mountain fortresses the Incas were unconquerable, but on the open plain the Spanish were in their element. The forces of Manco Inca were vanquished, and the Inca himself, along with the remnants of his army of supporters, retreated deep into the Urubamba valley northwest of Cuzco. Hernando Pizarro made one determined attempt to seize his fortress, Ollantaytambo, but his forces retreated in disarray from the Indian defence, a deluge of stones shot from slingshots and even gunfire from captured muskets. Never again did the Spanish attempt to storm the Incas in their mountain strongholds. Manco Inca and his men melted back into the Andes, and the Spanish were left in command of the fertile plains and coastal cities. But it had been a near thing – the Incas had come close to reclaiming their land.

It was probably then that Manco Inca retreated to the fortress of Machu Picchu and the stone city became, for a time, the royal residence. The most spectacular buildings there must have already been standing: the depleted resources at Manco Inca's command would not have permitted much ambitious construction. The stones are silent as to what role the city played before it became the fugitive Inca's refuge. Skeletons found in the burial caves near the city are almost entirely those of women, so perhaps the magnificent ruins were once a vast temple to the sun, populated mainly by the Chosen Women who devoted their lives to the rituals of worship. No one can now say if the Inca emperors before Pizarro made pilgrimages to the citadel in the mountains. But the presence of buildings much less carefully constructed than the superb central structures, suggests that the city was hastily enlarged to accommodate the loyal remnant of the Inca's followers who came with him to the city we now call Machu Picchu.

Meanwhile in the valleys below there was another Inca. The Spanish, still seeking a veil of legitimacy for their rape of the empire, elevated another surviving son of Huayna Capac. His name was Paullu Capac, and for 12 years, from 1537 to 1549, he cooperated with the Spanish in Cuzco. Paullu reasoned that the only possibility of Inca survival lay in some measure of collaboration with the Spanish, and he even fought with them against Manco Inca's forces in their desperate uprising. In 1543 he was baptised a Christian and became Don Cristobal Paullu Topa Inca. He was granted a Spanish coat of arms and founded the first chapel in Cuzco.

Manco Inca remained in the mountains. During these years the Spanish had other concerns which prevented them from stamping out the last pockets of Inca resistance. With the conquest virtually over the conquistadors fell upon one another, and for 11 long years, beginning in 1537 after the defeat of Manco Inca, the people of Peru watched helplessly as their new masters clawed and tore at each other, and the land sank deeper into anarchy. The chief rival to the power of the Pizarros, Diego de Almagro, was defeated and executed by Hernando Pizarro in 1538; three years later his vengeful supporters murdered Francisco Pizarro himself in his palace at Lima. Manco Inca was not untouched by the wrangling. In 1542, after the death of Pizarro, a handful of refugee Almagrists reached the outlying settlements of the Inca's truncated territory and, swearing loyalty to Manco Inca, were permitted to remain.

What followed was either stupid folly or deliberate treachery. The accounts vary, but most of them agree that the renegade Spaniards taught the Inca to play various European games – bowls, quoits, and even chess and checkers. Reportedly, Manco Inca had a bowling green made at the settlement where the Spanish refugees lived (there is no indication that the Spanish ever saw the city of Machu Picchu or knew that it existed). It was during one of these games that one of the refugees lost his temper in the heat of competition and insulted the Inca. Manco Inca struck the hot-tempered Spaniard and warned him to consider with whom he talked – and the furious Spaniard killed him, either with a dagger or with his bare hands. Titu Cusi, one of Manco's sons, claimed that the Spaniards deliberately set upon the Inca during a game of quoits and stabbed him to death – to win favour, it has been suggested, with the new Spanish viceroy of Peru.

Whatever the circumstances, Manco Inca was assassinated in 1545. His eldest son, Sayri Inca, succeeded him and ruled his mountain retreat in peace for 10 years. In 1555 he was coaxed out by the viceroy, who offered him a more comfortable residence nearer Cuzco. Sayri Inca seems to have been pleased with this opportunity to see more of the world that up to then he had only heard about, and he accepted the Spanish offer. But he lived only two years among the Spanish; although he was apparently well and respectfully cared for, he died of what the viceroy said was disease. His nobles claimed he had been poisoned.

His half-brother Titu Cusi remained in the mountains, safe-guarding a younger brother, Tupac Amaru, by placing him 'into the House of the Sun with the Chosen Virgins and their Matrons' – almost certainly in the city of Machu Picchu. Titu Cusi survived until 1571, meeting Spanish emissaries in his jungle city of Vilcabamba and listening to missionaries, always – the missionaries thought – on the verge of conversion, but never yielding in the end. He died of natural causes still supreme in his mountain stronghold.

The forehead fringe – the mark of Inca sovereignty – then passed to Tupac Amaru, but he proved no match for the Spanish. A new viceroy, Francisco de Toledo, had arrived in Peru in 1569, determined to regularise the administration of the colony by ending the power of the Incas for all time. He sent out an ambassador, and, unwisely, Tupac Amaru's men murdered him. The Spanish then dispatched a full-fledged expeditionary force to capture the Inca and take revenge. By then the Inca warriors had been reduced to a forlorn handful who had forgotten the tactics that had gained them an empire. They tried to hide their Inca in the jungle valley of the Pampas river, but it was not remote enough. The Spanish followed, and the last Inca was captured trying to protect his pregnant wife. Back in Cuzco she was mangled before his eyes. Tupac Amaru himself was baptised and beheaded, only 39 years after Atahualpa had been murdered by Pizarro.

Toledo gained little by his barbarism. When he returned to Spain the king refused to see him, saying he had been sent to serve kings, not to kill them. But the colonial system which Toledo established lasted for the next 200 years.

For how many of those years did the fortress city of Machu Picchu live? The city was stripped of all its furnishings, so it seems that at some time someone gave the order to abandon it. Was it Tupac Amaru? Were any of the Chosen Women left behind to continue their rituals and petitions to the sun god, who seemed to have forgotten his people? Did a last surviving priestess watch the sun rise and set as she waited patiently for death in the silent stone city?

No one knows. The years passed, and the jungle crept in over the stones. The terraces were overgrown and forgotten. The city remained, awaiting the visit of the scholar and archaeologist, the swarm of tourists, and rush of the 20th century. It stands as it has stood for centuries, an irrefutable monument to the grandeur of the Incas. They themselves may have perished, but their sun still shines upon their temple, and the stone city endures.

CHAPTER 18

THE HUNT FOR THE 'GILDED MAN'

If the Spanish rape of Peru and Mexico called down divine retribution, its form was as subtle as it was apt. The rumour of El Dorado (a native king so rich he could have himself coated with gold dust) infected the Conquistadors with a fever of greed. The reckless hunt to find and loot El Dorado's kingdom played-out like a Greek tragedy as the Spaniards suffered and died in the jungles, mountains and swamps of South America. Some found gold, but did they ever find El Dorado? Perhaps his land still lies undiscovered in the unexplored Brazilian interior.

It was in 1529 that reports of El Dorado – 'the gilded one' in Spanish – first reached the conquistadors, who were then establishing tiny settlements on the Caribbean coast of South America. It was said that a mountain city existed where the people possessed so much gold that they covered the body of their king with the glittering dust. The story was irresistible to the gold-hungry Spanish, who felt they were on the threshold of a world filled with incredible riches. In 1521 Hernando Cortes had conquered the Aztec empire in what is now Mexico; in 1526 Francisco Pizarro had at last discovered indisputable proof of the wealth of the Incas in Peru, and in 1529 he was in Spain obtaining King Charles V's authority for an expedition of conquest. Anything seemed possible – gold and glory were there for the taking.

As the years passed the story acquired more details. In his high mountain kingdom each year the chief would ceremoniously strip naked and be covered with a sticky resin. His attendants then blew clouds of gold dust over his bare body until he glittered with the dazzling magnificence of a living golden statue. Gilded and gleaming, the king then led his people in procession to the shores of a lake, and he was rowed out in a canoe to the centre. The king and his nobles threw gifts of emeralds and golden ornaments into the waters, and then, in a shimmering climax, the king himself plunged, shining, into the lake. When he emerged, the gold dust washed away, there was a festival of singing, dancing, and revelry.

The obvious question was where this splendid place was to be found. That it lay somewhere in the unexplored interior was not doubted from the moment the story was told. The image of a people so rich they could coat their king with gold and then carelessly wash it away was a magnet for soldiers of fortune, so there was no shortage of men eager to find the golden city and claim its treasure. One by one, year after year, they set off into the unknown jungle, with a marvellous golden vision dancing before their eyes.

The first man to try to find El Dorado was a red-bearded German, Ambrosius Ehinger. He had been a merchant, and it was as a representative of a bank that he came to America. The wealthy banking house of the Welsers had supported Charles V of Spain in his claim to the imperial title of Holy Roman Emperor, so when Charles V became emperor he repaid the Welsers in 1527 with the territory of present-day Venezuela, naming them as the proprietary lords in perpetuity. Ehinger, accompanied by one other German and a party of hired Spaniards, arrived early in 1529 to take possession of the Welser property at the newly founded town of Coro, about a hundred miles east of the Gulf of Venezuela. Almost immediately after his arrival Ehinger heard the first hazy version of the story and he promptly, that very summer, set off to locate the king and his treasure.

His quest was made considerably more difficult by the lack of knowledge of South American geography. Indeed, Ehinger believed that Venezuela was an island bounded on the south by the Pacific Ocean. Searching at random, he began by going west and setting up a garrison at the place where the Gulf of Venezuela meets Lake Maracaibo. From there he continued west, but after a year in which he found nothing he returned to Coro. He discovered that in the meantime he had been given up for dead, and a successor had been appointed as governor. However, as the successor had just died, there was no obstacle to Ehinger resuming his position.

Ehinger only remained in Coro for a year before he set out again in 1531. He retraced his earlier route, this time with several hundred Spaniards and a small army of Indian slave bearers, as far as Maracaibo and then turned southwest to the mountains. Although the terrain was difficult, Ehinger's advance was ruthless: he kept his Indian slaves together by means of a long iron collar that connected the chain of bearers in a single line, and if one bearer was unable to keep up because of illness or fatigue he was simply decapitated so as not to slow down the others. Ehinger met the attacks of hostile Indian tribes with the same methodical brutality, virtually depopulating whole villages as an example to others.

At Tamalameque, on the Rio Magdalena, Ehinger claimed a rich store of jewels and gold, which he wrested from terrified Indians who had sought refuge on islands in the flooded river. But the treasure did Ehinger little good. He sent the loot back to Coro with a small party of only 35 men, who blazed a new route rather than retrace their steps and face the vengeance of the Indians they had devastated. Almost immediately they lost their way and staggered through endless lagoons, swamps, and insect-infested rivers. The Indian porters escaped or collapsed and the Spaniards had to carry the heavy gold themselves. At last they could manage it no further and buried the treasure under a huge tree, hoping the tree would serve as a landmark. None of them ever reached Coro: reportedly one man survived, who was captured by the Indians and eventually adopted native ways. The treasure was never recovered, although many searchers came after it later.

Ehinger waited at Tamalameque for the party to return with

reinforcements from Coro but, finally concluding that he had been betrayed, he decided to press on regardless. He went south, where advance scouts had reported cool, heavily populated, mountainous country. It was the eastern Cordillera (mountain chain), one of the three that make up Colombia's Andean mountains. The change in altitude combined with the icy temperatures killed off most of the native porters and many of the Spaniards. Ehinger survived, as did a few dozen of his men. By this time they were starving as well as freezing and were plagued by hostile Indians. Near present-day Pamplona, Ehinger finally realised that it was futile to continue. He died on the return march, and only a handful of men stumbled into Coro in late 1533, gaunt and haggard. They had no gold to show for their ordeal.

Nikolaus Federmann, a young German agent for the Welsers who arrived during Ehinger's first expedition from Coro, was to fare rather better. In September 1530, while Ehinger was making the final preparations for his second attempt, Federmann (then only 25 years old) went south from Coro into the rugged foothills of the Sierra Nevada de Mérida, reaching the area around what is now Trujillo before Indian attacks made it impractical to continue. He returned in six months with some gold he had seized from the Indians and a tantalising story – soon to become bitterly familiar to the conquistadors – about the tremendous riches of a people who lived further west.

Ehinger's successor as governor was Georg Hohemut, from the German commercial town of Speyer. The Spaniards found his name totally unpronounceable (they had barely managed Ehinger, usually altering it to Alfinger or Dalfinger), and he is known in the Spanish chronicles simply as Jorge de Speyer (or Espira). Hohemut was as fascinated with the prospect of El Dorado as his predecessor had been. In May 1535, apparently relying on Indian reports of gold near the sources of the Río Meta, Hohemut set out with 400 men of whom a quarter were on horseback. Near what is now Barquisimeto (where Federmann had acquired his gold from the natives five years before) the expedition was decimated by fever in the hot, humid lowlands. Hohemut continued with less than 200 survivors, encouraged no doubt by the success of others – by this time Pizarro had conquered Peru with all its gold. Just beyond the Río Casanare he found some friendly Indians who told him that over the mountains to the west was a grassy plateau that was populated by a gold-rich people who kept sheep. They pointed in the direction of what is now Bogotá, where they said was a city with a temple full of precious objects. They offered to guide the Spaniards to a pass through the mountains but turned out to be less familiar with the territory than expected, and after a prolonged and futile search the attempt was abandoned when a group of hostile Indians made a savage attack on the party. Hohemut continued south, probing for any way across the forbidding mountains.

They encountered the Uaupés Indians, who possessed some gold and silver and also confirmed the stories of a fabulously wealthy golden kingdom across the mountains – but still no pass could be found by which to reach it. Hohemut doggedly marched on until he was within one degree of the equator, and by then he had only 50 men fit for service – the rest were pathetic invalids. Carrying the treasure he had managed to find, Hohemut headed back to Coro which he reached in 1538, three long years after he had departed. In the end Hohemut himself paid dearly for his gold: exhausted, he died within a year of his return.

By that time, however, the quest for El Dorado was in full swing, and in 1538 three expeditions were underway, each recklessly spending lives in an obsessive search for the golden man. Three single-minded men, each with his own armed force, were steadily moving toward a preposterous confrontation. All three had set out in the spring of 1536. The largest party to start was that of Gonzalo Jiménez de Quesada, an adventurous young lawyer from Granada who had arrived in Santa Marta, one of the oldest Spanish settlements on the northern coast, in 1535. The next April Quesada set out with 620 men on foot and 85 horsemen, despatched by his governor on an urgent search for gold to meet the town's debts. From the beginning they were harassed by Indians, and after a short march through the desert to the mouth of the Magdalena they found themselves in trackless jungle. The Spaniards had to hack their way through the vines with machetes, malarial mosquitoes buzzed around their sweating bodies, and inevitably racking fever tormented them. They reached Tamalameque where they were attacked by Indians who were embittered by their earlier experiences with Europeans. After a halt there – during which they received some additional supplies from Santa Marta, brought by brigantines up the Magdalena – Quesada went on, following the river south.

Fever, jaguars, alligators, and the ubiquitous Indians with poison-tipped arrows all took an appalling toll. After four months only 209 men were still alive. There were no towns to raid for food; game was scarce, and when an animal was killed it had to be eaten immediately, otherwise it turned putrid in the oppressive damp heat. A dismal air of futility came over the Spaniards as the months wore on. The jungle seemed to continue forever, and the exhausted men were probably incapable of carrying on much further or of surviving the return march to Santa Marta. It was not until January 1537, nearly 10 long months after they had begun, that the Spaniards moved out onto the high mountain plateau of Cundinamarca astride the Cordillera Oriental. The cultivated fields seemed like a miracle to the half-starved conquistadors. They had reached the mountain kingdom of the Chibchas.

Over a million Chibchas lived in their almost unapproachable highland plateau. Agriculturally self-supporting, their main foodstuff was the potato, and it was they who first introduced the Spanish to that useful tuber. They were expert in weaving and pottery, had developed an alloy of gold and copper which combined the greater strength of copper with the sheen of gold, and lived in substantial villages with large communal buildings. Realising the high level of this civilisation, the Spanish immediately looked for gold. The terrified Chibchas fled at their approach, first burying their gold. The soldiers pursued the Indians from settlement to settlement, capturing just enough gold to whet their appetite for more. At last they came to Tunja, which they approached so stealthily that the Spaniards were in the city before the inhabitants were able to hide their possessions.

It was truly a golden city: thin plates of gold tinkled musically outside the houses; the people were ornamented with golden pendants, earrings, and diadems of feathers embedded in gold. There were golden statues, gold-inlaid weapons, gold beads – and emeralds as well. Emeralds as big as walnuts were common. The soldiers ran wildly through the town, indiscriminately grabbing treasure. One man rushed up to Quesada, who was sitting quietly with the captured ruler of the city, and shouted in ecstasy, 'Peru, Sir General, Peru ! This is another Peru !'

Although they did not know it, they had found El Dorado. Just before coming into Tunja the conquistadors had passed beside Lake Guatavita – the very lake into which the gilded monarch had ceremoniously dived. But the real land of El Dorado had one major deficiency: it had no gold mines. The gold that so richly ornamented Tunja was all acquired by trade. Cundinamarca possessed salt mines, and the surrounding Indians readily traded gold for salt. Thus, after the Spanish had emptied the Chibcha cities of the gold that had been accumulated over generations, there was no more to be had. They learned this only gradually, and with that realisation came the firm conviction that Cundinamarca could not be El Dorado after all. The legendary city of gold must lie elsewhere.

Quesada and his men paused to decide what to do next. The Indians had told him of a temple, the House of the Sun, which held far more gold than all of Tunja. It lay to the west, and that seemed the most likely prospect. But as he was assembling his force disconcerting news reached him. Another party of Spaniards was approaching.

The other party turned out to be commanded by Sebastián de Belalcázar, who had been one of Francisco Pizarro's lieutenants in Peru. Belalcázar had been sent north by Pizarro after the overthrow of the Incas, and in 1534 on his own authority he had conquered Quito in what is now Ecuador. In Quito he heard rumours of the dazzling Colombian El Dorado, and in 1536, just as Quesada was leaving Santa Marta, Belalcázar had set out from Quito. He came by way of Popayán and Cali, leaving men to hold both outposts as he continued north. After leaving Cali he marched his 200 infantry and 100 horsemen through progressively more difficult country, hampered by the vast herd of swine which he had brought to provide food for his men. The little army, moving at a pig's pace, was harried by Indians who made lightning attacks armed with the poisoned arrows that brought inevitable and agonising death. They came through both icy mountains and jungle heat, and at last, in January 1539, they reached the high plateau of Cundinamarca. There they found Quesada's men, who had already conquered the Chibchas.

Incredibly, there was still more to come. Back in that same spring of 1536 a third force had set out for the golden city. Nikolaus Federmann, the young German based at Coro, had not waited for his governor, Georg Hohemut, to return from his expedition to the south before setting out himself with 400 men. He also went south, but he kept somewhat to the east of Hohemut's route. This took him through the grassy plains, or Llanos, of the Orinoco basin, territory later gold-hunters would come to know well. There are virtually no landmarks in the grassy marshes. In the dry season the heat is unremitting and almost unendurable; in the rainy months the rivers flood and the entire area becomes an appalling quagmire. Federmann and his men beat off attacks by Indians, their clothes rotted away on their backs, and their horses lost their shoes and stumbled on unshod.

Federmann wandered for nearly three years between the Llanos and the Cordillera, seeking a pass to the west. At last he came to the Indian village of Pasacote and discovered what he and Hohemut had both so profoundly hoped for – a pass into the high plateau. Only then did Federmann, in his turn, discover the galling reality – El Dorado was full of rival Spaniards. Then the final irony became apparent. Each of the three armies had exactly 166 survivors. Three precisely equal forces faced each other on the remote, mountain-encircled plateau.

In the end, although the rival armies muttered among themselves, the three generals met the unprecedented situation with grace. (The discovery that there were no gold mines in Cundinamarca probably helped to soothe relations.) Besides, all three were in a somewhat irregular position. Belalcázar had far exceeded his authority from Pizarro in continuing beyond Quito; Quesada had sent none of the gold he had seized back to Santa

Marta, where the governor was desperately in need of it; Federmann had left Coro while Hohemut was away and had made definite efforts to avoid his returning soldiers, when Hohemut might have reasonably anticipated some help. Therefore Belalcázar shared his pigs, Quesada shared some of his gold, and all three agreed to sail to Spain together where the king could distribute the governorships of the newly discovered lands. Prudently, they followed the Magdalena to Cartagena and sailed from there to Cuba – none of the three attempted to revisit the bases from which they had set out.

In Spain Belalcázar was given the governorship of Popayán. Federmann discovered he was out of favour with the Welsers, who felt aggrieved that he had abandoned his duties to wander in the Llanos for three years – without even reaching El Dorado in first place. Disappointed, Federmann never returned to South America. Quesada, indisputably the first to reach Cundinamarca and conqueror of the Chibchas, arrived at court to find that his claim to the governorship of New Granada (as he had named the plateau) was challenged by the son of the governor of Santa Marta. The governor had died in 1536, just after Quesada left, and his son (who had stolen Santa Marta's gold and escaped to Spain the year before) claimed not only the governorship of Santa Marta by right of inheritance but that of New Granada as well, saying it was as a representative of his father that Quesada had acted. The son had married well and had rich relatives to support him, and in 1540 the king gave both Santa Marta and New Granada to him. Quesada left Spain in disgust, and it was 10 years before he returned to South America.

When the three generals set off for Spain, Quesada's brother Hernán was left in command of New Granada, and he also attempted some further gold hunting. By this time Lake Guatavita had been identified as the lake of El Dorado, and in 1540 Hernán attempted to drain the lake to recover the golden objects that had been thrown into it. When tremendous efforts produced only a large quantity of thick mud and very little gold, Hernán concluded that it simply could not be the true lake of gold. El Dorado must lie elsewhere. As the Quesada expedition had explored west and north of the plateau and found nothing, and as Belalcázar had come from the south and not discovered the land of gold, Hernán decided that it must then lie to the east. (He ignored the awkward fact that Federmann had approached from that direction.) For a full year Hernán and nearly 300 Spaniards, with 5000 Indians, hunted through the Llanos and found nothing but Indian arrows and appalling heat. Half his men died; all the horses perished, and the expedition returned on foot, gaunt and haggard. They had discovered no gold.

Another younger brother who searched in the same general area was Gonzalo Pizarro, whose elder brother was the conqueror of Peru. Gonzalo left Quito in 1541 to follow the golden legend. By this time the tale had become so embroidered that the king was said to wear powdered gold as his ordinary attire, and the ceremony of the lake was disregarded. Seeking El Dorado, Pizarro and his men started out by crossing the eastern Cordillera, a ghastly experience in the course of which more than a hundred Indians froze to death. Once on the other side, Gonzalo became frustrated when the local Indians were unable to tell him where El Dorado lay, so he had them tortured on makeshift racks. When they still had no information to give, he had a few devoured by his dogs.

When word of his methods had spread from tribe to tribe he found no lack of extravagant reports of wealth, always possessed by a people who lived some distance to the east. Excited by the prospect of at last finding the golden city, the Spanish floundered further and further east through swamps and an endless maze of deep, fast-running creeks. Men and horses drowned, food was scarce, and even the ferocious hunting dogs were consumed as meat. So many of their Indian bearers died or deserted that the Spaniards were reduced to carrying their heavy equipment themselves. By this time they were following the wide Coca River, and Pizarro decided to build a boat to carry the surplus baggage and sick men downstream. A brigantine was built, and for a few weeks it moved slowly down the river beside the men, who marched wearily along the banks. Hunger was becoming a major problem, so just after Christmas 1541 the brigantine sailed ahead out of sight to search for settlements further on, where they could obtain food for the starving men upstream. But the brigantine, captained by Francisco de Orellana, never returned. Whether Orellana deliberately deserted Pizarro (as one of the men on the brigantine claimed), or whether he was unable to return upstream because of the fast-moving current (which he himself maintained), he went on to gain fame as the first to navigate the Amazon River. Pizarro, despairing at last and concluding that he had been betrayed, gave up the golden vision and struggled back in August 1542. Less than a third of the proud men who had set out returned to Quito, and those who did were in rags, wan and wasted beyond recognition.

While Pizarro was living out his nightmare east of Quito, another expedition was hunting for the same golden goal to the north. Philipp von Hutten, another young German, had been sent out by the Welsers from Coro to seek the golden 'temple of the sun', which was now believed to exist east of the Colombian Cordilleras. Hutten was no more successful than any of his predecessors, but he did hear from friendly Indians that a wealthy tribe called the Omagua lived along the northern shore of the Amazon. He even managed to get a glimpse of their city from a distance, and viewed from a hilltop the city did indeed seem to glitter like gold. But by that time he had only a few men left, and they were beaten back by the ferocious Omaguas. They straggled back to Coro in 1545 where they discovered a usurper in command, who had Hutten beheaded. It was the end of Welser rule in Venezuela: the Spanish authorities stepped in, and the usurper himself was seized and executed. But no more Germans came to search fruitlessly for El Dorado.

The next episode was particularly grisly and bizarre. The governor of Peru in the mid-16th century came to the sensible conclusion that the search for El Dorado was an excellent enterprise on which to send the unruly ruffians who had nothing to do but cause trouble once the conquest was complete. In 1559, therefore, an expedition set out headed for the upper Amazon, where El Dorado was then assumed to be located. The young nobleman given command, Pedro de Urzúa, had the misfortune to recruit among his disorderly rabble a homicidal maniac called Lope de Aguirre, and Urzúa himself was very soon hacked to death in a mutiny. His beautiful mistress (whom he had unwisely chosen to bring with him) and his successor Guzmán met a similar fate, and the madman took command himself. All thought of finding El Dorado was abandoned as the bloodthirsty pirate band groped north toward the coast of Venezuela. Aguirre garroted or stabbed anyone he suspected of disloyalty – and he was a suspicious man. When they reached the coast they crossed to the Spanish settlement on Margarita, an island just offshore. There they attacked, looted, and murdered their fellow countrymen. Aguirre sent off a long, rambling letter of defiance to the king of Spain, declaring one of his own followers (whom he nevertheless executed in time) 'Lord and Prince of Peru.' The angry Spanish authorities at last acted, and Aguirre found himself encircled. In his final desperation, just before he was captured and killed on the spot, Aguirre stabbed his own daughter to death.

The horrifying behaviour of Aguirre and his gory progress did not slow down other seekers of El Dorado – but each of them in the end met the same dismal fate. The jungles of the upper Amazon swallowed them up and the expeditions foundered, exhausted by heat, enfeebled by starvation and disease, and continually harassed by hostile Indians and their terrible poisoned arrows. Illusions were dissipated: Hutten's 'golden city', proved to be just another Indian town. Monotonously the skeletal survivors crept back to their home bases empty-handed, El Dorado ever elusive.

One of the most forlorn returns was that of Quesada, the conqueror of Cundinamarca, who had been dispossessed of his rightful title to New Granada at the court of Spain. In 1550 he had returned to Bogotá, the city he had founded, as a poor but highly respected man. Over the years he gradually acquired property, but he was as obsessed with the idea of the golden city as ever, and in 1568 he mortgaged all he possessed to launch out once more in search of El Dorado. He was still convinced that the city lay in the Llanos, in spite of the fact that the area had been crossed and recrossed by many expeditions. He was nearly 70 when he set out from Bogotá with a proud flourish, and four years later the pitiful fragments of his glittering procession crept back to the city. At their head was Quesada, still straight in his saddle, on a half-starved horse. He had staked everything on this final bid for glory, and he had lost it all. At least he was alive: of the 400 men who accompanied him from Bogotá only 25 returned.

Although Quesada himself never again led a search for El Dorado, his conviction that it existed never wavered. In his will – he died in 1579, at the age of nearly 80 – he made two bequests. One was for a well to be built on a hill in Peru, where the climate was hot and no water was available for wayfarers; Quesada had known his share of thirst. The other was the governorship of the unconquered land he had explored in his search for El Dorado, between the Orinoco and Amazon rivers. That he bequeathed to the husband of his niece, his only living relative, with the proviso that he continue the search for El Dorado.

Thus Don Antonio de Berrio, a professional soldier who was then about 60 years old, was catapulted into the quest for El Dorado by the indomitable determination of his wife's uncle. In 1580 he arrived in New Granada with his family and set about his inherited task. By this time the search for El Dorado had been going on for half a century, and Berrio, with the clearer vision of the outsider, considered that both the Andean plateaus and the Llanos to the east had been combed so thoroughly that there was no point in further investigation there. Berrio decided instead to try east of the Llanos, where there might be mountains. He had not forgotten – as many had – that the original reports of El Dorado had always mentioned a lake surrounded by mountains. In 1584 he set out to see. He crossed the eastern Cordillera from Tunja with only about 80 men and pushed briskly across the Llanos. Either he was more efficient than his predecessors or he had learned from their errors, because it took him only a few months to cross the maze of rivers and swamps that had so often defeated others. There before him were the mountains, east of the Orinoco River in what is now southern Venezuela. Although he reached the foothills, he was caught by the rainy season, and too many of his men fell ill with swamp fevers to try to go on. Berrio sensibly decided to retreat. He returned to New Granada 17 months after leaving, having lost only eight men.

He did not stay there long. In the summer of 1585 he was again on his way, crossing the Cordillera and the Llanos with his usual brisk despatch and, reaching the foothills again, marched along them for nearly 600 miles without finding a pass through the mountains. After two years of this his men rebelled, and most of them followed a mutinous captain back to New Granada. Thus reduced in manpower to below what he considered a safe level, Berrio abandoned further attempts at exploration and returned home himself. He was by now nearly 70 years old.

But in 1590 he was off again. By this time he knew exactly where he was going, and he travelled mainly by river. He went down the Pauto southeast to the Meta, and from there into the mighty Orinoco. His ranks thinned from day to day: some men died in the swift-running current, and others deserted. The horses had to be turned into rations for those who remained. But Berrio's leadership prevailed (the Englishman Sir Walter Raleigh, his opponent in days to come, wrote that he was 'a gentleman well-descended . . . of great assuredness, and of a great heart'). He had heard that behind that implacable mountain range was a lake where, said the Orinoco Indians, lived a tribe of great power and splendour; he was determined to reach it. What was more, he was told that these Indians had only arrived recently and had gained their power through military skill and payments in gold. For years it had been whispered that some of the Incas had escaped Pizarro and his terrible victory by fleeing eastward: Berrio must have imagined his quarry as Incas and El Dorado rolled into one.

He was told that the mountains came to an end near the mouth of the Caroni, a tributary of the Orinoco which joins the river just above the vast Orinoco estuary. But progress directly up the Caroni was impossible because a mighty waterfall blocked the way only a short distance upstream. Berrio therefore camped just beyond it. His manpower situation was again critical: only 50 of his men had survived, and of these scarcely a dozen were in good health. Although the Indians assured him that the riches of El Dorado lay within four days' march, Berrio was unable to advance. The gold was as unattainable as ever. Berrio sent letters via Indian guides to the governor of the island of Margarita (which Aguirre had brutalised 30 years before) asking for supplies and reinforcements, but there was no answer and no help. He watched his men grow more feeble and their provisions diminish daily, and eventually he had to abandon this attempt, too.

But this time instead of returning to New Granada, Berrio continued down the Orinoco to the sea and sailed to Margarita. There the old man, greatly tired by his monumental journey across the continent, discovered that Juan Sarmiento, the governor of Margarita, saw him as an obstacle in the governor's own path to the riches of El Dorado. It was Berrio, after all, who had the legal right to search the Orinoco area. He was of necessity Sarmiento's guest, but although he was aware of the threat of treachery beneath the cordial facade he was helpless to do anything except write letters seeking aid from the authorities.

In the midst of this unhappy situation occurred an extra-ordinary event which electrified the population of Margarita. It was rumoured that a man who called himself Juan Martinez had suddenly appeared, dressed as an Indian and speaking Spanish haltingly as if it were unfamiliar to him. He reportedly claimed that he had gone into the Llanos on a Spanish expedition over a decade before. Every man except himself had died, but he had been captured by Indians and lived among them for 10 years before he escaped. During this time he had actually been taken, blindfolded, to the great city of the Gilded Man and had seen with his own eyes the golden skin of the king and his courtiers. For seven months he had lived amid unimaginable wealth in a city he called Manoa. Then he was blindfolded again and allowed to leave, loaded with treasure. Unfortunately he had lost all of it to robbers on his way to Margarita.

The man was never actually seen by anyone in authority, and all the accounts agree that he died very shortly after his appearance. Still, it was an absorbing tale, almost too incredible for disbelief. To Berrio, this was confirmation of all he had hoped for; the possibility that Juan Martinez was lying or had lost his wits during his years in the jungle – or, indeed, that his story was a complete fabrication – seems never to have occurred to him.

Berrio had left the Orinoco late in 1592, and by the spring of 1595 he still had not managed to return. Every attempt to seek assistance had come to nothing, seemingly producing only more rivals. 'The devil himself is the patron of this enterprise,', Berrio declared in bitter frustration, according to Sir Walter Raleigh.

Raleigh himself was to become Berrio's most formidable rival. The English had made their presence felt first in 1594, when a party arrived at Trinidad, sent by Raleigh on a reconnaissance voyage to check out the possibilities of an English attempt on El Dorado. Berrio, who by then had managed to establish a garrison and was living at Trinidad, away from Sarmiento's malignant hospitality, received them peaceably enough; but later an ambush (whether engineered by Berrio or not is unclear) resulted in eight men having their throats cut. Sir Robert Dudley, another Englishman, arrived in February 1595 but was understandably wary. Again Berrio was friendly, but Dudley chose to stay on the opposite side of the island and used it as a base for a brief and abortive attempt on the Orinoco estuary, where his men collected a few golden trinkets. In April, unsuspected by Berrio, Raleigh himself landed on Trinidad. He defeated the few soldiers sent out to investigate and swept into Berrio's stronghold with the advantage of surprise. The garrison was burned, 20 Spaniards were killed, and Berrio found himself a prisoner on Raleigh's. ship.

Sir Walter Raleigh was a fascinating man. Courtier, philosopher, poet, soldier, and liar, he had been a favourite of Queen Elizabeth I until he provoked her wrath by secretly marrying one of her maids of honour. He and his new wife were promptly imprisoned in the Tower of London, and even after his release the queen looked upon him with cold dislike. Raleigh's attempt on El Dorado was his bid to regain her favour and win back her preference by heaping her with gold from the New World. Raleigh also, in common with most Britons of his era, deeply distrusted and despised the Spanish. He felt that it was imperative for the English to weaken Spain by drawing off some of her South American treasure, which might otherwise finance Spanish aggression in Europe.

While Berrio was his prisoner Raleigh developed a cautious respect for the old Spaniard, and verbally the two men fenced politely. Berrio was willing enough to talk of El Dorado, but he emphasised the hardships and exaggerated the distances. Berrio told Raleigh of the reports of Juan Martinez and his gold, but he also told him of the sandbars and swift currents of the Orinoco estuary. Raleigh concluded that Berrio was simply trying to discourage and mislead him.

But in the event he found the difficulties real enough, beginning with the fact that the waters of the estuary were too shallow for his boats. Using makeshift craft, he wandered vaguely through the complicated system of waterways. When the water was low, progress was slow because of the mud flats; when the water was high, the current pushed them back. In spite of it all, Raleigh pushed stubbornly on until he reached the mouth of the Caroni. Here the Indians told encouraging tales of the riches of Manoa, beside the lake on the other side of the mountains. Raleigh started up the Caroni but the falls stopped further progress. His men fanned out to gather ore samples that seemed to glitter like gold and stones that looked like sapphires. But the winter rains were beginning, and Raleigh decided it was time to return. The journey back to the coast was easier, as this time they travelled with the current.

In England he was given an unenthusiastic welcome. He had no gold, and many of the ore samples were worthless. The queen was even less favorably disposed toward him than before, and Raleigh was given no opportunity to return to South America. In 1596, the year after his return, he did manage to send back his lieutenant, Laurence Keymis, to maintain contact with Raleigh's Indian allies. Keymis discovered that Berrio had reached the mouth of the Caroni and had established a fortification there, which blocked access to the area in which Raleigh had found small amounts of gold ore. Later expeditions backed by Raleigh were no more successful.

Raleigh himself did not return to South America for nearly 20 years. In the meantime Berrio, after a series of disappointments, had died in his jungle fortress at the mouth of the Caroni, unable to penetrate further. In England Raleigh fared little better. After Queen Elizabeth died in 1603 her successor, James I, had him imprisoned in the Tower again at the instigation of his enemies. For 13 years he remained there, dreaming of the day he would be free to set out again for El Dorado.

When he did, in 1616, it was under almost impossible conditions. James was then following a pro-Spanish policy, and he released Raleigh for the expedition only with the proviso that he search for the gold of El Dorado without setting foot on Spanish territory or inflicting injury on any Spanish vessel. In addition, Raleigh still had a death sentence hanging over him, and he was not to be pardoned unless he returned successful.

Not surprisingly, he failed. Bad luck dogged him throughout: the voyage across the Atlantic was terrible, and at the end of it Raleigh – then well over 60 – was too ill to lead the expedition ashore himself. His faithful lieutenant Keymis went on with Raleigh's 24-year-old son Walter. For all his loyalty, Keymis brought both Raleigh and the expedition to the verge of disaster by blundering into a battle with the Spanish at the mouth of the Caroni. The English took the fort, but young Walter was killed and the terms of the commission had clearly been violated. To add to the debacle, there was no gold to be found. After wandering around aimlessly in bitter misery, Keymis at last brought his force back to the waiting Raleigh, who received his report of failure heaped upon failure with cold anger. In despair Keymis retired to his cabin, where he killed himself. Raleigh sailed back to England with a disappointed and mutinous crew. He was immediately imprisoned and, on October 29, 1618, he was beheaded.

Raleigh was to be the last of the heroic seekers after El Dorado. The Spanish abandoned the quest after the failure of Berrio; the Dutch, British, and French were more concerned with the tangible profits of trade and slaves in the Caribbean than with the illusory riches of El Dorado. Neither Raleigh nor any other man ever found El Dorado in the territory of Guiana. The golden myth had become a fatal will-o'-the-wisp leading men deeper and deeper into the jungle to their destruction. To the extent that the golden man – El Dorado – had ever existed, he existed in Cundinamarca on the high Andean plateau. But no reality could ever live up to the golden legend, and so – although the fabled lake was found early in the search – the quest went on and on, moving further eastward as each supposed site was found to be barren. There were no gold mines in Cundinamarca; there was no gold along the Amazon; and finally, when the mountains of Guiana were breached, it was discovered that there was no city of Manoa. The lake of which the Indians had told was simply formed when winter rains flooded the shallow banks of the rivers.

The interior of South America is only slightly less forbidding now than it was in the days of Quesada, Berrio, and Raleigh. The more remote Indian tribes are little more affected by civilisation. Even today some people wonder if somewhere in the deep jungle El Dorado might await discovery. The will to believe is still as curiously persistent as it ever was.

CHAPTER 19

THE DESERTED CITIES
OF THE MAYA

While Europe lay rotting in the stultifying grip of the Dark Ages, a civilisation half-way across the globe was enjoying its golden period. In the area now divided between southern Mexico and Guatemala the Maya raised sacred cities adorned with pyramids to rival those of ancient Egypt. Their buildings were bedecked with carvings of great intricacy and beauty, and Maya society seems to have been equally ceremonial and decorous. They were not, on the other hand, an impractical people – their astronomers made observations and calculations astounding by even modern standards. Yet, at the height of their achievements, they left their cities and vanished into the jungle. When the Spanish discovered the Maya cities in 18th century, they had been abandoned for a thousand years. Why did such a thriving, developed civilisation suddenly destroy itself?

If it were not for chewing gum, we would know even less than we do about the mysterious Maya of Central America. Their incredibly sophisticated civilisation rose to its greatest height in the six centuries after 300 AD and then inexplicably collapsed, completely and entirely. What had once been a thickly populated territory returned to virtually uninhabited virgin forest. The Maya cities are now nearly submerged in smothering vegetation. The tips of the tallest pyramids, green with creeping vines, may rise above the treetops, but most of the buildings are completely hidden, their locations suggested only by gentle swellings in the surface of the all-enveloping overgrowth. The only people who now walk the warm and humid forest paths are native chicleros, who collect the sap from the sapodilla trees which provides chicle, the base for chewing gum. The ancient Maya also gathered the sap centuries ago, but they used it as an adhesive.

Only the chicleros now know the forest paths, and they were the ones who guided the archaeologists to the half-forgotten Maya ruins. The once-bustling ceremonial courts, the patchwork of cultivated fields surrounding the cities, the multitude of scattered huts that housed artisans, craftsmen, builders, and farmers – all were abandoned abruptly to the forest, leaving only their enigmatic hieroglyphic carvings behind. What happened ? Where did the people go ? The forest is silent now, except for the chattering of birds and monkeys.

Archaeologists can offer only suppositions and theories for the many gaps in the history of the Maya. They were the only people of the New World to develop a true writing system for which they used hieroglyphs, but, maddeningly, most of what has been deciphered is simply numerical and calendrical calculations. The great preoccupation of the Maya seems to have been the passage of time. They learned to calculate millions of years into the past, and much of their writing records these computations. The rest is a mystery awaiting the gifted scholar who can finally crack the script, as a codebreaker cracks a code.

But without the clues to be found in their own writing about themselves, the Maya remain elusive. Using only stone tools they managed to build great cities in areas of jungle and forest where the victory over relentlessly encroaching undergrowth was not a single achievement but a daily battle. Though they never grasped the principle of the wheel, yet they charted the heavens accurately. They never learned to weigh a sack of corn, but their mathematicians contemplated eternity and performed elaborate calculations. They never made the short step from the corbelled to the true arch, but the magnificence of their architecture is visible still, even clothed in jungle vegetation.

Their accomplishments have fascinated those who stumbled

on the ruins of their greatness since the time of the Franciscan Diego de Landa, who in the 16th century burned all the Maya books he could seize because they 'contained nothing but superstitions and falsehoods of the Devil.' But after his return to Spain, where he was summoned to explain his excesses, he wrote a history of the Yucatan area in which he recorded the customs, religious beliefs, and history of the Maya calendar, illustrated with drawings of the glyphs. Thanks to his account we know something of these mysterious people, and from the three books (*codices*) which survived, and are now in European museums, we can piece out a bit more. But still we can only glimpse the Maya dimly, through the shifting perspectives of the past: even Landa, the earliest European, arrived seven centuries too late.

The Maya built their civilisation in the central lowlands of the Yucatán peninsula. They did not call it Yucatan – we do not know what they called it or what they called themselves. When the Spaniards first skirted the coastline and saw the well-constructed buildings, they asked (in Spanish) who had built them. The Indians answered, 'Ci-u-than,' which meant 'We don't understand you.' The Spanish took that to mean the land was called Yucatán.

Whatever it is called, the Yucatán peninsula, which now is divided between Mexico and Guatemala, is not a hospitable part of the world. The Maya people inhabited, as they still do, the entire peninsula as well as the adjoining mountainous spine of Central America. The land ranges from arid limestone in the Mexican states of Yucatan and Campeche and the territory of Quintana Roo to the volcanic ranges of highland Guatemala and neighbouring El Salvador. Between lies the central lowland area, which includes what is now the Peten district of Guatemala and the adjacent parts of Mexico and Belize. The territory is mainly low-lying limestone with only a thin layer of soil. It has been described as singularly lacking in natural resources – except, perhaps, for the limestone itself, which is an excellent building material.

Normally there is abundant rainfall during the rainy season, which begins in May and lasts until December or January, but water runs through the limestone quickly, and the supply of water was an abiding Maya concern. In January the dry season begins. Archaeologists have long limited their site work to the dry months; during the rainy season the swamps become an impassable morass. Even in the dry season the humidity is oppressive: one archaeologist working at Tikal, one of the best-excavated Maya cities, had continuous problems with his ear which were only resolved when a doctor removed several tiny mushrooms which had taken root in auditory canal.

No matter how unpromising the territory, it is an indisputable fact that at one time a substantial population lived in the now-abandoned central area. Their method of agriculture is one of the many controversial aspects of Maya life. The theories – and guesses – are based on the method of farming practiced by Maya farmers today, who live on the fringes of the central area. It is the system known as slash-and-burn agriculture or, in the Central American region, the *milpa*.

In the milpa cycle, the farmer cuts vegetation in either virgin forest or an abandoned field during the dry season. At the end of the dry season, but before the rains start, the dried debris is burned to produce ash that fertilises the soil. Then the farmer pokes holes in the cleared land with a digging stick and drops in grains of corn. With luck and under normal circumstances, the rains then come and water the fields, and the grain flourishes. But so poor is the soil – and so great the competition from stubborn clumps of grass that relentlessly return to the cleared land – that after a second year of cultivation the crop is no longer worth the effort expended, and the farmer abandons that plot to the forest and clears new ground. The abandoned field is left fallow for years, never less than three and most commonly between six and eight. By the time the field is again farmed, natural processes have built up its fertility again.

Such a system is obviously wasteful of land, since for every plot farmed in a given year there are three or four fallow. Among modern milpa farmers in lowland Central America, population density ranges from 25 to 100 persons per square mile in a highly decentralised pattern. Milpa farmers cannot live together in towns: the walk to the field cannot be so long that the farmer has no energy left for farming when he reaches it. One of the main problems for archaeologists trying to reconstruct the pattern of Maya life has thus been to explain the existence of Maya cities. It is true that they were not cities in the sense that New York or Amsterdam or Tokyo are cities, but they nonetheless represented concentrations of population. Almost all of the buildings in the excavated Maya cities appear to have been temples and ceremonial structures. The people lived outside the cities near their fields.

Even so, the concentration of homesteads around the ceremonial centres is far higher than the milpa system of farming apparently could support. Tikal is probably the largest of the central Maya centres and is one of the most thoroughly excavated. In the six square miles surrounding the site there are enough house mounds to have accommodated 11,000 residents. That works out at a density of about 1600 persons per square mile – 16 times the maximum density now living within a milpa system.

If the climate of the lowland area was similar to what it is now, and the bulk of the evidence seems to indicate that it has not changed, then it seems impossible that the Maya should have been able to gather thousands of workers to live near the ceremonial centres. But the centres are there, and for six centuries the people were, too.

Furthermore, theirs was not a bare subsistence economy. Millions of man-hours went into the construction of Maya cities which were built of stones joined together with pulverised limestone cement. These were then polished and glazed. A surplus of food would have been required to feed the builders. There were craftsmen and artisans – potters whose skills matched or surpassed those of ancient Greece, sculptors who carved images of astonishing vigour and beauty, and painters who produced vivid murals. There must also have been many priests. All these people had to be supported by a food production system which could supply more than the needs of the farmer and his family alone.

Many suggestions have been formulated to explain how Maya food production worked. Although corn, or maize, was the centre of Maya life, and the youthful corn god was a particularly revered member of the pantheon of deities, they might well have grown other crops as well – root crops such as yams, sweet potatoes, and cassava; and nuts from the ramon or breadnut tree, an excellent source of vegetable protein. The soil might conceivably have been more fertile until overfarmed, although in that case one would expect that over the centuries it would have reverted to its natural state. Or the fallow period in ancient times might have been much shorter than it is now. Which, if any, of these hypotheses are correct we do not know. With no direct evidence scholars can only theorise. Modern techniques, including the sophisticated analysis of ancient pollen, are no help here. Root crops leave no pollen and ramon trees exist abundantly in the natural vegetation, so the presence of their pollen would not be conclusive. The problem is simply one of many that presently remain unsolved.

Perhaps the most elementary of Maya mysteries, however, is where the tribes came from in the first place. There has been no dearth of suggestions. When they were first discovered, Europeans were convinced that the civilisations of the New World must have been transplanted from somewhere else. The sophisticated Maya artefacts were variously attributed to remnants of the Lost Tribes of Israel (by Bishop Landa himself), survivors of the 'lost continent' of Atlantis, and Phoenician settlers who crossed the Atlantic from the Mediterranean. In the 18th century it was suggested that American Indians in general were descended from Noah, and according to this school of thought the Ark was built in America. Another idea was that America had been colonised by survivors of one of Alexander the Great's fleets, recorded to have been lost in the 4th century BC; or perhaps crews from Kublai Khan's ships had been driven across the Pacific by a great storm in the 14th century; or the American peoples might have descended from Trojans, Etruscans, Chinese Buddhists, Norsemen, African Mandingos, Tartars, Irish, or Huns.

Amidst this plethora of proposed origins, most archaeologists today choose the less spectacular theory that the Maya were simply themselves, descendants of several scattered migrations from Asia to America over the then-existing land bridge which is now Bering Strait. The consensus of opinion holds that those migrations took place 10 to 20 thousand years ago. According to this interpretation, by 2000 BC the people who were to become the Maya were probably established in the southern part of what is now Maya territory, and over the next two millennia they developed in the same ways as their neighbours. Early researchers, dazzled by the magnificence of the Maya ruins, believed that Maya culture inexplicably blossomed on its own. But further excavation and study have indicated that the Maya and their neighbours to the north in what is now Mexico – the Zapotec of Oaxaca and the Olmec, centered at La Venta in the state of Tabasco – were developing at nearly the same time. The Olmec, in fact, almost certainly predated them, and many archaeologists now give them credit for beginning the development of what became the Maya calendar, and even for inventing writing.

Other archaeologists speculate that the Olmec in fact spoke Maya (one site in Belize in what was once British Honduras thought to be pre-Olmec, shows Maya building characteristics), and the problem of which group came first becomes yet more convoluted. In any case, focusing on the Olmec simply moves the mystery back in time: Olmec development is as enigmatic as that of the Maya, and their society collapsed just as suddenly around the beginning of the Christian era. In any case, the entire fragile structure of theoretical sequences and influences may change drastically at any time, since in the mile upon mile of uninvestigated jungle and forest the find of a single new site could conceivably alter much of the picture.

By about 250 AD the lowland Maya had evolved a 'civilised' culture. This was once believed to have been a sudden jump in development, which lent strength to the theories that Maya brilliance was an import from somewhere else. More recent study, however, has uncovered clues showing that Maya traits were being developed during the formative period which began around 500 BC. During that period the Maya were building pyramids, proper study of which is unfortunately greatly hindered by the

Maya custom of building later pyramids on top of existing ones. Their burials show that differences in social rank were emerging. The burials also share typical features with later Maya culture – the presence of stingray tail spines, for instance, which were imported for use in ceremonial blood-letting. In a child's burial the finger bone of an adult was found; this is interesting because throughout the Maya period and up to the Spanish conquest it was customary for a mother to bury one of her own terminal finger bones with her dead child. Clearly the tradition is very old.

By 1949 archaeologists had found many of the Mayas' long deserted pyramids in scrub and forest. In ancient Egypt, pyramids had served as royal tombs. But Amerindian people had topped their pyramids with temples in which they practiced rituals including human sacrifice. No Maya pyramid had also served as royal tomb – or so archaeologists believed in 1949, before Alberto Ruz explored Palenque's Temple of Inscriptions.

As an archaeologist working for the Mexican government, Ruz was supervising Palenque's restoration. He had to contend with decayed buildings, heavily invaded by the forests that grow fast in this warm, wet region on the frontier of Mexico and Guatemala. The task proved huge, for Palenque had been a big religious centre rich in strange stone temples, complete with a road, an aqueduct, and steam baths. Ruz found its Temple of Inscriptions especially intriguing. Like other Maya temples, this stone building was a steep-sided pyramid, with steps leading to a crowning temple. This was a small structure roofed by stones that overlapped to form a high but narrow arch, for the Maya never mastered the true arch, and thus could never build large vaults and domes. Stone panels bearing the longest known Maya inscription made the Temple of Inscriptions unique and inspired its present name. But something less obvious caught Ruz's eye.

Most Maya temple floors were faced with stucco. This one consisted of abutting flagstones. The centre stone was huge and at each end of it someone had drilled three holes, then plugged them with stones. Could the holes have held ropes for lowering the slab into position? If so. something important might be hidden beneath. Ruz determined to find out.

Beneath the slab Ruz first found a stairway leading down into the pyramid but the shaft was blocked with a great mass of rocks and earth. It took months of toil to shift this obstruction. At last Ruz cleared 45 steps that went down to a landing with a sharp bend. Then came 21 more steps. Ruz had now descended over 70 feet to the level of the base of the pyramid. Meanwhile he had been making some discoveries. At the top of the stairs people had left jade ear plugs and a reddened stone as an offering. At the foot of the stairs lay other offerings, a pearl, jade beads, pottery. and shells containing red paint. A stucco tube snaked mysteriously down the stairs and continued beyond.

Then came fresh obstacles: first a wall had to be demolished, then a stone-and-lime-packed corridor laboriously cleared. In a stone chest at the far end lay the bones of five youths and a girl, their heads artificially deformed and the teeth gem-encrusted, in the manner of the Maya nobility. Beyond these evidently sacrificial victims loomed a blank wall, several feet thick, its only entrance sealed by a triangular stone slab seven feet high. Ruz's heart beat faster as he tried to guess what lay beyond.

At last, on 15 June, 1952, men heaved the stone aside and Ruz stepped through into a wonderland. Torchlight revealed a roomy crypt 30 feet long, 12 feet wide, and over 20 feet high. To Ruz the man-made cave seemed carved from ice. Rainwater seeping through the limestone rocks over thousands of years had faced the crypt with a gleaming crust of calcium carbonate, while the floor and ceiling were festooned with stalactites and stalagmites. Study of the walls nonetheless revealed a procession of nine larger-than-life stucco reliefs, representing the Mayas' so-called lords of darkness.

Most of the crypt floor was taken up by what seemed to be a massive altar capped by a carved stone slab nearly 12 feet long, more than 6 feet across and weighing several tons. Reliefs carved on its surface revealed a young man lying on the head of a monster. Here, too, were symbols representing life and death, and hieroglyphs dating the work to about AD 700. Human heads masked in jade mosaic lay on the slab.

Below it was another monolith propped on six stone blocks.

Ruz now began to wonder whether the upper slab could conceal a burial. Lifting the slab would be difficult and dangerous, so instead, he had a workman drill through the lower slab to see if it was hollow. A wire thrust in the hole emerged with flakes of red paint. For the Maya red had stood for the east, the rising sun – and immortality. Ruz now knew that his altar was in fact a tomb. To see what lay within he somehow *had* to raise its five-ton lid. Ruz spent a sleepless night watching the lifting process, slowly accomplished with infinite care and patience by means of four truck jacks and tree-trunk sections wedged beneath the corners of the slab. At last the lid stood high enough for Ruz to peer down. He saw a polished oblong slab with projecting 'ears'. Ruz raised this inner lid, and marvelled at what proved to be the contents of a great stone coffin. Lying on its reddened floor was the bejewelled skeleton of a man aged over 40. A jade diadem had crowned his head. A realistic jade mosaic face mask with shells for lips covered his face. A collar of jade beads carved as fruits and flowers had hung about his neck. Jade bracelets, rings, and beads had adorned breast, wrists, and fingers. Even the hairs on his head had been combed out and threaded through jade tubes. The burial was plainly that of someone important – so important that the pyramid and temple had been built above his tomb after his burial, because measurements showed that the coffin would have been too big for men to have carried it down the narrow stairway. Most experts think the man had been a priest-king ruler of Palenque. The sacrifice of the noble youths and maiden would support this theory. So would the stucco 'snake' that crawled from his sarcophagus up through the pyramid – a 'soul duct' to let his spirit travel in and out. But, surprisingly for someone so exalted, the skull was not deformed and the teeth had not been filed and filled with jade as was the Maya custom with nobles. The shape of the body leads some anthropologists to doubt that he had been a Maya Indian at all.

The Maya were probably, then as now, a fairly homogeneous people. Their descendants speak about 15 Maya languages or major dialects, similar in their relationships with each other to those within the Romance group of European languages. Some dialects are mutually intelligible while others are only somewhat alike, as is the case with French and Italian. Generally speaking the Maya are stocky with broad faces, straight or slightly wavy black hair, and almond-shaped eyes. Many Maya have large, hooked noses and a slightly drooping lower lip, traits which were considered very beautiful by the ancient Maya and are faithfully recorded in their art. A broad, sloping forehead was considered so desirable that Maya infants were strapped between boards during their first few days of life in order to set their soft skulls in the required deformation. Slightly crossed eyes were also admired, so a ball would be suspended a short distance above the baby's nose for it to focus on.

However food production may have been organised, inevitably most labourers would have been involved in farming. They lived with their families in small, rounded huts built on low, stonewalled platforms, and it is the existence of these platforms which makes it possible to estimate the population during the peak of Maya development. Maya descendants to this day are exceptionally clean and place a high value on orderliness, and the archaeological evidence shows that this is no recent characteristic. The huts were built in small, neat clusters, often with carefully paved plazas in between. The riches of Maya civilisation seem to have reached the most humble social levels: in remote peasant households archaeologists have found hand-painted, multicolored pottery like that used in the ceremonial centres, as well as imported stone implements for grinding corn.

Wealthier people and priests probably lived closer to the main centres or in smaller centres which boasted their own temple pyramids and one or more 'palace' structures. What exactly these palaces were used for has not been satisfactorily determined. It seems unlikely that they were residential buildings, since many of the walls are massively thick and the rooms are small, ill-lit, and airless. Nor has any domestic debris from the classic period been uncovered within them. Some archaeologists have suggested that they might have been used for solemn religious ceremonies not held in public; others have theorised that they were used by the administrative and bureaucratic workers who must have gathered in the local centres and cities. Lacking any direct contemporary evidence, however, the suggestions remain only educated guesses.

The cities themselves were magnificent, clearly the jewel and pride of the Maya people. They were almost entirely devoted to religious worship, which seems to have been the centre of Maya life in general. Their all-powerful gods were worshipped, placated, and sacrificed to; a knowledge of their good or bad intentions was considered essential for the success of any enterprise. It seems clear that at the top of the social pyramid stood the priests, whose power and authority with the gods was supposed to guarantee the greatest possible benefits for the people. The conquering Spanish thought the Maya gods innumerable; certainly there were a great many. The Maya year was a rich tapestry of festivals, dances, and music devoted to the seasons of the gods. There were processions, ceremonies, and sacrifices. During the festivals the great cities must have been thronged with people drawn in from the neighbouring countryside. The great pyramids, with their steep narrow steps ascending precipitously to temple platforms at the top, must have been awe-inspiring when immaculately clean, shining in the sun. The great plazas and ball courts had stepped accommodation for spectators and must have been crowded with men, women, and children. To this day prayers and offerings remain an important feature of Maya religious life, now a curious amalgamation of Catholicism with aspects of the traditional pagan faith.

Sacrifices played a key part in the religious ritual, and the remains of offerings abound in Maya ruins. Human sacrifice was practiced during the classic period between 350 and 900 AD, though not to the same extent as in the decadent period which followed the Maya collapse; the surviving Maya were heavily influenced by the Mexican peoples' emphasis upon the need of the gods for human hearts. Self-sacrifice by blood-letting seems to have been immensely important throughout Maya history, however, and blood was apparently shed freely from the tongue, ears, elbows, and penis during preparation for and in the course of important festivals.

The Maya were obsessed by time to a degree not equalled by any other great pre-modern civilisation, and a prominent feature of all Maya cities are the *stelae*. These are limestone shafts carved or painted with stylised portraits of gods and hieroglyphic texts which report the inexorable passage of time. It is as if New York were to have a sequence of monuments down Fifth Avenue, each recording the date it was erected and the positions of the moon and the planets at the time, with information on ruling gods.

For the Maya, each day was not merely influenced by a god: each day *was* a god, or rather a number of gods. They visualised the divisions of time as burdens carried by relays of gods through eternity. For instance, imagine 10 May, 1979 carried by six bearers: the god of the number 10 carries May on his back; the god of number 1 carries the millennium; the god of number 9 carries the centuries; the god of 7 the decades; and the god of 9 carries the years. At the end of the day the May load is transferred to the god of the number 11, and after this momentary halt the procession moves off again. These burdens came to be equated with the expected good or ill fortune of the year: the day with which a new year started was its bearer, and the aspect of that god governed the year. If the year began with the god Kan it meant a good harvest, since Kan was an aspect of the maize god. On the other hand, a year beginning with Ix was likely to be disastrous because the god Ix was malevolent. To predict these matters and mollify the evil aspects of gods were clearly major concerns, and these seem to have been the basis for the elaborate Maya systems of calendrical and astronomical calculations. They believed that history was cyclical and that what had happened at a given point in the past would be repeated when that point was duplicated in a later cycle. Given the same influences, history would repeat itself.

These cycles were themselves greatly complicated. A Sacred Round was a cycle of 20 repeating days, each of which was a god, and 13 repeating numbers, which interlocked to form a total of 260 days. The secular year was divided into 18 months of 20 days each, ending with a period of five days which was considered almost outside the year and was desperately unlucky. While it lasted one tried to do as little as possible lest misfortune fall on one's enterprises; one devoted the time to fasting, continence, and prayer. These two calendars, of the Sacred Round and the secular year, intermeshed so that each date was expressed in terms of both: 1 Imix, 19 Pop – rather as if we used our ordinary calendar and a liturgical (Hebrew or Muslim) calendar simultaneously. The two Maya calendars only repeated the same coincidence of dates every 52 years, which was known as the Calendar Round. This poses a problem in deciphering Maya inscriptions in that they are sometimes dated according to the Calendar Round alone, rather like our habit of abbreviating dates – as in 15 May, 78 – so that its position is located within a century, but exactly which century is not indicated. As the Maya wanted to count time in long periods, they also had the Long Count method, which may have been invented by the Olmec. This system (which in its turn interlocked with the Calendar Round) included the *tun*, an approximate year of 360 days; a cycle of *katuns*, periods of 20 tuns or 7200 days; and *baktuns*, periods of 20 katuns or 144,000 days Larger measurements of time existed but were less commonly used.

The entire complicated system has been likened to a series of engaged cogwheels, with the reservation, of course, that the Maya themselves never visualised the process as mechanical but rather as a series of complicated interactions between the relevant gods who took turns ruling the world. To record these intricate calendrical calculations the Maya developed a positional system of representing written numbers, like our own. In our system the numbers 2001 and 1002 use the same digits, but their different positions give them different values. We use a decimal system; the Maya used 20 rather than 10 as their base and used bars and dots for notation. A bar was 5 and the dot was 1. Numbers could be written both vertically and horizontally. It was a much more flexible and subtle system than the contemporary Roman numeral system then in use in Europe, which had no concept of zero. The Maya mark for zero was usually a stylised figure of a shell.

Maya expertise in astronomy was as great as their skill with numbers and dates, and it is particularly impressive in view of the environment, in which it rains for nearly nine months of the year making consistent observation difficult. The Maya were mainly concerned with the movements of the moon and the planet Venus. As they had no concept of a round earth, the movements of heavenly bodies were seen simply as repeating events in the same way that time itself was repetitive. The astronomical patterns were another aspect of the Maya enthusiasm for working out parallel calculations and then intermeshing them. The surviving Maya works – the three codices and the multitude of carved glyphs on stelae and other sculptures – are filled with calendrical and astronomical information.

The last three centuries of the Maya classic period, from 600 AD to roughly 900, were years of rapidly expanding population growth and a significant increase in monumental architecture. Pyramids and temples as well as palace groups rose like mushrooms all over the lowlands. These buildings showed an interesting change in emphasis: whereas the earlier builders had apparently concentrated on temples, the later Maya increasingly replaced temples with secular palaces. There seems also to have been a rise in military activity. Although the presentation of prisoners had been a dominant theme in Maya art from the beginning, in the late classic period there are more scenes of actual fighting.

Who the opponents were is not clear. The individual Maya cities seem to have been self-ruling and independent and have often been compared to the ancient Greek city-states, but the evidence is not definite. There are indications of friendly relations between the cities, and they certainly shared the same language and culture, but until more of the Maya writing is deciphered we are unable to say what their political relationship was; warfare might, then, have occurred between the cities. During the late classic period none of their once-powerful non-Maya neighbours was strong enough to pose much of a threat.

Lacking details, therefore, we are left with the image of a society in full and flamboyant flower. The vast lowland area, once forest, must have been studded with countless ceremonial centres – from simple, thatched hut-temples to the vast grandeur of the massed pyramids, temples, and palaces of the great cities. The land would have been a busy patchwork of cleared fields and clusters of huts grouped together. The people were building, always building, erecting more stelae to mark the passage of time, more temples to honour the gods, and more palaces to reflect the power of the rulers. Sculpture expressed sensitivity; the pottery was the result of skilled experimentation with new techniques of shaping and decoration; buildings were spacious. The civilisation was reaching its climax.

Then it collapsed, quite abruptly, over the course of less than a century. In 790, at the end of one 20-year katun, 19 cities erected stelae (as was usual, although this was the largest number ever to do so). In 810 12 cities erected stelae; in 830 only three did so. The last stelae with full inscriptions from the Long Count dating system were carved in 889. Building stopped; house mounds in the countryside surrounding the cities were abandoned. The palace structures in the city of Tikal, though inhabited, were in a state far from their former glory. Roofs collapsed from lack of maintenance, and the debris was pushed to one side so that the impoverished inhabitants could continue to live in the rubble. Garbage piled up on stairways, in courtyards, and in abandoned rooms – all of which had once been swept clean. The survivors clung on for a while, but estimates suggest that a century later only 10 percent of the previous population remained.

Where did they go'? What could have happened? So far no single explanation seems conclusive. The increasing importance of military power might point to a series of suicidal civil wars, but there is no evidence that the cities were overthrown by force, and in fact there is no sign of anything but natural decay following abandonment. The peasants might have risen in revolt against increasingly powerful priests and nobles. There might have been invasion from abroad (of which there is no evidence). There might have been epidemics (but the endemic diseases of which we know – malaria, yellow fever, and hookworm – are almost certainly post-Columbian importations). Did the Maya simply overpopulate and overfarm their limited rain-forest environment? Of all the possibilities, overpopulation is generally accepted as at least one of the factors leading to the disaster.

For disaster it certainly was. Some of the people of the lowlands may have migrated to the surrounding areas, but there is no archaeological evidence to prove that they did, and in any case nowhere nearby could the total Maya population have possibly been accommodated. One authority does point out that we are not talking about jungles piled high with rotting corpses: the collapse, swift as it was, did extend over four or five generations, and it is an inescapable fact that each generation dies out in any population. The decline may have taken the form of a marked drop in fertility or disproportionately high death rates (perhaps due to malnutrition) among young women and children. Only in the Maya lowlands was the light snuffed out entirely. In Yucatán – or, more precisely, in the northern Maya area comprising the modern Mexican states of Yucatán, Campeche, and Quintana Roo – the civilisation actively continued, although it was altered and increasingly influenced by ideas from Mexico. While most of the Maya cities in Yucatan and Campeche were apparently abandoned about the same time as the lowland sites, some were revived later during the so-called Mexican period from about 975 to 1200. The Itzá, described as foreigners who spoke broken Maya, in 987 seized the famous Chichen Itza site, which had been a Maya city of some importance during the classic period.

Who the Itzá were is another topic of vigorous scholarly, debate. Most likely they were Toltecs, whose culture developed in Tula, about 50 miles north of modern Mexico City. Even if not actually Toltecs, they were clearly influenced by Toltec culture, for Chichén Itzá has Toltec ornaments and additions built on top of Maya structures. The name Chichén Itzá itself means *cenote* of the Itzá (meaning a natural limestone reservoir). Human sacrifices of young virgins were thrown into the depths of the Sacred Cenote, according to stories which circulated from the time of the conquest. Determined archaeologists dredged it, and, although they found human remains, of the 42 identifiable skeletons recovered half were of children, 13 were of men, and the remaining 8 were women, all but one apparently past the normal age of marriage.

Toltec domination of Chichén Itzá lasted for more than two centuries, but we do not know whether any other cities were taken over or how much of the surrounding countryside was under their control. They were succeeded by the rulers of Mayapán, a more recently established city not far from present-day Merida. For the next 250 years Mayapán governed Yucatán, keeping tight control over subject cities by requiring that their rulers live in Mayapán itself. Mayapán was an ordinary city in the sense that most of its buildings were residential. The ruins are extensive and are surrounded by a massive stone wall, now collapsing, which is over 5 miles long. Obviously a defensive device, the wall suggests that conditions were more dangerous.

The ruins of Chichén Itzá show a decline both in the quality of art and the craftsmanship of building, and in Mayapán both continued to degenerate. The Maya fires were burning low; revolts against Mayapán in the 15th century meant only that the independent chieftainships, which had succeeded its centralised rule, warred bitterly against each other. The intertribal rivalry was ended in 1525 with the coming of the Spanish. The conquest of Yucatán was complete 16 years later. Although the last Maya settlement, at Tayasal, a small island in Lake Petén Itzá in what is now northern Guatemala, was not conquered until 1697, the glory of the Maya was long past. But the strength of Maya traditions remained: imported Mexican gods were eventually forgotten, while the Maya rain gods were remembered in primitive ceremonies.

Today Maya ruins still lie in the rain forest, a tantalising reminder of a greatness we cannot grasp. The evidence remaining is incomplete and elusive and it involves trying to reconstitute a culture from a handful of calendars and three books – it is as if we were to use an almanac, *Pilgrim's Progress*, and a manual on astrology to try to visualise our own culture. The magnificence of the Maya accomplishment is indisputable, but what did it mean? What was it like to be a Maya? How did they see their world ?

If we are ever able to read their inscriptions we may come

closer to an answer. For the present the Maya remain one of history's enigmas. They took one of the world's most unpromising environments – the evergreen tropical rain forest – and built within it some of the world's most remarkable structures. But the forest has since swallowed nearly all traces of them and only their memory, incomplete as it is, remains.

CHAPTER 20

THE COUNTERWEIGHT CONTINENT

As soon as Europeans became aware that the earth was a globe, they wondered why most of the land sat in the northern hemisphere. Surely, they argued, this would make the world top heavy and prone to toppling-over. Logically there must be, somewhere in the southern hemisphere, a huge continent to counter-balance the lands of the north. Renaissance map makers would even add this land to the Pacific ocean marked Terra Incognita, the Unknown Land. As the riches of the New World fired the imaginations of explorers, many set-out to find and exploit the lost continent of the south.

Like most rumoured but unseen places, the 'Unknown Southern Land' glittered with promise. The Greeks had suggested its existence on their maps, and by the 16th century it carried a definite aura of reality. For one thing, voyages by the Portuguese and Spanish had established that the world was round, as knowledgeable men had long been aware from the traditions of antiquity. And, as the great 16th-century Flemish mapmaker Gerardus Mercator argued, the symmetry of the earth required a mass of land in the southern hemisphere to balance the immensity of land known to exist in the north; otherwise the world would topple over to destruction amid the stars.

For another thing, the previously unknown continent of America had been proved to exist: was it not reasonable to believe that another continent was waiting to be found? There was even space for it in a southern sea of unknown dimensions. The Portuguese, travelling east around Africa, reached the Spice Islands – the Moluccas – and looked out to the east over what we now call the Pacific Ocean in 1511 . Only two years later, Vasco Núñez de Balboa was taken by his Indian guide to a mountaintop in Panama where he could look out at the same ocean, stretching endlessly to the west. No one could more than guess at the distance between the two points, but it was certainly big enough to contain an Unknown Southern Land – *Terra Australis Incognita*. One small, rather undistinguished-looking man was convinced the distance was not overly large. His name was Fernão de Magalhães, better known in its anglicised form of Ferdinand Magellan. Magellan had an idea and an ambition. His idea was that it was possible to sail west past newly discovered America and reach the Moluccas. His ambition was that he would be the man to do it.

Although Magellan had spent long years in the service of the king of Portugal (he limped due to a wound received in Morocco), Don Manuel, strangely enough, did not like him. In 1512 he refused Magellan further employment, and, insultingly, told him he was free to enter any other service he chose. Magellan went to Spain.

This was to be unfortunate for Don Manuel. Back in 1493, just after Columbus' momentous voyage, Ferdinand and Isabella of Spain had asked the pope for his agreement to their monopoly over their new western possessions. At that time the pope divided the undiscovered world into two portions: all discoveries made to the west of the Cape Verde Islands belonged to Spain, and all to the east were the province of Portugal, which had pioneered the route around the tip of Africa to India. The Portuguese were not entirely happy with this arrangement, and after a year of negotiations the Treaty of Tordesillas was drawn up between Spain and Portugal, adjusting the line to some 340 miles west of the Cape Verde Islands. The problem then became how this affected the other side of the world. There was then no method of determining longitude at sea – a navigator simply guessed, based on his speed and latitude, his likely east/west position – so an absolutely accurate computation of location was impossible. In which half of the world did the Moluccas fall? Magellan was willing to support the Spanish argument that the Pacific was narrow enough for the islands to lie in their half, and to sail west to reach them.

He set out in September 1519 with a little fleet of five ships. 'Very old and patched', the Portuguese ambassador reported scornfully to his king, who by this time was seriously alarmed at the course events were taking. He ordered out his own ships to stop the traitor at the Cape of Good Hope, but Magellan had already sailed, and his route was not to be around Africa. He spent the first winter – from March to October in the southern hemisphere – off the coast of South America, where he had to quell an incipient mutiny. In late October he sailed south and after only four days entered a bay which proved to open into a strait. Luck was with him: in only 38 days he managed to thread his way through the strait now named after him, avoiding the innumerable possible dead ends among the lacework of islands that lie off the southern tip of South America. On 28 November, 1520 he sailed into what he named the Pacific Ocean, up to then simply called the South Sea.

But by this time he had lost two ships. One was wrecked during the winter; another deserted in the strait and fled back to Spain. The three survivors steered northward for the latitude of the Moluccas. It was an unfortunate route: on that course they missed most of the main archipelagoes of Pacific islands, and for 98 terrible days they sailed without touching land. The heat was blistering; food ran out; the water was foul and stinking. Rats were auctioned off between hungry men, but there were not enough. Scurvy, the terrible scourge of the sea, swept the crew.

In March 1521 they finally reached an island where they could anchor. The natives, fascinated by their unprecedented visitors, stole everything they could lay their hands on, and Magellan named the two islands in the group they sighted that day the Ladrones, or Thieves. (They were Guam and Rota, in the group now called the Marianas.) Refreshed by the fruit and fresh food, Magellan and his men sailed on to what is now the Philippines, first to Samar, then Cebu. On 27 April, 1521, Magellan undertook to aid his new Christian convert, the chief of Cebu, on a raid against a rebel in neighbouring Mactan. For all his Christian valour the battle went badly, and Magellan was covering the retreat of his men when he was speared and stabbed to death.

Without their commander, the surviving crew members sank one ship – there were too few of them left to man all three – and careered about the islands for seven months before they reached the Moluccas. Only the *Victoria* managed to return to Spain, arriving on 6 September, 1522 by way of the Cape of Good Hope. She had a cargo of 26 tons of cloves. There were only 31 men left of the 170 who had set out, but those 31 were the first men to circle the globe.

They had also proved that the Pacific Ocean was far wider than anyone had previously suspected, and the passage across it was more terrible. To modern eyes the difficulties they faced were appalling. Their ships were tiny and incapable of sailing close to the wind, and as a result they were completely dependent on the winds and the currents. They were made of wood, and in tropical waters the *Teredo navalis* (shipworm) was fearfully active. It was imperative every few weeks to find a beach or creek where the ship could be hauled up for careening and patching. On shipboard the men ate salted meat and biscuit, and the dreaded scurvy raged. The cause was then unknown (scurvy is now recognized as the inevitable result of a Vitamin C deficiency); seamen usually relied on the pragmatic remedy of fresh food, which again required that land be found. As it often was not, it was considered inevitable that a substantial percentage of an average crew would perish.

Navigation was such an imperfect science that ships were unable to determine accurately either where they were or where such land they did discover was, so that relocating previously charted islands was alarmingly haphazard. There were gifted pilots and navigators, and their successes are all the more remarkable considering the unreliability of their instruments. The crews, however, were less admirable. Often they were the dregs of piracy, prison, and the taverns of the world's ports. Mutiny runs like a black thread through the fabric of Pacific exploration. Whatever the rigours, however, there was the temptation of immeasurable riches. A Spaniard in Peru, Don Pedro Sarmiento de Gamboa, used the customary barbaric methods of inquisition on the natives and heard of an Inca tradition – marvellously wealthy islands that were supposed to lie to the west. It sounded promising enough to warrant an exploratory expedition, and in 1567 one was planned. Sarmiento, however, was not given command. Instead a young man in his twenties, Álvaro de Mendaña, the nephew of the viceroy, was appointed. Sarmiento was named as captain of the smaller of the two ships.

They sailed from Callao in Peru in November 1567 with 150 men, expecting to find land (according to Sarmiento's information) within 600 miles. They covered nearer 7000. For 80 days they saw only endless water. On 7 February, 1568 an island was sighted and named for Santa Ysabel, their patron saint. The islanders were initially friendly but were unwilling to provide food for two boatloads of hungry strangers. When human meat was provided – the arm and shoulder of a young boy – the Spanish were revolted and felt justified in savage retribution on such unnatural heathens. Misunderstandings fuelled ambushes, villages were burned, and the Spanish moved southward to two other islands, Guadalcanal and San Cristóbal. The same melancholy sequence of events was played out again, and it was on a lonely beach on San Cristóbal, watched by hostile islanders lurking in the surrounding undergrowth, that Mendana had the ships careened and cleaned while they decided what to do next.

Mendaña and Sarmiento had already quarrelled; now Sarmiento wanted to remain in the islands and establish a settlement while Mendana thought it wisest to return to Peru. It was true that the ships were worn and leaky; it was also true that ammunition was low, and without it settlers would probably be massacred. The decision was that the sea offered less danger, and they set sail to return. The wind was against them, and it was seven days before the islands disappeared behind them. It would be two centuries before these lands were rediscovered.

The return journey was a nightmare. The ships were badly

provisioned, the captains and pilots argued constantly about the course so that the ships veered indecisively back and forth, and in the end Sarmiento either fell behind or deliberately deserted. Lashed by hurricanes, they crept east across the vast expanse of sea. Their water turned putrid, the biscuit was rotten, and the inevitable scurvy ravaged the crew. Bodies were thrown over board daily. Mutiny was threatened, but at the point of crisis Mendaña prevailed, and at last Lower California was sighted on 19 December, 1568. Sarmiento's ship, equally enfeebled, crept into the bay of Colima to the same harbour the next day. The Spanish authorities viewed the results of the expedition with little enthusiasm. Mendaña had found some islands but no gold, silver or spices, and the inhabitants were naked cannibals.

It was not, by any stretch of the imagination, *Terra Australis* and, taken altogether, not particularly promising. Mendaña, understandably enough, did not see it that way. True, he had not reached the mysterious continent, but these could well be outlying islands. After all, the islands Columbus had reached were poor enough, yet the gold and silver of America were indisputable. He was determined to return.

He surely did not anticipate that he would have to wait 27 years. It was not until April 1595 that Mendaña sailed from Callao again to colonise his discovery, now known as the Solomon Islands. In the years since they had been sighted their attractions had been magnified greatly, and on his four ships Mendaña carried 378 men, women, and children to settle there. His colonists were a mixed lot: there were many unemployed adventurers, prostitutes, and soldiers as well as respectable married couples. Mendaña's wife, a disagreeable woman, also insisted on accompanying him. Only in his chief pilot, Pedro Fernandez de Quiros, was Mendaña fortunate.

The entire expedition was a disaster. In the first place, Mendaña did not know where his Solomons were – he anticipated finding them within 4500 miles of Peru. Twice he thought he'd found them: the first time was when they reached what he named the Marquesas, the second time at the Santa Cruz islands. In both places the relationship with initially friendly islanders became unmanageable. Soldiers restless for action after months at sea attacked at random. Quiros estimated that 200 Marquesans were left dead when the ships sailed away. At Santa Cruz, further west, expedition members turned on each other as well. At his wife's urging Mendana agreed reluctantly to the murder of his wilful camp master, and this led to general slaughter on all sides. In the frenzy the local chief, Malope, was pointlessly shot down in cold blood. Malaria swept the ranks of the survivors, and Mendaña himself was one of the many who died. The dreaded Doña Ysabel, his wife, took command, and with Quiros as pilot undertook to sail the tattered remnants of the fleet to the Philippines. She would not permit the smaller ships to be abandoned and the decimated, fever-ridden crews combined (one ship was lost and eventually discovered with sails set and all hands dead). She washed her clothes in the desperately short supply of drinking water. She sat in her cabin, praying and playing with the keys to the supply room in which she hoarded food, while those around her starved. Quiros' accurate navigation did in the end bring one ship into port at Manila on 11 February, 1596. On that ship alone 50 had died since they left Santa Cruz. Doña Ysabel complained bitterly about the survivors to a local magistrate.

In spite of it all, Quiros was confident that he now knew where the southern continent lay. He was convinced that the Santa Cruz islands, Mendaña's lost Solomons, and New Guinea (known to lie east of the Moluccas) were all close together, and that nearby was the unknown continent where an innumerable multitude of heathen waited to be saved. His mind became more and more fixed upon his missionary task. He petitioned steadily for nearly 10 years: finally at the end of 1605 he was given a fleet of three small ships, and he set out from Peru on a holy crusade. He would convert the inhabitants of *Terra Australis*. His second-in-command was Luis Vaez de Torres, a gifted navigator in his own right.

Quiros had already proved himself an exceptional seaman. He was, however, no leader of men, and as the months passed his crews became more and more restive. The ships passed many uninhabited atolls and stopped at three islands while sailing for

Santa Cruz; at the third they were told of a large land to the south. Full of joy, Quiros sailed to find it, and on 1 May, 1606 he entered a wide bay – 'big enough for all the fleets in the world,' Torres said. As they approached there seemed to be land to the south and southwest as far as the eye could see, and Quiros was convinced that he had found the southern continent at last. He named the river that flowed into the bay the Jordan and declared he would found a city there called New Jerusalem.

The natives did not appear to welcome their salvation. In the first encounters between them and the Spaniards several natives died, and after three weeks spent exploring, planting seeds, and building a church of branches, Quiros abruptly decided to explore the land to windward. The ships set off, but after a night of squalls Quiros' ship was blown out to sea and did not return. Quiros hoped to meet the other ships at the Santa Cruz islands, but as he was unable to locate either the islands or the ships he eventually sailed for Acapulco, which he reached in November 1606.

Torres, left behind with the ships near land, woke to find Quiros gone. He searched for wreckage far enough along the coast to confirm what some had already suspected: Quiros' new land was not the southern continent at all, but merely another group of islands. Three overlapping islands, in a group now known as the New Hebrides, had been mistaken for continuous coast. Torres searched as far south as 21° latitude looking for new land, but finding none he decided to reach the Philippines via the north coast of New Guinea. But, he observed simply, 'I could not weather the east point, so I coasted along to the westward on the south side.' By passing through the strait now named after him which separates New Guinea from Australia, Torres settled a major geographical question of the 17th century: New Guinea was not a projection of Terra Australis, but an island.

At the time no one recognized the significance. Torres reached Manila in May 1607, and from then on nothing more is known of him. His report was filed and forgotten. Quiros reached Peru and eventually returned to Spain. His many petitions to return to his southern land were an embarrassment to Spain, whose colonial fortunes were waning. At length he was allowed to return to Peru to organise an expedition; simultaneously, orders were given to the viceroy to keep him quiet with empty promises. Quiros died in Panama in 1615, unaware of this final betrayal.

As Spain yielded up her ambitions – her treasury was exhausted and her manpower depleted by the continuous demands of her empire – a new power was moving into the Pacific. In 1581 the Netherlands had declared its independence of the Spanish crown. By 1600 Dutch ships – sturdy, efficient ships in which the crews were not crowded and where standards of diet and cleanliness were remarkably high for the time – were sailing around the Cape of Good Hope to a profitable trade in Java. First the Portuguese and then the English were driven out of the East Indies, and after 1623 Dutch supremacy was assured.

But the Dutch were traders whose first priority was trade, not the elusive promise of exploration. The rumoured riches of *Terra Australis* were less productive than the certain returns to be made from Java. Such discoveries as were made tended to be accidental. From time to time ships sailing to Batavia (now Jakarta, Indonesia) went further than they intended and came up against the west coast of Australia – New Holland, they called it. The west and part of the north coast were gradually charted, but more pressing concerns kept the East India Company from investigating what lay inland of those coasts; the few reports they had were not encouraging.

One notable Dutch voyage into the Pacific was made during those early years, but it was not under the auspices of the East India Company. It was, in fact, in defiance of the company. A long-time critic, an Amsterdam merchant named Isaac Le Maire, succeeded in obtaining permission from the Dutch government to trade in Terra Australis and the islands of the South Sea – but he was barred from using either the passage around Africa or the Strait of Magellan. Le Maire consulted with an eminent navigator, Willem Cornelis Schouten, who believed that Tierra del Fuego, which lay south of Magellan's strait, was an island. In 1615 two ships set out to investigate, with Isaac's son Jakob Le Maire as commander and Schouten himself as navigator. By the next January the expedition – reduced to one ship, the *Eendracht*, after the other had burned at Port Desire in Patagonia – passed the opening of the Strait of Magellan. They coasted Tierra del Fuego and, to their satisfaction, came to the end of it. There was land to the east, but with a channel about eight miles wide between the headlands. They named the eastern coast Staten Landt (perhaps it was the southern continent?) and within five days found themselves in the Pacific. They had made the passage. They named the southernmost extremity of the American continent, then to the north of them, Cape Hoorn after their native town in Holland.

Their passage across the Pacific was competent and unremarkable. They passed through the Tuamotu archipelago, faring no better than the Spanish in their encounters with the islanders. In late May, however, they reached Futuna and Alofi, now known as the Horn Islands, and there they spent two weeks with hospitable natives. Le Maire thought these islands might be the Solomons, but they were actually between the groups now known as Fiji and Samoa. Le Maire wanted to sail west to reach the continent he was sure lay near at hand; Schouten was apprehensive of the unknown south side of New Guinea (Torres' report lay buried in Spanish files, inaccessible to foreigners) and felt it prudent to bear northwest around the more familiar north coast. Schouten's view prevailed, and after two months' sailing along the coast of New Guinea they reached the Moluccas, less than 17 months after leaving Holland.

The aftermath of the voyage was not happy. The East India Company refused to believe Le Maire and Schouten's account of the new strait and confiscated their ship and all their goods on the grounds that they had infringed the Company's monopoly. Jakob Le Maire died on the melancholy return to the Netherlands, and Isaac Le Maire, infuriated, sued the Company. After two years of wrangling he finally succeeded in recovering ship, cargo, and all costs with interest from the date of seizure. The Le Maire Strait was established beyond doubt.

Schouten and Le Maire had not, however, been any more successful than their predecessors in pinning down the elusive southern continent. In 1642 the East India Company itself undertook the project of investigation. The then governor general,

Anthony van Diemen, wanted to discover the relationship between the vaguely known coast of New Holland and whatever lay south and east of it. With the advice of one of the ablest Dutch navigators of the time, Franz Jacobszoon Visscher, plans were drawn up for a voyage under the command of Abel Janszoon Tasman, on which Visscher would accompany him.

In August 1642 they left the Netherlands, stopping at Mauritius in the Indian Ocean. From there their instructions were to sail south to latitude 54° unless they encountered the unknown southland before that. By 49°4', they had sighted no land, but the cold was so intense that they returned to 44° and sailed east; toward the end of November they sighted land to the north. They named it Van Diemen's Land – it is now Tasmania. They followed the coastline until it fell away to the northwest and then sailed east across what is now the Tasman Sea.

Two days later they saw more land, an inhospitable rocky shore which rose through forests to cloud-covered summits. The local inhabitants were no more welcoming than usual: when the ships approached the coast the Maoris attacked from their canoes and left four men dead. Tasman and Visscher scurried off to the north. As they coasted along, they named their discovery Staten Landt, believing it might be the western coast of the land Le Maire and Schouten had seen as they rounded Cape Horn. It was actually the south island of what is now New Zealand. Tasman and Visscher missed the strait between the islands and so charted them as a continuous coast with a deep bay.

Leaving the coast at the northern tip, the wind carried them northeast until they encountered the Tonga Islands. Here the islanders were cordial – Cook later renamed them the Friendly Islands – and Tasman was able to get badly needed water and fresh food. From there, Tasman and Visscher faced exactly the same problem Le Maire and Schouten had: should they sail west, which offered the possibility of new discovery but also the danger of unknown shoals, or should they vote for safety and sail along the known north coast of New Guinea? The weather was bad and, like their predecessors, they chose the familiar course. Using Schouten's charts, they followed the entire north coast of New

Guinea. From there they sailed straight for Java through the Moluccas. They arrived in June 1643. They had managed to circumnavigate Australia without ever once catching even a glimpse of the continent.

The company was not particularly pleased with their results. One of the discoveries hoped for had been a passage through to the South Sea whereby the Dutch could sail to Chile and perhaps plunder their old enemies, the Spanish. Although there might be such a passage north of Tasman's Staten Landt, it was not proven. Nonetheless, Tasman and Visscher were sent out again in 1644 to investigate whether there was a passage south of New Guinea. No detailed account survives, but apparently they missed Torres Strait and so reported that New Guinea was connected to the land to the south. It was the last of Tasman's long voyages and was no more enthusiastically received by the company than the other. The Amsterdam managers decided they had had enough of expensive and profitless exploration. The East Indies they already knew about possessed gold and silver enough, and the vision of a Dutch Pacific faded.

By the beginning of the 18th century the search for T*erra Australis* had primarily succeeded in mapping large areas where it was not to be found. The Spanish voyages had discovered nothing but open ocean and scattered island groups north of the Tropic of Capricorn. Schouten and Le Maire had eliminated the possibility that Tierra del Fuego was a projection of the southern continent by sailing south of it; in 1643 Henrik Brouwer found that Le Maire's Staten Landt was only a small island. Tasman's voyage had proved that New Guinea, even assuming it was connected to the land to the south, did not extend further south than Van Diemen's Land, and the existence of the Tasman Sea proved that New Holland (western Australia) did not stretch as far east as Tasman's Staten Landt (New Zealand). Curiously, as the southern continent was shown not to exist in more and more places, it was argued more fiercely than ever that it must exist somewhere else. In 1697 William Dampier, an English bucca-neer, published his journals as *A New Voyage Around the World*, in which he mentioned that another English pirate, Captain

Edward Davis, had told him of sighting land in 1687 about 1500 miles west of Chile in latitude 27°20'. The general public, fascinated by Dampier's tales of the Pacific, was intrigued, and in 1721 the Dutch explorer Jacob Roggeveen set off to find it. *Terra Australis* remained elusive, but he did find Easter Island, with its mysterious giant carved statues and friendly inhabitants.

He was followed by the Englishmen Samuel Wallis and Philip Carteret in 1766, who were no more successful. Like all the other sailing ships entering the Pacific around the tip of South America, their ships were forced by the strong winds and storms of the 'roaring forties' to head north before turning west. Carteret's course was the most southerly so far achieved, and he became convinced that Davis Land did not exist; Wallis discovered Tahiti, an earthly paradise of beautiful scenery and compliant island women.

None of this discouraged Alexander Dalrymple, an English geographer who had worked for the East India Company. He was inspired by the exploits of the Spaniard Quiros and echoed his conviction of the existence of the southern continent. Studying the writings of the Pacific explorers, Dalrymple decided that the coast of *Terra Australis* ran north (slightly west of the usual route from South America to the Juan Fernandez Islands) turned west at latitude 28°, joined the land Quiros had seen, and then probably extended south to the coast Tasman had charted (of New Zealand). The continent was thus 'of a greater extent than the whole civilised part of Asia, from Turkey eastward to the extremity of China,' he wrote enthusiastically in 1767.

A British expedition was being planned at that very time. The transit of Venus between the earth and the sun was to take place on 3 June, 1769 and would be best visible from the southern hemisphere. Wallis' Tahiti was selected as the most suitable location for observation; and such an expedition to the South Seas would clearly also be able to search for the southern continent. Dalrymple himself hoped to lead the expedition, but he insisted on entire control of the ship, and his seagoing experience was limited. The admiralty insisted on the prerogatives of the navy, and so in the end the command was given to a

Captain James Cook

Yorkshire-born lieutenant who had risen through the ranks, James Cook.

Cook's ship, the *Endeavour*, sailed from Plymouth in August 1768, and after a smooth journey around Cape Horn it reached Tahiti the following April. Her men were physically in very good condition: Cook had a passion for maintaining the cleanliness and proper diet of his crew, on the sensible grounds that only with a healthy crew could the ship follow the course she had been given. They spent three months in Tahiti, making observations of Venus as directed and enjoying the land and its people, whose charm was only exceeded by their expertise in thievery. They even stole Cook's stockings from under his pillow. Cook surveyed Tahiti and the neighbouring islands, reprovisioned the ship, and on 9 August, 1769 the *Endeavour* sailed off to fulfil the second, and secret, part of its orders.

Cook had been instructed to proceed south to 40° and then west. He did so, thus sailing through what Dalrymple had claimed was the western part of *Terra Australis*. His crew saw no land until 6 October, when they sighted the north island of New Zealand. Cook then proceeded methodically around the coastline, mapping as he went. He paused in the deep bay Tasman had seen to clean and repair the ship, and he thus discovered the strait that separated the two islands. Sailing through, he continued surveying around the south island.

When all 2400 miles of coast had been charted – in less than six months – he turned west in the hope of encountering New Holland's unknown eastern coast. He landed near what is now Botany Bay and worked his way northward up the coast, until to his dismay he discovered himself within the Great Barrier Reef. The ship struck a coral reef of terrifying sharpness and remained impaled on it. All hands turned to the pumps and the ship's gear, and after 23 hours the *Endeavour* was heaved off into deep water. A makeshift plug held the water out until the ship could be safely beached. Cook, usually moderate in his praise as in all else, said that no men had ever behaved better than his ship's company had done in that crisis.

The ship repaired, Cook managed by luck and superb navigation to work his way painstakingly west through the reefs and shoals to a passage between small islands, and so past the south shore of New Guinea. He had proved again that New Guinea and New Holland were separated, 160 years after Torres.

When Cook returned to England the admiralty was astounded at his achievement. He had charted 5000 miles of coastline; he had fixed the position of that coastline with a precision not yet achieved in most of the civilised world; and until he reached Batavia, with its malaria and dysentery, not a single man had been lost through sickness. He had not discovered the southern continent, but his work made most men wonder if it existed to be discovered. Dalrymple's huge continent was disintegrating.

Cook's second voyage, in the *Resolution* and the *Adventure*, began in 1772 and lasted three years, and with it the dream of an unknown southern continent was finally destroyed. From the Cape of Good Hope, Cook turned south, searching for any indication of land. There was nothing but ice fields as they worked further south than anyone had been before, crossing the Antarctic Circle for the first time. They continued in the high southern latitudes until they came to the longitude of New Zealand, when they turned north. After a brief pause near Cook Strait between the north and south islands, Cook moved off to the east.

Approaching from the west, Cook was able to use the winds that had for so long pushed other ships north. Through June, July, and part of August he searched fruitlessly between latitudes 41° and 46°. After a pause in Tahiti, he returned to New Zealand to refit the *Resolution* for another plunge into the Antarctic. Leaving in late November 1773, Cook soon found himself among icebergs. Once again he dipped below the Antarctic Circle, sailing further south than the previous summer. The cold was frightful – the ship was encased in ice and the men covered in frozen snow. Cook zigzagged back and forth until, at 71°10'S., their progress was absolutely stopped by the ice. There was no land.

He found no land to the northeast either, except for Roggeveen's Easter Island. After a final sweep through latitudes 54° to 55° on his way home past Cape Horn, when they spent

Christmas in a cove off Tierra del Fuego, Cook gave up the search. Back in England after his three-year voyage he wrote, 'I have now done with the Southern Pacific Continent, and flatter myself that no one will think that I have left it unexplored.'

The unavoidable conclusion was that there was no Terra Australis – at least not the continent the ancients had postulated and generations of men had hoped to find. The land of milk and honey, gold and silver, and jewels and spices simply did not exist. At the southernmost extremity of the world lay only frozen, icebound Antarctica. Across the rest of the vast expanse that European geographers had thought must be land, spread the shimmering waters of the Pacific Ocean, broken only by occasional islands. Across that emptiness had sailed dreamers, villains, mystics, and fortune hunters. One by one the islands were charted and the routes marked, often by men who were dying of thirst or hunger or trembling with the enfeebling curse of scurvy. In the end, with the ease of genius, Cook made it all look easy. The quest was over, and the mysterious *Terra Australis Incognita* slipped into history.

CHAPTER 21

THE MYSTERY OF ATLANTIS

The tale of Atlantis has fascinated people for thousands of years, but is it just a fairy story? The first mention of the lost continent is found in Plato's discourses and some believe that he invented the tale to illustrate a philosophical point: that of a utopian society which went bad. As we saw in the last chapter, people are ready to go to extraordinary lengths to chase after myths. Perhaps the so-called Atlantists are as deluded as the hunters of Terra Australis Incognita. On the other hand, we have also seen how cultures around the world — the Sumerians, the Egyptians, the Megalith-Builders, the Dogon, the Maya and the Olmec — seem to have spontaneously utilised skills well beyond their apparent level of development. Did they inherit this knowledge from a previous culture now beyond our power to investigate because it was totally destroyed in a cataclysm? Over the next few chapters, we will look closely at the evidence for and against the theory of the lost continent.

Of all the world's unsolved mysteries, Atlantis is probably the biggest. Said to have been a huge island continent with an extraordinary civilisation, situated in the Atlantic Ocean, it is reported to have vanished from the face of the earth in a day and a night. So complete was this devastation that Atlantis sank beneath the sea, taking with it every trace of its existence. Despite this colossal vanishing trick, the lost continent of Atlantis has exerted a mysterious influence over the human race for thousands of years. It is almost as though a primitive memory of the glorious days of Atlantis lingers on in the deepest recesses of the human mind. The passage of time has not diminished interest in the fabled continent, nor have centuries of scepticism by scientists succeeded in banishing Atlantis to obscurity in its watery grave. Thousands of books and articles have been written about the lost continent. It has inspired the authors of novels, short stories, poems, and movies. Its name has been used for ships, restaurants, magazines, and even a region of the planet Mars. Atlantean societies have been formed to theorise and speculate about the great lost land. Atlantis has come to symbolise our dream of a once golden past. It appeals to our nostalgic longing for a better, happier world; it feeds our hunger for knowledge of mankind's true origins; and above all it offers the challenge of a genuinely sensational detective story.

Today the search for evidence of the existence of Atlantis continues with renewed vigour, using 20th-century man's most sophisticated tools in the hope of discovering the continent that is said to have disappeared around 11,600 years ago. Did Atlantis exist, or is it just a myth? Ours may be the generation that finally solves this tantalising and ancient enigma.

Atlantis is said to have been the nearest thing to paradise that the earth has seen. Fruits and vegetables grew in abundance in its rich soil. Fragrant flowers and herbs bloomed on the wooded slopes of its many beautiful mountains. All kinds of tame and wild animals roamed its meadows and magnificent forests, and drank from its rivers and lakes. Underground streams of wonderfully sweet water were used to irrigate the soil, to provide hot and cold fountains and baths for all the inhabitants – there were even baths for the horses. The earth was rich in precious metals, and the Atlanteans were wealthier than any people before or after them. Their temples and public buildings were lavishly decorated with gold, silver, brass, tin, and ivory, and their principal royal palace was a marvel of size and beauty. Besides being skilled metallurgists, the Atlanteans were accomplished engineers. A huge and complex system of canals and bridges linked their capital city with the sea and the surrounding countryside, and there were magnificent docks and harbours for the fleets of vessels that carried on a flourishing trade with overseas countries.

Whether they lived in the city or the country, the people of Atlantis had everything they could possibly want for their comfort and happiness. They were a gentle, wise, and loving people, unaffected by their great wealth, and prizing virtue above all things. In time, however, their noble nature became debased. No longer satisfied with ruling their own great land of plenty, they set about waging war on others. Their vast armies swept through the Strait of Gibraltar into the Mediterranean region, conquering large areas of North Africa and Europe. The Atlanteans were poised to strike against Athens and Egypt when the Athenian army rose up, drove them back to Gibraltar, and defeated them. Hardly had the Athenians tasted victory when a terrible cataclysm wiped out their entire army in a single day and night, and caused Atlantis to sink forever beneath the waves. Perhaps a few survivors were left to tell what had happened. At all events, the story is said to have been passed down through many generations until, more than 9200 years later, it was made known to the world for the first time.

The man who first committed the legend to paper was the Greek philosopher Plato, who, in about 355 BC, wrote about Atlantis in two of his famous dialogues, the *Timaeus* and the *Critias*. Although Plato claimed that the story of the lost continent was derived from ancient Egyptian records, no such records have ever come to light, nor has any direct mention of Atlantis been found in any surviving records made before Plato's time. Every book and article on Atlantis that has ever been published has been based on Plato's account; subsequent authors have merely interpreted or added to it.

Plato was a master storyteller who put his philosophical ideas across in the form of apparently real-life events with well-known characters, and his Atlantis story might well have been firmly relegated to the realms of fiction. The very fact that it is still widely regarded as a factual account 2300 years after he wrote it shows the extraordinary power of Plato's story. It has inspired scholars to stake their reputation on the former existence of the lost continent, and explorers to go in search of its remains. Their actions were prompted not by the Greek story alone, but also by their own discoveries, which seemed to indicate that there must once have been a great landmass that acted as a bridge between our existing continents.

Why, ask the scholars, are there so many remarkable similarities between the ancient cultures of the Old and New Worlds? Why do we find the same plants and animals on continents thousands of miles apart when there is no known way for them to have been transported there? How did the primitive peoples of many lands construct technological marvels, such as Stonehenge in Britain, the huge statues of Easter Island in the Pacific, and the strange sacred cities of the Andes? Were they helped by a technically sophisticated race that has since disappeared? Above all, why do the legends of people the world over tell the same story of an overwhelming natural disaster and the arrival of godlike beings who brought with them a new culture from afar? Could the catastrophe that sank Atlantis have sent tidal waves throughout the globe, causing terrible havoc and destruction? And were the 'gods' the remnants of the Atlantean race – the few survivors who were not on or near the island continent when it was engulfed?

Even without Plato's account, the quest for answers to these mysteries might have led to the belief by some in a 'missing link' between the continents – a land-bridge populated by a highly evolved people in the distant past. Nevertheless, it is the Greek philosopher's story that lies at the heart of all arguments for or against the existence of such a lost continent.

Plato intended writing a trilogy in which the Atlantis story plays an important part, but he completed only one of the works, *Timaeus*, and part of the second, *Critias*. Like Plato's other writings, they take the form of dialogues or playlets in which a group of individuals discuss various political and moral issues. Leading the discussion is Plato's old teacher, the Greek philosopher Socrates. His debating companions are Timaeus, an astronomer from Italy, Critias, a poet and historian who was a distant relative of Plato, and Hermocrates, a general from Syracuse. Plato had already used the same cast of real-life characters in his most famous dialogue, *The Republic*, written some years previously, and he planned his trilogy as a sequel to that debate, in which the four men had talked at some length about ideal government. Plato set the meeting of the four men in Critias' house in June 421 BC. *Timaeus* begins on the day following the debate recorded in *The Republic*, and the men start by recalling their previous conversation. Then Hermocrates mentions 'a story derived from ancient tradition' that Critias knows. Pressed for details, Critias recalls how, a century and a half earlier, the great Athenian statesman Solon had visited Egypt. (Solon was a real person and he did visit Egypt, although his trip took place around 590 BC, some 20 years earlier than the date given by Plato.) Critias says that while Solon was in Sais, an Egyptian city having close ties with Athens, a group of priests told him the story of Atlantis – 'a tale that, though strange, is certainly true.' Solon made notes of the conversation, and intended recording the story for posterity, but he did not do so. Instead he told it to a relative, Dropides, who passed it on to his son, Critias the elder, who eventually told his grandson, another Critias – the man who features in Plato's dialogues.

In *Timaeus* Critias gives a brief account of what the priests had told Solon. According to ancient Egyptian records there had been a great Athenian empire 9000 years earlier (that is, in about 9600 BC). At the same time, there had been a mighty empire of Atlantis based on an island or continent west of the Pillars of Hercules (the Strait of Gibraltar) that was larger than North Africa and Asia Minor combined. Beyond it lay a chain of islands that stretched across the ocean to another huge continent.

The Atlanteans ruled over their central island and several others, and over parts of the great continent on the other side of the ocean. Then their armies struck eastward into the Mediterranean region, conquering North Africa as far as Egypt and southern Europe up to the Greek borders. 'This vast power, gathered into one, endeavoured to subdue at one blow our country and yours,' said the Egyptian priests, 'and the whole of the region within the strait. . . .' Athens, standing alone, defeated the Atlanteans. 'But afterward there occurred violent earthquakes and floods; and in a single day and night of destruction all your warlike men in a body sank into the earth, and the island of Atlantis in like manner disappeared in the depths of the sea. For which reason the sea in those parts is impassable and impenetrable, because there is so much shallow mud in the way, caused by the subsidence of the island.'

Socrates is delighted with Critias' story, which has 'the very great advantage of being a fact and not a fiction.' However, the rest of *Timaeus* is taken up with a discourse on science, and the story of Atlantis is continued in Plato's next dialogue, the *Critias*, where Critias gives a much fuller description of the island continent. He goes back to the island's very beginning when the gods were apportioned parts of the earth, as is usual in ancient histories. Poseidon, Greek god of the sea and also of earthquakes, was given Atlantis, and there he fell in love with a mortal maiden called Cleito. Cleito dwelled on a hill in Atlantis, and to prevent anyone reaching her home, Poseidon encircled the hill with alternate rings of land and water, 'two of land and three of water, which he turned as with a lathe.' He also laid on abundant supplies of food and water to the hill, 'bringing up two springs of water from beneath the earth, one of warm water and the other of cold, and making every variety of food to spring up abundantly from the soil.'

Poseidon and Cleito produced 10 children – five pairs of male twins – and Poseidon divided Atlantis and its adjacent islands among these 10 sons to rule as a confederacy of kings. The first-born of the eldest twins, Atlas (after whom Atlantis was named), was made chief king. The kings in turn had numerous children, and their descendants ruled for many generations.

As the population of Atlantis grew and developed, the people accomplished great feats of engineering and architecture. They built palaces and temples, harbours and docks, and reaped the rich harvest of their agricultural and mineral resources. The kings and their descendants built the city of Atlantis around Cleito's hill on the southern coast of the island continent. It was a circular city, about 11 miles in diameter, and Cleito's hill, surrounded by its concentric rings of land and water, formed a citadel about three miles in diameter, situated at the very centre of the impressive city.

The kings built bridges to connect the land rings, and tunnels through which ships could pass from one ring of water to the next. The rings of land were surrounded by stone walls plated with precious metals, and another wall ran around the entire city. The outermost ring of water became a great harbour, crowded with shipping.

A huge canal, 300 feet wide and 100 feet deep, linked the great harbour with the sea at the southern end, and joined the city to a vast irrigated plain, sheltered by lofty mountains, which lay beyond the city walls in the north. This rectangular plain, measuring 230 by 340 miles, was divided into 60,000 square lots, assigned to farmers. The mountains beyond housed 'many wealthy villages of country folk, and rivers, and lakes, and meadows, supplying food for every animal, wild or tame, and much wood of various sorts, abundant for each and every kind of work.' The inhabitants of the mountains and of the rest of the country were 'a vast multitude having leaders to whom they were assigned according to their dwellings and villages.' These leaders and the farmers on the plain were each required to supply men for the Atlantean army, which included light and heavy infantry, cavalry, and chariots.

Plato and Critias paint a vivid picture of Atlantean engineering and architecture with an attention to detail that bears the hallmark of a very factual account. Critias tells how the stone used for the city's buildings was quarried from beneath the central island (Cleito's hill) and from beneath the outer and inner circles of land. 'One kind of stone was white, another black, and a third red, and as they quarried they at the same time hollowed out docks within, having roofs formed of the native rock. Some of their buildings were simple, but in others they put together different stones which they intermingled for the sake of ornament, to be a natural source of delight.' But it was into their magnificent temples that the Atlanteans poured their greatest artistic and technical skills. In the centre of the citadel was a holy temple dedicated to Cleito and Poseidon and this was surrounded by an enclosure of gold. Nearby stood Poseidon's own temple, a superb structure covered in silver, with pinnacles of gold. The roof's interior was covered with ivory, and lavishly decorated with gold, silver, and *orichalc* – probably a fine grade of brass or bronze – which 'glowed like fire'. Inside the temple was a massive gold statue of Poseidon driving a chariot drawn by six winged horses and surrounded by 100 sea nymphs on dolphins. This was so high that its head touched the temple roof. Gold statues of Atlantis' original 10 kings and their wives stood outside the temple.

Critias tells of the beautiful buildings that were constructed around the warm and cold fountains in the centre of the city. Trees were planted between the buildings, and cisterns were designed – some open to the heavens, others roofed over – to be used as baths. 'There were the kings' baths, and the baths of private persons, which were kept apart; and there were separate baths for women, and for horses and cattle, and to each of them they gave as much adornment as was suitable. Of the water that ran off they carried some to the grove of Poseidon, where were growing all manner of trees of wonderful height and beauty, owing to the excellence of the soil, while the remainder was conveyed by aqueducts along the bridges to the outer circles; and there were many temples built and dedicated to many gods; also gardens and places of exercise, some for men, and others for horses in both of the two islands formed by the zones [rings of water]; and in the centre of the larger of the two there was set apart a racecourse of a stadium [about 607 feet] in width, and in length allowed to extend all around the island, for horses to race in.'

At alternate intervals of five and six years the 10 kings of Atlantis met in the temple of Poseidon to consult on matters of government and to administer justice. During this meeting a strange ritual was enacted. After offering up prayers to the gods, the kings were required to hunt bulls, which roamed freely within the temple, and to capture one of them for sacrifice, using only staves and nooses. The captured animal was led to a bronze column in the temple, on which the laws of Atlantis were inscribed, and was slain so that its blood ran over the sacred inscription. After further ceremony, the kings partook of a banquet and when darkness fell they wrapped themselves in beautiful dark-blue robes. Sitting in a circle they gave their judgments, which were recorded at daybreak on tablets of gold.

In the course of time, the people of Atlantis began to lose the love of wisdom and virtue that they had inherited from Poseidon. As their divine nature was diluted and human nature got the upper hand, they became greedy, corrupt, and domineering. Whereupon, says Plato, 'Zeus, the god of gods, who rules by law, and is able to see into such things, perceiving that an honourable race was in a most wretched state and wanting to punish them that they might be chastened and improve, collected all the gods into his most holy abode, which, being placed in the centre of the universe, sees all things that partake of generation. And when he had called them together he spoke as follows. . . .'

And there, enigmatically and frustratingly, Plato's story of Atlantis breaks off, never to be completed. Some scholars regard the *Critias* dialogue as a rough draft that Plato abandoned. Others assume he intended to continue the story in the third part of his trilogy, but he never even started that work. He went on, instead, to write his last dialogue, *The Laws*.

Controversy has raged over Plato's story ever since he wrote it, 2300 years ago. Was his account fact, part-fact, or total fiction? Each explanation has its adherents, and each has been hotly defended over the centuries. Plato's story certainly presents a number of problems. Critics of the Atlantis theory claim that these invalidate the story as a factual account. Supporters maintain that they can be accepted as poetic license, exaggeration, or understandable mistakes that have crept in during the telling and retelling of the story over many centuries before Plato reported it.

The greatest stumbling block is the date that the Greek philosopher gives for the destruction of Atlantis. The Egyptian priests are said to have told Solon that Atlantis was destroyed 9000 years before his visit, in about 9600 BC, which is far earlier than any known evidence of civilisation. Supporters of Atlantis point out that modern discoveries are constantly pushing back the boundaries of human prehistory and we may yet discover that civilisation is far older than we think. However, Plato makes it clear that in 9600 BC Athens was also the home of a mighty civilisation that defeated the Atlanteans. Archaeologists claim that their knowledge of Greece in the early days of its development is sufficiently complete to rule out the possibility of highly developed people in that country as early as 9600 BC. Their evidence suggests that either Plato's story is an invention or he has the date wrong.

Assuming that Plato's facts are right but his date wrong, what evidence do we have to support his account of the origin of the Atlantis story? Bearing in mind that the war was principally between Atlantis and Athens, it seems odd that there were no Greek records of the battle, and that the account should have originated in Egypt. However, Plato has an explanation for this. The Egyptian priests are said to have told Solon that a series of catastrophes had destroyed the Greek records, whereas their own had been preserved. The problem here is that if the Egyptian records existed at the time of Solon's visit, they have since disappeared as completely as Atlantis itself.

Supposing that Solon did hear about Atlantis during his Egyptian trip, is it credible that such a detailed story could have been passed down through the generations as Plato asks us to believe? This is not impossible, because the art of accurate oral transmission was highly developed in the ancient world. Moreover, Solon is said to have taken notes of his conversation with the priests, and Critias claims that these were handed down to his relatives. However, here again we encounter a difficulty. For whereas in one place Critias states that he is still in possession of Solon's notes, in another he declares that he lay awake all night ransacking his memory for details of the Atlantis story that his grandfather had told him. Why didn't he simply refresh his memory from Solon's notes? And why didn't he show the notes to his three companions as incontrovertible proof of the truth of his rather unlikely story?

Yet another problem is that Plato dates the meeting of Socrates, Timaeus, Critias, and Hermocrates, during which Atlantis is discussed, as 421 BC. Plato may have been present during their conversation, but as he was only six years old at the time, he could hardly have taken in much of their discussion, let alone made detailed notes of it. Either his account is based on records made by someone else, or the date is wrong, or this part of his story at least is an invention.

Critics of the Atlantis story believe that it is simply a myth invented to put across the great philosopher's views on war and corruption. Plato used real people in his other dialogues, and put his words into their mouths, too, as a dramatic device to present his ideas. There is no reason, say the detractors, to assume that *Timaeus* and *Critias* are different in this respect. But Plato seems to expect his readers to draw different conclusions. He is at great pains to stress the truth of his account, tracing it back to Solon, a highly respected statesman with a reputation for being 'straight-tongued', and having Critias declare that the Atlantis story, 'though strange, is certainly true.' And why, if his sole intention was to deliver a philosophical treatise, did Plato fill his account with remarkable detail and then stop abruptly at the very point where we would expect the 'message' to be delivered? In spite of the errors and contradictions that have found their way into Plato's account, his story of Atlantis can still be viewed as an exciting recollection of previously unrecorded events.

As we saw in the introduction, history certainly provides us with other examples of supposedly mythical places subsequently being discovered. In 1871 the German archaeologist Heinrich Schliemann excavated in Hissarlik in northwestern Turkey and uncovered Troy just where Homer had placed it over 1000 years previously in his epic poems the *Iliad* and the *Odyssey*. Homer wrote or recited his poems some 500 years before Plato wrote about Atlantis! Schliemann, then, found the historical basis for what European scholars had long dismissed as pure fantasy. Subsequent research has shown that Homer's account of the Trojan War was based on real historical events. As the Irish scholar J. V. Luce observes in his book *The End of Atlantis*: 'Classical scholars laughed at Schliemann when he set out with Homer in one hand and a spade in the other. But he dug up Troy and thereby demonstrated the inestimable value of folk memory. Sir Arthur Evans did much the same thing when he found the labyrinthine home of the Minotaur at Knossos.' Indeed, Sir Arthur Evans revealed that a highly advanced European civilisation had flourished on the island of Crete long before the time of Homer, some 4500 years ago.

This should be justification enough to keep an open mind on Plato's account. The problem is that whereas Troy and Knossos were simply buried, Atlantis could be submerged hundreds or even thousands of feet beneath the waves. And the force of the destruction may have destroyed the remains beyond recognition. However, if Plato's account is based on fact, then we know that the Atlanteans traded with their neighbours. In this case there should be some evidence of their influence and culture in lands that survived the catastrophe. Believers in Atlantis have furnished us with a formidable array of such 'proofs'. Certainly there are enough puzzling architectural and technical achievements scattered around the globe to lend support to the idea of a highly advanced, Atlantean-type civilisation that was responsible.

Although Plato appears to place Atlantis in the Atlantic Ocean, and early cartographers did likewise, numerous scholars and other Atlantis enthusiasts have since scoured the globe for more likely sites. Surprisingly, these have not always been in the ocean. The lost kingdom of Atlantis has been 'found' at various times in the Pacific Ocean, the North Sea, the Sahara Desert, Sweden, southern Spain, Palestine, Cyprus, Crete, the West Indies, and Peru, to name but a few.

Inevitably, with a lack of physical evidence of Atlantis, the occultists have been busy for centuries producing a wealth of information about the lost civilisation. They believe that the past is accessible to properly attuned psychics, who can delve into history and see events happening clairvoyantly. Using such methods a number of individuals have produced vivid descriptions of life on Atlantis. Some merely expanded Plato's account. Others gave descriptions so astonishing that it can only be presumed that they were tuning in to some other lost civilisation than the one immortalised by Plato. In the 1890s, for example, the English occultist W. Scott-Elliot used astral clairvoyance to reveal that Atlantis occupied most of what is now the Atlantic, more than one million years ago. It was inhabited by warrior tribes, including Rmoahals, black aboriginals who stood 10 to 12 feet tall. The ruling race, Scott-Elliot reported, were the Toltecs, who, though only eight feet tall, made slaves of the Rmoahals. Some 200,000 years ago groups of Toltecs emigrated to Egypt and Mexico as well as visiting England. The rulers of Atlantis then took to black magic, and suffered retribution in the form of earthquake and flood, but the emigrants were safe in their new homelands.

Another seer who added to the literature on Atlantis was Edgar Cayce, the famous American clairvoyant prophet and psychic healer who died in 1945. While in a deep trance Cayce gave thousands of 'psychic interviews' concerning the supposed previous incarnations of his clients. According to Cayce some of his clients were former Atlanteans, and in describing their lives he added fascinating details of the great civilisation. These include references to the Atlanteans' use of what seem to be lasers and masers, described by Cayce in 1942, many years before modern scientists had developed them.

The gist of the many Cayce writings dealing with Atlantis is that the Atlanteans were technically as advanced as we are, and it was the tremendous energies that they developed – possibly nuclear – which brought about their destruction. Many people laugh at Cayce, just as they scoff at Plato's story, but the seer's followers expect to have the last laugh. They believe the earth has begun to undergo major upheavals that will cause large parts of Atlantis to rise again from the sea. In 1940 Cayce predicted that these changes would start around 1968 and 1969, when part of the 'western section of Atlantis' would reappear near the Bahamas. Strangely enough, in 1968 a number of underwater formations, including what appeared to be ruined buildings, were sighted off Bimini in the Bahamas. Cayce's followers claim that these 'finds' are a fulfillment of the seer's prophecy, and that far more dramatic discoveries will occur over the next 30 years or so. Unfortunately Cayce also predicted that the very upheavals that would uncover the lost continent would also submerge many parts of our existing land, including most of New York City and Japan.

The mystery of Atlantis will not be solved by the study of Plato alone. Clues from a tremendous number of disciplines, and theories from the orthodox to the occult, deserve an objective appraisal. There are those who believe that the quest for the lost continent is merely an expression of mankind's need to believe in a golden age when life was idyllic and men and women were perfect. For them, Atlantis is a dream without foundation. But there are others who view man's ancient legends and mysterious monuments very differently. In their opinion our picture of evolution and civilisation is totally inadequate. We choose to ignore the puzzles that do not conform to our cozy picture of development, without realising that these very enigmas hold the key to a far greater understanding of our past. The missing link, according to this argument, is Atlantis, and that is why the lost continent still excites such astonishing interest. Find Atlantis, they say, and everything will fall into place. And find Atlantis we may well do, for there is a growing body of people who believe from the clues so far produced that we are now on the very brink of rediscovering the lost civilisation.

CHAPTER 22

THE SEARCHERS FOR ATLANTIS

The Industrial Revolution bred a new species of Atlantist. Although still characterised by an inclination to chase their dreams, these modem Atlantis hunters had a better grounding in scientific method. Their well-presented arguments won new respect for the theory of Atlantis with both the general public and with many influential scientists. Following the revelations of Darwinism people were more inclined to consider world-shaking ideas. Thus the great Atlantis debate began in earnest.

In 1912 the *New York American* published a sensational article. It was written by Dr Paul Schliemann, grandson of Heinrich Schliemann, the man who discovered Troy. Paul Schliemann announced that he had in his possession coins and an inscribed metal plate belonging to the Atlantean culture. Here at last, it seemed, was proof of the existence of Atlantis.

In his article entitled 'How I Discovered Atlantis, the Source of All Civilisation', Paul Schliemann explained that the Atlantean artefacts had been left to him by his famous grandfather, who had discovered them during his excavations. Heinrich Schliemann had died before completing his search for evidence of the lost continent. However, he had left his family a sealed envelope containing a number of secret papers about Atlantis, together with an ancient, owl-headed vase. A note on the envelope warned that it should be opened only by a member of the family prepared to swear that he would devote his life to researching the matters dealt with in the papers. Paul Schliemann made that pledge and opened the envelope.

His grandfather's first instruction was to break open the owl-headed vase. Inside he found several square coins of platinum-aluminum-silver alloy and a plate made of a silverlike metal that bore the inscription, in Phoenician: 'Issued in the Temple of Transparent Walls.' Heinrich Schliemann's notes told of finds made on the site of Troy, including a huge bronze vase containing coins and objects made of metal, bone, and pottery. The vase and some of its contents were inscribed with the words: 'From King Cronos of Atlantis.'

'You can imagine my excitement,' wrote the young Schliemann. 'Here was the first material evidence of that great continent whose legend has lived for ages. . . .' He went on to state that, by following up these clues with his own investigations, he had finally solved the Atlantis mystery. However, his 'research' would appear to have gone no further than a study of the arguments of the pro-Atlantis enthusiasts, because the rest of his article consisted of material clearly culled (without acknowledgment) from their works. Like others before him, Paul Schliemann claimed the cultures of the New and Old Worlds had a common origin in Atlantis. He said he had read the *Troano Codex*, an ancient Mayan text that until then had defied translation. It told of the sinking of an island named Mu, and he had found corroboration of this account in a 4000-year-old Chaldean manuscript from a Buddhist temple in Tibet.

It was at this point that the experts began to have misgivings. Paul Schliemann claimed to have read the *Troano Codex* in the British Museum – but it is preserved in the National Museum of Madrid. And his 'translation' was remarkably similar to that made by an eccentric French scholar, which seemed to owe more to a vivid imagination than to a linguistic talent.

Schliemann promised to divulge the full story of his discoveries in a forthcoming book. Like Atlantis, the book never appeared. Nor did the vase, coins, and other precious relics ever see the light of day. Although the Schliemann story was clearly a hoax, this has not stopped the more credulous pro-Atlantists from using it to support their claims, sometimes confusing Paul with his famous grandfather to make matters worse.

This rather sad episode is typical of the numerous false leads that have bedeviled genuine attempts to uncover the truth about Atlantis. Time and again, men of apparent erudition and integrity have claimed the discovery of vital clues. Using ancient manuscripts, folklore, and legends, they have pieced together impressive 'evidence' about the sinking of the island continent, the appearance of its inhabitants, what happened to the survivors, and, above all, the true site of Atlantis. Some of these theories, based on inaccurate information, have been rapidly demolished by fellow scholars. Others are so revolutionary in their implications that, if they were proved correct, the entire history of the world would need to be rewritten.

Ever since Plato's time writers, scholars, and explorers have sought – and 'found' – Atlantis in almost every corner of the globe. Francis Bacon, the 17th-century English philosopher and statesman, thought that Plato's Atlantis was America. Another 17th-century scholar, the Swede Olof Rudbeck, wrote a lengthy treatise 'proving' that Atlantis was Sweden. In the 18th century, French astronomer Jean Bailly – a victim of the French Revolution – traced Atlantis to Spitsbergen in the Arctic Ocean. Francis Wilford, a British officer in India in the 19th century, was convinced that the British Isles were a remnant of the lost continent, and his theory was enthusiastically adopted by the poet William Blake. Other leading theorists and investigators – some of whom have devoted their lives to the subject – have placed Atlantis in North Africa, South Africa, Central America, Australia, France, the North Sea, Sardinia, Israel and Lebanon, Malta, the Sahara, East Prussia and the Baltic, Siberia, Greenland, Iraq, Iran, Brazil, and the Pacific and Indian Oceans. The peoples of these regions naturally had a vested interest in such theories, because the location of Atlantis in or near their country would give them a reasonable claim to be descended from Atlantean survivors.

It may seem odd that most of the Atlantis theorists mentioned above have chosen *land* areas as the site of a supposedly drowned continent. There are a number of reasons for this, including the obvious one that until recent times extensive underwater exploration has not been possible. Some theorists base their choice on a reinterpretation of Plato's story, believing that he built his account on the memory of some ancient disaster of relatively limited proportions. Others point out that vast areas of our present landmasses were once under water; similarly, areas that are now submerged were once above sea level. According to this argument, Atlantis was submerged, as Plato said, but has since reappeared as one of the countries or areas listed. However, geological evidence does not support this theory. Most geologists agree that, although the earth's surface has undergone many major changes, these have occurred only very gradually over millions of years. As far as they are concerned, large landmasses do not rise and sink rapidly enough to account for the overnight drowning of Atlantis and its re-emergence as one of our present day land areas.

The Atlantis-seekers mentioned so far are, however, in a minority. By far the greater number of scholars who have studied the Atlantis enigma agree with Plato. If the lost continent was anywhere, they believe, it was in the Atlantic Ocean – and they have produced a wealth of material to support their case.

Of all the theorists who have placed Atlantis in the Atlantic, none has argued more persuasively or made a greater impact on the study of Atlantis than the American Ignatius T. T. Donnelly, sometimes called the Father of Scientific Atlantology. Donnelly's enormous physical and intellectual energy brought him success at an early age. Born in Philadelphia in 1831, he studied law and was admitted to the bar at the age of 22. Three years later he and his bride went to Minnesota, where Donnelly and a group of friends had purchased some land near St Paul and hoped to found a great Middle West metropolis, Nininger City. As part of the campaign to publicise this dream, Donnelly edited and published *The Emigrant Journal*. But Nininger City was never developed, possibly because of the financial depression that occurred in the 1850s.

Instead, the chubby dynamic Donnelly turned his attention to politics, and was elected Lieutenant-Governor of Minnesota at the age of 28. Four years later he was sent to Congress, where he served for eight years. Donnelly was renowned as a brilliant, forceful, and witty speaker, and rapidly earned the respect of fellow members of the House of Representatives.

Behind the public image, however, Donnelly was experiencing a period of intense loneliness. Soon after his arrival in Washington, his wife had died, and Donnelly turned to study for solace. During his two terms as the member from Minnesota, he spent long hours in the magnificent Library of Congress, soaking up all the information he could.

After his defeat in the election of 1870, Donnelly returned to his home in the ghost town of Nininger City. There, surrounded by his notes and a large personal library, he began writing the books that were to make him famous throughout the world. After years of isolation and poverty during which he persevered with the task in hand to the exclusion of all else, Donnelly produced his masterpiece: *Atlantis, the Antediluvian World*. Published in 1882, this unique study of the lost continent became an overnight sensation. The following year another book, *Ragnarok, the Age of Fire and Gravel,* joined his first as a best seller. This dealt with the cosmic aspects of natural cataclysms such as that which supposedly submerged Atlantis. The extent of Donnelly's influence on the study of Atlantis can be judged by the enormous and continuing success of his books. His first work, for example, has been reprinted 50 times and is still in print today, nearly a century after it was written. Donnelly transformed what had been, until then, a subject of speculation mainly among intellectuals into a popular cult, and one that has survived ever since.

This giant of Atlantology did more than look for confirmation of Plato's story. He used it as the basis for a picture of Atlantis that went far beyond anything stated – or that could even have been imagined – by the Greek philosopher. His theories were distilled into 13 'theses':

'1. That there once existed in the Atlantic Ocean, opposite the mouth of the Mediterranean Sea, a large island, which was the remnant of an Atlantic continent, and known to the ancient world as Atlantis.

'2. That the description of this island given by Plato is not, as has been long supposed, fable, but veritable history.

'3. That Atlantis was the region where man first rose from a state of barbarism to civilisation.

'4. That it became, in the course of ages, a populous and mighty nation, from whose overflowings the shores of the Gulf of Mexico, the Mississippi River, the Amazon, the Pacific coast of South America, the Mediterranean, the west coast of Europe and Africa, the Baltic, the Black Sea, and the Caspian were populated by civilised nations.

'5. That it was the true Antediluvian world; the Garden of Eden; the Gardens of the Hesperides; the Elysian Fields; the Gardens of Alcinous; the Mesomphales; the Olympes; the Asgard of the traditions of the ancient nations; representing a universal memory of a great land, where early mankind dwelt for ages in peace and happiness.

'6. That the gods and goddesses of the ancient Greeks, the Phoenicians, the Hindoos, and the Scandinavians were simply the kings, queens, and heroes of Atlantis; and the acts attributed to them in mythology are a confused recollection of real historical events.

'7. That the mythology of Egypt and Peru represented the original religion of Atlantis, which was sun-worship.

'8. That the oldest colony formed by the Atlanteans was probably in Egypt, whose civilisation was a reproduction of that of the Atlantic island.

'9. That the implements of the ''Bronze Age'' of Europe were derived from Atlantis. The Atlanteans were also the first manufacturers of iron.

'10. That the Phoenician alphabet, parent of all the European alphabets, was derived from an Atlantis alphabet, which was also conveyed from Atlantis to the Mayas of Central America.

'11. That Atlantis was the original seat of the Aryan or Indo-European family of nations, as well as of the Semitic peoples, and possibly also of the Turanian races.

'12. That Atlantis perished in a terrible convulsion of nature, in which the whole island sank into the ocean, with nearly all its inhabitants.

'13. That a few persons escaped in ships and on rafts, and carried to the nations east and west tidings of the appalling catastrophe, which has survived to our own time in the Flood and Deluge legends of the different nations of the old and new worlds.'

Donnelly, it seems, had not only 'discovered' Atlantis but also succeeded in solving nearly all the mysteries of the past at the same time. He maintained that Atlantis was the source of all civilisation (Plato made no such claim) and as such, had inspired the myths and legends of numerous races – many of which are indeed remarkably similar.

Donnelly argued that the resemblances between many species of American and European animals and plants are due to their having a common origin – Atlantis. Quoting a number of authorities to support his case, he stated that such plants as tobacco, guava, cotton, and bananas were not confined to one hemisphere before Columbus – as was generally thought – but had long been grown in both the New and the Old World. In his view these plants must have crossed the Atlantic by means of an Atlantean land-bridge.

Donnelly also believed that the civilisation of ancient Egypt emerged suddenly rather than evolving gradually over thousands of years, thus indicating that it was imported from elsewhere. He quoted the opinion of the 19th-century French writer Ernest Renan to support this view: 'Egypt at the beginning appears mature, old, and entirely without mythical and heroic ages, as if the country had never known youth. Its civilisation has no infancy, and its art no archaic period.' That opinion together with 'evidence' drawn from the religious and cultural beliefs of the ancient Egyptians and from their magnificent achievements, was sufficient to convince Donnelly that Egypt was colonized by survivors of Atlantis who brought with them a ready-made civilisation modelled on their former life.

In Donnelly's view, the Mayas of Central America were also of

Atlantean origin, partly because they possessed what he believed to be a phonetic alphabet similar to the Old World alphabets, and also because they 'claim that their civilisation came to them *across the sea in ships from the east*, that is, from the direction of Atlantis.'

Another important feature of Donnelly's argument was the incidence of similar culture traits among New and Old World peoples, which he assumed to have a common origin. He cited as evidence the appearance on both sides of the Atlantic of pyramids, pillars, burial mounds, metallurgy, ships, and various other cultural developments. 'I cannot believe that the great inventions were duplicated spontaneously . . . in different countries,' he argued. 'If this were so, all savages would have invented the boomerang; all savages would possess pottery, bow and arrows, slings, tents, and canoes; in short, all races would have risen to civilisation, for certainly the comforts of life are as agreeable to one people as another.'

Finally, this wide-ranging scholar claimed to have proved the connection between Atlantis and other civilisations through a study of linguistics. New World languages, he declared, are closely related to tongues of the Old World, and he composed parallel tables of words to back his case. For those who had wanted to believe in Atlantis but had felt Plato's account left too many questions unanswered, Donnelly had put flesh on the bones of the legend. Almost every writer on Atlantis who came after him has borrowed from Donnelly's work, which remains the bible of Atlantology. But does it deserve that reputation?

Donnelly's forceful style, his undoubted learning, his enthusiasm, and his air of absolute conviction tend to sweep the reader along with him and mask the false or shaky foundations of some of his arguments. According to L. Sprague de Camp, author of one of the best critical studies of Atlantis, *Lost Continents*, 'Most of Donnelly's statements of fact, to tell the truth, either were wrong when he made them, or have been disproved by subsequent discoveries.'

De Camp points out that Donnelly was mistaken in asserting that the Peruvian Indians had a system of writing, or that the cotton plants native to the New and Old Worlds belong to the same species. Donnelly's comparisons between New and Old World alphabets were based on an inaccurate and discredited representation of a so-called 'Mayan alphabet', further distorted by Donnelly to create 'intermediate forms' between Latin and allegedly Mayan letters. Nor is there a resemblance between the Otomi language of Mexico and Chinese, despite a table of 'similarities' that Donnelly published. 'I don't know what he used for Chinese,' says de Camp, ' – certainly not the standard Northern Chinese, the language usually meant by the term.'

Errors such as these have gone largely unnoticed, and Donnelly still enjoys a sizable following. Soon after the publication of his first book his correspondence reached gigantic proportions. Even the British Prime Minister William E. Gladstone is said to have written to express his appreciation. Gladstone was so impressed by Donnelly's arguments that he tried to persuade Parliament to vote funds for an expedition to go in search of Atlantis. On the strength of such reactions, Donnelly took to the lecture platform with equal success. Then he turned his back on lecturing to return home and continue writing. Later, he re-entered politics, helping to found the Populist Party and twice running for Vice-President of the United States on the Populist ticket. This remarkable, largely self-taught man died in 1901, knowing that he had shaped and laid the foundation stone of modern Atlantology.

Others soon followed, of whom the most outstanding was Lewis Spence, a Scottish mythologist who launched a shortlived magazine called *Atlantis Quarterly* and wrote five books on Atlantis. Spence never achieved the popular appeal of Donnelly, but his theories have won almost as much acclaim among fellow Atlantologists. Even the sceptics have a high regard for Spence. L. Sprague de Camp, for instance, calls Spence 'a sane and sober writer,' and describes his major work, *The Problem of Atlantis*, as 'about the best pro-Atlantis work published to date.' Like Donnelly, Spence takes a serious and scientific approach to his subject. In *The Problem of Atlantis*, which appeared in 1924, he set out to prove four points:

'1. That a great continent formerly occupied the whole or

major portion of the North Atlantic region, and a considerable portion of its southern basin. Of early geological origin, it must, in the course of successive ages, have experienced many changes in contour and mass, probably undergoing frequent submergence and emergence.

'2. That in the Miocene (Later Tertiary) times [from 25 to 10 million years ago] it still retained its continental character, but towards the end of that period it began to disintegrate, owing to successive volcanic and other causes.

'3. That this disintegration resulted in the formation of greater and lesser insular masses. Two of these, considerably larger in area than any of the others, were situated (a) at a relatively short distance from the entrance to the Mediterranean; and (b) in the region of the present West Indian Islands. These may respectively be called Atlantis and Antillia. Communication between them was possible by an insular chain.

'4. That these two island-continents and this connecting chain of islands persisted until late Pleistocene times, at which epoch (about 25,000 years ago, or the beginning of the post-glacial epoch), Atlantis seems to have experienced further disintegration. Final disaster appears to have overtaken Atlantis about 10,000 BC. Antillia, on the other hand, seems to have survived until a much more recent period, and still persists fragmentally in the Antillean group, or West Indian Islands.'

In order to make these theses acceptable, Spence had to throw out some aspects of Plato's account. Atlantis, he asserted, did not vanish in a day and a night. Its disappearance – the last of many disasters affecting the continent – probably occurred gradually over many years. Nor did he attempt to confirm Donnelly's claim that Atlantis was the source of all civilisation. Although he believed the Atlanteans had a developed culture, he was prepared to accept that they were a Stone Age people, despite Plato's reference to their skilful use of metals.

If Atlantis did exist in the Atlantic Ocean, Spence argued, and disintegrated gradually – finally disappearing at about the time Plato gives (around 10,000 BC) – then there should be evidence of its survivors taking refuge in other lands. In the early phases of

Atlantis' destruction, man was not a seafarer, and the Atlantean landmass must have been near the coast of other continents to make the journey possible. Spence is able to produce some fascinating evidence for just such an exodus.

The missing link between the Atlanteans and present-day man, according to Spence, consisted of three races of people, the Cro-Magnon, the Caspian, and the Azilian. Quoting a variety of experts Spence demonstrates that none of these races developed in the country where their remains are now to be found. Because most of their settlements were in coastal areas of southwestern France and northern Spain, around the shores of the Bay of Biscay, Spence concluded that they came from a country to the west. None exists there now, and it must have been Atlantis.

The Cro-Magnons were the first to arrive in Europe, at the close of the Ice Age about 25,000 years ago. They appear to have wiped out the Neanderthal people who then inhabited the area, which is hardly surprising because the Cro-Magnons were vastly superior in physique and intellect. The average height of the Cro-Magnon men was 6 feet 1$^1/_2$ inches. They had short arms – a sign of high racial development – and skulls that indicate an exceptionally large brain capacity. Their faces were very broad, with massive chins, high foreheads, and beak noses. The Cro-Magnon people produced amazingly realistic cave paintings – usually of animals, including the bull – and carved equally impressive pictures on their tools and utensils.

This remarkable race flourished for 15,000 years until it was displaced by the Caspian and Azilian invasions. According to Spence, these peoples were also fleeing from Atlantis at later periods in the island's violent history. The Azilians appeared in exactly the same European areas as their predecessors, but archaeologists have found evidence that, unlike the Cro-Magnon people, the Azilians were fishermen, capable of deep-sea fishing. If subsequent cataclysms had destroyed the land-bridge that brought the Cro-Magnons to Europe, said Spence, their successors now had boats in which to flee. Azilian culture appeared in Europe around 10,000 BC, which ties in approximately with Plato's date for the destruction of Atlantis. Significantly, the

Azilians were always buried facing west – toward their home-land, according to Spence.

Spence argued that the Azilians probably founded the civiliza-tions of Egypt and Crete. He believed that Atlantean town plan-ning, as described by Plato, was reflected in the great ancient cities of Carthage and Knossos. In Spence's view, the Mayan culture too derived from Atlantis – as Donnelly had claimed before him. He explained the enormous time gap between the destruction of Atlantis around 10,000 BC, and the appearance of the Mayan civilisation just before the Christian Era by suggesting that some Atlantean refugees had fled westward to Antillia (the second island continent in his theory) and had remained there for thousands of years. It was only when Antillia too was destroyed that they moved on to Central America. Spence believed that the Mayan culture, like that of Egypt, was imported, because it showed no evidence of gradual evolution.

Mankind may have largely forgotten Atlantis over the centuries, argued Spence, but certain animals did not. As an example, he pointed to the curious behaviour of the Norwegian lemming. When the lemming population outgrows its local food supply, these small rodents gather in great masses and swim out to sea until they all drown. In Spence's view the lemmings are responding to an instinctive memory of a land that used to exist in the west, where fresh food could be found.

Despite his praise of Spence's book, L. Sprague de Camp is quickly on hand to raise a few healthy objections to some of the author's conclusions. 'Even if we confine ourselves to Spence's facts, they turn out less impressive than they seem at first,' he writes. 'For one thing, Cro-Magnon culture has now been found in the East – in Palestine. Furthermore, despite all these assertions that the cultures of Egypt, Yucatán, and Peru sprang into existence suddenly without a slow transition from primitive culture, modern archaeology has disclosed the gradual evolution of all these cultures from more primitive levels. You can, for instance, trace the growth of Egyptian culture from the neolithic Merimda people, who wore animal skins, lived in mud houses, and farmed in a crude manner, to the highly civilised men of the Fourth Dynasty.'

It is easy enough to make mistakes about the development of cultures, says de Camp, simply because relics of more recent times are more numerous and easier to find, and are frequently bigger and more durable than those built in a culture's earlier stages. In Spence's defence, however, modern Atlantologists point to numerous relics and artifacts that do not appear to fit in with the archaeologists' neat and orderly pattern of development. As for the lemmings in search of a lost land, de Camp points out that when they become starved by overpopulation they set of willy-nilly in any direction, often swimming rivers in search of food. When they reach the sea they no doubt mistake it for another river and carry on swimming until they drown. Swedish lemmings, he adds, try to swim the Baltic in the opposite direction, which makes nonsense of Spence's theory . . . unless, of course, Atlantis was in the Baltic, as one researcher has suggested.

Lewis Spence, who died in 1955, would probably not have been too perturbed by such criticisms. Although he had worked hard to assemble facts on which to hang his theories, he realised that ultimately they would probably not be sufficient to convince the sceptics. His books do not openly deal with the occult aspects of Atlantology, but Spence was certainly aware that many had endeavoured to solve the riddle of the lost continent by non-material methods. Indeed, before writing his first book on Atlantis, Spence had completed an excellent *Encyclopedia of Occultism*, in which he made a first cautious reference to Atlantis.

In time, Spence grew tired of the demand for facts. He began suggesting that the durability of the Atlantis theory might be due to a common 'folk-memory' that could actually be inherited rather than preserved through oral or written accounts. There is 'a world-intuition regarding the existence of a transatlantic continent,' he said, and 'we are dealing with a great world-memory, of which Plato's story is merely one of the broken and distorted fragments. . . .' Elsewhere he declared himself in favour of 'inspirational methods,' which would become 'the Archaeology of the Future.' In his opinion, 'The Tape-Measure School, dull and full of the credulity of incredulity, is doomed,' and 'the day is passing when mere weight of evidence alone, unsupported by considerations which result from inspiration or insight, can be accepted by the world.'

Many Atlantis enthusiasts have been satisfied with inspiration alone, of course, but Spence's views rather clouded his reputation as a scholar. Spence did little to allay his critics when, in 1942, he published a book entitled *Will Europe Follow Atlantis?* This argued that God had destroyed Atlantis because of the wickedness of the Atlanteans and (with the Nazi atrocities in mind) He would do the same to Europe unless it reformed.

For all his idiosyncrasies Spence is probably still the best guide to the Atlantis story. His knowledge of the subject was such that he was consulted by Sir Arthur Conan Doyle during the latter's preparation of his exciting romance *The Lost World*, which concerns an expedition to the Brazilian jungle in search of a mysterious, hidden world. Spence also conducted a correspondence with an English explorer, Colonel Percy H. Fawcett, who was planning a very similar expedition. Fawcett believed that South America might be part of Atlantis, or that the mysterious cities reported to exist in the dense jungles of the Amazon might have been built by Atlanteans who had fled their stricken land.

Fawcett was not alone in linking ancient America with Atlantis. Both Donnelly and Spence had used the Mayan culture as evidence in their arguments, and the mysterious early civilisations of the Americas still fascinate and puzzle us today.

CHAPTER 23

THE AMERICAN LEGACY

The origin of native civilisations of Central and South America has long been the source of controversy. The Olmecs, the earliest known American city dwellers, left no sign of their previous cultural development; they seem to be an example of spontaneous generation. Or could it be that we have been looking in the wrong places, and the inhabitants of Central and South America inherited the culture of refugees from another continent – the 'white gods' who were revered in legend from the east to the west coast?

High on a desolate plateau in the Andes stand the ruins of an ancient city, silent, shadowy, and mysterious. This is Tiahuanaco, near La Paz in modern Bolivia. Set at the dizzying altitude of 13,000 feet, amid a wild expanse of barren rock, framed by volcanic mountains, Tiahuanaco is one of the loneliest and most inhospitable places on earth. Yet this city was once the heart of a mighty civilization, built by an unknown people who lived on the shores of Lake Titicaca hundreds – and perhaps many thousands – of years before the arrival of the Incas. Legend has it that Tiahuanaco was built for the worship of Viracocha, the White God, who came to the Indians in the distant past, bringing them all the arts and laws of an advanced civilisation. Then Viracocha disappeared across the sea, never fulfilling his promise to return.

Tiahuanaco already lay partly in ruins when the Incas found it in the early 13th century AD. Three hundred years later the Spanish conquistadors destroyed more of the city in their search for gold. The destruction of Tiahuanaco continued at the end of the 19th century, when most of its remaining treasures were plundered; its fabulous buildings and massive statues were blasted away to provide building materials for the city of La Paz and a roadbed for its railroad. However, enough was recorded by Spanish chroniclers and by travellers from later times for us to be able to gain some impression of the former majesty of this great city and of the powerful and gifted people who built it

Tiahuanaco now stands about 15 miles from Lake Titicaca, but the level of the lake has dropped considerably over the centuries and its waters once lapped the very walls of the ancient city. Stairs led from the water up the side of a massive step pyramid, about 150 feet tall, topped by a huge temple. Palaces, temples, and other great buildings stood on the shores of the lake. One Spanish chronicler, Diego d'Alcobaca, reported seeing a paved court 80 feet square, with a covered hall 45 feet long running down one of its sides. The court and hall had been hewn from a single block of stone. 'There are still many statues to be seen here today,' wrote d'Alcobaca. 'They represent men and women, and are so perfect one could believe the figures were alive.' Another chronicler held that, 'One of the palaces is truly an eighth wonder of the world. Stones 37 feet long by 15 feet wide have been prepared without the aid of lime or mortar, in such a way as to fit together without any joins showing.' The Spanish discovered that the colossal stone blocks – some of them weighing as much as 200 tons – used in these buildings were held in place by silver rivets. (It was the removal of these rivets by Spanish mercenaries that caused many of Tiahuanaco's great buildings to collapse in subsequent earthquakes.) The blocks were brought from the volcanic Kiappa region, 40 miles from Tiahuanaco, and, as writer and explorer of South America Pierre Honore comments in his book *In Quest of the White God*, 'As with the pyramids in Egypt, thousands of men must have worked for hundreds of years to erect the enormous buildings of Tiahuanaco, slave labour forced to build on an ever larger, taller, more powerful scale.'

The most impressive feature of Tiahuanaco that is still standing is the Gate of the Sun, which may have been the entrance to the city or to its main palace. Cut from a single block of stone, 10 feet high, 6 feet wide, and weighing over 10 tons, it is the largest carved monolith on earth. The gate is crowned by a deeply carved frieze of beautiful and intricate designs, including human figures, animals, birds, and symbols thought by some investigators to denote astronomical observations. Over the centre of the gate is a stylised jaguar with human features, holding what may be symbols of thunder and lightning. The frieze was originally inlaid with gold, and the eyes of the figures were made of semi-precious stones. Some of the carvings have been left unfinished, as if something had suddenly interrupted the work of the artists.

According to Spanish chroniclers, the walls and niches of Tiahuanaco's palaces and temples were adorned with statues and ornaments of gold, copper, and bronze, and with stone and clay masks that hung from large-headed gold nails. The holes made by these nails can still be seen today, and some of the nails and other precious objects salvaged from the ruins of Tiahuanaco are on view in La Paz in the Posnansky Museum – named after Arthur Posnansky, a German engineer who tried to save Tiahuanaco from further destruction during the quarrying operations of the 19th century. Pieces in the museum and in private collections include six-foot-high statues covered all over with reliefs, gold figurines weighing between four and six pounds, gold animals and birds, and gold cups, plates, and spoons. These few remaining treasures testify to Tiahuanaco's former magnificence, and other groups of ruins, including step pyramids, in the highlands and on the coast of present-day Bolivia and Peru indicate the power and extent of the ancient Tiahuanacan civilisation.

Tiahuanaco has puzzled archaeologists and historians ever since its discovery. Although our knowledge of the history and development of the civilisation of South and Central America has increased enormously in recent years, and the experts have been able to answer some questions about the majestic city, the riddle of its age and of the people who built it is by no means solved.

When archaeologists and explorers of the 19th and early 20th century began rediscovering the magnificent stone citadels of once flourishing civilisations in Central and South America, the effect was electrifying. Most Europeans and North Americans, accustomed to regarding the Middle East as the cradle of civilization, found it hard to believe that the American Indians could possibly have developed such a high degree of cultural and technical achievement without outside help. In the 1840s, when the American traveller John Lloyd Stephens first uncovered the awesome vestiges of Mayan civilisation deep in the Honduran jungle, he declared himself convinced that the local inhabitants could not have built such structures. Whenever the remains of advanced civilisations were found in the Americas, they were attributed to the influence of Old World peoples such as the Egyptians, the Phoenicians, the Irish, or the Vikings – or to the Atlanteans. Atlantists were quick to seize on the discovery of American pre-Columbian civilisations as further evidence for the existence of a lost Atlantic continent. After all, Plato had mentioned another great continent that lay beyond Atlantis on the other side of the ocean, and had said that Atlantean influence extended to parts of that continent. Direct contact between the Old World and the New prior to the arrival of Columbus in 1492 must have been chancy and sporadic, if it occurred at all, the Atlantists argued, simply because of the vast expanses of ocean that lie between the two. But if the Atlanteans were even half as powerful as Plato had described them, a voyage from their Atlantic home to the Americas would have been easy, especially considering the chain of islands that were said to stretch across the ocean between Atlantis and the outer continent.

Did the Atlanteans influence the civilisations of Central and South America? It is a possibility that has to be considered in any attempt to unravel the mysteries of the ancient ruins in this part of the world. If we reject the theory, we are still faced with the questions: Who built these fabulous cities? And how did they acquire the technical skills to do so?

In trying to answer these questions we have to take into account the theory of cultural diffusion. This is based on the belief that separate civilisations would not develop along similar lines without contact with each other. Where we find two or more cultures with the same or similar beliefs, customs, art forms, architecture, or technologies, we can assume, according to the theory, that the people concerned acquired their knowledge from each other or from a common source. This was the cornerstone of Ignatius Donnelly's arguments about Atlantis, and although there are many diffusionists who do not believe in Atlantis, almost all latter-day Atlantists believe in diffusion because it fits their case so well. It is because of some remarkable cultural similarities that the civilizations of the Americas share among themselves and with those of the Old World, that most believers in Atlantis look upon the now ruined citadels of Central and South America as outposts of the once great Atlantean culture.

Orthodox scholars challenge this view. Today many scholars believe that the pre-Columbian civilizations of the Americas were developed by the American Indians themselves, independent of any chance contact they may have had with the outside world. The only trouble from the scholars' point of view is that they have so far been unable to trace with any certainty the starting point of civilization in the Americas. No sooner do they uncover the origins of one civilization in this part of the world than another equally advanced civilization appears right behind it. This, of course, comes as no surprise to Atlantologists, who are convinced that a fully developed civilization was imported into the Americas in the first place.

Before examining this claim in detail, we need to take a look at what archaeologists know of the people in whose lands the mysterious citadels of the Americas have appeared. They are principally the Olmecs, the Mayas, the Incas, and the Aztecs. The Olmec civilization is the oldest so far known in the Americas, and was founded along the Gulf of Mexico in what are now the states of Veracruz and Tabasco. No one knows where the Olmecs came from, but their civilization is thought to have flourished from about 1300 BC to 400 BC, and their colossal monuments and sculptures show them to have been gifted artists and engineers. They also possessed a written language, apparently resembling that of the Mayas, whose origins are equally mysterious. The Mayan culture arose in Guatemala some time between 400 and 100 BC and flourished there for 1000 years, during which the

Mayas built over 100 city-states with magnificent temples, palaces, pyramids, and plazas. The Mayas called themselves 'lords of the earth', and their influence quickly spread toward the north, west, and southwest, covering a large part of Central America. Then, between AD 700 and 1000, for reasons that are still unknown, they abandoned their homeland and its thriving cities and moved to the arid and inhospitable Yucatán. Their attempts to rebuild their empire were thwarted by invasions and internal strife, and the Mayan civilisation gradually declined. By the time the Spaniards arrived in 1511 it possessed only a shadow of its former greatness.

The Aztecs of Mexico were relative latecomers on the American scene. Their civilization flourished from about 1350 until the Spanish conquest of 1521. They inherited much of their culture from their predecessors, but their own art and architecture was so splendid that the leader of the Spanish conquistadors declared their capital Tenochtitlán (now the site of Mexico City): 'The most beautiful city in the world.' While the Aztecs were building Tenochtitlán, the Incas of South America were establishing their considerable empire that stretched from the Columbia-Ecuador border to central Chile, taking in parts of present-day Peru, northern Argentina, Bolivia, Chile, and Ecuador. The Incas, who founded their capital of Cusco around AD 1200 and whose empire crumbled before the Spaniards in 1537, traced their ancestry back in legend to the builders of Tiahuanaco, which they regarded as the cradle of their civilization.

The history books, then, paint a picture of a whole series of rapidly developing American civilizations, far less ancient than those of the Old World, and archaeological examination of the ruins generally confirms this simplified view of the various peoples of the Americas. But some scholars disagree. Tiahuanaco, for example, has been the centre of debate for decades because the experts cannot agree about when the city was built. At one time it was widely believed to date from around 1000 BC. Today, the generally accepted view is that its impressive buildings were erected several centuries after the beginning of our era – estimates vary from about AD 100 to 800. Some scholars believe several cities were built on the same site. Arthur Posnansky, who made valiant efforts to preserve the ruins of Tiahuanaco, came to the conclusion that the last city was built 16,000 years ago. Other researchers claim that Tiahuanaco is a quarter of a million years old.

It has been suggested that Tiahuanaco was originally built at sea level and that the land on which it now stands and Lake Titicaca were thrust upward a distance of about two miles during a convulsion of the earth many thousands of years ago. This theory is based on the discovery of a 'water mark' line on the surrounding mountains, which stretches for over 300 miles and consists of the calcified remains of marine plants, indicating that these slopes were once part of the seashore. Significantly Lake Titicaca has a very high salinity and oceanic fauna, as do other lakes in the area. This theory would certainly account for the presence of what appears to be a ruined seaport close to Tiahuanaco and might also explain why the city was abruptly abandoned by its builders and how it first fell into ruin.

According to some German and local archaeologists, Tiahuanaco was abandoned around 9000 or 10,000 BC – which conveniently coincides with the date given by Plato for the destruction of Atlantis. Atlantologists conclude that the catastrophe that caused Atlantis to sink into the ocean also pushed a large area of the west coast of South America some two miles above sea level. If this theory were proved correct and Tiahuanaco was built before the catastrophe, it would be over 11,000 years old.

Another curious feature of the area has not escaped the cultural diffusionists and the Atlantologists. The boats that sail on the salty waters of Lake Titicaca are identical with the papyrus boats of ancient Egypt. Their shape, the material used, and the method of construction are the same. Coincidence? Evidence of direct contact between ancient Egypt and the New World? Or one more clue that a long-lost civilization once influenced great areas of the globe?

South America is probably one of the last places on earth to be keeping its secrets from us. Many lost cities have been found in the dense, almost impenetrable jungle since the turn of the century, and no one can guess how many more, filled with treasures and works of art, are hidden beneath the thick and tangled canopy of tropical vegetation. It is an area that cannot easily be mapped from the air, and explorers enter this 'Green Hell' at their peril.

Among the adventurers who have dared to risk death in their search for ancient ruins, the name of Colonel Percy H. Fawcett is particularly remembered because of the mystery surrounding the fate of his final expedition to South America. Fawcett was convinced that the ruins of Atlantis or some of its daughter cities lay beneath the jungles of Brazil, and in the 1920s, after 20 years in the British Army as a military surveyor, geographer, and engineer, he turned to exploration. He went on several expeditions to Brazil, during which he travelled extensively through uncharted country populated by hostile tribes. Fawcett was an acknowledged expert on the area and how to survive its hazards.

During these explorations a map came into his possession. It was said to have been 150 years old and to have been drawn by a man who had found a lost city deep in the Mato Grosso region of southwest Brazil. The city was said to be surrounded by a wall and to stand in acres of cultivated land. In 1925, accompanied by his 20-year-old son Jack and a young friend named Raleigh Rimmel, Fawcett set off in search of this city, which he was sure would prove to have links with Atlantis. Before his departure, he declared: 'Whether we succeed in penetrating the jungle and come out alive, or whether we leave our bones there, of this I am certain: the key to the mystery of ancient South America, and perhaps of the whole of prehistory, can be found if we are able to locate these old cities ... and open them up to science. Their existence I do not for a moment doubt – how could I? I myself have seen a portion of one, and that is the reason why I observed it was imperative for me to go again. The remains seemed to be those of an outpost of one of the largest cities, which I am convinced is to be found together with others, if a properly organised search is carried out. Unfortunately I cannot induce scientific men to accept even the supposition that there are traces of an old civilization in Brazil. But I have travelled through regions unknown to other explorers and the wild Indians have told me time and again of the buildings, the characteristics of their old inhabitants, and the strange things to be found there.'

With those words, Fawcett and his two companions left for their last great adventure. Their final message came from Dead Horse Camp in the Xingu Basin, where they reported hearing of yet another ruined city on the edge of a large lake. Then they disappeared into the jungle, never to be seen again. The chances are that they were captured and killed by hostile Indians or that they all died from fever. But as the world waited for news of the Fawcett expedition, other theories were advanced. Some believed that the party had found the lost city but, for reasons best known to themselves, had decided not to return to England. Others suggested that the Indians had taken the explorers to the lost city but had either killed them or held them prisoner afterward so that no one else would come looking for the secret. Mediums tried to contact Fawcett in the next world, but their psychic explorations shed little light on the true outcome of his expedition.

Nevertheless, one alleged spirit communication does stand head and shoulders above the others. This purports to be a long communication from Fawcett, dictated over a number of years through the hand of a woman who was to become one of the world's most famous automatic writing mediums.

Geraldine Cummins, a young Irish writer, was already a well-known medium when her friend, E. Beatrice Gibbes, asked her to try communicating with the lost explorer. Miss Cummins would go into a light trance during which her hand would be allegedly controlled by spirit people who would write messages. It was 10 years after Fawcett had disappeared when the two women first attempted to establish contact with him. They apparently succeeded, but Fawcett told them he was not dead. He was in a semi-conscious state, still in the South American jungle, but his spirit was able to communicate. Four communications were made in 1936, after which they were abandoned for 12 years. When Fawcett again communicated, in 1948, he said he had died.

It would be easy to dismiss these messages as utter nonsense if it were not for the fact that Geraldine Cummins was a very talented psychic widely respected in psychical research. She submitted to numerous tests during her long lifetime, and was apparently able to receive communications of incredible detail and accuracy from people about whom she knew nothing. Researchers are still debating whether in the best of these cases Geraldine Cummins was really in touch with the dead person, or whether she was using clairvoyance to discover information that she could not know normally. There is no doubt, however, that she did possess remarkable paranormal powers. So, even if she was not in touch with Fawcett, the possibility exists that she did have supernormal access to facts about the fate and findings of his expedition.

The communicator claiming to be Fawcett wrote that he had seen pyramids in the jungle. He had apparently been given drugs that enabled him, when in the vicinity of a certain pyramid, to travel back in time. The forest would become transparent and another landscape would appear before his eyes, superimposed on the jungle. He could then see the pyramids as they had been in the distant past and the people who lived at that time. He described the pyramids as Egyptian in appearance.

'You must accept my assurance that the last relics of an ancient civilization, Egyptian in character, are to be found in central South America,' he wrote. 'With my living eyes I have seen these ruins. . . . I believe that, if the climate were not so oppressive and we could bring gangs of men here, excavating under skilled direction, a whole ancient civilization would be revealed – the secret of the Lost Continent would be divulged; a flood of light thrown on a period that is prehistoric, and our origins more clearly realized.'

The communicator said that sun worship was the basic principle of this civilisation, and he added: 'The Atlanteans knew more or less the nature of electricity, which is dependent on the sun yet is allied to other air forces. Of course, there is more than one kind of electricity. The kind that is known to men was discovered by these Atlanteans, but they used their kind of electricity in a different way from us. They realised that it might be used, not

Colonel Percy H. Fawcett

merely to give light – queer globular lights – but that it might also be employed in connection with the shifting of weights. The building of the pyramids is solved when you know that huge blocks of stone can be manipulated through what I might call blast-electricity. . . . You will think me mad. . . but I, who have seen this ancient world, walked through its streets, halted before the porticoes of its temples, descended into the great subterranean world wherein electricity and air are combined and fused, can assure you that the men who came before modern history was recorded knew more about matter and light, about the ether and its properties, than the scientists of the 20th century can ever know or imagine.'

The scripts went on to claim that it was not natural forces but massive explosions in these subterranean electricity reservoirs that destroyed Atlantis. Do these writings give us a fantastic glimpse of Atlantis, or are they simply the outpourings of a highly imaginative brain? It is not a question we can answer with certainty. There is undoubtedly a widespread belief that ancient peoples were able to move great weights by unknown means, though scholars have come back with quite mundane solutions to such problems. The ancient Egyptian pyramids have often been cited in this connection despite the experts' assurances that thousands of labourers were capable of moving and assembling the huge blocks used in their construction.

In the Americas, too, we find immense buildings made of huge blocks of stone, often greater than those of the Egyptian pyramids. Time and again we learn that the stones were cut with such precision that the joins between them were scarcely detectable, and required no mortar. Yet the people who designed and built these architectural masterpieces possessed neither iron nor steel. Nor was bronze in general use, for either tools or weapons. Many temples, and even cities, were built high in the mountains, where the problems of terrain and altitude made their construction even more difficult.

Of all these cyclopean structures, the one that raises the biggest question mark over the Americas is undoubtedly the pyramid. Understandably, the sight of these impressive monuments calls to mind the Egyptians. Is it possible that two quite separate civilizations, living at different times, evolved the same structure and the technique to build it?

L. Sprague de Camp can be relied on to throw cold water on any Atlantis or other diffusionist theory not backed by scientific evidence. 'Mayan architecture, like that of Egypt three or four thousand years earlier, began by developing stone structures in imitation of the existing wooden houses . . .' he writes in *Lost Continents*. 'Their structures included astronomical observatories, ball-courts in which they played a kind of cross between basket-ball and soccer, dance-platforms, vapour-baths, shrines, reviewing-stands, stadiums, city walls, causeways, and pyramids, comparable in bulk, though not in height, with those of Egypt. However, the pyramids of the Mayas and Aztecs have nothing to do with those of Egypt, which were built several thousands of years earlier and moreover evolved from tombs, while the New World pyramids evolved from temple platforms.'

But for once, de Camp cannot have the last word. Despite his assertion that Egyptian and American pyramids differ in that the former evolved from tombs and the latter from temples, some New World pyramids were used for burial in a similar way to those in Egypt. And that, say the Atlantologists, is stretching coincidence too far.

It was in 1952, when Professor Alberto Ruz Lhullier was investigating the Mayan ruins near Palenque in southeast Mexico, that the burial aspect of American pyramids was confirmed. Among the ruins in Palenque is an impressive step pyramid known as the Temple of the Inscriptions. Inside this pyramid, Lhullier found a passage blocked with rubble. When this was removed and the professor had reached what he took to be the base of the pyramid, he discovered a heavy stone door. Behind it lay a chamber, 12 feet by 7 feet, whose floor consisted of a slab decorated with reliefs. Using an elaborate system of ropes and pulleys, Lhullier and his team finally managed to lift the 12-cwt slab. Beneath it they found a large, red stone sarcophagus containing the skeleton of a man, and a quantity of jade treasure, including a death mask placed over the man's skull. The walls of the tomb were covered with stucco relief figures of men in archaic costume – possibly ancestors of the Mayans who built the city near Palenque.

Commenting on this remarkable find, Michael Coe, Professor of Anthropology at Yale University, writes in his book *The Maya*: 'It is immediately evident that this great man, certainly a late seventh- or early eighth-century ruler of Palenque, had the Funerary Crypt built to contain his own remains; further, that he might have had the entire temple pyramid above it raised in his own lifetime. Thus it seems that the Temple of the Inscriptions was a funerary monument with exactly the same primary function as the Egyptian pyramids. And this, of course, leads one to look upon most Maya temple pyramids as sepulchral monuments, dedicated to the worship of deceased kings.'

A similar find was made as early as 1896 by Edward H. Thompson, the US Consul in Yucatán and one of the early explorers of the great Mayan city of Chichén Itzá. Among the ruins of Chichén Itzá, Thompson discovered a small pyramid containing the bones of seven human skeletons, and a cave housing a tomb.

The Egyptian connection does not end there. One of the most brilliant sites of American civilization, built by a people who apparently had close ties with the Mayas, is a city known by its Aztec name of Teotihuacan. It is an extraordinary place near Mexico City, consisting of a vast complex of ruins that were already overgrown when the Spaniards reached America. It is dominated by pyramids, one dedicated to the sun and another to the moon. The base of the sun pyramid measures 740 feet by 725 feet – exactly the same as the base of the Cheops pyramid in Egypt. The height of the Mexican structure is 215 feet, half that of the Egyptian one. Again we have to ask if this is just a strange coincidence or does it have tremendous significance?

Teotihuacán was a city of 100,000 people. Its streets and houses were laid out to a precise grid plan, and the homes of the wealthy were decorated with paintings and frescoes. The city's major buildings were constructed sometime between AD 100 and 300, and Teotihuacan was sacked and burned in AD 856 by the

Toltecs – contemporaries of the Mayas who later overran much of the Mayan empire in Yucatán.

In the Mayan city of Tikal in Guatemala the pyramids are of a height and steepness that astonished the early explorers. One rises to 230 feet, making it the highest known building in the Americas before the construction of New York's first skyscrapers. And in nearby Uaxactún, the oldest Mayan city yet excavated, archaeologists discovered a feature unique in the world: a pyramid within a pyramid.

The Mayas erected *stelae* – carved stone columns – bearing inscriptions that recorded important events. At Tikal a series of stelae was raised to mark the passage of each 20 years between AD 629 and 790. On each was the date, the age of the moon, and symbols of the gods ruling at the time. Stelae are not unique to the Mayas. They are an Asian device that the Egyptians, Greeks, and Romans also used.

One of the greatest puzzles about the past is how so many ancient peoples, without our modern technical aids, were able to transport massive building stones over great distances, fashion them precisely, and erect them with such ability that they have stood for thousands of years. The island of Malta in the Mediterranean, for example, is rich in megalithic remains. The primitive men who erected Malta's giant monuments also dug large underground tunnel networks and subterranean chambers. We do not know who these people were or why they carried out this work. Stonehenge is perhaps the most famous example of Stone Age skill that is beyond our comprehension. This ancient circle of stones in southern England, built about 1800 BC, attracts a quarter of a million visitors a year. 'We today can name no man or tribe who had all these qualifications [to erect the stones] at any time in the period of British prehistory,' says the official guide to Stonehenge. A recent theory suggests that a party of Egyptians was responsible for its construction because a basic measurement used by its builders was also used by the Egyptians. It is widely believed that the builders of Stonehenge, whoever they were, possessed a considerable knowledge of astronomy. We find a similar knowledge among the peoples of Central America. In the opinion of French historian Raymond Cartier, 'In many fields of knowledge the Mayas outclassed the Greeks and Romans. They were expert astronomers and mathematicians, and thus brought to perfection the science of chronology. They built domed observatories with a more exact orientation than those of 17th-century Paris, e.g. the Caracol erected on three terraces in Chichén Itzá. They had a precise calendar based on a 'sacred year' of 260 days, a solar year of 365 days, and a Venusian year of 584 days. The exact length of the solar year has been fixed, after long calculation, at 365·2422 days; the Mayas estimated it at 365·2420 days, i.e. correct to three places of decimals.'

The Mayas showed astonishing mathematical skill. While the Romans were still using a cumbersome method of counting, the Mayas invented a system of numbering that has all the features of modern arithmetic. Yet they used only three symbols: a bar for the number five, dots for each unit up to four, and a stylised shell for zero. Above all, the Mayas developed a form of picture-writing, based on a similar system to that used in Egyptian hieroglyphs. Because Diego de Landa, a Spanish monk who became Bishop of Yucatán, burned all the Mayan literature he could lay his hands on, only three Mayan books remain for study, and Mayan writing is still largely undeciphered.

While acknowledging the remarkable achievements of the early American civilizations and their striking similarities to Old World cultures, it is only fair that we also consider the features they did *not* share with Old World civilizations. They had no plough, very few metal tools, no Old World diseases, no Old World domestic animals, and no wheels – except on toys. Indeed it is one of the great mysteries of the American cultures that they never extended the use of wheels from toys to full-size vehicles. Atlantologists and other diffusionists make much of the supposed resemblances between Mayan and ancient Egyptian writing, but although the two scripts are based on similar principles, the signs and language are completely different. Those who argue that the early American civilizations developed under the influence of a greater people, such as the Atlanteans or the Egyptians, must explain all these anomalies.

Probably the most important objection to the theory that Atlantean refugees founded the cultures of the Americas is the enormous time-lag between the date given by Plato for the destruction of Atlantis and the emergence of the civilizations of the Olmecs and Mayas, let alone those of the Aztecs and Incas. Either we must believe, like Lewis Spence and others, that the Atlanteans escaped to another continent and only moved on to the Americas at a much later stage, or we must accept that these cultures were the echo of others equally great that date back many thousands of years – as some investigators of Tiahuanaco maintain. Atlantologists point out that the peoples of the Americas seem to have been content to reproduce the same patterns of art and architecture over and over again, as if they were copying models provided by others, and that they do not seem to have progressed from an advanced starting point. However, orthodox scholars contest the view that the civilizations of the Americas sprang up suddenly, and are convinced that these cultures evolved, albeit rapidly, from more primitive beginnings. Certainly the claim by some Atlantologists that the Mayas derived their peaceful nature from the Atlanteans does not stand up to close examination. The Mayas may not have been as bloodthirsty as the later Aztecs, but they were undoubtedly warlike and they indulged in human sacrifice.

On the other hand we cannot ignore the persistent legends of the ancient American peoples that tell of visits from fair-skinned 'gods' with beards who came from across the sea in the mists of prehistory, bringing the Indians the arts of civilization. This tradition was common to the Mayas, Aztecs, Incas, and other culturally advanced peoples of pre-Columbian America, though each culture called the White God by a different name. To the Mayas he was Kukulcan; the Toltecs and Aztecs knew him as Quetzalcoatl; and the Incas called him Viracocha.

The discovery of artifacts depicting men with beards and narrow, beaked noses, who look quite un-Indian, appears to some investigators to back up the legends and to provide further evidence that another people influenced American culture. The famous Norwegian anthropologist and diffusionist Thor

Heyerdahl, is reportedly convinced that 'a people, or more exactly a group of men, with fair skin, aquiline noses, and bushy beards exercised a decisive influence on the development of the American civilizations and in particular on those that flourished in the Andes, in ancient Peru.'

The legends of the White God were the undoing of these great civilizations, for they welcomed the fair-skinned Spanish conquistadors as gods, and their kingdoms crumbled.

Dr Michael Coe, a leading expert on Olmec civilisation, believes that the earliest site of the Olmecs is in San Lorenzo, Mexico. Radiocarbon dating of samples from San Lorenzo indicates that the monuments at this site were constructed no later than 900 or 800 BC, and perhaps considerably earlier. 'We have, therefore, found the oldest civilized communities thus far known in Mesoamerica,' says Dr Coe. 'Nonetheless, by pushing back the earliest Olmec civilization to such an early date – to a time when there was little else but simple village cultures in the rest of Mexico and Central America – the lack of antecedents is an embarrassing problem. We now have no idea where the Olmec came from or who built the mounds and carved the sculptures of San Lorenzo. Whoever they were, these pioneers must have been unusually gifted in engineering as well as art. ....'

So, despite attempts to make the civilizations of ancient America appear normal, if remarkable, it seems that there is a mystery that remains unsolved. Perhaps the South American jungles will provide more ruins and more clues. Or perhaps Atlantis will be found, and give us the answers. Unless, of course, the answer lies not in the Atlantic but in the Pacific, in the shape of yet another lost continent.

CHAPTER 24

THE MONUMENTS OF MU

Were the explorers who searched for the Counterweight Continent a few thousand years too late? Are the archipelagos of Pacific islands the former mountain tops of a sunken land? In the nineteenth century some of the seekers for a lost continent looked on the other side of the globe, to the world's largest ocean, for their vanished civilization. Indeed a study of surviving Mayan texts had even provided the new land with a name – Mu. Pure imagination, perhaps – yet there are a number of intriguing puzzles that could be explained by the notion of a Pacific land-mass that vanished beneath the waves . . .

In the evening twilight of Easter Sunday 1722, a Dutch fleet chanced upon a tiny island in the South Pacific – and launched a controversy that has lasted ever since. Admiral Jaakob Roggeveen and his men reached the island too late in the day to explore. They dropped anchor and waited until dawn next day before moving closer to the shore to look for signs of life. At first light they saw a series of small fires on the shore. Then, as the sun climbed slowly above the horizon, an astonishing sight met their eyes. All along the shore, people of different skin colours were apparently worshipping in front of colossal statues.

Roggeveen named the island Paasch Eyland, or Easter Island, because of the day on which his fleet had first sighted it. He and his men spent only a few hours there, but they did take a closer look at the enormous statues. These proved to be huge elongated heads, all very similar and of varying heights. Roggeveen was able to break a piece from one of the statues with his bare fingers and the Dutch explorers concluded it was made from clay and soil mixed with pebbles. In fact, the statues were made from solid rock that had deteriorated with age and erosion. This was discovered by a Spanish expedition under Felipe Gonzalez, which reached the island in 1770. The Spaniards hit the statues with pickaxes, causing sparks to fly.

If the Easter Island statues had been moulded, as the Dutch explorers believed, there would have been no mystery. But with the realization that the statues had been hewn from rock a problem arose. How did the inhabitants of this tiny island develop the skill to sculpt the statues and, more important, how did they transport the huge heads and erect them on an island devoid of trees and ropes large enough for the purpose? Later European explorers discovered that, although the Easter Islanders held the statues in awe, they seemed to know nothing about their construction. And as time went by, a new enigma emerged. The Easter Islanders possessed a number of engraved wooden boards, known as *rongorongo* boards or 'singing tablets,' that appeared to be inscribed with a form of picture-writing. Yet none of the islanders could read the boards with any exactness, and they remain undeciphered. Where did this writing come from? Was it invented by the statue-builders? Is it really writing at all? These and other questions about the perplexing Easter Island civilization have exercised the minds of scholars for 200 years.

Easter Island is dominated by three extinct volcanoes, Rano Raraku, Rano Kao, and Rano Aroi. It is only 13 miles long and 7 miles across at its widest points, and it rises out of the South Pacific in splendid isolation. Its nearest inhabited neighbour is Pitcairn Island – refuge of the *Bounty* mutineers – 1200 miles to the west. In the opposite direction, 2300 miles of open ocean lie between Easter Island and the coast of northern Chile.

Yet a people settled on this barren stretch of land, with its boulder-strewn landscape and porous soil. There are no freshwater rivers or streams and the strong, salt-laden winds prevent the growth of tall plants or trees. There was no animal life to hunt, and life for the early settlers must have been arduous in the extreme. But they multiplied, and apparently developed (or had brought with them) a form of writing. They built roads, temples, and a solar observatory, and carved some 600 massive stone heads with elongated ears. Many of these statues were set up along the coast of the island. Some were erected on the slopes of Rano Raraku, and others appear to have marked the island's roads. The largest of the coastal statues is 33 feet high and weighs 80 tons. It was once surmounted by a 12-ton cylindrical topknot, carved from red stone and measuring six feet high by eight feet wide.

It is hardly surprising, then, that Easter Island has figured prominently in numerous theories about the earth's early civilizations and their origins, particularly as the island's inhabitants at the time of its discovery – who bore no resemblance to the stone colossi – seemed as mystified by the statues as the visitors. Nearly 200 stone heads, including one 66 feet high, are still in the quarry, suddenly abandoned during production, adding one more intriguing element to the enigma.

In the absence of any immediate acceptable solution to the Easter Island problem, scholars and visionaries have been free to give their imagination full rein in an attempt to find the answer. Many have speculated that the island is either part of a sunken Pacific continent, or an outpost of such a lost land. Inevitably, because the Americas sit between the Atlantic and Pacific oceans, much of the 'evidence' for a lost Atlantic continent that influenced the cultures of ancient America has been offered in support of a vanished Pacific civilization, also supposed to have carried its arts and skills to the American Indians.

In 1864 a French scholar, the Abbé Charles-Étienne Brasseur de Bourbourg, came across an abridged copy of a treatise on the Mayan civilisation in the library of the Historical Academy of Madrid. This treatise, entitled *Account of the Affairs of Yucatán*, had been written by Diego de Landa, the Spanish Bishop of Yucatán, who destroyed all but three books of the Mayans' extensive literature and substituted Christian teachings. After this appalling act of vandalism, de Landa became interested in the

Mayan culture and tried to learn Mayan writing – a complicated system combining ideographic signs and phonetic elements to produce word-glyphs. As a result he compiled a 'Mayan alphabet' and included it in his treatise.

The discovery of this alphabet excited Brasseur. He already had a considerable interest in the civilizations of the New World, and he believed he could use de Landa's alphabet to decipher the three surviving Mayan books. Armed with the alphabet and aided by a lively imagination, he immediately set about translating one of the books, the *Troano Codex* – half of the two-part *Tro-Cortesianus Codex* preserved in Madrid. Soon he revealed that the book told of a volcanic catastrophe and of a land that sank beneath the waves. But there were two symbols in the Mayan manuscript that Brasseur was unable to account for. They bore a very faint resemblance to de Landa's 'M' and 'U,' so he put them together and produced Mu – the name he gave to the submerged land.

Naturally, Brasseur's discovery of the de Landa alphabet caused excitement among historians and scholars, but this quickly turned to disappointment when attempts to translate other Mayan writing with this 'key' produced incoherent nonsense. To this day only about one third of the Mayan glyphs are understood, but enough is now known about the language to assert that the *Troano Codex* deals with astrology and not with the destruction of Mu. The other two books – the *Dresden Codex* and the *Codex Perezianus*, preserved in Dresden and Paris respectively – appear to concern astronomy and religious ritual. Although de Landa's alphabet has been shown to be based on erroneous principles, and Brasseur's translation has been discredited, the story of Mu has survived and grown, as others have sought to prove the existence of a lost continent, using the same tools. Whereas Brasseur believed Mu to be the name once used for Atlantis, others have adopted it for a South Pacific continent.

Brasseur's contemporary and fellow countryman Augustus Le Plongeon, a physician and archaeologist of some repute, was the first man to excavate Mayan ruins in Yucatan, where he and his American wife Alice lived for many years. Le Plongeon, a resplendent figure with a waist-length beard, attempted his own translation of the *Troano Codex*, drawing a good deal of his inspiration from the work of Brasseur and from a liberal interpretation of pictures found on the walls of ruins in the Mayan city of Chichén-Itzá. Le Plongeon's 'translation' retraced the story of the sunken continent of Mu with an extravagance that made Brasseur's account pale in comparison. At the heart of his account is the rivalry of two Muvian princes, Coh and Aac, for the hand of their sister Moo, the Queen of Mu. Prince Coh won, but was killed by his jealous brother who immediately took over the country from Queen Moo.

At the height of this drama, the continent began to sink. Moo fled to Egypt, where she built the Sphinx as a memorial to Prince Coh, and, under the name of Isis, founded the Egyptian civilization. Other Muvians escaped from their sinking homeland to Yucatán, where they recorded their history and erected temples to their leaders. Le Plongeon claimed that Egyptian hieroglyphs and Mayan writings were alike – a belief not shared by the specialists in these languages – and even maintained that Jesus spoke Mayan on the Cross.

In the 1880s, Augustus and Alice Le Plongeon settled down in Brooklyn to write several books on their experiences and discoveries. The best-known of these was Le Plongeon's *Queen Moo and the Egyptian Sphinx* – published in 1896 and still in print – which included the author's claim to have found the charred entrails of Prince Coh, preserved in a stone urn, during his excavations of Mayan ruins.

Le Plongeon's 'translation' of the *Troano Codex* was far more readable – if no more reliable – than Brasseur's. Here is the part of Le Plongeon's version that deals with the destruction of Mu: 'In the year 6 Kan, on the 11th Muluc in the month Zac, there occurred terrible earthquakes, which continued without interruption until the 13th Chuen. The country of the hills of mud, the land of Mu was sacrificed; being twice upheaved it suddenly disappeared during the night, the basin being continually shaken by the volcanic forces. Being confined, these caused the land to sink and to rise several times in various places. At last the surface gave way and ten countries were torn asunder and scattered. Unable to stand the force of the convulsion, they sank with their 64,000,000 inhabitants 8060 years before the writing of this book.'

According to the Frenchman, he found records in Yucatán stating that 'the Hieratic head [high priest] of the land of Mu prophesied its destruction, and that some, heeding the prophecy, left and went to the colonies where they were saved.'

Like Brasseur, Le Plongeon believed that Mu and Atlantis were one and the same land. Basing his argument on his interpretations of Mayan wall paintings and inscriptions, he placed the sunken continent in the region of the Gulf of Mexico and the Caribbean Sea, to the east of Central America.

At about the same time, another Frenchman, Louis Jacolliot, was also writing about a lost continent. He had a new name for it, Rutas, and a new source, a collection of Sanskrit myths collected during a stay in India. According to Jacolliot, these myths told of a land named Rutas that sank in the Indian Ocean. But he interpreted them as referring to a Pacific landmass that formerly covered the region now occupied by the Polynesian islands. Plato's Atlantis story, he argued, was merely an echo of this tremendous event, and the sinking of Rutas caused India and other lands to rise from the sea.

From the 1880s onward, support for the existence of a lost Pacific continent began to appear with surprising frequency, and from sources that were even more surprising. A New York dentist, Dr John Ballou Newbrough, claimed angelic inspiration for his account of a vanished land called Pan. Newbrough, a spiritualist medium, published the story of Pan in *Oahspe*, a book allegedly produced by automatic writing (hand writing said to occur without the individual's conscious control). The book was subtitled *A Kosmon Bible in the Words of Jehovah and his Angel Ambassadors*. It was first published in 1882, and has since been largely ridiculed for its misinformation and unfulfilled prophecies.

According to *Oahspe*, man appeared on earth 72,000 years ago as a result of the union between the angels and a species of seal-like animals. Newbrough's book contains a map of the earth in antediluvian times showing the triangular continent of Pan in the North Pacific. Pan sank beneath the waves 24,000 years ago. However, it is scheduled to rise again in the very near future. *Oahspe* tells us that Pan will begin to resurface in 1980, and when its cities and the records of its civilization are finally exposed, we will have no difficulty in deciphering its books or learning about its culture, because *Oahspe* very thoughtfully supplies us with a Panic dictionary and a Panic alphabet.

Not all proponents of a lost Pacific continent needed the help of angels to formulate their ideas. A New Zealander, Professor J. MacMillan Brown, drew upon his knowledge of geology, archaeology, and anthropology to explain the mystery of Easter Island. He argued that there had once been either a continent or a densely populated archipelago in the South Pacific, inhabited by white men, and that Easter Island had served as a collective burial ground for the people of neighbouring islands. The professor pointed to similarities between the monuments and customs of the Polynesian people and those of the Peruvian civilizations, believing that South American culture had reached that continent from the west. Although Professor Brown has been described as 'a man with a mind both simple and excessively imaginative', parts of his theory find support today in a new interpretation of Polynesian culture by modern experts.

The professor published his theory in the form of a book, *Riddle of the Pacific*, which appeared in 1906. Shortly afterward, between 1908 and 1926, the German explorer Leo Frobenius made discoveries in Yorubaland – part of Nigeria – that led him to believe he had discovered Atlantis. He identified the Nigerian god Olokon with Poseidon, and argued that the Yoruba culture contained many elements, such as the short bow and tattooing, that he said were non-African. He went on to state his belief that civilization had begun on a lost Pacific continent. It had spread from there to Asia, then to the west, giving rise to the Egyptian and Atlanto-Nigerian civilizations.

All these protagonists had merely set the stage for the appearance of the most outrageous supporter of a vanished Pacific continent. James Churchward, a small, thin Anglo-American, was already in his 70s when he first revealed the results of a lifetime's research on the subject. His first book, *The Lost Continent of Mu*, published in 1926, made fascinating reading, though acceptance of its contents demands a high degree of gullibility on the part of the reader. Nevertheless, Churchward's name is now almost synonymous with Mu's, and his book is still in print.

Churchward based his theory on two sets of tablets, one of which no one has had the privilege of studying except a priest in whose temple the tablets were allegedly preserved. In his first book Churchward claims to have seen these 'Naacal tablets' in an Indian temple; elsewhere he says he studied them in Tibet. The other set of tablets is a collection of some 2500 stone objects found in Mexico by an American engineer named William Niven. These objects, which look like flattened figurines, were made in great numbers by the Aztecs and other Mexican peoples. No one else seemed to think there was anything on them worth deciphering, but Churchward claimed to be able to 'read' their bumps and curlicues. They are symbols that originated in Mu, he said, and they convey deep and mysterious meanings. He dated the Niven tablets as at least 12,000 years old, and claimed that they and the Naacal tablets contain extracts from the Sacred Inspired Writings of Mu. Churchward's first book begins with these compelling words: 'The Garden of Eden was not in Asia but on a now sunken continent in the Pacific Ocean. The Biblical story of creation – the epic of the seven days and the seven nights – came first not from the peoples of the Nile or of the Euphrates Valley but from this now submerged continent, Mu – the Motherland of Man.

'These assertions call be proved by the complex records I discovered upon long-forgotten sacred tablets in India, together with records from other countries. They tell of this strange country of 64,000,000 inhabitants, who, 50,000 years ago, had developed a civilization superior in many respects to our own. They described, among other things, the creation of man in the mysterious land of Mu.'

Churchward explains that he saw the sacred Naacal tablets during a stay in India (or Tibet, depending on which of his books we are reading). While he was studying the bas-reliefs in a certain temple, he became friendly with the temple's high priest. He discovered that the man was interested in archaeology and ancient records, 'and had a greater knowledge of those subjects than any other living man.' The high priest began teaching Churchward how to read the peculiar inscriptions on the temple walls, and Churchward spent the next two years studying this strange language, which 'my priestly friend believed to be the original tongue of mankind.' Churchward learned that only two other priests in India knew this language.

Interpreting the temple writings proved difficult, because many apparently simple inscriptions had hidden meaning, 'which had been designed especially for the Holy Brothers – the Naacals – a priestly brotherhood sent from the motherland [Mu] to the colonies to teach the sacred writings, religion, and the sciences.' One day, in the course of a conversation with Churchward, the priest revealed that there were a number of ancient tablets in the temple's secret archives, which were believed to have originated either in Burma or in the vanished land of Mu itself. He had never seen the tablets, only the containers in which they were kept. Although he was in a position to examine the tablets, the high priest had not done so because they were sacred records not to be touched.

Churchward argued that the tablets might not be packed away properly and could be deteriorating, a view that the priest eventually shared, and so the containers were opened. According to Churchward the tablets, written in the same dead language that he had been studying, described in detail the earth's creation, the appearance of man, and the land on which he evolved – Mu.

Having learned that more tablets were preserved in other Indian temples, Churchward set off on an unsuccessful quest for them. He then turned to a study of the writings of old civilizations, which confirmed his belief that the Chaldeans, Babylonians, Persians, Egyptians, Greeks, and Hindus had been preceded by the civilisation of Mu.

'Continuing my researches, I discovered that this lost continent had extended from somewhere north of Hawaii to the south as far as the Fijis and Easter Island, and was undoubtedly the original habitat of man. I learned that in this beautiful country there had lived a people that colonized the earth, and that the land had been obliterated by terrific earthquakes and submersion 12,000 years ago, and had vanished in a vortex of fire and water.'

According to Churchward, Mu was a beautiful, tropical country with vast plains covered with rich grazing grasses and tilled fields. There were no mountains, 'for mountains had not yet been forced up from the bowels of the earth,' but there were low, rolling hills, shaded by tropical vegetation. Many 'broad, slow-running streams and rivers, which wound their sinuous ways in fantastic curves and bends around the wooded hills and through the fertile plains,' watered the land and produced luxuriant flowers and shrubs.

Churchward peoples his graphic picture of the vanished continent with gaudy-winged butterflies, humming birds, lively crickets, mighty mastodons and elephants, and a population of 64,000,000 noble human beings enjoying 'a gay and happy life.'

The inhabitants of Mu consisted of ten tribes all under one government, ruled by an emperor, the Ra Mu. 'The dominant race in the land of Mu was a white race, exceedingly handsome people, with clear white or olive skins, large, soft, dark eyes, and straight black hair. Besides this white race, there were other races, people with yellow, brown, or black skins. They, however, did not dominate.'

The Muvians built broad, smooth roads running in all directions like a spider's web, and the stones from which the roads were constructed were matched so perfectly that not a blade of grass could grow between them. They were great navigators, and they made all the other countries on the planet their colonies. It was an idyllic life, and on cool evenings pleasure ships, filled with gorgeously dressed, jewel-bedecked men and women, rejoiced at their good fortune. 'While this great land was thus at its zenith,' Churchward's account continues, 'centre of the earth's civilization, learning, trade and commerce, with great stone temples being erected, and huge statues and monoliths set up, she received a rude shock; a fearful visitation overtook her.'

Earthquakes and volcanic eruptions shook the southern parts of the continent, destroying many cities. Tidal waves flooded the land, and the lava piled up into high cones that are still to be seen today in the form of the Pacific islands. Eventually the Muvians were able to rebuild these cities, and life returned to normal. Then, many generations later, a similar but far greater catastrophe struck Mu, and 'the whole continent heaved and rolled like the ocean's waves.' Churchward is not one to miss the drama of such an event. 'With thunderous roarings the doomed land sank,' he writes. 'Down, down, down she went, into the mouth of hell – a tank of fire'. Then 50 million square miles of water poured over the continent, drowning the vast majority of its noble inhabitants.

The only visible remains of the great continent were its lava cones, which formed chains of small islands, covered to capacity with the survivors of the cataclysm. With no clothing, no tools, no shelter, and no food, these formerly peace-loving people had to become cannibals in order to survive. The colonies that Mu had founded continued for a while, but without the help of the mother-land they eventually flickered out. Churchward asserts that Atlantis was one of these colonies, and suffered a similar fate to Mu 1000 years later.

Churchward claimed that his findings solved the mysteries surrounding the first inhabitants of the South Sea islands and the origins of the ancient American civilizations. 'On some of the South Sea Islands, notably Easter, Mangaia, Tongatabu, Panape, and the Ladrone or Marianas Islands' he writes, 'there stand today vestiges of old stone temples and other lithic [stone] remains that take us back to the time of Mu. At Uxmal, in Yucatán, a ruined temple bears inscriptions commemorative of the 'Lands of the West, whence we came;' and the striking Mexican pyramid southwest of Mexico City, according to its inscriptions, was raised as a monument to the destruction of these same 'Lands of the West'.'

Even those readers prepared to believe that Churchward was privileged to see the ancient Naacal tablets may wonder how he was able to decipher them – and the Niven tablets that also supplied part of his story – so quickly. However, Churchward has an explanation for this. Like many occultists, he believed that it is possible for a suitably gifted person to decipher the secret language of symbols (said to have been used by all the ancients to record their wisdom) simply by staring at the symbols until their meaning emerges from the student's inner consciousness. It was this technique, in which he was aided by the teachings of the Indian (or Tibetan) high priest, that enabled Churchward to recover the forgotten history of Mu.

In considering the possibility that there was once a huge continent in the Pacific, we need to take a fresh look at the islands now occupying that area. The place deserving the closest scrutiny is undoubtedly Easter Island with its huge sculptures and associated mysteries. Why did the people of such a tiny island build so many very similar stone heads? Why, instead of carving them one at a time, were they producing as many as 200 simultaneously in their quarry when they suddenly abandoned their work ?

Some have suggested that the island was part of Mu, and the place at which the stone monuments were carved before being transported to other parts of the continent. Others believe Easter Island to have been a burial ground, a sacred area of Mu that became an island when the rest of the continent sank.

The man who has done most in our time to popularize Easter Island and to solve its riddles is Thor Heyerdahl, the Norwegian anthropologist who, in 1947, led the famous Scandinavian *Kon-Tiki* expedition from South America to Polynesia. He subsequently organized expeditions to the Galápagos Islands in 1952 and to Easter Island in 1955. Heyerdahl was convinced that all the Polynesian islands were originally settled by people from South America. When he first published his theory, in 1941, most scientists disregarded the possibility of South American influence on Polynesia because of the vast expanse of ocean that lies between South America and the nearest South Pacific islands. It seemed unlikely, to say the least, that the South American Indians with their frail reed and balsa wood craft could have crossed thousands of miles of ocean to carry their culture to Polynesia. Most authorities believed that the Polynesians had come from the other direction, from Asia. Heyerdahl agreed that Asian immigrants *had*

Norwegian anthropologist, Thor Heyerdahl

reached the Polynesian islands, but he was convinced that they were preceded by colonisers from South America.

To help prove his case, Heyerdahl and his team built the balsa wood raft *Kon-Tiki* based on the traditional materials and techniques used in the construction of South American boats. In 1947, he and five companions set out aboard the raft from Callao, Peru. They spent 101 days at sea, allowing the South Equatorial Current and the prevailing trade winds to carry them 4300 nautical miles to the little Polynesian atoll of Raroia in the Tuamotu Archipelago.

The voyage made Heyerdahl famous, but many scientists remained sceptical. To show a thing can be done is not the same as proving it was done, said the critics. And even if people from South America had reached Polynesia, this did not prove that there was regular contact across the ocean or that the sailors from Peru founded the culture of the Polynesian islands, as Heyerdahl suggested. Orthodox scientists were even more outraged when Heyerdahl suggested that the civilizers from Peru might have been the fair-skinned, bearded men enshrined in Indian legend, who had previously influenced the development of the American civilizations.

However, Heyerdahl was a careful scientist, and he had carried out a great deal of research among the American Indians and the Polynesians in order to provide evidence for his theories. His expedition to Easter Island in 1955 was the first to undertake a thorough archaeological study, including modern techniques such as radiocarbon dating, and he combined his examination of the island's past with a practical approach to such problems as how the Easter Island statues were transported.

Why is it that Easter Island, the most remote and inaccessible of all the countless Polynesian islands, should be the very one among them to possess the most abundant and spectacular archaeological remains? And why, alone in Polynesia, should it have a system of writing? asked Heyerdahl. He believed that the key to these questions lay in the island's situation. Of all the inhabited Polynesian islands, Easter Island is the nearest to South America – and the farthest from Asia. It is likely to have been the first island colonised by settlers from South America, whereas migrants from Asia would have reached it last.

Heyerdahl's excavations, backed up by radiocarbon dating tests, showed that a considerable population lived on Easter Island around AD 380 – about 1000 years earlier than anyone had hitherto suspected. Heyerdahl believed that these people came from Peru, bringing with them their stoneworking techniques. They built temples, roads, and a solar observatory that resemble the magnificent constructions found in ancient Peru. Their temples were astronomically oriented, altarlike elevations, evidently built by specialized stonemasons.

This cultural period was succeeded by another around AD 1100, when a new wave of immigrants overran the island. These people showed similar – but not identical – stone-carving skills to their predecessors, and Heyerdahl believes that they too came from Peru. It was during this period that the giant statues were carved and placed on terraced stone platforms that contained burial vaults. The huge heads, depicting long-eared men, recall the practice among the Inca and other Peruvian Indians of elongating the ears by inserting ornamental plugs into the lobes.

According to Heyerdahl, the statue-builders controlled the island for nearly 600 years, but around 1680 the production of statues stopped abruptly, and from then on the giant heads were gradually toppled or destroyed. In Heyerdahl's view, this occurred as the result of another invasion of the island, this time by Polynesians arriving from the direction of Asia. Archaeological evidence suggests that from about 1680 onward the island underwent a period of decadence and warfare, and Easter Island legends tell of a lengthy conflict between 'the short ears' (whom Heyerdahl identified with the Polynesian invaders) and 'the long ears' (the statue-builders). The 'short ears' eventually won, wiping out the 'long ears' and destroying their civilization. The Polynesians were left in control of the island, unable to carve the statues or read the rongorongo boards left by their predecessors. Apart from the remaining statues, the only picture we now have of the earlier settlers is the wood carving, produced by the hundred for commercial purposes by today's Easter

Islanders. It shows an emaciated person with goatee beard, aquiline nose, and long ear lobes. The islanders claim that these were the people their ancestors found and exterminated.

Apart from the early date ascribed to Easter Island civilization, one of the most remarkable discoveries made by Heyerdahl was that when the first settlers arrived on Easter Island there were trees in abundance. The settlers had to cut them down in order to clear the way for the transportation of stones from the quarry. The trees were still there when the statue-builders arrived. Thus the means of moving and erecting the giant statues is no longer a mystery. Indeed Heyerdahl arranged for some of the present-day inhabitants to erect a fallen statue by levering it up with long poles and ropes and gradually blocking piles of small rocks underneath it. It took 12 men 18 days to raise the 25-ton statue – but they did it.

Heyerdahl still has his detractors. Critics point out that, despite the apparent similarities between the stoneworking techniques of Easter Island and Peru, there are fundamental differences between the two. The Easter Islanders built rubble walls that they faced with thin slabs of stone, whereas the Peruvians built with solid blocks of stone. What is more, the Peruvians could not have brought writing to Easter Island, because they themselves had no written language. Indeed, many scholars believe that the inscriptions on the rongorongo boards are not, strictly speaking, a system of writing at all, but rather a device to jog the memory of the storytellers or hymn-singers who used the symbols as reminders of the key elements of their story when reciting lengthy ritual chants. Above all, the critics attack Heyerdahl's use of legend to support his theories, because the legends themselves are often contradictory. They also point out that the Easter Islanders and the Peruvian Indians were not alone in elongating their ear lobes. This practice is also found in Polynesian islands much closer to Asia.

Nevertheless, Heyerdahl's tireless endeavours in support of his claims and his undoubted contribution to our knowledge of Easter Island have led to a re-evaluation of the idea of cultural contact between South America and Polynesia, and a number of scientists now accept at least part of his theory concerning the history of Easter Island.

Heyerdahl has shown that it is possible to explain the mysteries of Easter Island without recourse to a lost continent. But even if his claims are correct, they need not mean that such a continent never existed in the Pacific. If the continent sank 12,000 years ago, as Churchward maintained, it could well have taken all evidence of its existence with it. Easter Island may be one of its peaks, even if the cultures whose remains now litter its surface appear to have no connection with Mu.

The Pacific region seems so rich in unsolved mysteries and enigmatic finds that almost any theorist, however outlandish, will probably find some 'evidence' for his ideas in this part of the globe. Until a more thorough archaeological examination of the area has been carried out, it would be unwise to jump to any firm conclusions. After all, in many ways the huge Pacific Ocean – the world's largest at 68,000,000 square miles – with its volcanic history and strings of islands, might seem to be a more promising site for a vanished continent than the much smaller Atlantic (31,830,000 square miles).

CHAPTER 25

LEMURIA: THE HOME OF THE MISSING LINK

Ever since the mid-19th century, men have puzzled over the lemur. This small mammal, halfway between a monkey and a squirrel, is found mainly in Madagascar, but also in Africa, India, and the Malay Archipelago. How, argued the biologists, could the identical animal have settled in such widely scattered territories? The answer was simple. They proposed Lemuria, a lost continent spanning the Indian Ocean, as the only feasible solution. Where they right? And assuming they were, what would such a lost land mean in terms of the origins of mankind itself? This chapter explores the arguments and the evidence.

The descendants of a long-lost race from a vanished continent are alive and well and living on the slopes of Mount Shasta in northern California. So claimed an article in the *Los Angeles Times Star* of 22 May, 1932. The writer of the article, reporter Edward Lanser, said he had first learned about these people while travelling at night on the *Shasta Limited*, the train taking him to Portland, Oregon. From the train's observation car Lanser had seen strange red and green lights illuminating Mount Shasta. The conductor of the train told him that these were the work of 'Lemurians holding ceremonials'. Understandably intrigued, and sensing a scoop for his newspaper, Lanser made an expedition into the Mount Shasta wilderness in search of these mysterious beings, said to be the last descendants of the earth's first inhabitants.

Lanser drove to the town of Weed where he heard tell of a 'mystic village' on Mount Shasta and talked to other investigators who had seen the Lemurians' ceremonial lights, during the daytime as well as at night. But no one had ever been able to enter the 'sacred precincts' of the Mount Shasta colony – or if they had, they had not returned to tell the tale. One man, however, had managed to become an expert on this strange Lemurian settlement: 'the eminent scientist Professor Edgar Lucin Larkin'. According to Lanser, Professor Larkin, 'with determined sagacity, penetrated the Shasta wilderness as far as he could – or dared – and then, cleverly, continued his investigations from a promontory with a powerful long-distance telescope.'

Peering through his telescope, the professor had seen a great temple in the midst of the Lemurian village. It was a splendid piece of architecture, carved from marble and onyx, which rivalled the beauty of the magnificent Mayan temples in Yucatán. Although the investigators seemed frightened to trespass on the Lemurians' sacred terrain, the evidence was that they were a peace-loving, friendly community, apparently leading the same kind of life as their ancestors had done before their homeland sank beneath the sea.

Lanser reported that the people of Weed had occasionally met Lemurians and were able to give a good description of them. They were 'tall, barefoot, noble-looking men, with close-cropped hair, dressed in spotless white robes.' The town's storekeepers had good reason to like them. The Lemurians purchased huge quantities of sulphur, salt, and lard, paying with large gold nuggets – worth far more than the merchandise – that they apparently mined from Mount Shasta.

How had this ancient people been able to remain undetected for so long? Lanser provided the answer in his remarkable account. The Lemurians, he said, possessed 'the secret power of the Tibetan masters,' which enabled them to blend with their surroundings and vanish at will, and they encircled their village with an 'invisible protective boundary' to keep intruders out. According to Lanser, the Lemurians' scientific knowledge was far greater than ours. And although they had lived in America –

which they called Gustama – for several hundred thousand years, they had not forgotten their homeland. Their strangely lit ceremonials on the slopes of Mount Shasta were held in honour of the long-lost Lemuria.

Those readers of the *Los Angeles Times Star* who took Lanser's story without a pinch of salt were to be disappointed. Lanser's report contains the only allegedly eye-witness account of the Mount Shasta Lemurians ever published, and no subsequent investigators have found the mystic village or its strange inhabitants. Either these mysterious people never existed or they have since blended irretrievably into their surroundings. Professor Larkin, who studied the Lemurians through his telescope, turns out to be no 'eminent scientist,' as Lanser claimed, but an elderly occultist who ran the Mount Lowe Observatory in California. Unlike its neighbour, the Mount Wilson Observatory, which is a great scientific institution, the Mount Lowe Observatory was a tourist attraction operated by the Pacific Electric Railway, and Larkin's job was to show visitors the stars through a small telescope. Larkin died in 1924 – eight years before the publication of Lanser's article.

Mount Shasta had already been a subject of mystical speculation long before Lanser wrote his Lemurian story. In 1894 a writer named Frederick Spencer Oliver published an occult novel entitled *A Dweller on Two Planets*, under the name 'Phylos the Tibetan'. In this book the narrator meets his Master, a Chinese named Quong, on Mount Shasta, where sages have established a community to preserve the wisdom of the ancients. Having inducted him into their order, the sages take the narrator to visit Venus in his spiritual body and also teach him to remember his previous incarnations. These include a life on Atlantis, where he rose from miner's son to prince of the realm. He then got involved with two women at once, which proved to be his undoing.

Although we can dismiss the Lanser story as a fascinating piece of fiction based on another piece of fiction, we cannot discard the Lemurians in the same way. Their country of origin, Lemuria, was first suggested in the mid-1800s by scientists trying to account for striking resemblances between the rocks and fossils of Central India and South Africa and for the spread of certain fauna and flora between these continents. One animal that puzzled them particularly was the lemur, a small mammal related to both men and monkeys. The lemur, which looks like a cross between a monkey and a squirrel, lives mainly on the island of Madagascar, but is also found in Africa, India, and the Malay archipelago.

The debate over the lemur emerged in the wake of Charles Darwin's great thesis on evolution, *On The Origin of Species*, published in 1859. At this time there were two schools of thought: either God had created the various species and put them on earth in the form that we know them, or they had evolved over millions of years. If the former were the case, then God could put His creations wherever He liked – limiting similar species to a particular area of the globe, or placing them on continents thousands of miles apart. But if similar species had evolved in one place from a common ancestor, as Darwin and his supporters thought, the geographical spread of those species had to be in accordance with the limitations of the global picture. In the evolutionists' scheme of things, the lowly lemur presented a problem, because some means had to be found by which it could have crossed the ocean to its present areas of distribution.

Biologists were quick to come up with the obvious solution to the dilemma. The areas now inhabited by the lemur must once have been connected in one vast continent, which still existed at the time when mammals were evolving. The English zoologist Philip L. Sclater suggested that the continent be called 'Lemuria' in honour of the lemur.

Many eminent people were ready to accept the possibility of such a continent. Alfred Russel Wallace, who independently developed the theory of evolution simultaneously with Darwin, wrote: 'This is undoubtedly a legitimate and highly probable supposition, and it is an example of the way in which a study of the geographical distribution of animals may enable us to reconstruct the geography of a bygone age. . . . It [Lemuria] represents what was probably a primary zoological region in some past geological epoch; but what that epoch was and what were the limits of the region in question, we are quite unable to say. If we are to suppose that it comprised the whole area now inhabited by Lemuroid animals, we must make it extend from West Africa to Burmah, South China and Celebes, an area which it possibly did once occupy.'

Among the most ardent supporters of Lemuria was the German naturalist Ernst Heinrich Haeckel. In a burst of enthusiasm he suggested that if Lemuria had existed it could solve a hotly disputed matter of far greater significance than the spread of the lemurs – namely, the origin of man.

'Of the five now existing continents,' Haeckel wrote in the 1870s, 'neither Australia nor America nor Europe can have been this primeval home (of man), or the so-called 'Paradise' the 'cradle of the human race'. Besides Southern Asia, the only other of the now existing continents which might be viewed in this light is Africa. But there are a number of circumstances (especially chronological facts) which suggest that the primeval home of man was a continent now sunk below the surface of the Indian Ocean, which extended along the south of Asia, as it is at present (and probably in direct connection with it), towards the east, as far as Further India and the Sunda Islands; towards the west as far as Madagascar and the southeastern shores of Africa. We have already mentioned that many facts in animal and vegetable geography render the former existence of such a South Indian continent very probable. . . . By assuming this Lemuria to have been man's primeval home, we greatly facilitate the explanation of the geographical distribution of the human species by migration.'

At the height of the great debate on evolution no fossil remains of man, or of forms intermediate between apes and man, had been identified. (Although fragments of Neanderthal man had already been found, they were only later identified.) Some scientists therefore concluded that the land on which man evolved had disappeared, taking the evidence with it, and Lemuria seemed a good candidate for the site of man's emergence. Our subsequent knowledge of man's family tree and his gradual evolution has done away with the need for a Lemuria-type place of origin, just as other theories have been found to account for the distribution of the lemur, but this information came too late to stop Lemuria taking its place alongside Atlantis and Mu as a great lost continent. No sooner had scientists made the cautious suggestion that Lemuria might have existed than the occultists brought it to life with vivid accounts, derived from supernormal sources, of its inhabitants and their civilization. As a result, Lemuria is now an apparently imperishable feature of the thinking of most leading occult groups.

Madame Helena Petrovna Blavatsky, the greatest of modern occultists and founder of the occult group known as the Theosophical Society, started the ball rolling. In 1888 she published a vast work, *The Secret Doctrine*, which set out her philosophy and gave its readers an insight into the ancient wisdom imparted to her by the Brotherhood of Mahatmas, ethereal beings who were said to run the world from their Tibetan headquarters. Madame Blavatsky maintained that her book was based on an ancient work called the *Book of Dzyan*, which the Mahatmas had shown her during the astral visits they paid her. The *Book of Dzyan*, she says, was written on palm-leaf pages, and had been composed in Atlantis in the now forgotten Senzar language. Besides describing Atlantis it dealt with the lost continent of Lemuria.

It is not easy for the reader to understand the full meaning of Madame Blavatsky's writings, or those of the mysterious *Book of Dzyan* from which she quotes at length. She writes: 'After great throes she cast of her old Three and put on her new Seven Skins, and stood in her first one. . . . The Wheel whirled for thirty crores more. It constructed Rûpas; soft Stones that hardened, hard Plants that softened. Visible from invisible, Insects and small Lives. . . .'

Describing the emergence of life on earth, Madame Blavatsky declares that we are the 'Fifth Root Race' to inhabit the earth, and that our planet is destined to have seven such races, each composed of seven subraces. The First Root Race, invisible beings made of fire-mist, lived on an Imperishable Sacred Land. The Second, who were just visible, inhabited the former Arctic continent of Hyperborea. The Third Root Race was the Lemurians, gigantic, brainless, apelike creatures. The Fourth

Root Race was the fully human Atlanteans, who were destroyed through black magic. We are the Fifth, and the Sixth will evolve from us and return to live on Lemuria. After the Seventh Root Race, life will leave our planet and start afresh on Mercury.

According to Madame Blavatsky, some of the Lemurians had four arms, and some had an eye in the back of their heads, which gave them 'psychic vision'. They had no spoken language, using telepathy instead as their method of communication. They lived in caves and holes in the ground, and although they had no proper brain they could use their willpower literally to move mountains. Their homeland, Lemuria, occupied practically the whole of the Southern Hemisphere, 'from the foot of the Himalayas to within a few degrees of the Antarctic Circle.' Although their continent was swept away before the Eocene epoch – which occurred from 60 million to 40 million years ago – their descendants survived to become the Australian Aborigines, Papuans, and Hottentots.

After Madame Blavatsky's death in 1891 her successor, Annie Besant, wrote at length on the subject of Lemuria and its people, as did another leading British Theosophist, W. Scott-Elliot. He put the flesh on the bones of Madame Blavatsky's Lemuria with an astonishing account based on occult revelations he had received from the 'Theosophical Masters'. He was helped further by having had 'the privilege . . . to be allowed to obtain copies – more or less complete' of a set of maps showing the world at critical stages of its history. They form the basis of six world maps reproduced in Scott-Elliot's book *The Story of Atlantis* and *The Lost Lemuria*, published in 1896 and still kept in print by the Theosophical Society.

Scott-Elliot enlarged on Madame Blavatsky's description of Lemuria. He said that this huge continent took shape when the great northern continent of Hyperborea – his and Madame Blavatsky's designated home of the Second Root Race – broke up. The Manus, the unseen supervisors of the universe, then chose Lemuria for the evolution of the Third Root Race. Their first attempt at producing human life resulted in jellylike creatures, but in time the Lemurians' bodies hardened and they were able to stand up.

From Scott-Elliot's description the Lemurians were far from beautiful. They were between 12 and 15 feet tall. Their faces were flat, apart from a protruding muzzle, and they had no foreheads. Their skin was brown, and their eyes were set so wide apart that they could see sideways as well as forward. As for the Lemurians' third eye in the back of the head, that now forms the pineal gland in our brains. The capacity to see out of the backs of their heads was particularly useful to the Lemurians, because their heels stuck out so far at the back that they could walk backward as well as forward.

The Lemurians started out as egg-laying hermaphrodites, but by the time their fifth subrace evolved they were reproducing as we do. However, during their sexual progress they foolishly interbred with beasts, producing the apes that still populate our planet. This upset the Lhas, supernatural beings whose duty it was, at this stage of the cosmic plan, to incarnate on earth in human bodies to help the evolving Lemurians. So the Lhas refused to carry out their appointed task. Beings from Venus saved the day by offering to take the place of the Lhas. The Venusians – called 'Lords of the Flame' – had already developed a highly advanced civilization on their own planet, and they taught the Lemurians how to achieve individual immortality and reincarnation. By the time of the seventh subrace, the Lemurians had mastered the basic arts of civilization and had begun to look human. The Lapps and the Australian Aborigines are among their descendants on earth today.

During the period of the sixth and seventh subraces Lemuria began to break up as various parts of the continent sank. But a peninsula of Lemuria that extended into the North Atlantic grew into Atlantis. Then the Fourth Root Race, the Atlantean, appeared on what was left of Lemuria. Some of its first subrace, the Rmoahals, moved to Atlantis. Others stayed behind and interbred with the Lemurians to produce a race of half-breeds, who looked like blue-skinned American Indians. The Rmoahals were black-skinned, and stood between 10 and 12 feet tall. The Rmoahals who settled in southern Atlantis waged continual war on the remaining Lemurians, but as time went on some Rmoahals moved to the north of Atlantis, where their skins became lighter and their stature shorter. Their descendants were the Cro-Magnons of Europe.

Next to arrive on the scene, according to Scott-Elliot, were the Tlavatlis. This second Atlantean subrace originated on an island off Atlantis that is now the site of Mexico. Gradually the human race was feeling its way toward self-government, and the appearance of the third subrace, the Toltecs, ushered in the golden age of Atlantis. The Toltecs enjoyed a superb culture for 100,000 years until they resorted to sorcery and phallic worship. There was a rebellion, and the followers of the 'black arts' overthrew the emperor and replaced him with their own king. The Toltecs then degenerated, and were soon at war with the Turanians, the fourth subrace, who had meanwhile emerged on Atlantis. The Turanians were a brutal and ruthless people, and practiced complete sexual promiscuity in order to boost their population for warfare. Their direct descendants were the Aztecs.

During these wars – some 800,000 years ago – a great catastrophe caused most of Atlantis to disappear, reducing it to a relatively small island. At the same time, a number of islands began to grow in size on their way to becoming the continents we know today. Many of the surviving Turanians left for Asia where they evolved into the more civilized seventh subrace, the Mongolians. In the meantime, the fifth and sixth subraces, the Semites and the Akkadians, came into being on Atlantis. The Semites inhabited the northern region of Atlantis, which is now Scotland and Ireland, and were a quarrelsome people who constantly provoked fights with their neighbours, the peaceful Akkadians.

Another disaster 200,000 years ago split what was left of Atlantis into two islands – Ruta, ruled by surviving Toltec sorcerers, and Daitya, occupied by Semite sorcerers. The next phase in the destruction occurred 80,000 years ago when a further catastrophe submerged Daitya and made Ruta an even smaller island. It was the final sinking of Ruta – also called Poseidonis – in 9564 BC that inspired Plato's story. Before the disaster that destroyed Daitya, a selected band of Semites moved into Central Asia where they evolved into the Aryans, the Fifth Root Race, who include the modern Hindus and Europeans.

There was far more to Scott-Elliot's story than this complex account of racial evolution. He was able to list the great achievements of the Atlanteans, such as the domestication of leopard-like animals and the creation of the banana. Atlantean alchemists made huge quantities of precious metals. Atlantean scientists invented gas-bombs and aircraft propelled by jets of *vril*-force, a mentally directed, invisible force first dreamed up by a Victorian novelist. These aircraft, owned only by the rich, flew at 100 mph and had a ceiling of 1000 feet. They were even capable of vertical takeoff, and Scott-Elliot's description of this aeronautical feat is not too different from the 'jump jet' technique used today.

Another detail-packed interpretation of the lost continents of Atlantis and Lemuria came from the pen of Rudolf Steiner, a tall, dark-eyed Austrian who broke away from the Theosophists in 1907 to form his own Anthroposophical Society. Steiner's *Cosmic Memory: Atlantis and Lemuria*, published in 1923, is still in print through Rudolf Steiner Publications, the publishing enterprise that also prints other Atlantis classics such as the works of Donnelly and Le Plongeon. Steiner claimed to have derived his view of the lost continents from consultation of what he called the 'Akasha Chronicle' – a spiritual record of the past available only to the initiated. Nevertheless, many of his ideas are obviously drawn from the work of Madame Blavatsky.

Steiner's Lemurians were feeble-minded, but they had enormous willpower by which they could lift heavy weights. Young Lemurians were taught to bear pain as an aid to developing this willpower. The Lemurians were endowed with souls, and they slowly developed the rudiments of speech. During their period as egg-laying hermaphrodites, the Lemurians made do with a single eye, but their vision improved along with their discovery of sex. According to Steiner, while their souls dominated their bodies, the Lemurians remained bisexual, but when the earth entered 'a certain stage of its densification', the increasing density of matter forced a division of the sexes. The Lemurians were unenthusiastic about this change, and for a long time they regarded sexual intercourse as a sacred duty rather than a pleasure. The Lemurian women remained far more spiritual than their menfolk.

Steiner's Atlanteans, like the Lemurians, were unable to reason but they did possess good memories. They were educated in a way that enabled them to hold a vast store of images in their minds, and each problem was solved by remembering a precedent. When confronted with a novel situation, however, this system left them floundering. The Atlanteans had learned to control the 'life force,' which they were able to use to power their aircraft.

They had also discovered the magical power of certain words, which they used to heal the sick or to tame wild animals. They wove the branches of living trees to form their houses and cities. Toward the end of their racial history, when the Semites emerged, the Atlanteans had begun to lose their mastery of the life force and were allowing individualism to take over. However, the Semites developed reasoning and a conscience to take themselves a step further along the evolutionary scale, and their descendants, the Aryans, refined these qualities further still.

So what began as mere speculation in the minds of biologists looking for a land-bridge in the Indian Ocean has developed into a complex occult world picture centred on both Atlantis and Lemuria, which – depending on whose account is regarded as the most authoritative – might once have been joined together in a single massive continent that covered practically the entire Southern Hemisphere and stretched all the way into the North Atlantic. It would be easy to dismiss Blavatsky, Scott-Elliot, and Steiner as cranks or fools, and their accounts as highly romanticised fiction with mass appeal. But would that be entirely fair? Do we know enough about man's spiritual and mental abilities to rule out the possibility of being able to step back in time? The field of parapsychology is a thriving if frustrating one, but there are certainly enough paranormal phenomena now under study for us to keep an open mind on the possibility of astral clairvoyance. Indeed some occultists have claimed that Plato himself might have used this method in compiling his Atlantis story.

It is intriguing to note that many early maps of the world showed a continental landmass in the Southern Hemisphere, long before anyone had ever mentioned Lemuria. The landmass, placed in the South Pacific, was named *Terra Australis Incognita*, 'the great unknown southern continent', and no one was more surprised than the European explorers of the 16th and 17th centuries to discover little but sea in the vast Pacific Ocean. It has been argued that the belief in *Terra Australis Incognita* originated in the human desire for symmetry, which caused the Greeks to suppose that equal amounts of land were distributed, in symmetrical fashion, around the globe. Although this idea was modified by the voyages of Columbus and others, most people continued to think it reasonable that the same amount of land should be found below the equator as above it. The discovery of Australia in the 17th century failed to solve the problem, being too small and too barren a land to fulfill people's expectations about the great southern continent, and even when the great British explorer Captain James Cook had shown beyond doubt that no such continent existed in the South Pacific, some people clung to the idea that it must once have been there. Believers in this lost continent argue that our very desire for symmetry may be a manifestation of a deep, latent knowing – a collective subconscious memory of the land on which our ancestors evolved.

The problem with the occultists is that their stories go back so far in time. Scientists assure us that if such enormous changes in the earth's surface as the occultists describe did occur, they would have taken place long before man appeared on the planet. By the time our species was emerging the earth's crust was relatively peaceful, and has remained so ever since.

Probably most people today would prefer to fall in with an orthodox view of the earth backed by scientific evidence. But before we dismiss the occultists and their beliefs there is one important question that requires all answer: Why do the ancient myths and legends of practically every people tell of a tremendous catastrophe that once shook the earth? Perhaps the scientists are mistaken after all.

CHAPTER 26

LEGENDS OF DESTRUCTION

The psychologist Carl Jung noted the recurrence of Great Flood myths in cultures around the world. Was this, he wondered, some kind of racial memory dating to a time when most of our ancestors were living in the same small area? The alternative seemed to suggest that the whole world had suffered tremendous flooding at some point. This appeared patently ridiculous unless, perhaps, a huge land mass had sunk beneath the ocean, raising sea levels worldwide. Is the sinking of a whole continent possible and, if so, what could have been the cause?

The earth was at peace. A mild climate enveloped the planet and man had responded well to the beneficence of nature. He had learned to cultivate and harvest his crops. He had domesticated animals to help make his life easier. Various civilizations were beginning to blossom. Then a terrible and all-encompassing catastrophe shook the earth.

The sky lit up with a strange celestial display. Those who saw in this a portent of disaster fled for shelter. Those who watched and waited perished as the sky grew dark and a fearful rain fell upon the earth. In places the rain was red like blood. In others it was like gravel or hailstones. And it brought down fire from the sky, too. Nothing escaped this global holocaust. Men and animals were engulfed. Forests were crushed. Even those who reached the caves were not safe. Darkness gripped the earth and tremendous quakes convulsed the planet. Mountains were thrown up to the heavens and continents were sucked beneath the seas as the stricken earth rolled and tilted. Hurricane winds lashed the planet's wretched surface and tidal waves swept across vast stretches of land. Fearful explosions shook the world as molten lava spewed out from the broken crust. A terrible heat hung over the planet and in places even the sea boiled.

Some, miraculously, lived through this horrific turmoil. After many long days of darkness the mantle of gloom was lifted from the earth and the survivors slowly began rebuilding their lives. A catastrophe of such proportions would account for the sinking of a huge continent such as Atlantis – but did such an event ever take place?

If it did, we might expect to find evidence of it in the myths, legends, and folklore of the people who survived. It is a remarkable fact that almost all races have a tradition, handed down through countless generations, of a catastrophe that nearly ended the world. Not only are these legends similar in essence, they are also frequently similar in detail, to such an extent that it is tempting to assume they all share a common origin: a terrifying event of global proportions.

The Babylonian *Epic of Gilgamesh*, which is around 4000 years old and records traditions of an even earlier age, tells of a dark cloud that rushed at the earth, leaving the land shrivelled by the heat of the flames: 'Desolation . . . stretched to heaven; all that was bright was turned into darkness. . . . Nor could a brother distinguish his brother. . . . Six days . . . the hurricane, deluge, and tempest continued sweeping the land . . . and all human life back to its clay was returned.'

From ancient Hindu legend comes an account of the appearance in the sky of 'a being shaped like a boar, white and exceedingly small; this being, in the space of an hour, grew to the size of an elephant of the largest size, and remained in the air.' After some time the 'boar' suddenly uttered 'a sound like the loudest thunder, and the echo reverberated and shook all the quarters of the universe.' This object then became a 'dreadful spectacle,' and 'descended from the region of the air, and plunged head-foremost into the water. The whole body of water was convulsed by the motion, and began to rise in waves, while the guardian spirit of the sea, being terrified, began to tremble for his domain and cry for mercy.'

Hesiod, a Greek poet of the 8th century BC writes of a legend involving the earth and the heavens. The story centres around a fiery, serpentlike creature, an aerial monster mightier than men and gods alike, that wreaks terrible havoc upon the earth: 'Harshly then he thundered, and heavily and terribly the earth re-echoed around; and the broad heaven above, and the sea and streams of ocean, and the abyss of earth. But beneath his immortal feet vast Olympus trembled, as the king uprose and earth groaned beneath. And the heat from both caught the dark-coloured sea, both of the thunder and the lightning, and fire from the monster, the heat arising from the thunderstorm, winds, and burning lightning. And all earth, and heaven, and sea were boiling. . . .'

From Iceland we have further evidence of a global catastrophe in the *Poetic Edda*, a collection of ancient Scandinavian legendary poems of unknown antiquity:

'Mountains dash together,
Heroes go the way to Hel,
and heaven is rent in twain. . . .
The sun grows dark,
The earth sinks into the sea,
The bright stars from heaven vanish;
Fire rages,
Heat blazes,
And high flames play
'Gainst heaven itself.'

The legends of the Cashinaua, the aborigines of western Brazil, tell of the time when 'The lightnings flashed and the thunders roared terribly and all were afraid. Then the heaven burst and the fragments fell down and killed everything and everybody. Heaven and earth changed places. Nothing that had life was left upon the earth.'

In North America, the Choctaw Indians of Oklahoma have a tradition about the time when 'The earth was plunged in darkness for a long time.' A bright light eventually appeared in the north, 'but it was mountain-high waves, rapidly coming nearer.'

The Samoan aborigines of the South Pacific have a legend that says: 'Then arose smell . . . the smell became smoke, which again became clouds. . . . The sea too arose, and in a stupendous catastrophe of nature the land sank into the sea.... The new earth (the Samoan islands) arose out of the womb of the last earth.'

The Bible, too, contains numerous passages that refer to terrible conflagrations. Psalms 1 8: 7- 1 5 is one example: 'Then the earth shook and trembled; the foundations also of the hills moved and were shaken. . . . The Lord also thundered in the heavens, and the Highest gave his voice; hail stones and coals of fire. . . . Then the channels of waters were seen, and the foundations of the world were discovered. . . .'

These are but a few of the vast number of legends dealing with great cosmic events and cataclysmic destruction on the face of the earth. The ancient records of Egypt, India, and China, the mythology of Greece and Rome, the legends of the Mayas and the Aztecs, the biblical accounts, and those of Norway, Finland, Persia, and Babylon, all tell the same story. So, too, do the people of widely separated countries, such as the Celts of Britain and the Maoris of New Zealand.

What on earth, or in heaven, could have caused such seemingly worldwide catastrophe? The accounts quoted above are taken from two masterly works on the subject, both of which offer the same explanation. One is Ignatius Donnelly's *Ragnarok: The Age of Fire and Gravel*, published in 1883, whose title is drawn from the legend of Ragnarok (wrongly translated as 'the darkness of the gods' and 'the rain of dust') contained in the Scandinavian *Poetic Edda*. The other is *Worlds in Collision*, which appeared in 1950, and is the most famous of several books by Immanuel Velikovsky, a Russo-lsraeli physician whose theories have made him as controversial a character as Donnelly before him. Both men suggest that a comet which came into close proximity with the earth caused the terrible events remembered by the ancient peoples of the world. They agree on many points of evidence, such as the myths and legends, and the sinking of Atlantis features in both works. But they take different stands in their search for scientific proof of their theories.

Donnelly devotes a large part of his book to a discussion of the drift, or *till* – a vast deposit of sand, gravel, and clay that lies above the stratified rocks of the earth's surface. The origin of the till puzzled many geologists, and Donnelly's explanation was that it had rained down from the heavens as the earth passed through a comet's tail. He argued that the comet's tail would have been moving at close to the speed of light when the earth passed through it, so only half the planet would have been covered by the till, and he sought to produce evidence to confirm his theory.

Velikovsky, though agreeing that a close earth-comet encounter lay behind the ancient catastrophe legends, has no use for the till theory – which was a foundation stone of Donnelly's treatise – and he observes: 'Donnelly . . . tried in his book *Ragnarok* to explain the presence of till and gravel on the rock substratum in America and Europe by hypothesising an encounter with a comet, which rained till on the terrestrial hemisphere facing it at that moment. . . . His assumption that there is till only in one half of the earth is arbitrary and wrong.'

Neither Donnelly nor Velikovsky was the first to argue that a comet had caused havoc on this planet. The English scientist William Whiston, who succeeded Sir Isaac Newton at Cambridge, wrote a book in 1696, *New Theory of the Earth*, which attempted to prove that a comet caused the biblical Flood. There was also a belief, at the time of Aristotle, in the 4th century BC, that a comet had joined the solar system as a planet.

But Velikovsky has pieced together a far more startling picture of cosmic activity. It began, he believes, when a planetary collision caused Jupiter to eject a comet, which went into an eccentric orbit. This brought it close to the earth in about 1500 BC, causing global catastrophes. The comet returned 52 years later and did further damage to the earth. Its approaches even caused the planet to stop and then rotate in the opposite direction, changing the position of the poles and altering the earth's orbit. The hydrocarbon gases of the comet's tail showered down on the earth in a rain of gravel and fire that formed the petroleum deposits we now use to power our automobiles and airplanes.

The comet, having left much of its tail behind, then had a close encounter with Mars, causing that planet to leave its orbit and, in turn, to come dangerously close to the earth in the 8th and 7th centuries BC. Meanwhile the comet joined the solar system as a planet – the one we now call Venus.

When this theory was first published, in 1950, it caused a sensation. Since then Velikovsky has become something of a cult figure, particularly among young people, though the scientific community has largely dismissed his ideas as nonsense. L. Sprague de Camp probably expresses the opinion of most orthodox scientists and scholars in his succinct and damning appraisal of Velikovsky's 'mad' theory. He writes in *Lost Continents*: 'Despite the impressive build-up . . . Velikovsky neither establishes a case nor accounts for the success of the Copernicus-Newton-Einstein picture of the cosmos which he undertook to supersede. Some of his mythological references are wrong (for instance he uses the Brasseur 'translation' of the *Troano Codex*); the rest merely demonstrate once again that the corpus of recorded myth is so vast that you can find mythological allusions to back up any cosmological speculation you please. The Babylonians left clear records of observations of Venus 5000 years ago, behaving just as it does now. . . . Moreover, the theory is ridiculous from the point of view of physics and mechanics. Comets are not planets and do not evolve into planets; instead they are loose aggregations of meteors with total masses less than a millionth that of the earth. Such a mass – about that of an ordinary mountain – could perhaps devastate several counties or a small state if struck, but could not appreciably affect the earth's orbit, rotation, inclination, or other components of movement. . . . And the gas of which the comet's tail is composed is so attenuated that if the tail of a good-sized comet were compressed to the density of iron, I could put the whole thing in my briefcase!'

So that disposes of Velikovsky – or does it? Seven years after his book was published, man made his first tentative steps into space. Since then earthlings have landed on the moon, and space vehicles have probed our nearest planetary neighbours. So far, these explorations appear to have confirmed some of Velikovsky's predictions about our planetary system. He had stated that, because Venus is a newcomer to the system, it is still giving off heat. This was thought to be nonsense at the time, and the consensus of astronomical opinion was that the surface temperature of Venus was around 65°F. Radio astronomy and the arrival of space vehicles in the vicinity of the planet have proved Velikovsky right. Mariner II, when it passed Venus in December 1962, detected a temperature of over 800°F, and subsequent investigations have revealed a temperature of approximately 990°F.

The results of the Mariner probe – the first to provide reliable information about the planet – showed that, just as Velikovsky had maintained, Venus is enclosed in an envelope of hydrocarbon gases and dust. It was also revealed that Venus rotated retrogradely, a sign that either it had been disturbed or it had evolved in a different way from other planets. A Russian probe that softlanded on the planet in October 1975 was able to relay information for 53 minutes before the extremely high pressure of the atmosphere caused it to stop transmitting. But it was enough for the Russian scientists to declare that Venus is a young planet, and still 'alive'.

Interviewed about these findings by a British newspaper, Velikovsky commented that they confirmed his theory. His book contained many other predictions about Mars, Jupiter, the earth, and the moon. 'And about 30 of them have since been proved right,' he claimed. If subsequent probes confirm other details of his theory, it would not be the first time that science has had to change its thinking about the history of the earth and its partners in the solar system.

Velikovsky weaves the destruction of Atlantis into his theory by suggesting that the continent sank as a result of the first approach of the Venus comet, though in order to make this idea fit his scheme he has to alter Plato's dating of the Atlantis catastrophe. There is one zero too many in Plato's date, says Velikovsky. Atlantis sank not 9000 years before Solon's trip to Egypt, but 900 years before Solon – in about 1500 BC.

Immanuel Velikovsky, author of Worlds in Collision

The idea that a comet destroyed Atlantis was not a new one. It had previously been put forward in 1785 by the Italian scholar Gian Rinaldo Carli – although he dated the catastrophe at 4000 BC – and was taken up again in the 1920s by a German writer called Karl George Zschaetzch, whose main aim was to prove the racial superiority of the Aryans by providing them with a pedigree that went all the way back to Atlantis.

Another theory to account for the Atlantis catastrophe came from Hanns Hörbiger, an Austrian inventor and engineer. Hörbiger maintained that the universe is filled with 'cosmic building stuff', consisting of hot metallic stars and 'cosmic ice'. The collision between a hot star and a block of cosmic ice generates a tremendous explosion, throwing pieces of star material and ice particles into space. These bodies spiral inward toward the sun, causing another explosion, which covers the nearest planets with a thick coating of ice. Hörbiger believed the Milky Way to consist of ice particles, and maintained that Venus and Mercury were sheathed in ice, as was the moon. According to Hörbiger's theory, the earth had possessed several moons before the present one. Each of these moons caused violent earthquakes and floods on the earth at the time of its capture by our planet, and finally shattered, showering its fragments onto the earth's surface. These events gave rise to the catastrophe myths, and it was the capture of our present moon that caused both Atlantis and Lemuria to sink. Hörbiger predicted that the eventual breakup and fall of our present moon would probably wipe out life on earth.

Hörbiger's theory, published in 1913, attracted millions of followers, and made him as much of a cult figure as Velikovsky is today. But whereas space exploration and our increased knowledge of the universe have disproved most of Hörbiger's assertions, many of Velikovsky's ideas are still living up to the expectations of his followers, who foresee them becoming the accepted scientific thinking of a future era. Unless and until that day comes, however, we need to examine the catastrophe legends and the theories of lost continents in the light of current scientific belief. The picture then becomes far less promising.

Orthodox scientists dismiss the idea of a global catastrophe of the kind described by Velikovsky and others. How, then, do they explain the legends? The answer is that, universal though the disaster legends may seem, they are descriptions of separate events that occurred at different times and were fairly localized. They concern tremendous earthquakes, great volcanic eruptions, massive flooding of river valleys, and inundation of areas below sea level. These events spanning many centuries and not linked in any way, gave rise to the legends, which were doubtless exaggerated as they were handed down from one generation to the next.

Take Noah's flood, for example. According to the Bible, this great deluge drowned every living thing on earth – apart from the few survivors in the ark. It is now considered likely that this story was based on a real flood that submerged something like 40,000 square miles of the Euphrates Valley some time between 5400 and 4200 BC. China and the lowlands of Bengal have seen similar great floods, and these, too, could have given rise to deluge legends. Many geologists believe that the Mediterranean was once a fertile valley below sea level, which was flooded long ago by the Atlantic in one terrible rush. The flooding of the former Zuider Zee (now Ijssel Lake) in the Netherlands is a more recent example of this kind of catastrophe. A storm in 1282 broke the natural dykes that protected this area of sub-sea-level land, and let in the North Sea, which submerged it in a single day.

In this century alone there have been a number of earthquakes that have taken in excess of 100,000 lives, and there are records of even more disastrous quakes in the past. The Chinese earthquake of 1556 is said to have killed 830,000 people. It would be surprising if similar quakes in ancient times did not give rise to catastrophe legends. To those living in the affected areas it must certainly have seemed as if the whole world were coming to an end. An earthquake beneath the sea may cause a tidal wave. In mid-ocean the gentle slopes of a tidal wave may go undetected, but as the wave approaches and meets the shore it surges up into a massive, sometimes skyscraper-high, wall of water. In 1737, a 210-foot tidal wave was recorded in Kamchatka in southern Russia and many others have been reported between 50 and 100 feet tall. Volcanic eruptions, in addition to wreaking their own havoc, may also set up tidal waves. The Krakatoa eruption of 1883 caused a huge wave that drowned 36,380 people living on the shores of the nearby Indonesian islands.

So, our history is rich in natural disasters that have taken a tremendous toll of human life – as they still do – and that may well have given rise to the legends. But could any of these pestilences account for the sinking of a great continent such as Atlantis? Most scientists think it extremely unlikely. An earthquake might have destroyed part of the island continent, or caused landslides around its shores. but the total area devastated by even a violent earthquake is relatively limited, and a quake that would have destroyed a huge landmass is unheard-of. Had Atlantis been an island with a very low profile it might have been at least partly submerged by flooding, but Plato describes Atlantis as a mountainous country. A tidal wave might have washed over Atlantis, but it would not have washed it away. And a volcanic eruption could have blown part of the continent into the ocean, but if Atlantis had been anywhere near the size claimed by Plato, much would still be towering above the sea. In the scientists' view even a whole series of massive earthquakes, volcanic eruptions, and flooding would take many thousands of years to sink an island of anything approaching continental size – and a low, flat island at that.

The only other possibility would seem to be that the earth's crust is capable of opening up and swallowing areas of land. Small islands have been submerged in living memory, and others have suddenly appeared. Could the same forces have been responsible for wiping Atlantis from the face of our planet? To answer this question we need to look at present opinion on the way the world has developed, and at the processes by which continents take shape.

According to current geological theory, the earth is encased in a crust of rock that becomes hotter and hotter as we go down toward the centre of the planet. Some 50 to 100 miles beneath the surface the rock has become white-hot. From that point down the earth consists of a hot, glasslike substance called *magma*, which surrounds the nickel-iron core of the earth, a sphere about 4000 miles in diameter. The cool exterior rocks consist in general of two types: dense, heavy, magnesium-bearing rocks, called *sima*, which form most of the ocean floors, and light, aluminum-bearing rocks, called *sial*, which form most of the land areas. Geologists see the continents as beds of sial 'floating' on a crust of sima. The continental blocks descend deeply into the sima, showing a comparatively small amount above the surface, just as icebergs do in water.

Over a century ago, it became apparent to some geologists that the face of our globe has not always been as it now appears. The evidence for this assumption was the same that led many biologists of the time to consider the possibility of a lost continent: namely, the existence of fossils of similar fauna and flora on continents thousands of miles apart.

Geologists who accepted fossil evidence of ancient land connections between the continents put forward the idea of a former gigantic landmass, which they called Gondwanaland, comprising present-day South America, Africa, India, Australia, and Antarctica. A second landmass, consisting of North America and Europe, was also suggested and given the name Laurasia. However, the proponents of this theory were unable to offer any convincing evidence as to how these two supercontinents might have broken up, and their idea attracted little support among fellow scientists.

Nevertheless, in the early years of the 20th century, a number of scientists began thinking along similar lines, and in 1915 the German astronomer, geophysicist, and meteorologist Alfred Wegener published the modern theory on continental drift. Wegener argued that if the continents float like icebergs on the sima crust, why should they not also drift like icebergs across the face of the earth? He suggested that all the modern continents were once joined in a single giant landmass. They have since drifted apart, and the drift is continuing; millions of years from now, the face of our planet will look very different from the way it does today.

Wegener's theory has rocked the geological establishment, and its revolutionary effect on the geological sciences has been compared to the effect of Darwin's theory of evolution on the biological sciences a century ago. But for several decades after its publication the majority of scientists continued to reject the idea of continental drift, mainly because they found it hard to envisage forces strong enough to move the continents around. (After all, even the smallest continent, Australia, weighs around 500 million million million kilograms.) In due course, however, a plausible explanation – involving convection currents driven by radioactive heat from within the earth – was put forward to account for the continental movement and a mass of impressive evidence began piling up in support of Wegener's theory, so that most scientists now accept the reality of continental drift.

In the late 1960s, computers were used to show how the continental jigsaw pieces might fit together to form the original gigantic landmass. This was not an easy task, because the shape of the continents has altered over the ages. Some minor parts of the jigsaw are missing, some have been added, and the true edges of the continents generally lie far below sea level and have not yet been plotted in detail. Nevertheless, the computer pictures showed an extremely good fit between South America and the western coast of Africa, and between Antarctica, Australia, and India. The fit of these last three continents against south and eastern Africa was less satisfactory, and some adjustment was needed to improve the fit across the North Atlantic, linking Britain and the rest of Europe with North America.

In their book *Continental Drift*, leading British geophysicist D. P. Tarling and his technical journalist wife M. P. Tarling write: 'By studying the size and composition of particles in old sedimentary rocks it is possible to work out the direction and type of land from which they were derived. In Britain, we find that the source of many Caledonian Mountain sediments was a very extensive landmass which must have lain to the north and west where there is now the deep Atlantic Ocean. In North America, the sources of many Appalachian rocks lay to the south and east. To explain this before the acceptance of continental drift, geologists supposed that a continent, 'Atlantis', must have occupied the present position of the Atlantic. This continent was thought to have sunk beneath the Atlantic waves. [But] there can be no question of the existence of a sunken continent in the Atlantic. By reconstructing the jigsaw we not only fit together the Caledonian Mountain chain, but also explain the sources of the sediments which formed it.'

Most scientists agree that as we push the continents back to their original places, we effectively squeeze Atlantis off the map. So, could Atlantis have been North America, which, having drifted away, was thought to have been submerged in the Atlantic? No. The continents are moving apart at the rate of between one and six inches a year – hardly enough to give rise to Plato's account of the submergence of Atlantis in a day and a night. What is more, the original landmass is thought to have broken up before the Mesozoic era, some 200 million years ago, and the continents probably reached approximately their present positions by the beginning of the Cenozoic era, around 70 million years ago – long before man appeared on the face of the earth.

Could Atlantis have been in the Pacific, where Mu was said to have sunk, or in the Indian Ocean, where the early Lemuria enthusiasts placed yet another lost continent? Our present knowledge of the earth seems to rule out these possibilities, too. Bearing in mind the geologists' belief that the ocean floors are mostly formed of sima and the landmasses of sial, a sunken continent should be easy to detect because its rocks would be different from surrounding rocks in the deep ocean. However, geological investigation has so far revealed that the greatest areas of deep sima are in the Central Pacific, the southern Indian Ocean, and the Arctic Ocean, making these the least likely sites on earth for a vanished continent.

Not surprisingly, believers in Atlantis hotly contest the findings of modern science that seek to dismiss the existence of the lost continent. In considering the theory of continental drift they point to gaps and seeming misfits in the linking of continents across the Atlantic that might still leave room for Atlantis. Nor are they impressed by the failure of oceanographers to find evidence of a sunken civilization beneath the Atlantic. In his book *The Mystery of Atlantis*, Charles Berlitz points out that even the underwater cities of the Mediterranean have been discovered only comparatively recently and in relatively shallow water. How much more difficult, then, to discover the ruins of Atlantis beneath the far larger Atlantic, where they would be smothered by sedimentation and mud accumulated over thousands of years.

If a once-derided theory such as continental drift can eventually earn the backing of the respectable scientific community, the Atlantists argue, might not other theories, now regarded as nonsensical, one day gain the same acceptance? Perhaps man existed long before the scientists, estimates. Perhaps there was some extraordinary global catastrophe of a nature quite outside the bounds of cautious scientific conjecture. Indeed, a recent report by the internationally renowned geologist Professor Alexander Tollman of the University of Vienna, seems to back Velikovsky's rogue comet theory to a striking degree. Tollman's study of the worldwide distribution of *tektites* – splinters of molten rock thrown up by an impact to the Earth's surface – convinced him that the planet must have suffered a major space collision around twelve thousand years ago. A sudden increase in radioactive carbon-14 found in fossilised trees from the period also seems to back his conclusions. Tollman believes that seven pieces of a disintegrating comet (much like the comet Shoemaker-Levey that struck Jupiter in 1994) intersected with Earth's orbit with calamitous results. Quoted in the *Sunday Times* (21 August 1996) he said: 'The consequence of the impact explosions appears to have included a chain of up to a dozen individual catastrophes, including earthquakes, geological deformation, a vapour plume and tidal waves.' He also believes that the disaster caused the mass extinction of many prehistoric species, like the mammoth and sabre-toothed tiger. Of course, being a respectable scientist, Professor Tollman does not mention Atlantis in his report, but it is interesting to note that his geological research points to the impact taking place around 9600 BC – the same year Plato gives for the sinking of the lost continent.

Recent scientific findings and theories may have helped modern man put the search for Atlantis into perspective, but they have not proved the lost continent to be a myth. In fact, some investigators among scientists themselves believe they have now discovered the true site of Atlantis, far away from the huge ocean so long regarded as its resting place.

CHAPTER 27

THE LOST EMPIRE IN THE AEGEAN

To the Greeks of Plato's day – and the Egyptians of Solon's – the tideless Mediterranean was the centre of the world, while the Atlantic was an unexplored enigma. Did the ancient story tellers, in the days before writing, somehow exaggerate the size and change the location of Plato's lost continent, moving it from their own familiar world to the centre of the Atlantic ocean? In the twentieth century, the rediscovery of a once legendary civilization has caused many to believe Atlantis has been found on Plato's own doorstep.

Until the beginning of this century, most historians regarded the island of Crete as an unimportant place. True, the ancient Greeks had numerous stories and legends about this mountainous island at the southern end of the Aegean Sea. They looked upon Crete as the one-time home of a mighty seafaring people ruled by King Minos, the son of Zeus and the mortal maiden Europa. Legend had it that a bronze robot, with a man's body and a bull's head, patrolled Crete's rocky coastline, keeping invaders at bay by hurling boulders at them. There, too, was the labyrinth in which King Minos imprisoned the Minotaur, the monstrous bull-man who annually devoured seven Greek youths and seven Greek maidens, and who was finally slain by the Greek hero Theseus.

To most historians these stories were nothing more than colourful myths. It took the excavations of British archaeologist

Sir Arthur Evans to prove that the legends were founded on fact. In 1900, Evans began uncovering astonishingly beautiful and sophisticated buildings on the island of Crete. His discoveries, together with subsequent finds, revealed that a highly advanced civilization had existed on Crete 4500 years ago. Evans gave this civilization the name Minoan for the legendary King Minos.

Minoans ruled the Aegean while the Greeks were still barbarians. Not only traders, but also colonisers, they were able to extract tribute from less advanced peoples such as the Greeks, and were known as far away as northern and western Europe, as well as in Egypt and the eastern Mediterranean, for their seagoing power, their wealth, and their gracious style of living.

Knossos, near modern Heraklion, about three miles from the coast of northern Crete, was the Minoan capital, and in 2500 BC it probably housed about 100,000 people. The palace of Knossos, home of the king and queen and a centre of Minoan government, was a magnificent complex of buildings covering six acres. The elaborate plan of its rooms, halls, and courts, with their stately porticoes, shrines, tapered columns, and terraces, built on many different levels and linked by stairways and twisting passages, could well have given rise to Greek tales of a labyrinth on the island of Crete. The palace's huge storerooms contained supplies of grain, wine, and oil. Some jars kept there were able to hold up to 79,000 gallons of olive oil. The palace was also a religious and artistic centre, with homes for priests and priestesses and workshops for artists and craftsmen, who held a highly respected place in Minoan society. The palace walls were resplendent with brilliantly coloured paintings of birds, beasts, flowers, and young men and women in fashionable dress. Frescoes and pottery found in Knossos and elsewhere express the Minoans' love of bright colours and swirling shapes, their keen observation of nature, and their zest for living. Their paintings show dancing and feasting, celebrations and sport, plants and animals, rather than battles or sieges – and everywhere their regard for the bull is apparent. Murals and vases show young, unarmed Minoans fearlessly leaping over the back of a bull, and a particularly striking ritual vessel is made in the form of a bull's head with golden horns.

Other magnificent treasures, including beautifully wrought gold jewellery, and tools and ornaments inlaid with gold and ivory, testify to the reality of the Minoans' legendary wealth.

Not only did the Minoans live in beautiful surroundings but they enjoyed comforts unmatched until modern times. The palace in Knossos had flushing toilets, running water, and a well-planned drainage system for rainwater and sewage. Its rooms were ingeniously lit by windows opening onto light wells – possibly the earliest example of indirect lighting. The palace was surrounded by a town of 22 acres, containing the houses of sea captains, merchants, and shipowners, and a paved road with drains on either side ran all the way from Knossos to the south coast. Near the southern shore of Crete stood another magnificent city called Phaistos, and about 100 smaller cities or towns were scattered across the island. Archaeological studies have established that the civilization of Crete flourished for about 2000 years, but that it suffered an abrupt collapse around 1500 to 1400 BC.

Here, for the first time, was evidence that a people very similar to the Atlanteans described by Plato had once existed. It was not long before some scholars were asking if a memory of this great culture had given rise to the Atlantis legend. Both Atlantis and Crete were island kingdoms and great sea powers, and both had suffered a sudden downfall. There seemed to be links, too, between the bull ceremonies depicted in Minoan art and the ritual hunting of the bull said to have taken place on Atlantis.

The first man to point out the similarities between Plato's Atlantis and the Minoan civilization was K. T. Frost, professor of classical history at Queen's University, Belfast. In 1909 Frost wrote in *The Times* of London about the need to reconsider the whole scheme of Mediterranean history as a result of the excavations on Crete, adding: 'The whole description of Atlantis which is given in the *Timaeus* and the *Critias* has features so thoroughly Minoan that even Plato could not have invented so many unsuspected facts.'

Recalling Plato's story, Frost went on to observe: 'The great harbour, for example, with its shipping and its merchants coming from all parts, the elaborate bathrooms, the stadium, and the solemn sacrifice of a bull are all thoroughly, though not exclusively, Minoan; but when we read how the bull is hunted 'in the temple of Poseidon without weapons but with staves and nooses, we have an unmistakable description of the bull-ring at Knossos, the very thing which struck foreigners most and which gave rise to the legend of the Minotaur. Plato's words exactly describe the scenes on the famous Vapheio cups which certainly represent catching wild bulls for the Minoan bull-fight which, as we know from the palace itself, differed from all others which the world has seen in exactly the point which Plato emphasises – namely that no weapons were used.'

But Crete is not in the Atlantic. It is nowhere near the size of the great island continent described by Plato. And it has not disappeared beneath the waves. Frost argued that the sudden eclipse of Minoan power was probably caused by invasions from the Greek mainland – a point of view shared by most of his fellow scholars – but few were prepared to accept his suggestion that the loss of contact with their Minoan trading partners had led the Egyptians to believe that Crete had sunk beneath the sea. Frost's theory was therefore dismissed by the academic world, and after his death in World War I his ideas were forgotten.

Thirty years after the publication of Frost's theory, however, Professor Spyridon Marinatos, later Director-General of the Greek Archaeological Service, put forward new evidence that appeared to strengthen Frost's case. In an article entitled 'The Volcanic Destruction of Minoan Crete', published in the British journal *Antiquity* in 1939, Marinatos told how, during his excavations in Amnisos, the site of an ancient harbour close to Knossos, he had discovered a pit full of pumice stone. He also found evidence that a vast mass of water had washed over the site, dragging large objects out of place. Marinatos became convinced that Crete's downfall was due not to foreign invaders, as most scholars still assumed, but to a tremendously violent natural catastrophe. He was also able to point an accusing finger at the probable source of this devastation: a small volcanic island named Thera, just 75 miles north of Crete, and the most southerly island in the archipelago of the Cyclades.

Thera has been given a number of names. Some people today know it as Santorini, a name derived from Saint Irene, the patron saint of the island. In the past, it has been called Kallistē ('the very beautiful island') and Strongulē ('the circular island'). Although these two names preserve a memory of how the island used to look, neither description is appropriate today. Once a circular island, about 11 miles across, covered by cone-shaped peaks, with woods and good vegetation, Thera now consists of three fragments of its former glory. The largest is a crescent-shaped island, Thera proper, which has a population of around 5000. A much smaller island, Therasia, situated to the northwest, has only two villages. The third portion, Aspronisi, is an uninhabited white fragment. Viewed from the air these three pieces of land still show the circular outline of the former island, but the central area is now a deep bay. Towering cliffs form an inner rim around this expanse of sea, dropping steeply into the water as if sliced through by some gigantic knife. In the centre of the bay a dark dome broods and smoulders, a constant reminder that Thera is the only active volcano in the Aegean Sea.

The island has probably had a very long history of volcanic disturbance, but geological evidence suggests that the eruption, or series of eruptions, that tore out the centre of the island and created the bay may well have been the greatest the world has ever known. It began with a burst of pumice, which built up to a height of 12 feet in some parts of the island. Then there was probably a period of quiescence, followed by another enormous outburst, which covered the island and a vast surrounding area in a mass of fine white ash known as *tephra*. On parts of Thera this tephra is over 200 feet thick. Once the vast magna chamber beneath the earth's crust had ejected this material, its roof – the island of Thera – collapsed, and part of it fell into the sea, forming the central, sea-filled bay known to scientists as a *caldera*.

We can gain some idea of the appalling, widespread devastation caused by such an eruption from eye-witness accounts of a similar event in 1883. In May of that year the island of Krakatoa – a volcano of the same type as Thera – began erupting. Krakatoa is situated in the Sunda Strait, between Java and Sumatra, close to a main sea route between the China Sea and the Indian Ocean. There were therefore a number of ships in the vicinity at the time of the eruption, and their crews were able to give first-hand accounts of it. Krakatoa was uninhabited, and had been dormant for about 200 years, but the 1883 outbreak was preceded by six or seven years of severe earthquakes. Then, on 20 May, 1883, the volcano began erupting with booming explosions that rattled doors and windows 100 miles away. Two days later a column of dust and vapour was seen rising from the island to an estimated height of seven miles, and falls of dust were recorded 300 miles away. Observers who landed on the island a week later found it covered by a thin layer of white ash, and the trees stripped of branches by the falling pumice. Activity continued throughout June and July, and at the beginning of August another visitor to Krakatoa reported that all vegetation had been completely destroyed. The climax came on 26 and 27 August, beginning with a black, billowing cloud that rose to a height of 17 miles. Violent explosions were heard throughout Java, and warm pumice fell onto ships in the area. During the night of the 26th the crew of the ship *Charles Bal*, sailing about 15 miles east of Krakatoa, saw 'balls of white fire' rolling down the rim of the island. The air became hot and choking with a sulphurous smell, and the sky was 'one second intense blackness, the next a blaze of fire.' Throughout the night the noise was so great that the inhabitants of western Java could not sleep. Krakatoa quietened a little toward dawn but early on the morning of the 27th there were four stupendous eruptions, the third of which was heard on the island of Rodriguez, 3000 miles away, and was the loudest noise ever recorded on earth. A cloud of dust rose 50 miles, dispersing its contents over a huge area. An estimated five cubic miles of material was blown out of the volcano, and two thirds of it fell within a 10-mile radius, piling white tephra to a height of 185 feet on the parts of Krakatoa that had survived the devastation. The rest of the ejected material caused a pall of darkness that rapidly spread, reaching Bandong, 150 miles away, late on the same day. Windborne dust was still falling 12 days later at a distance of 3300 miles.

Blast waves from the great explosion shattered windows and broke walls up to 100 miles away and were detected all over the globe. But it was the ensuing tidal wave that caused the greatest destruction. In areas bordering the Sunda Strait, 300 towns and villages were destroyed and 36,380 people died as a giant wave ripped through their lands. Tides rose steeply on shores as much as 7000 miles away, and a slight rise was recorded as far away as the English Channel. Sea-borne pumice floated over scores of thousands of square miles, and large amounts were reported all over the Indian Ocean for many months after the eruptions. For many months, too, people all around the world saw the strange phenomena created by dust retained in the upper atmosphere – the sun rose green and then turned blue, the moon was green or blue, and glorious sunsets and afterglows set the sky ablaze.

When visitors ventured to the island after this great cataclysm they found that the northern part of Krakatoa had collapsed into the sea, creating a caldera, and the remainder of the island had been split in half.

How does the Thera eruption compare with the paroxysm of Krakatoa? The Thera caldera is deeper than that formed in Krakatoa, and its surface area is four times as large. Although this does not mean that the Thera eruption was four times as powerful, the structure of the caldera and the extent of the pumice deposits at Thera indicate that the eruption there was at least as violent as, and probably even more destructive than, that of Krakatoa.

Pumice dust from Thera, mixed with lime, produces a very durable cement, and during the 1860s Therasia provided vast quantities of pumice for the construction of the Suez Canal and the new harbour in Port Said. In the course of the quarrying operations, engineers found themselves hindered by numerous stone blocks that marked the lower limit of the pumice. These were the tops of ancient walls buried by fallout from the great eruption, and they might well have been destroyed in the interests of commerce had it not been for another eruption, which began in 1866 and brought a group of scientific observers to the island. As a result of their interest in the ancient walls, excavations were begun, notably by the French vulcanologist Ferdinand Fouqué, who went on to uncover part of a Bronze Age settlement in Akrotiri in northeast Therasia. Fouqué was the first to provide evidence that Thera had suffered its dramatic volcanic collapse sometime in the Bronze Age, 3000 to 1000 BC.

Fouqué's finds were made before Sir Arthur Evans uncovered the glories of the Minoan civilisation on Crete, and their full significance was not realised for a long time afterward. Indeed 100 years were to pass before Professor Marinatos began important new excavations in Akrotiri. In the meantime, however, Thera was not entirely neglected. In 1956 a severe earthquake disturbed the lower strata of a quarry on the main island of Thera, exposing the ruins of an ancient building. Human bones, teeth, and charred wood were found nearby and a Greek seismologist, Dr Angelos Galanopoulos, arranged for these to be submitted to the carbon-14 dating test, which gives the approximate age of an object by detecting when it 'died' and stopped absorbing carbon from the atmosphere. This showed the relics to be about 3500 years old. Further tests of this kind carried out in 1967 on a variety of objects found on Thera have enabled scholars to put the date of the Thera eruption at between 1500 and 1450 BC. And that coincides with the period when the great Minoan civilization suddenly declined.

In his book *The End of Atlantis*, a scholarly study of the Atlantis legend, Professor J. V. Luce discusses the effects of the Thera eruption on Crete: 'We do not know what happened on Crete and on the islands and coasts of the Aegean, but I consider it a safe guess that the loss of life and damage to property were no less [than from Krakatoa]. They may well have been many times as great. We can say with reasonable assurance that Crete had ceased to be a great maritime power after the middle of the 15th century BC. Is it not reasonable to suppose that the Thera eruption was a major factor in her downfall?'

Supporting evidence for this point of view has come from cores of sediment taken from the floor of the Eastern Mediterranean. It was published in 1965 by two American scientists, D. Ninkovich and B. C. Heezen of the Lamont Geological Observatory, Columbia University, who concluded from the distribution of the volcanic ash found in these deposits that the Thera explosion was a major catastrophe for Minoan Crete. In their opinion, this catastrophe led directly to a transference of power in the area from the Minoans to the mainland Greeks – the Mycenaeans.

The remarkable buildings, frescoes, and pottery found on Thera indicate that it was part of the Minoan island empire. Discussing the 1967 excavations made by Professor Marinatos in Akrotiri, J. V. Luce comments: 'Enough evidence has been accumulated for us to say with some assurance that the settlement has distinctly Minoan features, and was clearly in close contact with Crete. It is likely to have been a Minoan colony or dependency, possibly the seat of the Minoan ruler of the island.'

Luce, like a number of other scholars who have studied the exciting finds on Thera and Crete, believes that Plato's Atlantis story is a composite picture of the Minoan downfall. The 'disappearance' of Atlantis is really the sudden fall from power of the Minoans, coupled with the cataclysmic events on part of their island empire. Luce remarks that he does not look for the lost Atlantis under the surface of Thera bay. 'For me 'lost Atlantis' is a historical rather than a geographical concept.'

Greek seismologist Dr. Angelos Galanopoulos takes a more literal view of the legend, and has gone a long way toward satisfying many critics of the Atlantis-in-the-Aegean theory with an ingenious hypothesis. Galanopoulos interprets Plato's story as a description of two islands. The larger is the 'royal state' – Crete. The smaller is the metropolis, or capital city and religious centre – Thera. Plato says that the metropolis of Atlantis was about 11 miles in diameter. This is the same as the former size of Thera. But Galanopoulos noted that other measurements in Plato's account seemed to be far too great in comparison. However, he found that if all measurements over 1000 were divided by 10, they would neatly reduce Atlantis to a size consistent with that of the Minoan empire. Therefore Galanopoulos argued that at some time a tenfold error had crept into the Atlantis story – either when the Egyptians recorded it, or after they gave the story to Solon, who handed it down through a number of generations. Galanopoulos believes that in the translation of Egyptian scripts by Solon, or possibly of Minoan scripts from which the Egyptians obtained the story, the symbol for 100 was rendered as 1000. A modern example of this sort of confusion is the difference between the American billion, which is one thousand millions, and the British billion, which is one million millions.

This mistake, if it occurred, would affect not only the size of Atlantis and its population but also the date of its destruction. Take off the final zero in Plato's figures over 1000, says Galanopoulos, and we find that the date of the submergence of Atlantis coincides with that of the Thera eruption. Instead of sinking 9000 years before Solon's visit to Egypt – a date that caused most people to dismiss the account as a myth because there is no evidence of an advanced civilization existing at such an early period – Atlantis disappeared only 900 years before Solon's trip. Because Solon's journey took place around 600 BC, this would mean that Atlantis was destroyed around 1500 BC – just when the experts believe Thera erupted and Crete suffered its downfall.

Galanopoulos first put forward his hypothesis in 1960, and it is interesting to recall that the 1500 BC date for the destruction of Atlantis had already been suggested 10 years earlier by Immanuel Velikovsky in his book *Worlds in Collision*. Writing before the present Atlantis-Thera-Crete theory had evolved, Velikovsky also believed that there was one zero too many in Plato's date.

If Atlantis was in the Aegean, why did Plato apparently situate it in the distant Atlantic Ocean? And why, if Atlantis sank so close to the Greek mainland, were the Greeks so vague about its existence, having to rely on the Egyptians for information about the 'lost continent'?

It has been suggested that Plato placed Atlantis in the Atlantic simply because, according to his figures, it was too big to fit anywhere else. Alternatively, there is the possibility of yet another misinterpretation originating with Solon. Plato's account states that Atlantis lay 'beyond the Pillars of Hercules' – the name given to the Strait of Gibraltar in Plato's time. Thus his readers automatically assumed that Atlantis was in the Atlantic. But Dr Galanopoulos has pointed out that the name 'Pillars of Hercules' was also once applied to two promontories on the south coast of Greece (ancient Mycenae), facing Crete. If Plato's account refers to these, says Galanopoulos, then the Minoans are almost certainly the Atlanteans.

Archaeological evidence shows that the Minoan culture began to acquire strong Mycenaean characteristics around the time of its downfall, and that the Minoans were starting to lose their dominance of the Aegean. The Minoans and the Mycenaeans may well have been rivals, just as Plato described the Athenians and the Atlanteans to be. Whether the Mycenaeans had conquered parts of Crete, or whether the two cultures underwent a more peaceful integration, discoveries in Knossos show that, after the fall of Crete, the Mycenaeans took the Minoans' place as the major force in the Aegean. The Mycenaeans would even appear to have taken control of the palace in Knossos, which, though damaged, had survived because it was inland.

The Greeks, however, were still too young a people to recall the history of these events with any clarity, though with hindsight we can find some of the story in their legends. J. V. Luce comments that, 'The Greeks remembered very little at all about the 15th century BC. Their national consciousness was then only in an early formative stage. Their main saga cycles date from the 13th century when, under the leadership of Mycenae, they had become a major power in the eastern Mediterranean.' Luce adds that 'even the Mycenaean world as a whole was only dimly remembered by the later Greeks.' The Egyptians, a much older race, had long been trading with the Minoans and recorded the visits of Minoans to Egypt. So it is perhaps not surprising if the Egyptians knew more than the Greek themselves about their talented forebears.

According to Plato, the Egyptian priests told Solon: 'You remember only one deluge though there have been many, and you do not know that the finest and best race of men that ever existed lived in your country; you and your fellow citizens are descended from the few survivors who remained, but you know nothing about it, because of the many intervening generations silent for lack of written speech.'

In the opinion of some scholars, that quotation supplies further evidence for the Atlantis-in-the-Aegean theory, and for the Egyptian origin of the Atlantis story. The Egyptians are apparently referring to a literacy gap that has since been confirmed. Scripts known as Linear A and B were used in Crete, Greece, and the Aegean islands during the second millennium BC, but they disappeared from use after 1200 BC. They do not appear to have been replaced by any other form of writing until around 850 BC, when the Greek archaic script appeared. So it seems that, even had there been any local records of the Thera explosion and the fall of Crete, they would have been written in a language that the Greeks of Plato's time would not have understood.

As a result of the discoveries in the Aegean, a number of scholars are now prepared to believe not only that Plato's account is based on historical reality, but that it is an astonishingly accurate record of events that occurred over 1000 years before he wrote his story. Until further information about the Minoan culture emerges, however, even the Atlantis-in-the-Aegean theory is open to different interpretations. Professor Galanopoulos, for example, believes that Thera was as important to the Minoans as Crete was. He regards Thera as the centre of Minoan life and Crete as its larger adjunct. Galanopoulos pictures the slopes of the small volcanic island teeming with life and adorned with the white temples and palaces of a majestic city. When the eruption came, these great feats of architecture – equal to those discovered on Crete – would have been buried in fallout, then submerged beneath the waters that now fill the Thera basin.

Attempts to detect submerged harbours and canals at Thera similar to those described by Plato have been made, using the latest sonar equipment. In 1966, Dr. James W. Mavor of the Woods Hole Oceanographic Institution was given permission to carry out runs across the bay with the research vessel *Chain*. The findings of the *Chain* are related in Mavor's book *Voyage to Atlantis*. Although they have added to our understanding of the shape and depth of the caldera and the volcanic deposits beneath the sea, they could not provide the evidence needed to support Galanopoulos's theory. Pending the discovery of new evidence, no one can say for sure that the Atlantis mystery has been solved. But excavations now in progress may soon be able to show whether the Minoans – possibly the most accomplished and inventive race the world has ever known – were not only the forefathers of Greek civilization, and ultimately of Europe, but also the lost and fabled Atlanteans.

CHAPTER 28

THE NEW DISCOVERIES

The evidence presented in the last chapter suggests that the mystery of Atlantis is finally solved. Yet discoveries made since the 1960s have raised many startling new possibilities. Are we about to witness the most radical rewriting of history since Darwin's Origin of Species? Will we or our children be the first to excavate Atlantis? And just how old is human civilization?

In 1968 two commercial airline pilots flying over the Bahamas spotted what appeared to be several underwater buildings coming to the surface. The pilots made their sighting just off the coast of Bimini and photographed the underwater formations from the air. Their discovery was immediately hailed by some as the fulfilment of a 28-year-old prophecy concerning the reappearance of Atlantis. Indeed, one of the pilots had been keeping a lookout for underwater structures while flying his regular assignments because he believed Atlantis was about to re-emerge from the Atlantic in this very area.

The man concerned is a member of the Association for Research and Enlightenment, an organisation based in Virginia Beach, Virginia, which is dedicated to the study of the teachings and 'psychic readings' of the late Edgar Cayce, the 'sleeping prophet' and psychic healer. Between 1923 and 1944 Cayce made numerous references to Atlantis in the course of trance interviews concerning the alleged former lives of the people who consulted him. These interviews were recorded verbatim, and much of the material about Atlantis has been published in a book called *Edgar Cayce on Atlantis*, by Cayce's son Edgar Cayce. It includes this prediction, made in June 1940: 'Poseidia will be among the first portions of Atlantis to rise again. Expect it in '68 and '69; not so far away!'

According to the Cayce readings, Poseidia was the 'western section of Atlantis', and the area off Bimini is the highest point of this sunken land. So the ARE is naturally delighted about the underwater find in the Bahamas, just where and when the famous prophet said something would appear. Until this and similar discoveries have been thoroughly explored, we have to admit that Thera may yet have an equally plausible rival for the title of Atlantis, right where most people always considered the long-lost continent to be in the Atlantic.

In his book *The Mystery of Atlantis* Charles Berlitz comments that: 'Other underwater ruins have subsequently been found near other Caribbean islands, including what appears to be an entire city submerged off the coast of Haiti, and still another at the bottom of a lake. What appears to be an underwater road (or perhaps a series of plazas or foundations) was discovered in 1968 off north Bimini beneath several fathoms of water. From these numerous findings, it would appear that part of the continental shelf of the Atlantic and Caribbean was once dry land, sunk or flooded during a period when man was already civilized.'

Not everyone accepts these underwater features as being of man-made origin. The so-called 'Bimini road' is dismissed by sceptics as nothing more than beach rock that just happens to have produced an unusual effect. Berlitz and Dr Manson Valentine, the American archaeologist and oceanographer who discovered the 'road', do not agree. 'It should be pointed out,' writes Berlitz, 'that beach rock does not form great blocks which fit together in a pattern, that haphazardly splitting rock does not make 90-degree turns, nor does it normally have regularly laid-out passageways running between sections of it. Nor, above all, are 'natural' beach rocks, lying on the ocean floor, likely to be found supported by stone pillars precisely placed beneath them!'

Other sightings made off Bimini, at distances up to 100 miles from the shore, include what appear to be vertical walls, a great arch, and pyramids or bases for pyramids under the sea. Some 10 miles north of Andros, another island in the Bahamas, pilots have photographed formations on the seabed that look like great circles of standing stones, reminiscent of Stonehenge. Off the coasts of eastern Yucatán and British Honduras seemingly man-made roads stretch far out to sea, and off Venezuela a 100-mile 'wall' runs along the ocean bottom. However, geologists have declared many of these to be natural features, and deem the Venezuelan wall 'too big to be considered man-made'. According to Berlitz, the Russians have explored an underwater building complex covering over 10 acres of the sea floor north of Cuba, and the French bathyscaphe *Archimede* has reported sighting flights of steps carved in the steep continental shelf off northern Puerto Rico.

Do these intriguing finds indicate that Atlantis was, after all, in the Atlantic? It seems we must keep an open mind until they have been investigated more thoroughly. Meanwhile, let us take a fresh look at the Atlantic Ocean to see if the theory of continental drift might still leave room for a missing continent there. When a computer was used to reassemble the continental jigsaw, the fit across the Atlantic was found, with some adjustment, to be fairly satisfactory. But that picture does not take account of a fascinating underwater feature known as the mid-Atlantic Ridge. This mountainous ridge, nearly two miles high and hundreds of miles wide, runs in an S-curve down the Atlantic midway between the Americas and Africa and Europe, following the contours of those continents and marking its course above water with a number of islands, such as the Azores, Ascension Island, and Tristan da Cunha.

As early as 1883 Ignatius Donnelly suggested that the mid-Atlantic Ridge was a remnant of Atlantis. But most modern geologists and oceanographers consider that, far from being the relic of a continent that sank beneath the sea, the ridge was forced upward from the ocean floor, probably by volcanic activity. One theory is that as the continents drifted apart they produced a huge fault line that is a centre of earthquake and volcanic action. Some of the earth's molten centre has erupted through this crack and built up into a ridge, even rising above the waves in several places. However, there is evidence that this explanation may have to be reviewed before too long.

Seabed cores taken from the mid-Atlantic Ridge in 1957 brought up freshwater plants from a depth of two miles. And in one of the deep valleys, known as Romanche, sands have been found that appear to have been formed by weathering when that part of the ridge was above water level. In 1969, a Duke University research expedition dredged 50 sites along an under-water ridge running from Venezuela to the Virgin Islands, and brought up granitic rocks, which are normally found only on continents. Commenting on this discovery, Dr Bruce Heezen of the Lamont Geological Observatory said: 'Up to now, geologists generally believed that light granitic or acid igneous rocks are confined to the continents and that the crust of the earth beneath the sea is composed of heavier, dark-colored basaltic rock. . . . Thus, the occurrence of light-coloured granitic rocks may support an old theory that a continent formerly existed in the region of the eastern Caribbean and that these rocks may represent the core of a subsided, lost continent.'

A cautious report on the nature of the Atlantic seabed appears to confirm that there is at least part of a former continent lying beneath the ocean. Under the headline 'Concrete Evidence for Atlantis?', the British journal *New Scientist* of June 5, 1975 reported: 'Although they make no such fanciful claim from their results as to have discovered the mythical mid-Atlantic landmass, an international group of oceanographers has now convincingly confirmed preliminary findings that a sunken block of continent lies in the middle of the Atlantic Ocean. The discovery comes from analysing dredge samples taken along the line of the Vema offset fault, a long east-west fracture zone lying between Africa and South America close to latitude 11°N.'

The report goes on to state that in 1971 two researchers from the University of Miami recovered some shallow-water limestone fragments from deep water in the area. Minerals in the limestone indicated that they came from a nearby source of granite that was unlikely to occur on the ocean floor. More exhaustive analysis of the dredge samples revealed that the limestones included traces of shallow-water fossils, implying formation in very shallow water indeed, a view confirmed by the ratios of oxygen and carbon isotopes found in the fragments. One piece of limestone was pitted and showed evidence of tidal action.

The researchers believe that the limestone dates from the Mesozoic era (between 70 and 220 million years ago) and forms a cap 'on a residual continental block left behind as the Atlantic spread out into an ocean.' The *New Scientist* observes that 'the granitic minerals could thus have come from the bordering continents while the ocean was still in its infancy. Vertical movements made by the block appear to have raised it above sea level at some period during its history.'

It would therefore seem that there is a lost continent in the Atlantic, but unfortunately for Atlantists, it evidently disappeared long before man appeared on earth. Most scientists remain convinced that there is no likelihood of finding the Atlantis described by Plato in the area of the mid-Atlantic Ridge. As L. Sprague de Camp comments in his *Lost Continents*, nearly all of the ridge, except for the small and mountainous Azores region, is under two or three miles of water, 'and there is no known way to get a large island down to that depth in anything like the 10,000 years required to fit in with Plato's date for the sinking of Atlantis.' He also points to a report published in 1967 by Dr Maurice Ewing of Columbia University, who announced that 'after 13 years of exploring the mid-Atlantic Ridge,' he had 'found no trace of sunken cities.'

Atlantists reply that Dr. Ewing could have been looking in the wrong places, or perhaps too close to the centre of the destructive forces that plunged Atlantis into the ocean. Some Atlantists have suggested that the original Atlantic landmass broke up into at least two parts, one of which sank long after the other. Perhaps Plato's Atlantis was a remnant of the continent that oceanographers now appear to have detected in the Atlantic, and perhaps it was not submerged until very much more recent times. The bed of the Atlantic is, after all, an unstable area and one that has given birth to numerous islands, then swallowed them up again. In 1811, for example, volcanic activity in the Azores resulted in the emergence of a new island called Sambrina, which shortly sank back again into the sea. In our own time, the island of Surtsey, 20 miles southwest of Iceland, has slowly risen from the ocean. Surtsey was formed during a continuous underwater eruption between 1963 and 1966.

If Atlantis did exist in the Atlantic above the great fault line that runs between the present continents, it would certainly have been plagued by earthquakes and volcanic eruptions. Is it mere coincidence that Plato should have situated his lost continent in an ocean that does apparently contain such a continent, and in an area subject to the very kind of catastrophe he describes? Atlantists think not.

On the other hand, there are some Atlantists who believe that the destruction of Atlantis was brought about not by geological events but by a man-made disaster, such as a nuclear explosion. According to the Cayce readings the Atlanteans achieved an astonishingly high level of technology before the continent sank, around 10,000 BC. They invented the laser, aircraft, television, death rays, atomic energy, and cybernetic control of human beings, and it was the misuse of the tremendously powerful natural forces they had developed that caused their destruction.

Cayce is best-known for his apparent ability to diagnose illness even in people whom he had never met. This ability was tested by a group of physicians from Hopkinsville and Bowling Green, Kentucky. They discovered that when Cayce was in a state of trance, it was sufficient to give him the name and address of a patient for him to supply a wealth of information about that person, often drawing attention to medical conditions of which the physicians were then unaware, but that subsequent tests on the patient proved to be correct. This work alone would appear to justify the description of Cayce as America's most talented psychic. And if one aspect of his clairvoyant powers could prove so successful, it seems reasonable to give a fair hearing to other psychic statements he made, however fantastic.

Cayce's sons, who help run the organisation set up to study his work, admit that their life would be far simpler if Edgar Cayce had never mentioned Atlantis. Hugh Lynn Cayce comments: 'It would be very easy to present a very tight evidential picture of Edgar Cayce's psychic ability and the helpfulness of his readings if we selected only those which are confirmed and completely validated. This would not be fair in a total, overall evaluation of his life's work. My brother and I know that Edgar Cayce did not read Plato's material on Atlantis, or books on Atlantis, and that he, so far as we know, had absolutely no knowledge of this subject. If his unconscious fabricated this material or wove it together from existing legends and writings, we believe that it is the most amazing example of a telepathic clairvoyant scanning of existing legends and stories in print or of the minds of persons dealing with the Atlantis theory.' Edgar Evans Cayce makes the comment that 'unless proof of the existence of Atlantis is one day discovered, Edgar Cayce is in a very unenviable position. On the other hand, if he proves accurate on this score he may become as famous an archaeologist or historian as he was a medical clairvoyant.'

If, as his sons and thousands of followers believe, Edgar Cayce's readings were supernormal, and not the product of reading the works of others, it is certainly an intriguing case. There are, for example, some fascinating similarities between Cayce's descriptions of Atlantis and those of occultists such as Madame Blavatsky, Rudolf Steiner, and W. Scott-Elliot, including references to the Atlanteans' telepathic and other supernormal powers, their advanced technology, their moral disintegration, and the civil strife and misuse of their powers that finally caused their demise. Cayce's readings also mention Lemuria, or Mu. Either Cayce was psychically reading the works of these earlier writers, or he – and they – really were 'tuning in' to the past.

Whatever the result of future investigations around the splendid temples and palaces of Crete, or in the depths of the Thera basin, there will still be people who continue to look for Atlantis in the Atlantic Ocean. Scholars may have made out a convincing case for the identification of Plato's Atlantis with the

Minoan civilization of the Aegean, but their opponents argue that the existence of such a civilization – however striking its similarities with Atlantis – does not preclude the existence of an even greater civilization in the Atlantic. The strange finds in the Bahamas and the discovery of a sunken block of continent in the middle of the Atlantic add some weight to their argument. On the other hand, it has been argued that both camps rely too exclusively on Plato's dialogues. The two-and-a-half-thousand year hunt for the continent described in the *Timaeus* and *Critias* has inspired many theories, but no solid evidence. The search for Atlantis remains a purely speculative pursuit, and will probably stay that way as long as Atlantis enthusiasts concentrate on an unfinished story supplemented by pure imagination.

Meanwhile, researchers working in more down-to-earth fields, like archaeology and anthropology, have found enough anomalies in our present view of prehistory to suggest that an important part of the story remains untold.

The problem is one that has recurred throughout this volume: how civilizations can reach a high degree of sophistication in what looks like a single leap. Alexander Marshack, a researcher from the Peabody Museum, begins his book *The Roots of Civilisation* – dealing with our Cro-Magnon ancestors – by noting that he began by questioning what he calls 'a series of suddenlies' – how science began 'suddenly' with the Greeks, how mathematics and astronomy appeared 'suddenly' among the Egyptians, and how civilization itself began 'suddenly' in the fertile crescent of the Middle East.

Examining a 35,000 year old bone engraved with curious markings, Marshack came to the conclusion that they were notations of the phases of the moon. But why would our cave-man ancestors be interested in the phases of the moon? It would seem that the origins of astronomy are tens of thousands of years older than we have always assumed. A classic study of mythology, *Hamlet's Mill* by Gorgio de Santillana and Herta von Dachend, starts from the proposition that mythologies from all over the world contains coded references to the phenomenon known as 'precession of the equinoxes', which (as we saw earlier) is caused by the slight wobble of the earth's axis, and which causes the stars to slowly change their positions. Without this wobble, precisely the same constellations of the zodiac would rise at dawn year in and year out, for all eternity. As it is, they change very slowly, taking more than two thousand years to do so, so that we move from the 'Age of Aries' (when Aries rose with the sun at the spring equinox) to the 'Age of Pisces' (our present age) to the coming 'Age of Aquarius'.

Santillana argues that this knowledge of 'precession' seems to date back thousands – perhaps tens of thousands – of years, which suggests that our remote ancestors were studying the heavens with extreme attention. But why should they? What does a cave man care about the stars? The answer, apparently, was: a great deal. In a remarkable book called *Forbidden Archaeology*, Michael Cremo surveys the archaeological evidence for the length of time man has lived on earth, and for the assumption that homo sapiens has been around for less than a hundred thousand years, and demonstrates that the late Victorians suppressed a great deal of evidence that creatures like ourselves existed millions of years ago. All this evidence seems to point in the same direction: that civilization may be far older than we think.

In 1966, a book entitled *Maps of the Ancient Sea Kings*, by an American academic, Charles H. Hapgood, caused widespread controversy. The reason becomes clear from the title of the final chapter: 'A Civilisation that Vanished', which begins:

'The evidence presented by the ancient maps appears to suggest the existence in remote times, before the rise of any known culture, of a true civilisation, of an advanced kind, which either was localised in one area but had worldwide commerce, or was, in a real sense, a worldwide culture. This culture, at least in some respects, was more advanced than the civilisations of Greece and Rome. In geodesy, nautical science, and mapmaking it was more advanced than any known culture before the 18th century of the Christian Era. It was only in the 18th century that we developed a practical means of finding longitude. It was in the 18th century that we first accurately measured the circumference of the earth. Not until the 19th century did we begin to send out ships for exploration into the Arctic or Antarctic Seas and only then did we begin the exploration of the bottom of the Atlantic. The maps indicate that some ancient people did all these things.'

The maps Hapgood refers to are called portolans, meaning 'from port to port', and were used by mariners in the Middle Ages. Before the development of accurate navigation methods, ships were forced to hug the coastlines to be certain where they were. When unfavourable winds blew them temporarily out of the sight of land they might be quite lost when they returned. Under such circumstances, navigators needed highly accurate coastline maps to compare points of reference. In 1889, a scholar named E. E. Nordenskjold was compiling a book of surviving portolans when he noticed an interesting fact: that the maps dating from the 16th century showed no sign of development from those of the 14th century. It was as if both had been copied from the same set of older charts rather than being elaborated by subsequent generations of navigators.

In 1554, when the Turkish pirate Piri Re'is was beheaded, his hoard of treasure passed into the hands of the authorities. In 1929 a portolan said to belong to him was found in the Topkapi Palace Museum, in Istanbul, and in 1956, a copy of the same map was presented to the United States Navy Hydrographic Office by a Turkish naval officer. The U.S.N.H.O.'s cartographic expert, in turn, showed it to a friend named Captain Arlington H. Mallery, who studied old maps as a hobby. What the captain saw astounded him. The painted parchment, dated 1513, accurately showed the deeps of the Atlantic Ocean, parts of West Africa, most of the coast of South America and what appeared to be the continent of Antarctica. Quite apart from the fact that South America was supposedly unmapped in 1513, leaving aside the fact that Antarctica was not discovered until 1818, forgetting that the Atlantic was not plumbed until the late nineteenth century – what really startled Mallery was the recognition that the map showed Antarctica as it was *before it was covered with ice*.

Today, all geographers are familiar with the coastline of the Antarctic continent, despite the fact that it lies hidden beneath a huge polar ice sheet. For Captain Mallery, however, the sight was relatively new. It was only in 1949, seven years before, that an international mapping expedition had managed to penetrate the Antarctic ice – in places a mile thick – using sonar equipment.

How did a 16th century pirate come by this information? The obvious answer was that he couldn't have – the map must be a modern fake. At least, this was the opinion of critics taking part in a radio debate that Charles Hapgood heard in September 1956, following Mallery's announcement of his discovery. Hapgood, an American professor of the history of science, was particularly fascinated because he was, at the time, trying to prove a theory concerning the polar ice caps. He had suggested that the great masses of ice around the poles had built up fairly quickly – in thousands as opposed to the millions of years. Hapgood's theory further stated that this rapid build-up of ice would regularly (every fifty to a hundred thousand years) make the Earth's entire crust unstable, causing it to shift en masse like the skin on cold soup.

The Earth's crust – that is the segmented layer of cold rock that comprises the sea bed and the foundation of the continental land-masses – rests, unanchored, on a layer of molten rock called magma. A sudden large build-up of ice at the two poles could, Hapgood suggested in *Earth's Shifting Crust* (1959), make the crust prone to slip around on the viscous magma. Hapgood thought that when such a crisis point is reached the entire Earth's crust might move thousands of miles from its original position, like a man's wig slipping over his eyes in a strong wind. As a result, much of the destabilising polar ice would be moved into warmer climes where it would melt. The crust would lose its iner-tial velocity and come to a rest and the whole process would begin again. (This fits neatly with Chaos Theory, which states that wildly unpredictable changes result from too much energy being stored-up in any system. When the excess energy is discharged, order and predictability are restored.)

Hapgood's theory explained certain problems about the great Ice Ages. These are periods when, for reasons we have yet to fully understand, ice from the poles advances towards the equator, grinding intervening landmasses beneath armies of glaciers. The damage left after the retreat of the ice sheets can be seen in any atlas – glacially produced mountain ranges, coastal fjords and flattened, gravelly stretches of plainsland. The problem, as Hapgood saw it, was that certain areas of the globe that should have been well within the reach of the ice sheets seem to have been left unmarked. This was, he suggested, because they had once been further from the poles, but had since been moved closer by an earth crust displacement.

To support his hypothesis, Hapgood cited geologic evidence that Hudson Bay once rested over the North Pole, and could quote from a 1954 magnetic survey of British rocks which seemed to show that the British Isles were once two thousand miles further south. Soviet scientists had been surprised by their discovery that the North Pole had been positioned as far south as 55 degrees latitude 60 million years ago and, most striking of all, that during the last Ice Age, areas of Africa and India were crushed by ice sheets while Siberia basked in a temperate climate. Hapgood's explanation fitted all these anomalies into an understandable pattern.

Even before he heard about the Piri Re'is map, Hapgood had concluded that the last such a catastrophe had, among other things, moved Antarctica 2,500 miles away from the equator and closer to the south polar zone. Was the pirate's map, he wondered, copied from another made by the inhabitants of Antarctica before the time of the great disaster? If it was, the historians were in for a shock. As we have seen, archaeologists believe the earliest developed culture was that of the Sumerians, beginning around 4000 BC. Farming began about six thousand years before that. And before 10,000 BC, the history books take it for granted that our ancestors were primitives who lived by hunting and fishing. Yet Hapgood estimated the earth crust displacement that doomed the once temperate continent of Antarctica had started about 15,000 BC, eleven thousand years before the 'birth of civilisation'. So if the inhabitants of Antarctica had made the pre-Ice Age maps, that continent had been the home of a sophisticated civilization millennia before the Sumerians.

From Captain Mallery, Hapgood learned more about the

portolan's history. Piri Re'is (Re'is was Turkish for admiral) claimed that he had made the map himself, basing it on twenty others: nineteen surviving from the great library of Alexandria (burned by a Muslim army in 640 AD) and one which had belonged to Christopher Columbus. The global portolan found in Istanbul in 1929, and later given to the US Navy Hydrographic Office, dated from the 16th century, and there was no reason to believe it was not drawn by Piri Re'is. But whoever drew the map, it could not be disputed that it contained information that was not known to Europeans at the time it was made.

Provided with a copy of the map, Hapgood showed it to his students and asked them to examine it for clues. The first thing they noticed was that, as Piri Re'is had said, the map was obviously copied from many smaller maps. The copier, uncertain as to how to fit them together, had occasionally allowed them to overlap ,and, as a result, added stretches of coast that did not exist. For example, a 900-mile stretch of the south American coastline had been missed-out in one area, but the River Amazon had been included twice.

Another interesting question concerned the 'centre' of the map. It should be explained that before the invention of latitude and longitude by Gerald Mercator in 1569, maps were based on a central point – Jerusalem or Mecca for example – and fanned outward from there. The problem with this method – as we live on a sphere – is that two-dimensional maps become more inaccurate the further they stretch from their original centre. (If we imagine removing the skin of an orange in longitudinal strips, and then placing it flat on a table, the problem becomes obvious).

In the case of the Piri Re'is map the centre was not even shown – it lay off the map. But it could be inferred, and trigonometric projection eventually showed the 'centre' to be the Egyptian town of Syene – now the site of the great Aswan Dam. It was an insignificant place in the 16th century, but one that held an interesting significance in ancient history.

Around 200 BC, the Greek scholar Eratosthenes heard of that at midday on 21 June the towers of Syene had no shadows and the sun was reflected at the bottom of the town's deepest well. This, he realised, was because the sun was then directly overhead. Yet, 500 miles north in Alexandria at the same moment, the buildings had a perceptible shadow. If the earth was flat, Alexandria would have been as shadowless as Syene, therefore, Eratosthenes reasoned, the Earth's surface must be curved. (Fortunately he took it for granted that the sun was big enough or far enough away for its rays always to strike the Earth in parallel.) Knowing the exact distance between the two towns and angle of shadows in Alexandria at midday, 21 June, allowed him to calculate the curvature and thus the circumference of the Earth. He estimated it at 24,000. (It is actually closer to 25,000, but he was amazingly close.)

Now Eratosthenes had made a small error of 4.5 degrees. Piri Re'is had clearly been influenced by Eratosthenes, for he not only centred his map on Syene, but also miscalculated the curvature of the planet by 4.5 degrees. When Hapgood corrected for this mistake, the Piri Re'is map became even more accurate. The implication was stunning: the original mapmakers had known the exact circumference of the Earth before Eratosthenes. (We saw in Chapter 2 that the ancient Egyptians encoded the same information in the design of the Pyramid of Cheops in the third millennium BC.)

In the course of this research, Hapgood arranged to visit the US Library of Congress to view their portolans. His surprise was considerable when he was led into a room containing hundreds of them. Moreover many contained information historians insist was unknown at the time they were made. In fact, a few were as startling as Piri Re'is's map of Antarctica. A chart made by Oronteus Finaeus in 1531 not only showed Antarctica before it was covered with ice, but also showed mountain ranges and rivers flowing into the sea. Another Turkish map, by Hadji Ahmed, dated 1550, showed the world from a northern 'projection, (a point-of-view hovering over the North Pole), in which Alaska and Siberia were joined across the Bering Strait. Such a land bridge actually existed before it vanished under the sea at the end of the last great Ice Age, but that was between twelve and fourteen thousand years ago. Why had these documents been ignored for so long?

Because no one had taken the trouble to study them closely. Hapgood, alerted by the Piri Re'is map, was the first to take them seriously.

He concluded that they had been copied from much earlier maps, and that these, in turn, had been copied from still older maps. And the original maps, it seemed, had been made by a civilization of ocean-navigating sailors who lived at a time when the Antarctic continent was still free of ice. As far as Hapgood could determine, that was at least six thousand years ago, possibly more.

In *Earth's Shifting Crust*, published in 1959, Hapgood considers such evidence as fossil corals in the Arctic Ocean and fossil waterlilies from Spitzbergen to support the argument that the Earth's poles have not always been where they are at present. Geological evidence shows, for example, that there was a great ice cap in the Congo, in Central Africa, during the Permo-Carboniferous period, around 300 million years ago. The African ice sheet once reached the present equator. As to Antarctica, the present ice that covers it began to form about 4000 BC. Before that, back as far as 15,000 BC – the beginning of the end of the last great Ice Age – it seems to have been free of ice. Meanwhile, the North American ice cap disappeared at about the time when the Antarctic began to freeze over. That, says Hapgood, seems to suggest that the Earth's crust itself slipped, pushing North America closer to the equator and Antarctica further away, towards and over the South Pole. He believed the 'slippage' of the crust was due to the weight of ice that built up in the polar regions. Albert Einstein was sufficiently impressed by the theory to write an introduction to the book.

Hapgood went on to write *Maps of the Ancient Sea Kings*, (1966), which (as we have seen) argued for the existence of a great seagoing civilization before 7000 BC, and suggested that its centre was Antarctica. This book had the misfortune to appear shortly before a book called *Chariots of the Gods?* by Erich von Daniken, which argued that the Giza pyramids and various other ancient monuments were built by visitors from outer space; Daniken actually cited Hapgood and his ancient maps to support his case. And since Daniken's book was full of absurd inaccuracies (such as multiplying the weight of the Great Pyramid by five), and was savagely criticised, Hapgood found himself tarred with the same brush, and bracketed with Daniken and the 'ancient astronaut' theorists.

In the early 1970's a Canadian librarian called Randy Flemming, waiting to hear if he had secured a job at Victoria University, passed the time writing a novel about Atlantis set in 10,000 BC. Without having heard of Hapgood's work, he decided that, for the sake of the plot, he would identify Atlantis with the Antarctic continent. A few years later, coming on the *Maps of the Ancient Sea Kings*, he was amazed to learn that his fictional theory had a sound basis in fact. Actually, Hapgood had never mentioned that his pre-Ice Age civilization sounded like Plato's Atlantis, as it would have invited ridicule from his academic colleagues.

Hapgood responded in a friendly manner to a letter from Randy Flemming – who now decided to write a serious book about Atlantis – but cautioned him from placing too much emphasis on the 'lost continent'. He felt that it made no difference what the ancient civilization was called, and was aware that excessive emphasis on Atlantis would get the Flemmings (Randy was collaborating with his wife Rose), classified with the lunatic fringe.

Flemming was to ignore that advice. Over the next few years he and Rose – also a librarian – started to collect their own evidence for Hapgood's unfairly discredited thesis. The Flem-Aths (a combination of the couple's pre-marital surnames, Flemming and De'Ath) found supporting data across a wide spectrum of different fields – geology, archaeology, the history of agriculture and world mythology – which they would publish in 1995 in *When the Sky Fell*.

They found evidence, for example, in the *National Atlas of Canada*, that during the last Ice Age, while glaciers were grinding deep into North America, the now frozen Yukon and some Arctic islands had been free from ice. They also came across archaeological evidence that, during the same period Siberia was warmer than it is today. They state that 'of thirty-four species known to have lived in Siberia before 9600 BC including mammoths, giant deer, cave hyena and cave lions, thirty-eight were adapted to temperate conditions.' Siberia is now, of course, a sub-temperate region of frozen tundra, wind-blown steppes and dense coniferous forests.

The Flem-Aths also looked into the possible side-effects of a earth crust displacement. As we saw in Chapter 26, many ancient cultures around the globe share 'catastrophe myths'. Focusing specifically on Native American mythologies, the Flem-Aths found many strikingly similar cataclysm stories in peoples as far apart and as unlike as the nomadic Cherokee in North America and the city-dwelling Incas of Peru. For instance, they found many tribes shared the tale of 'the time of the wayward sun', when the sun looked 'shattered' and proceeded to rise, move across the sky and set in the wrong places – literally wandering about the sky.

The Flem-Aths noted that a large proportion of Native American Indians had handed-down stories of great earthquakes, (many myths stating that they were preceded by a wandering of the sun), followed by floods so terrible that only those in the mountains survived. (A side-effect of an earth crust displacement would, of course, be world-wide flooding as billions of tons of Arctic and Antarctic ice melted and raised the sea levels.) The Flem-Aths point out that the many thousands of human sacrifices performed by the Incas, Mayas and Aztecs were an attempt to persuade the gods – and most particularly the Sun God – not to allow such a catastrophe to happen again.

Perhaps the most striking evidence cited by the Flem-Ath's to support the 'universal flood' thesis comes from the study of early agriculture. The modern scientific account of the origin of agriculture dates the first primitive farmers to around 10,000 BC, at the very end of the last great Ice Age. The Flem-Aths note that several different types of domestic plants seem to have been cultivated around the globe – rice in the Far East, corn in the Americas and wheat on the continent of Europe – at exactly the same time, by peoples who can have had no possible contact.

The Flem-Aths note another curious fact about these experiments in agriculture; the early farmers chose upland areas rather than the more fertile plains and valleys. When the Soviet botanist Nikolai Ivanovich Vavilov conducted a study of over fifty-thousand wild plants from around the globe, he concluded that they had all originated from eight separate areas, all in mountain ranges. Of course, if the lowlands were flooded, the early farmers would have been forced to use uplands.

It is true, of course, that melting ice sheets at the end of the last Ice Age would have caused sea levels to rise, probably by about 300 feet; but this would not be enough to drive farmers into the mountains.

Rand Flem-Ath observed that in Plato's *Laws*, there is a description of a great deluge which wiped out the lowland cities and forced survivors into the mountains; it was there, he says, that they discovered the techniques of farming. Plato does not mention Atlantis in the *Laws*, so we cannot link the great flood he describes with the sinking of the 'lost continent', but it is interesting to note that 9600 BC – the date he says Atlantis was destroyed – is also the date of the spontaneous rise of agriculture.

Lake Titicaca, 13,000 feet above sea level in the Andes, is one of the 'birthplaces of agriculture'. It was also the place where Inca civilization originated (see Chapter 17), and is the site of the ancient city of Tiahuanaco – home of Viracocha, the 'White God' credited with bringing the arts of civilization to South America (see Chapter 23). On the other side of the globe – exactly opposite Lake Titicaca – is another centre of early agricultural development, in the mountains of Thailand. In *Earth's Shifting Crust*, Hapgood had suggested that both these areas had known relative peace following the last earth crust displacement – ideal for resettlement after a catastrophic series of natural disasters.

The Flem-Aths argue that the last great earth crust displacement took place between 15,000 and 9600 BC, ending with a violent upheavals around the globe. At that time, according to Hapgood, the tropical regions of China, India, Sumeria, Crete and Egypt became temperate, while the warm continent of Antarctica moved away from the equator towards the South Pole. Did these newly hospitable regions become host to the earliest civilizations by coincidence, ask the Flem-Aths, or was it because survivors from Antarctica chose them to found new colonies? Perhaps here we see the origin of the myths of the American 'White Gods', the fish-gods who brought civilization to the Babylonians and the Dogon of Mali, and the architect-priests of the ancient Egyptians and the Megalith people of western Europe.

But where is the actual physical evidence to support these revolutionary theories? Until the early 1990s, it was virtually non-existent. But one student of Egyptology, John Anthony West, had raised a fascinating question. In a book called *Serpent in the Sky* (1979), he had noted the argument of a maverick Egyptologist called Rene Schwaller de Lubicz, that Egyptian civilization – and the Sphinx in particular – was thousands of years older than historians believe. Schwaller had devoted the latter part of his life to demonstrating that the ancient Egyptians possessed 'a grand, interrelated and complete system of knowledge.' West writes:

'Schwaller de Lubicz observed that the severe erosion of the body of the Great Sphinx at Giza is due to the action of water, not of wind and sand.

'If the single fact of water erosion of the Sphinx could be confirmed, it would in itself overthrow all accepted chronologies of the history of civilization, it would force a drastic re-evaluation of the assumption of 'progress' – the assumption upon which the whole of modern education is based. It would be difficult to find a single, simple question with graver implications. The water erosion of the Sphinx is to history what the convertibility of matter into energy is to physics.'

The problem is that although this final chapter of the book is called 'Egypt: Heir to Atlantis', it actually says very little about such a possible link. The most important comment about this occurs in the Introduction:

'Following an observation made by Schwaller de Lubicz, it is now possible virtually to prove the existence of another, and perhaps greater civilization ante-dating dynastic Egypt – and all other known civilizations by millennia. In other words, it is now possible to prove 'Atlantis', and simultaneously, the historical reality of the Biblical Flood. (I use inverted – by commas around 'Atlantis' since it is not the physical location that is at issue here, but rather the existence of a civilization sufficiently sophisticated and sufficiently ancient to give rise to the legend.)'

So West was not, in fact, necessarily talking about Plato's mythical Atlantis, but simply about the possibility that civilization may be millennia older than historians accept.

The Sphinx is a 240 foot long by sixty-six feet high and lies in a rectangular trench formed when it was carved out of the limestone bedrock. Its lion's body and human head are solid limestone, although it has been repaired with bricks and mortar several times over its lifetime. It faces eastward, towards the sunrise, and gazes over a temple built from limestone blocks removed during the carving of the statue. Some of these blocks weigh over two hundred tons.

Egyptologists believe that the Sphinx and the Sphinx temple were built by the son of the pharaoh Cheops, Chefren or Khafre – who also constructed the second great pyramid of Giza – around 2500 BC. This assumption is based solely on a carved stela (a stone plaque) found between the paws of the Sphinx and bearing the name 'Khef...' In fact, the stela is so badly damaged that we can no longer tell what words surrounded the name of Chefren; it is simply assumed that he was claiming credit for the construction.

In a book called *Sacred Science*, Schwaller de Lubicz had remarked that the Sphinx was not eroded by wind-blown sand, but by water. It seemed to West that this ought to be easy enough to prove or disprove, since water-weathering is quite distinct from wind-weathering. Porous rock is like a layer cake, with an alternation of hard and soft layers. The wind scours out the soft layers, so that the rock has an undulating vertical profile.

Rain also weathers the soft rock more than the hard. But in flowing downward, it also cuts vertical channels, so that the protruding layers look rather like a row of buttocks.

This type of weathering can be seen very distinctly on the Sphinx and – even more – on the Sphinx enclosure, the walls of the 'pit' out of which it has been dug. But then, West was not a geologist, and felt he could easily be wrong.

Nevertheless, he approached an expert on weathering at Oxford, and showed him a photograph of the Sphinx, in which the head and the paws had been covered with masking tape. 'Would you say this is wind or rain weathering?' The expert took one look and said: 'Undoubtedly, rain.' West then stripped off the masking tape, and the expert said: 'Oh. . .' He declined to comment further on the grounds that this was not his field.

After a long search, West found a geologist who was willing to go and see for himself: Robert Schoch, of the University of Boston. In June 1990, they visited the Giza plateau together. And Schoch's preliminary judgment was that the Sphinx was weathered by rain.

If true, this would have immense implications. It is not known when the Sahara changed into a desert – it was once as green as northern Europe – but a conservative estimate is 3500 BC. So if the Sphinx was built in 2500 BC, then rain weathering would be out of the question.

West gathered a team of experts and returned to Giza. They noted that the weathering on Old Kingdom tombs – dating from about 2500 BC – was far less severe than on the Sphinx, which suggested that it was far older. On the other hand, the weathering on two temples in front of the Sphinx – the Valley Temple and the Sphinx Temple (the latter built from the blocks that were removed from around the Sphinx) was also very severe. All this suggested that the Sphinx and its temples were far older than the surrounding temples and tombs. Schoch's guess was that the Sphinx was carved around 7000 BC – doubling its age.

West presented evidence about the age of the Sphinx to a geological conference at San Diego in October 1991. The result is summarised in the *Los Angeles Times* for 26 October. 1991:

EGYPT SERVES UP NEW TWIST TO
MYSTERY OF THE SPHINX
San Diego, Wednesday

New evidence that Egypt's Great Sphinx may be twice as old as had been thought has triggered a fierce argument between geologists who say that it must be older and archaeologists who say that such a conclusion contradicts everything we know about ancient Egypt.

Geologists who presented their results at the Geological Society of America Convention yesterday found that weathering patterns on the monument were characteristic of a period far older than had been believed. But archaeologists and Egyptologists insist that the Sphinx could not be much older because people who lived there earlier could not have built it.

Most Egyptologists believe that the Sphinx was built during the reign of the 'Pharaoh' Kafre [Chefren] in approximately 2500 BC. But scientists who conducted a series of unprecedented studies at the Giza site said their evidence shows that the Sphinx was already there long before Kafre came to power.

The evidence suggests that Kafre simply refurbished the Sphinx.

Boston geologist Robert Schoch said his research suggests that the Sphinx dates back to between 5000 BC and 7000 BC. That would make it double the age of the Great Pyramid and make it the oldest monument in Egypt, he said.

But California archaeologist Carol Redmount. who specialises in Egyptian artifacts, said 'There's just no way that could be true.'

The people of that region would not have had the technology or the will to have built such a structure thousands of years earlier. she said.

Other Egyptologists said that they cannot explain the geological evidence, but they insist that the theory simply does not match up with the mountains of archaeological research they have carried out in that region. If the geologists are right, much of what the Egyptologists think they know would have to be wrong.

By now, West was fairly certain that the Egyptologists were wrong.

They fought back. One of them argued that the Sphinx and the surrounding tombs are made of different kinds of limestone. But an independent expert, hired by the BBC before West's programme about the Sphinx was presented, verified that the tombs were made of precisely the same flaky limestone as the Sphinx.

Dr Mark Lehner, one of the leading experts on the pyramids, attacked West's theory in the *National Geographic Magazine*, comparing the face of the pharaoh Chefren with a computer image in which the Sphinx's face had been 'completed'. This comparison, he said, showed that the Sphinx and Chefren were the same person.

West countered by getting a New York police artist, an expert on facial reconstruction, to go and look at the Sphinx, and compare its face with a statue of Chefren in the Cairo Museum. Domingo asked: 'What if I say they are the same person?' 'If that's what you say, that's what I'll print', said West. Domingo went to look at the Sphinx, and compared with Chefren. He concluded that they were not the same person – the Sphinx has a more prominent chin, and a line drawn from the ear to the corner of the Sphinx's mouth sloped at 32 degrees, while a similar line on Chefren's face was only 14 degrees.

All this was of great interest to a British writer named Graham Hancock who, on a visit to the Great Pyramid in 1993, had concluded that its builders were far more technically accomplished than anyone has realised. Hancock had come across West's *Traveller's Guide to Ancient Egypt* and read his comments about Schwaller de Lubicz, and his belief that the Sphinx was built by survivors fleeing from the destruction of Atlantis about 10,000 BC.

Hancock had also read about the legends of ancient Mexico and South America, attributing their civilization to 'white gods' from the east, and their leader Viracocha (or Quetzalcoatl, or Kon Tiki). Hancock persuaded a publisher to give him an advance, and he and his wife Santha flew to South America to study its monuments at first hand. He was deeply impressed by the legends of some great catastrophe which took place thousands of years ago, and which darkened the sun and caused tremendous floods. The arrival of the 'white god' Viracocha followed soon after.

Hancock had also read the Flem-Ath's book *When the Sky Fell* in typescript, and Bauval's *The Orion Mystery*, arguing that the pyramids of Giza were a 'reflection' of Orion's belt. He had been especially impressed by one of Bauval's most powerful arguments: that the pyramids of Giza had been planned – and perhaps partly built – in 10,500 BC.

His reasoning was based on the phenomenon called the precession of the equinoxes. In 2500 BC, when the Great Pyramid was built, the three pyramids of Giza were not an accurate 'reflection' of Orion's belt. 'Precession' not only causes the constellation of Orion to rise in the sky over a period of 12,500 years, but to change its position as if it was attached to the hand of a clock. The only time the Giza pyramids were a faithful reflection of Orion's belt was in 10,500 BC, at the beginning of the precessional cycle, when Orion was closest to the horizon.

For some reason, Bauval believed, the ancient Egyptians who built the pyramids wanted to remind us of the belt of Orion as it was in 2500 BC. Why?

The reason, he argued, was that 10,500 BC was Zep Tepi, the 'First Time' – the time of the Egyptian Garden of Eden. This was when their history began.

He thought it a reasonable assumption that when the Giza pyramids were planned, the planners also built the Sphinx, a lion, which faced the constellation of Leo when it rose at dawn on the date of the spring equinox.

In effect, Graham Hancock was bringing together the theories of Schwaller de Lubibcz, John Anthony West, Robert Bauval and Rand and Rose Flem-Ath. He was arguing that some great catastrophe occurred around 10,500 BC, a catastrophe that sent its survivors fleeing to Egypt and South America. In South America they were known as the Virachochas – or people of Virachocha – and taught the Mexicans and the inhabitants of Peru to build pyramids and temples. In Egypt they built the Sphinx, and planned and began to build the pyramids of Giza. (Hancock noted that the lower part of the Chefren pyramid is built of far more massive blocks than the upper half.)

Is there, in fact, any evidence to link ancient Egypt and South America? There are at least two astronomical pieces of evidence. Brasseur de Bourbourg, a French abbé who translated the *Popol*

Vuh, the sacred book of the Quiché Indians (descendants of the Mayas) in 1864, found evidence in Mayan documents of an ancient seafaring civilization that predated Middle Eastern civilization, whose religion involved the dog star Sirius, whom the Egyptians identified with Isis. And Dr Phillis Pitluga, of Chicago's Adler Planetarium, after making computer-aided calculations of the alignments of the Nazca lines of Peru, concluded that the great spider is a terrestrial diagram of the constellation of Orion. Brasseur also found evidence in Mayan writings of a legend of some great catastrophe that had convulsed Central America (Mexico) in the remote past, and Brasseur placed the date at 9937 BC. He had met Indians who still had an oral tradition of the destruction of a great continent in the Atlantic, and went on to speculate that it was from this continent that the civilizations of Egypt and Central America originated. Brasseur also suggested that Quetzalcoatl (Viracocha), the white god, came from Atlantis.

In a manuscript he discovered in the College of San Gregorio, in Mexico City, which he called the *Chimalpopoca Codex*, Brasseur read that a great catastrophe that had occurred around 10,500 BC was only one of a series of at least four catastrophes that caused the destruction of Atlantis.

But we are still left with a major problem. If 'Atlanteans' built the Sphinx and planned the Giza pyramids in 10,500 BC, why did they wait another eight thousand years – until 2500 – until they built the Great Pyramid?

In a book called *Keeper of Genesis* (1996), Robert Bauval and Graham Hancock suggest a convincing solution to this problem.

In the Pyramid texts, they found references to Osiris 'when his name becomes Sokar'. Now Sokar is the ancient Egyptian name for the necropolis of Memphis, one of the two Egyptian centres sacred to Osiris. Abydos, in the south, was the other. The legend declared that after his murder, the body of Osiris drifted up the Nile, from Abydos to Memphis.

If we now compare the map of Egypt with the sky map, in which the Nile is the Milky Way, we discover that precession of the equinoxes causes the constellation of Orion to 'float' up the Milky Way over the millennia.

Bauval and Hancock suggest that there is a highly convincing astronomical reason why the Sphinx was built in 10,500 BC. Standing at dawn between the paws of the Sphinx during spring equinox of 10,500 BC, and looking due east, we would see the constellation of Leo – the lion – rising above the horizon behind the sun. But if we wanted to see Orion, we would have to turn through a right angle, due south, whereupon we would see Orion near the horizon, at the nadir of his precessional cycle.

The Pyramid Texts often refer to the *Duat*, which is usually translated as heaven. Bauval and Hancock make a strong case for arguing that the *Duat* actually refers to a specific part of the heavens – the area of Orion and Sirius.

The Egyptian priesthood who built the Sphinx – and who seem to have been known as the Companions of Osiris – were interested in the time when the spring equinox would occur in the region of Orion. Then, at last, the great plan could be brought to fruition, and the temple of Osiris could be built on the ground. From this temple – the Great Pyramid – the soul of Osiris would go to rejoin his consort Isis in the sky. This great event, Bauval and Hancock argue, was the culmination of Egyptian history.

In *From Atlantis to the Sphinx* (1996), Colin Wilson has offered a summary of what happened next.

'And where was the vernal point [the spring equinox] at this time? Exactly where was the hand of the precessional clock pointing?

'Between 3000 and 2500 BC, the vernal point was on the 'west' bank of the Milky Way, moving slowly past the head of the bull Taurus. This 'head' is formed by a group of stars known as the Hyades, in which two stars stand out as the brightest.

'If we now look down from the sky to its reflection in the land of Egypt, we see the Nile and the 'land of Sokar', which includes Memphis, Heliopolis and Rostau (Giza.) And if we look down today, at the place where those two bright stars of the Hyades are 'reflected', we also see two pyramids – the so-called 'Bent Pyramid' and the 'Red Pyramid' at Dashur, built by the pharaoh Snefru, the father of Cheops.

'Bauval and Hancock, suggest, very reasonably, that Snefru

built them in that place for a purpose – to signal the beginning of the great design.

'And where is Osiris (Orion) at this time? He has also arrived virtually in 'Sokar'. The vernal point and the constellation of Orion – and the star Sirius (Isis) – are now in the same area of the sky.

'It was not so in 10,500 BC. As you faced due east towards Leo which is where the vernal point was situated – you had to turn through a full 90 degrees to look at Orion. Now, four thousand years later, they have come together.

'This, say Bauval and Hancock, is why the Great Pyramid was built eight thousand years after the Sphinx. The 'heavens' were finally ready for it. And their logic seems virtually irrefutable. Provided you agree that the ancient Egyptians knew all about precession – and no one now seriously doubts this – and that Orion was their most important constellation, then it is impossible to disagree that the moment when the vernal point moved into the same area as Orion was perhaps the most important moment in Egyptian history.

'What followed was the building of the pyramids at Rostau (Giza) with their arrangement pointing back clearly to the 'first time' in 10,500 BC.

'And what happened then?

'What happened, of course, was the ceremony that the pharaoh now undertook to send Osiris back to his proper home, which would also gain immortality for himself and for his people.

'This ceremony took place at the time of the dawn-rising of Sirius. But it began ten weeks earlier. Sirius was absent for seventy days below the horizon (due, of course, to the fact that the earth is tilted on its axis.) So, of course, was its near neighbour Orion – Osiris.

'It seems highly probable that a ceremony to 'rescue' Osiris took place every year. But the ceremony that took place at the time of the summer solstice – the event that announced the flooding of the Nile – in the year after the completion of the Great Pyramid, would have been climactic.

'The Horus-pharaoh – presumably Cheops – had to undertake a

journey to bring his father Osiris back to life. In his form as the sun, he had to cross the great river – the Milky Way – in his solar boat, and journey to the eastern horizon, where Osiris was held captive. In his form as the king, he had to cross the Nile in a boat, then journey to Giza, to stand before the breast of the Sphinx.

'Bauval and Hancock write:

"As the 'son of Osiris' he emerged from the womb of Isis, i.e. the star Sirius, at dawn on the summer solstice . . . It was then – and there both at the sky-horizon and the earth "Horizon" that the Horus-King was meant to find himself in front of the Gateway to Rostau (Giza). Guarding that Gateway on the earth-Horizon he would encounter the giant figure of a lion – the Great Sphinx. And guarding that Gateway in the skyhorizon his celestial counterpart would find – what?"

'The answer, of course, is the constellation of Leo.

'The Pyramid texts explain that the beginning of the journey of Horus into the Underworld occurred seventy days before the great ceremony. Twenty five days later, the sun has crossed the 'river' – the Milky Way – and is now moving east towards the constellation of Leo. And forty five days later – the end of the 70 days – the sun is between the paws of Leo.

'On the ground, the pharaoh stands on the east bank of the Nile, crosses it in the solar boat – perhaps the boat found buried near the pyramid in 1954 – the makes his way, via the two pyramids at Dashur, to the breast of the Sphinx.

'At this point, according to the texts, he has to face a ritual ordeal, rather like those of the Freemasons described in Mozart's *Magic Flute*. He is given a choice of two ways, either by land or by water, by which he can journey to the Underworld to rescue his father.The land route, the authors believe, was an immense causeway (of which there are still remains) linking the Valley Temple with the Great Pyramid. It was once roofed with lime-stone slabs and had stars painted on its ceiling.

'The "water route" is still undiscovered – but the authors believe that it was an underground corridor that was kept half filled (or perhaps more than half) with water drawn by capillary action from the Nile. (They cite a French engineer, Dr Jean

Kerisel, who suggests that the Sphinx may stand over a 700 metre-long tunnel leading to the Great Pyramid.)

'What happened next is pure conjecture – except that it must have ended with the reappearance of Orion and Sirius over the eastern horizon. Bauval and Hancock believe that this ceremony was the symbolic uniting of Upper and Lower Egypt – that is, of heaven and earth. Clearly, the priests who planned it saw it as the central event of Egyptian history after "the first time".'

Bauval and Hancock have one more interesting suggestion. Again, I quote Colin Wilson:

'Where precisely, they asked the computer, was the vernal point situated in 10,500 BC? The answer was "that it lay exactly 111.111 degrees east of the station that it had occupied at 2500 BC." Then it had been at the head of the Hyades-Taurus, close to the right bank of the Milky Way; 8000 years earlier it lay directly under the rear paws of the constellation of Leo.

'And if this point has an "earthly double", then it would seem to hint at some undiscovered secret below the rear paws of the Sphinx. The Coffin Texts speak about "a sealed thing, which is in darkness, with fire about it, which contains the efflux of Osiris, and is put in Rostau." Could it be that "something hidden" – in a chamber under the rear paws of the Sphinx – is a "treasure" that will transform our knowledge of ancient Egypt? Edgar Cayce predicted the discovery of a "Hall of Records" beneath the Sphinx towards the end of the 20th century, and Hancock and Bauval speculate whether this is not even now being investigated by the team of "official Egyptologists" who are the only ones permitted near the Sphinx.

'So *Keeper of Genesis* – as is perhaps inevitable – ends on a question mark. For the real question that lies behind this search into the remote past is: what does it all mean? We have to recognize that even the most precise knowledge of the Egyptian precessional code and their religion of resurrection still brings us no closer to answering some of the most obvious questions about their achievement – even one as straightforward as how they raised two hundred ton blocks . . .'

Wilson has his own suggestion of how this was achieved. He

cites evidence concerning the 'hunting magic' of primitive man –
how our Cro-Magnon ancestors made drawings on the walls of
his caves (like those at Lascaux) whose purpose was to guarantee
that the hunter trapped his prey. Anthropologists now know that
these cave drawings of deer and bison were part of a magic ritual;
the shaman or priest, wearing a skin of an animal, took part in a
dance whose purpose was somehow to guide the hunters to the
prey – or perhaps even to guide the prey to the hunters. Wilson
cites examples from modern anthropological literature that
appears to show that such 'magic' can actually work – how the
Amahuaca Indians of Brazil can lure their prey by means of
'magic ritual', and how the natives of the Gilbert Islands, in the
Pacific, engage in a ceremony called 'the Calling of the
Porpoises', in which the shaman can cause the porpoises to swim
ashore and beach themselves.

There is no evidence that the more primitive Neanderthal Man
made cave drawings. But his successor, Cro-Magnon man – our
direct ancestor – did.

Wilson suggests that it was this use of ritual magic that turned
Cro-Magnon Man into a far more purposive creature – that
'humanised' him. Magic was a kind of early science; it gave him
a new sense of control over nature.

Moreover, it would be inevitable that the shaman (or priestess)
would become the leader of the tribe. He or she would unite the
tribe and endow it with a new sense of purpose. (Adolf Hitler
provides an interesting – if dubious – modern parallel.)

Wilson goes on to suggest that these primitive tribes shared the
same kind of 'communal consciousness' as a flock of birds,
which can turn simultaneously in the air, without any obvious
signalled communication, or a shoal of fishes turning in the water.
In the introduction to a book about the Amahuaca Indians, *Wizard
of the Upper Amazon*, the American psychologist Andrew Weil
argues that the book provides evidence that their 'magic' is an
example of Jung's 'Collective Unconscious'. Citing evidence
from the anthropologist Edward T. Hall (who studied American
Indians), Wilson argues that all human beings were once united
by the Collective Unconscious, but that modern man, through the

development of analytical thought, has gradually lost – or suppressed – this capacity. He suggests that the Egyptians at the time of the Old Kingdom were a culmination of this 'collective' development.

'We have to understand what it means to be a civilization that is totally unified by its religion.' Schwaller de Lubicz emphasises that the Egyptians of this period were the most 'religious' civilization known to history: 'Ancient Egypt did not have a 'religion' as such; it was religion in its entirety, in the broadest and purest acceptation of the term.'

This, he suggests, could explain how they were able to lift 200 ton blocks, offering as a parallel the activities of modern 'shamans' or psychics:

'It is 1979, and Dr Larissa Vilenskaya, an experimental psychologist, is in the Moscow apartment of Dr Veniamin Pushkin, where the Soviet film maker Boris Yermolayev intends to demonstrate his peculiar powers in front of a small audience of scientific observers.

'Yermolayev drinks some vodka to relax, then, by way of a warm-up, proceeds to a card-guessing experiment, which proceeds so fast that Dr Vilenskaya cannot follow it. Then Yermolayev asks one of the observers to give him some light object; he is given a cigarette packet. He holds his hands in front of him and stares at his spread fingers with such tension that perspiration appears on his forehead. Then he takes the cigarette packet between fingers of both hands and stares at it. He opens his hands, and the packet falls to the ground. He picks it up and holds it again, talking to it in an inaudible whisper. Then he opens his hands, and the cigarette packet remains suspended in the air for between 30 and 40 seconds, before it falls to the ground.

'Yermolayev explains that he tries to establish a rapport with the object. He 'persuades' it, and tries to project a part of himself into it.

'In the same paper, Dr Vilenskaya describes how Elvira Shevchuk, a 40 year old woman from Kalinin, is able to suspend various objects in the air in the same way – including a beaker of liquid. In one case she took a stick provided by Dr Pushkin, rested it at an angle of 45 degrees on the floor, then slowly removed her hands. The stick remained at 45 degrees for over a minute.

'The evidence for such feats, performed under experimental conditions, is overwhelming. An Amahuaca or Hopi Indian would not express surprise – he would shrug and comment that Yermolayev and Madame Shevchuk are merely natural shamans, and are performing feats that shamans have performed since time began.

'Am I, then, suggesting that the ancient Egyptians "levitated" two hundred ton blocks of stone by exercising the 'group mind'? Not quite. It is not as simple as that. It is probable that they were not even aware that they were doing anything unusual. They prepared to move some vast block, probably with levers, ropes and rollers, the priest uttered "words of power", and then they all exerted themselves in concert, and the block moved smoothly, just as they all knew it would.' The 'great period' of ancient Egypt came to an end. Within two hundred years of building the Great Pyramid, their level of technical achievement had deteriorated. And Egypt became subject to a spiritual malaise, a new kind of individual self-consciousness. The innocence – and power – of the 'collective' was evaporating. Modern man was being born.

Yet, as Wilson emphasises, there is evidence that modern man has not lost these powers:

'In fact, modern computer science can provide an insight into this paradoxical notion of a collective unconscious. In *Out of Control* (1994), Kevin Kelly describes a conference in Las Vegas, in which five thousand computer enthusiasts came together in one hall. On the stage facing the audience is a kind of vast television screen in which the audience can see itself. Every member of the audience holds a cardboard wand, red on one side and green on the other. As the audience waves the wands, the screen dances with colours. Individual members of the audience can locate themselves by changing the colour of their wands from red to green and back.

'Now the Master of Ceremonies flashes on to the screen a video game called Pong – a kind of ping pong, with a white dot bouncing inside a square, while two moveable rectangles on either side act as ping pong bats. The MC announces: "The left side of the auditorium controls the left bat, and the right side controls the right bat."

'The whole audience then proceeds to play electronic ping pong. Each bat is controlled simultaneously by two and a half thousand people. The collective unconscious is playing the game. Moreover, it plays an excellent game, as if there were only one player on each side. As the ball is made to bounces faster, the whole audience adjusts, and increases its pace.

'Next, the MC causes a white circle to appear in the middle of the screen, and asks those who think they are sitting inside it to try to create a green figure five. Slowly, a blurred five materialises on the screen, then sharpens until it is quite distinct. When the MC asks for a four, then three, two, one, zero, the figures emerge almost instantly.

'Now the MC places a flight simulator on the screen, so the whole audience is looking through the pilot's eyes at a tiny runway in the midst of a pink valley. This time the left side controls the plane's roll, and the right side the pitch. But as five thousand minds bring the aircraft in for landing, it is obvious that it is going to land on its wing. So the whole audience aborts the landing and makes the plane raise its nose and try again.

'As Kelly comments: "Nobody decided whether to turn left or right . . . Nobody was in charge. But as if of one mind, the plane banks and turns wide."

'A second landing makes the wrong approach and is again aborted. "The mob decides, without lateral communication, like a flock of birds taking off . . ." And simultaneously, everyone in the audience decides to see if they can make the plane loop the loop. The horizons veers dizzily, but they succeed, and give themselves a standing ovation.

'So modern man can achieve group-consciousness, and moreover, achieve it almost instantaneously. It is obvious that we have not lost the trick. In effect – as Kelly observes – the audience turns into flocking birds. Presumably this could be explained in terms of individual feedback, but for all practical purposes, it is group telepathy.'

So it would be untrue to say that modern man has 'fallen' from his former level. We have achieved new powers that our remote ancestors did not possess: powers of reason and imagination. (A 'collective' does not need imagination.) And if we can begin to understand these secrets of the past, and the story of man's evolution in the past half million years (during which his brain size increased so much that scientists refer to it as 'the brain explosion'), there is no reason why we should not learn to combine the 'collective' consciousness of our ancestors with the more powerful analytical consciousness of modern man.

The conclusion would seem to be that 'Atlantis' is not an absurd irrelevance, an unsubstantiated myth that has turned into a modern romantic obsession. If Schwaller de Lubicz and West and Bauval and Hancock are correct, the Sphinx and the pyramids are the key to the mystery of Atlantis. And Atlantis, in turn, is one of the most important keys to the mystery of the 'brain explosion' and to human evolution not merely to man's evolution in the past, but in the future.

LIST OF ILLUSTRATIONS